ANNUAL EDITIONS

Early Childhood Education 09/10

Thirtieth Edition

W9-BPL-070

EDITOR

Karen Menke Paciorek

Eastern Michigan University

Karen Menke Paciorek is a professor of early childhood education at Eastern Michigan University in Ypsilanti. Her degrees in early childhood education include a BA from the University of Pittsburgh, an MA from George Washington University, and a PhD from Peabody College of Vanderbilt University. She is the editor of *Taking Sides: Clashing Views in Early Childhood Education (2nd. Ed.)* and co-edits, with Joyce Huth Munro, *Sources: Notable Selections in Early Childhood Education* both published by McGraw-Hill. She has served as president of the Michigan Association for the Education of Young Children, the Michigan Early Childhood Education Consortium and the Northville School Board. She presents at local, state, and national conferences on curriculum planning, guiding behavior, preparing the learning environment and working with families. She has served as a member of the Board of Education for the Northville Public Schools, Northville, Michigan since 2002 and is on the Board of Directors for Wolverine Human Services serving over 600 abused and delinquent youth in Michigan. Dr. Paciorek is a recipient of the Eastern Michigan University Distinguished Faculty Award for Service.

 **Higher Education**

Boston   Burr Ridge, IL   Dubuque, IA   New York   San Francisco   St. Louis
Bangkok   Bogotá   Caracas   Kuala Lumpur   Lisbon   London   Madrid   Mexico City
Milan   Montreal   New Delhi   Santiago   Seoul   Singapore   Sydney   Taipei   Toronto

The McGraw-Hill Companies

Mc Graw Hill **Higher Education**

ANNUAL EDITIONS: EARLY CHILDHOOD EDUCATION, THIRTIETH EDITION

Annual Editions® is a registered trademark of The McGraw-Hill Companies, Inc.

Annual Editions is published by the **Contemporary Learning Series** group within the McGraw-Hill Higher Education division.

1 2 3 4 5 6 7 8 9 0 QPD/QPD 0 9

ISBN 978–0–07–812764–9
MHID 0–07–812764–5
ISSN 0270–4456

Managing Editor: *Larry Loeppke*
Senior Managing Editor: *Faye Schilling*
Developmental Editor: *Dave Welsh*
Editorial Coordinator: *Mary Foust*
Editorial Assistant: *Nancy Meissner*
Production Service Assistant: *Rita Hingtgen*
Permissions Coordinator: *DeAnna Dausener*
Senior Marketing Manager: *Julie Keck*
Marketing Communications Specialist: *Mary Klein*
Marketing Coordinator: *Alice Link*
Project Manager: *Sandy Wille*
Design Specialist: *Tara McDermott*
Senior Production Supervisor: *Laura Fuller*
Cover Graphics: *Kristine Jubeck*

Compositor: Laserwords Private Limited
Cover Images: © Photoalto/PictureQuest/RF (inset); © Dory/Alamy/RF (background)

Library in Congress Cataloging-in-Publication Data
Main entry under title: Annual Editions: Early Childhood Education 2009/2010.
 1. Early Childhood Education—I. Menke Paciorek, Karen, *comp*. II. Title: Early Childhood Education.
658'.05

www.mhhe.com

Editors/Advisory Board

Members of the Advisory Board are instrumental in the final selection of articles for each edition of ANNUAL EDITIONS. Their review of articles for content, level, currentness, and appropriateness provides critical direction to the editor and staff. We think that you will find their careful consideration well reflected in this volume.

Preface

In publishing ANNUAL EDITIONS we recognize the enormous role played by the magazines, newspapers, and journals of the public press in providing current, first-rate educational information in a broad spectrum of interest areas. Many of these articles are appropriate for students, researchers, and professionals seeking accurate, current material to help bridge the gap between principles and theories and the real world. These articles, however, become more useful for study when those of lasting value are carefully collected, organized, indexed, and reproduced in a low-cost format, which provides easy and permanent access when the material is needed. That is the role played by ANNUAL EDITIONS.

Annual Editions: Early Childhood Education has evolved over the 30 years it has been in existence to become one of the most used texts for students in early childhood education. This annual reader is used today at over 550 colleges and universities. In addition, it may be found in public libraries, pediatricians' offices, and teacher reference sections of school libraries. I work diligently throughout the year to find articles and bring you the best and most significant readings in the field. I realize this is a tremendous responsibility to provide a thorough review of the current literature—a responsibility I take very seriously. I am always on the look out for possible articles for the next Annual Editions: Early Childhood Education. My goal is to provide the reader with a snapshot of the critical issues facing professionals in early childhood education.

Early childhood education is an interdisciplinary field that includes child development, family issues, educational practices, behavior guidance, and curriculum. Annual Editions: Early Childhood Education 09/10 brings you the latest information in the field from a wide variety of recent journals, newspapers, and magazines. There are four themes found in the readings chosen for this thirtieth edition of Annual Editions: Early Childhood Education. They are: (1) the effects of poverty on the lives and particularly the education of children, (2) the strong focus on early learning standards and the need for teachers to align their curriculum and learning experiences to meet the standards while still providing an environment that is engaging and meaningful, (3) the increasing focus on developing critical thinking skills through inquiry-based learning, and (4) the need for inclusive classrooms that meet the needs of all learners.

It is especially gratifying to see issues affecting children and families covered in magazines other than professional association journals. The general public needs to be aware of the impact of positive early learning and family experiences on the growth and development of children.

Continuing in this edition of Annual Editions: Early Childhood Education are selected World Wide Web sites that can be used to further explore topics addressed in the articles. I have chosen to include only a few high-quality sites. The reader is encouraged to explore these sites on their own, or in collaboration with others for extended learning opportunities.

Given the wide range of topics, Annual Editions: Early Childhood Education 09/10 may be used by several groups—undergraduate or graduate students, professionals, parents, or administrators—who want to develop an understanding of the critical issues in the field.

The selection of readings for this edition has been a cooperative effort between the editor and the advisory board members. I appreciate the time the advisory board members have taken to provide suggestions for improvement and possible articles for consideration. The production and editorial staff of McGraw-Hill, led by Larry Loeppke and David Welsh ably support and coordinate my efforts.

To the instructor or reader interested in the history of early childhood care and education programs throughout the years, I invite you to view my other books, also published by McGraw-Hill. Sources: Notable Selections in Early Childhood Education, 2nd edition (1999) is a collection of 46 writings of enduring historical value by influential people in the field. All of the selections are primary sources, which allow you to experience first hand the thoughts and views of these important educators. Taking Sides: Clashing Views on Controversial Issues in Early Childhood Education, 2nd edition (2008) contains eighteen critical issues facing early childhood professionals or parents. The book can be used in a seminar or issues course.

I appreciate the readers who have corresponded with me about the selection and organization of previous editions. Comments and articles sent for consideration are welcomed and will serve to modify future volumes. Take time to fill out and return the postage-paid article rating form on the last page. You may also contact me at: kpaciorek@emich.edu.

I look forward to hearing from you.

Karen Menke Paciorek

Karen Menke Paciorek
Editor

Contents

Preface   iv

Correlation Guide   xi

Topic Guide   xii

Internet References   xv

UNIT 1
Perspectives

Unit Overview   xviii

1. **Early Education, Later Success,** Susan Black, *American School Board Journal,* September 22, 2008

   What used to be called K-12 education has dipped down to include the very critical **preschool** years. School districts are beginning to **align** their PK-third grades into an ECE PK-3 unit. Schools committed to **achievement** and **best practices** find a cohesive approach to education for their youngest learners most effective.   3

2. **The Changing Culture of Childhood: A Perfect Storm,** Joe L. Frost, *Childhood Education,* Summer 2007

   Joe L. Frost was a keynote speaker at the 2006 Annual Conference for the Association for Childhood Education International. Included is an expanded version of his address focusing on the decrease of **play,** the increase of **academics,** the effects of **poverty,** and other issues affecting young children.   5

3. **Joy in School,** Steven Wolk, *Educational Leadership,* September 2008

   With the focus on academic **achievement,** teachers are feeling the pressure to teach so that students learn. For many teachers that means an academic approach where the joy and passion for learning is void. Wolk reminds educators to plan **developmentally appropriate** activities that encourage children to develop lifelong learning habits.   11

4. **Accountability Comes to Preschool: Can We Make It Work for Young Children?,** Deborah Stipek, *Phi Delta Kappan,* June 2006

   Many early childhood educators view the introduction of **standards** into **preschool** settings as a sign that a **play-based** experiential approach to learning is soon to be a thing of the past. Stipek explains that standards applied to early childhood programs can be compatible with **developmentally appropriate practices.** Good programs can be **accountable** and appropriate at the same time.   16

5. **No Child Left Behind: Who's Accountable?,** Lisa A. DuBois, *Peabody Reflector,* Summer 2007

   No Child Left Behind (NCLB) is half way to the year 2014, when the **federal** law requires that 100 percent of public school students **achieve** proficiency in reading, math, and science. **Accountability** and **best practices** of NCLB are discussed by researchers at Peabody College of Vanderbilt University.   21

6. **Preschool Comes of Age: The National Debate on Education for Young Children Intensifies,** Michael Lester, *Edutopia,* June 2007

   Close to two-thirds of **preschool** children have a school experience prior to entering kindergarten. The data on **achievement** levels and **readiness** for future learning of children who attend preschool programs is well documented. Data on the long-term **cost effectiveness** of preschool programs is also striking, yet, there are children without access to quality preschool programs. Michael Lester questions why more young children do not attend preschool.   25

The concepts in bold italics are developed in the article. For further expansion, please refer to the Topic Guide.

UNIT 2
Young Children, Their Families and Communities

Unit Overview   28

7. **Class Matters—In and Out of School,** Jayne Boyd-Zaharias and
   Helen Pate-Bain, *Phi Delta Kappan,* September 2008
   The effects of *poverty* on school *achievement* can be abated by *collaboration*
   between school administrators and community leaders. Quality instruction starting in
   the *preschool* years and *lower class sizes* are effective practices.   30

8. **Meeting of the Minds,** Laura Pappano, *Harvard Education Letter,*
   July/August 2007
   Making *parent-teacher* conferences a win-win situation for the *teacher, family,* and
   student is the key for developing positive relationships. Pappano provides strategies
   that teachers can use to take full advantage of the opportunity available for parents and
   teachers to meet.   35

9. **Making Long-Term Separations Easier for Children and Families,**
   Amy M. Kim and Julia Yeary, *Young Children,* September 2008
   The numbers of children separated from family members by military deployment are
   staggering. Long deployments, injuries and death of a *family* member have an impact
   on the *social, emotional,* and *cognitive development* of children. *Teachers* can work
   with the family to help alleviate the *stress* children are experiencing.   38

10. **Supporting Grandparents Who Raise Grandchildren,**
    Jennifer Birckmayer et al., *Young Children,* May 2005
    Grandparents raising their grandchildren often report that parenting isn't any easier,
    and that in fact, it is often more challenging the second time around. Grandparents have
    special support issues such as isolation, physical limitations, *stress, poverty,* and *disci-
    pline.* Teachers can offer special services aimed at this unique groups of *parents.*   43

11. **Children of Teen Parents: Challenges and Hope,** Barbara A. White,
    Mimi Graham, and Seaton K. Bradford, *Zero to Three,* March 2005
    When *parents* are children themselves, special services are needed to support these
    vulnerable parents of *infants and toddlers.* Their children are often at risk from lack of
    prenatal care, *poverty, violence,* and other developmental delays as a result of being
    raised in a teen parent *family.*   46

UNIT 3
Diverse Learners

Unit Overview   48

12. **Whose Problem Is Poverty?,** Richard Rothstein, *Educational Leadership,*
    April 2008
    There has been much focus on how best to close the *achievement gap* found in
    children living in *poverty.* Rothstein argues that schools alone will not solve the prob-
    lem. *Collaboration* between *families,* educators, *health* professionals, the *federal
    government,* and community agencies is needed.   50

13. **Learning in an Inclusive Community,** Mara Sapon-Shevin,
    Educational Leadership, September 2008
    Moving to develop an *inclusive* learning community that meets the needs of all students
    is the focus of this article. Included are ten suggestions for *teachers* to consider when
    designing classrooms that support the *diversity* of the children.   54

The concepts in bold italics are developed in the article. For further expansion, please refer to the Topic Guide.

14. **Including Children with Disabilities in Early Childhood Education Programs: Individualizing Developmentally Appropriate Practices,** John Filler and Yaoying Xu, *Childhood Education,* Winter 2006/2007

Integrating young children with *disabilities* in early childhood programs requires *teachers* who work closely with *families* to accommodate the special needs of each child. *Teachers* skilled in *differentiating* will be best able to make the practice of *inclusion* successful and a positive learning experience for all children in the classroom.　　**59**

15. **Creative Play: Building Connections with Children Who Are Learning English,** Sara J. Burton and Linda Carol Edwards, *Dimensions of Early Childhood,* Spring/Summer 2006

Children who are *English Language Learners* need many opportunities to engage in creative *play* experiences. Burton and Edwards provide suggestions for *teachers* to help *families* and children from other *cultures* as they acquire English language skills.　　**66**

UNIT 4
Supporting Young Children's Development

Unit Overview　　**72**

16. **Twelve Characteristics of Effective Early Childhood Teachers,** Laura J. Colker, *Young Children,* March 2008

Laura Colker provides 12 characteristics or dispositions found in skilled early childhood *teachers.* The author describes the characteristics: passion, perseverance, flexibility, and love of learning. All teachers should assess the effectiveness of their own teaching characteristics.　　**74**

17. **Health = Performance,** Ginny Ehrlich, *American School Board Journal,* October 2008

Ehrlich links students' *academic achievement* to their overall *health* and wellness. A strong physical presence and a strong body make one better able to acquire *cognitive* skills. School administrators who focus on offering healthy *food and nutrition,* providing ample opportunities for *physical development,* and partner with staff and *families* to be positive role models will see progress in moving to overall healthy students.　　**78**

18. **Which Hand?: Brains, Fine Motor Skills, and Holding a Pencil,** *Texas Child Care,* Spring 2007

Helping *parents* understand the needs of their child when developing *physical skills,* specifically related to handedness, is an important job for teachers. Strategies for helping children feel competent and comfortable with their choice to use either their left or right hand for fine motor skills are included.　　**80**

19. **What Can We Do to Prevent Childhood Obesity?,** Julie Lumeng, *Zero to Three,* January 2005

Childhood *obesity* is increasing at an alarming rate. Teachers and caregivers can educate *families* on how to provide *healthy* meals for their children, especially infants and toddlers. Research has found overweight three-year-olds are likely to be overweight adults.　　**84**

20. **When Girls and Boys Play: What Research Tells Us,** Jeanetta G. Riley and Rose B. Jones, *Childhood Education,* Fall 2007

As many teachers and administrators are deciding to eliminate *play* and *recess,* there is strong evidence supporting the many benefits of child-initiated, free choice play. Children specifically benefit *physically, socially,* and creatively when given an opportunity to engage in free play.　　**91**

The concepts in bold italics are developed in the article. For further expansion, please refer to the Topic Guide.

UNIT 5
Educational Practices

Unit Overview   96

21. **What Research Says about . . . Grade Retention,** Jane L. David,
Educational Leadership, March 2008

Retention, or repeating a grade, has been increasing as schools work to meet Adequate Yearly Progress (AYP). There is a great difference between countries such as Great Britain, Denmark, Japan and Sweden with zero children retained each year and the United States with over two million K-12 grade children retained each year. Significant research studies have found retention to not be a positive experience and that it doesn't lead to successful results in *achievement.* Additional strategies for educators to help struggling students are included.   98

22. **Back to Basics: Play in Early Childhood,** Jill Englebright Fox,
Earlychildhood NEWS, March/April 2006

The basics, to which Englebright refers, are the benefits of a variety of *developmentally appropriate play* experiences for young children. Freely chosen and supported by a knowledgeable staff, children who are allowed to engage in a variety of play will experience benefits in their cognitive, social, creative, physical, and emotional *development.*   100

23. **Scripted Curriculum: Is It a Prescription for Success?,** Anita Ede,
Childhood Education, Fall 2006

In light of the *NCLB* requirements that students are to achievie by 2014, many school districts have adopted *scripted curriculum* programs for *teachers* to use when teaching reading specifically. The use of these programs is most prevalent with *at-risk learners.*   103

24. **Using Brain-Based Teaching Strategies to Create Supportive Early Childhood Environments That Address Learning Standards,**
Pam Schiller and Clarissa A. Willis, *Young Children,* July 2008

Creative *primary teachers* can provide quality *inquiry-based* learning experiences where students can achieve content *standards.* Good teachers *differentiate* activities. The authors provide many suggestions for *brain-based* learning activities.   107

25. **Successful Transition to Kindergarten: The Role of Teachers and Parents,** Pam Deyell-Gingold *Earlychildhood NEWS,* May/June 2006

Helping young children make a smooth transition to *kindergarten* is a goal of every preschool teacher and parent. When kindergarten teachers prepare environments that are *ready* to accept a variety of *developmental* levels, children can be successful. A *play*-based setting with a focus on the *social and emotional development* of young children will allow them to be successful, lifelong learners.   111

26. *Rethinking* **Early Childhood Practices,** Francis Wardle,
Earlychildhood NEWS, January/February 2005

Francis Wardle makes us think and challenges us to reflect on everyday practices occurring in most programs for young children. Only after careful examination of the benefits of an activity or *curricular* practice should we continue doing things in classrooms that have been general practice for years without much thought to their efficacy.   115

27. **The Looping Classroom: Benefits for Children, Families, and Teachers,**
Mary M. Hitz, Mary Catherine Somers, and Christee L. Jenlink,
Young Children, March 2007

Educators often try different practices with improving academic *achievement* as their ultimate goal. The benefits of *teachers* moving up to the next grade with their class of children are many. Skilled teachers are able to provide *developmentally appropriate environments* and best serve *English Language Learners* and other *diverse learners. Families* often like the consistency that comes form their children having the same teacher for two or more years. *Retention* can be decreased when children have the opportunity to continue for another year with the same teacher in the next grade level.   120

The concepts in bold italics are developed in the article. For further expansion, please refer to the Topic Guide.

UNIT 6
Helping Children to Thrive in School

Unit Overview   **124**

28. **Play: Ten Power Boosts for Children's Early Learning,** Alice Sterling Honig,
    Young Children, September 2007
    Dr. Honig, an icon in the early childhood field, provides ten reasons why *play* is critical
    for young children. The reasons cover all areas of development and are very appropri-
    ate to share with *parents* and administrators questioning the benefit of play for young
    children's development.   **126**

29. **Ready or Not, Here We Come: What It Means to Be a Ready School,**
    Paula M. Dowker, with Larry Schweinhart and Marijata Daniel-Echols,
    Young Children, March 2007
    For years good early childhood educators have known that we don't get children ready
    for school, we get schools ready for children. School *readiness* takes on a whole new
    meaning when it is viewed from the perspective of how all learners will be accepted and
    accommodated. *Developmentally appropriate practices* that best serve all children
    are necessary for positive learning experiences to occur.   **131**

30. **"Stop Picking On Me!": What You Need to Know about Bullying,**
    Texas Child Care, Spring 2008
    Teachers have a responsibility to educate children about *bullying.* Risk factors as well
    as protective factors for aggressive behavior are provided along with strategies for
    teachers to use in preventing bullying.   **133**

31. **"You Got It!": Teaching Social and Emotional Skills,** Lise Fox and
    Rochelle Harper Lentini, *Young Children,* November 2006
    Fox and Lentini include excellent strategies for *teachers* to use when fostering *social
    and emotional development* in their *preschoolers.* Children who are confident learn-
    ers will be most successful in all endeavors.   **138**

32. **Fostering Positive Transitions for School Success,** Jayma Ferguson
    McGann and Patricia Clark, *Young Children,* November 2007
    Colleges and Universities have, for years, provided well-organized transition programs
    for incoming students. *Preschools* and elementary schools are just beginning to see the
    importance of helping children transit to their first or next school experience. The benefits
    of *social and emotional development* as well as establishing a positive connection with
    families are some of the results seen with an organized transition program.   **144**

33. **A Multinational Study Supports Child-Initiated Learning: Using the
    Findings in Your Classroom,** Jeanne E. Montie, Jill Claxton, and
    Shannon D. Lockhart, *Young Children,* November 2007
    A result from a study in 15 countries of over 5,000 preschoolers provides striking
    findings for educators everywhere. Applying four key findings can lead to increased
    achievement. Education of the teachers, opportunities to make choices, minimal time
    spent in large group activities and classrooms with a variety of materials all led to higher
    language and or cognitive achievement.   **146**

34. **The Power of Documentation in the Early Childhood Classroom,**
    Hilary Seitz, *Young Children,* March 2008
    Documentation takes many forms and should be collected throughout the year. It allows
    others to gain an understanding of the many learning opportunities in a classroom and
    shows specific ways in which children benefited from participation in various learning
    experiences.   **151**

The concepts in bold italics are developed in the article. For further expansion, please refer to the Topic Guide.

UNIT 7
Curricular Issues

Unit Overview   156

35. **Got Standards?: Don't Give up on Engaged Learning!,**
Judy Harris Helm, *Young Children,* March 2006
Judy Harris Helm walks teachers through a planning process where early learning
standards can be integrated into a child-initiated, ***inquiry based*** approach to learning.   159

36. **The Plan: Building on Children's Interests,** Hilary Jo Seitz,
Young Children, March 2006
Teachers who carefully listen and observe the children will find a wealth of possibilities
for the development of an ***emergent curriculum.*** When the ***curriculum*** is based on the
interests of the children and allows for extended ***projects*** there are many rich discover-
ies waiting for both the children and the teacher.   165

37. **One Teacher, 20 Preschoolers, and a Goldfish: Environmental
Awareness, Emergent Curriculum, and Documentation,**
Ann Lewin-Benham, *Young Children,* March 2006
Lewin-Benham takes the reader inside a ***preschool*** classroom and follows the children
and teacher as they embark on an ***emergent curriculum*** journey exploring a goldfish and the environment. There are many excellent suggestions for carrying out an
emergent curriculum and ***documentation*** of a learning experience.   169

38. **Fostering Prosocial Behavior in Young Children,** Kathy Preusse,
Earlychildhood NEWS, March/April 2005
Teaching children ***prosocial behaviors*** not only provides them with the ability to be
successful in group settings, but also help them to be lifelong learners. Strategies are
provided for ***teachers*** to help children learn to make choices, negotiate conflicts, and
develop self-control. Altruistic behaviors are those prosocial skills that will enable children to be fit to live with as they move through life.   174

39. **Constructive Play: A Value-Added Strategy for Meeting Early Learning
Standards,** Walter F. Drew et al., *Young Children,* July 2008
Constructive ***play*** is play in which children work to make an original creation or show
an understanding of a concept. ***Creativity,*** imagination, and ***inquiry*** are all parts of
constructive play. Teachers have found that early learning ***standards*** can be achieved
by fostering constructive play in their classrooms.   179

40. **Early Literacy and Very Young Children,** Rebecca Parlakian,
Zero to Three, September 2004
The focus on ***early literacy*** has moved down to programs for very young children.
Parlakian examines strategies and effective techniques to introduce young children to
reading. She encourages ***teachers*** to intentionally plan literacy experiences in the class-
room and to provide a scaffold for children's learning with a supportive environment.   185

41. **Using Picture Books to Support Young Children's Literacy,**
Janis Strasser and Holly Seplocha, *Childhood Education,* Summer 2007
Getting great picture books into the hands of young children and ***reading*** the stories
to them is a critical part of the job for any early childhood educator. ***Early Literacy***
experiences are best fostered in a supportive ***environment*** that is well stocked with
appropriate picture books.   191

42. **Calendar Time for Young Children: Good Intentions Gone Awry,**
Sallee J. Beneke, Michaelene M. Ostrosky, and Lilian G. Katz,
Young Children, May 2008
When ***teachers*** develop more experience and an understanding of young children's development, they begin to examine traditional classroom practices. The authors explore
calendar time and provide suggestions for making the experience more ***developmentally appropriate*** and authentic for young children.   196

Test-Your-Knowledge Form   200
Article Rating Form   201

The concepts in bold italics are developed in the article. For further expansion, please refer to the Topic Guide.

Correlation Guide

The *Annual Editions* series provides students with convenient, inexpensive access to current, carefully selected articles from the public press. **Annual Editions: Early Childhood Education 09/10** is an easy-to-use reader that presents articles on important topics such as *young children and their families, diverse learners, educational practices,* and many more. For more information on *Annual Editions* and other *McGraw-Hill Contemporary Learning Series* titles, visit www.mhcls.com.

This convenient guide matches the units in **Annual Editions: Early Childhood Education 09/10** with the corresponding chapters in two of our best-selling McGraw-Hill Early Childhood Education textbooks by Gonzalez-Mena.

Annual Editions: Early Childhood Education 09/10	Foundations of Early Childhood Education: Teaching Children in a Diverse Society, 4/e by Gonzalez-Mena	Diversity in Early Care and Education: Honoring Differences, 5/e by Gonzalez-Mena
Unit 1: Perspectives	**Chapter 4:** Facilitating Young Children's Work and Play **Chapter 8:** Setting Up the Physical Environment **Chapter 13:** Language and Emergent Literacy	**Chapter 1:** Perceiving and Responding to Differences
Unit 2: Young Children, Their Families and Communities	**Chapter 2:** First Things First: Health and Safety through Observation and Supervision **Chapter 5:** Guiding Young Children's Behavior **Chapter 7:** Modeling Adult Relationships in Early Childhood Settings **Chapter 9:** Creating a Social-Emotional Environment Chapter 10: Routines	**Chapter 4:** A Framework for Understanding Differences **Chapter 5:** Attachment and Separation **Chapter 7:** Socialization, Guidance, and Discipline
Unit 3: Diverse Learners	**Chapter 10:** Routines **Chapter 11:** Developmental Tasks as the Curriculum: How to Support Children at Each Stage	**Chapter 1:** Perceiving and Responding to Differences **Chapter 6:** Differing Perspectives on Learning through Play
Unit 4: Supporting Young Children's Development	**Chapter 1:** Early Childhood Education as a Profession **Chapter 4:** Facilitating Young Children's Work and Play **Chapter 8:** Setting Up the Physical Environment **Chapter 11:** Developmental Tasks as the Curriculum: How to Support Children at Each Stage	**Chapter 4:** A Framework for Understanding Differences
Unit 5: Educational Practices	**Chapter 4:** Facilitating Young Children's Work and Play **Chapter 6:** The Teacher as Model **Chapter 8:** Setting Up the Physical Environment **Chapter 12:** Observing, Recording, and Assessing	**Chapter 3:** Working with Diversity Issues
Unit 6: Helping Children to Thrive in School	**Chapter 3:** Communicating with Young Children **Chapter 13:** Language and Emergent Literacy	**Chapter 5:** Attachment and Separation
Unit 7: Curricular Issues	**Chapter 13:** Language and Emergent Literacy **Chapter 14:** Providing Developmentally Appropriate Experiences in Math and Science **Chapter 15:** Integrating Art, Music, and Social Studies into a Holistic Curriculum	**Chapter 7:** Socialization, Guidance, and Discipline

Topic Guide

This topic guide suggests how the selections in this book relate to the subjects covered in your course. You may want to use the topics listed on these pages to search the Web more easily.

On the following pages a number of Web sites have been gathered specifically for this book. They are arranged to reflect the units of this Annual Editions reader. You can link to these sites by going to *http://www.mhcls.com*.

All the articles that relate to each topic are listed below the bold-faced term.

Accountability
4. Accountability Comes to Preschool: Can We Make It Work for Young Children?
5. No Child Left Behind: Who's Accountable?

Achievement/academic achievement
1. Early Education, Later Success
2. The Changing Culture of Childhood: A Perfect Storm
3. Joy in School
6. Preschool Comes of Age: The National Debate on Education for Young Children Intensifies
7. Class Matters—In and Out of School
12. Whose Problem Is Poverty?
17. Health = Performance
21. What Research Says about . . . Grade Retention
27. The Looping Classroom: Benefits for Children, Families, and Teachers
33. A Multinational Study Supports Child-Initiated Learning: Using the Findings in Your Classroom

Alignment
1. Early Education, Later Success

Assessment
4. Accountability Comes to Preschool: Can We Make It Work for Young Children?

At-risk children
2. The Changing Culture of Childhood: A Perfect Storm
5. No Child Left Behind: Who's Accountable?
23. Scripted Curriculum: Is It a Prescription for Success?

Best practices
1. Early Education, Later Success
5. No Child Left Behind: Who's Accountable?

Brain development and brain-based learning
24. Using Brain-Based Teaching Strategies to Create Supportive Early Childhood Environments That Address Learning Standards

Bullying
30. "Stop Picking On Me!": What You Need to Know about Bullying

Cognitive development
17. Health = Performance
33. A Multinational Study Supports Child-Initiated Learning: Using the Findings in Your Classroom

Collaboration
7. Class Matters—In and Out of School
12. Whose Problem Is Poverty?

Cost, educational
6. Preschool Comes of Age: The National Debate on Education for Young Children Intensifies

Creativity
39. Constructive Play: A Value-Added Strategy for Meeting Early Learning Standards

Cultures
15. Creative Play: Building Connections with Children Who Are Learning English

Curriculum
36. The Plan: Building on Children's Interests

Development
11. Children of Teen Parents: Challenges and Hope
22. Back to Basics: Play in Early Childhood
25. Successful Transition to Kindergarten: The Role of Teachers and Parents

Developmentally appropriate practice
3. Joy in School
4. Accountability Comes to Preschool: Can We Make It Work for Young Children?
22. Back to Basics: Play in Early Childhood
27. The Looping Classroom: Benefits for Children, Families, and Teachers
42. Calendar Time for Young Children: Good Intentions Gone Awry

Differentiation
14. Including Children with Disabilities in Early Childhood Education Programs: Individualizing Developmentally Appropriate Practices
24. Using Brain-Based Teaching Strategies to Create Supportive Early Childhood Environments That Address Learning Standards

Discipline
10. Supporting Grandparents Who Raise Grandchildren

Disabilities
14. Including Children with Disabilities in Early Childhood Education Programs: Individualizing Developmentally Appropriate Practices

Diverse learners/diversity
13. Learning in an Inclusive Community
14. Including Children with Disabilities in Early Childhood Education Programs: Individualizing Developmentally Appropriate Practices
27. The Looping Classroom: Benefits for Children, Families, and Teachers

Documentation
34. The Power of Documentation in the Early Childhood Classroom
37. One Teacher, 20 Preschoolers, and a Goldfish: Environmental Awareness, Emergent Curriculum, and Documentation

Emergent curriculum
36. The Plan: Building on Children's Interests
37. One Teacher, 20 Preschoolers, and a Goldfish: Environmental Awareness, Emergent Curriculum, and Documentation

English language learners

15. Creative Play: Building Connections with Children Who Are Learning English
27. The Looping Classroom: Benefits for Children, Families, and Teachers

Environment

27. The Looping Classroom: Benefits for Children, Families, and Teachers
41. Using Picture Books to Support Young Children's Literacy

Families

8. Meeting of the Minds
10. Supporting Grandparents Who Raise Grandchildren
11. Children of Teen Parents: Challenges and Hope
12. Whose Problem Is Poverty?
14. Including Children with Disabilities in Early Childhood Education Programs: Individualizing Developmentally Appropriate Practices
15. Creative Play: Building Connections with Children Who Are Learning English
17. Health = Performance
19. What Can We Do to Prevent Childhood Obesity?
27. The Looping Classroom: Benefits for Children, Families, and Teachers
32. Fostering Positive Transitions for School Success

Federal government

5. No Child Left Behind: Who's Accountable?
12. Whose Problem Is Poverty?

Food

17. Health = Performance

Grandparents

10. Supporting Grandparents Who Raise Grandchildren

Guidance

10. Supporting Grandparents Who Raise Grandchildren

Health/Safety

12. Whose Problem Is Poverty?
17. Health = Performance
19. What Can We Do to Prevent Childhood Obesity?

Inclusive education

13. Learning in an Inclusive Community
14. Including Children with Disabilities in Early Childhood Education Programs: Individualizing Developmentally Appropriate Practices

Infants and toddlers

11. Children of Teen Parents: Challenges and Hope

Inquiry-based learning

24. Using Brain-Based Teaching Strategies to Create Supportive Early Childhood Environments That Address Learning Standards
35. Got Standards?: Don't Give up on Engaged Learning!
39. Constructive Play: A Value-Added Strategy for Meeting Early Learning Standards

Kindergarten

25. Successful Transition to Kindergarten: The Role of Teachers and Parents

Literacy

41. Using Picture Books to Support Young Children's Literacy

Lower class size

7. Class Matters—In and Out of School

No Child Left Behind (NCLB)

5. No Child Left Behind: Who's Accountable?
23. Scripted Curriculum: Is It a Prescription for Success?

Obesity

19. What Can We Do to Prevent Childhood Obesity?

Parenting/parents

10. Supporting Grandparents Who Raise Grandchildren
11. Children of Teen Parents: Challenges and Hope
18. Which Hand?: Brains, Fine Motor Skills, and Holding a Pencil
28. Play: Ten Power Boosts for Children's Early Learning

Physical development

17. Health = Performance
18. Which Hand?: Brains, Fine Motor Skills, and Holding a Pencil
20. When Girls and Boys Play: What Research Tells Us

Play

2. The Changing Culture of Childhood: A Perfect Storm
4. Accountability Comes to Preschool: Can We Make It Work for Young Children?
8. Meeting of the Minds: The Parent Teacher Conference
15. Creative Play: Building Connections with Children Who Are Learning English
20. When Girls and Boys Play: What Research Tells Us
22. Back to Basics: Play in Early Childhood
25. Successful Transition to Kindergarten: The Role of Teachers and Parents
28. Play: Ten Power Boosts for Children's Early Learning
39. Constructive Play: A Value-Added Strategy for Meeting Early Learning Standards

Playgrounds

20. When Girls and Boys Play: What Research Tells Us

Poverty

2. The Changing Culture of Childhood: A Perfect Storm
7. Class Matters—In and Out of School
10. Supporting Grandparents Who Raise Grandchildren
11. Children of Teen Parents: Challenges and Hope
12. Whose Problem Is Poverty?

Preschool

1. Early Education, Later Success
4. Accountability Comes to Preschool: Can We Make It Work for Young Children?
6. Preschool Comes of Age: The National Debate on Education for Young Children Intensifies
7. Class Matters—In and Out of School
31. "You Got It!": Teaching Social and Emotional Skills
32. Fostering Positive Transitions for School Success
37. One Teacher, 20 Preschoolers, and a Goldfish: Environmental Awareness, Emergent Curriculum, and Documentation

Primary grades

24. Using Brain-Based Teaching Strategies to Create Supportive Early Childhood Environments That Address Learning Standards

Project approach

36. The Plan: Building on Children's Interests

Reading

41. Using Picture Books to Support Young Children's Literacy

Readiness

6. Preschool Comes of Age: The National Debate on Education for Young Children Intensifies
25. Successful Transition to Kindergarten: The Role of Teachers and Parents
29. Ready or Not, Here We Come: What It Means to Be a Ready School

Recess

20. When Girls and Boys Play: What Research Tells Us

Research

21. What Research Says about . . . Grade Retention

Retention/red-shirting

21. What Research Says about . . . Grade Retention
27. The Looping Classroom: Benefits for Children, Families, and Teachers

Scripted curriculum

23. Scripted Curriculum: Is It a Prescription for Success?

Social/emotional development

20. When Girls and Boys Play: What Research Tells Us
25. Successful Transition to Kindergarten: The Role of Teachers and Parents
31. "You Got It!": Teaching Social and Emotional Skills
32. Fostering Positive Transitions for School Success

Standards

4. Accountability Comes to Preschool: Can We Make It Work for Young Children?
24. Using Brain-Based Teaching Strategies to Create Supportive Early Childhood Environments That Address Learning Standards
35. Got Standards?: Don't Give up on Engaged Learning!
39. Constructive Play: A Value-Added Strategy for Meeting Early Learning Standards

Stress

10. Supporting Grandparents Who Raise Grandchildren
11. Children of Teen Parents: Challenges and Hope
30. "Stop Picking On Me!": What You Need to Know about Bullying

Teachers/teaching

8. Meeting of the Minds: The Parent Teacher Conference
13. Learning in an Inclusive Community
14. Including Children with Disabilities in Early Childhood Education Programs: Individualizing Developmentally Appropriate Practices
15. Creative Play: Building Connections with Children Who Are Learning English
16. Twelve Characteristics of Effective Early Childhood Teachers
23. Scripted Curriculum: Is It a Prescription for Success?
24. Using Brain-Based Teaching Strategies to Create Supportive Early Childhood Environments That Address Learning Standards
30. "Stop Picking On Me!": What You Need to Know about Bullying
31. "You Got It!": Teaching Social and Emotional Skills
36. The Plan: Building on Children's Interests
42. Calendar Time for Young Children: Good Intentions Gone Awry

Teenage parents

11. Children of Teen Parents: Challenges and Hope

Violence

11. Children of Teen Parents: Challenges and Hope

Internet References

The following Internet sites have been selected to support the articles found in this reader. These sites were available at the time of publication. However, because Web sites often change their structure and content, the information listed may no longer be available. We invite you to visit http://www.mhcls.com for easy access to these sites.

Annual Editions: Early Childhood Education 09/10

General Sources

Children's Defense Fund (CDF)
http://www.childrensdefense.org

At this site of the CDF, an organization that seeks to ensure that every child is treated fairly, there are reports and resources regarding current issues facing today's youth, along with national statistics on various subjects.

Connect for Kids
http://www.connectforkids.org

This nonprofit site provides news and information on issues affecting children and families, with over 1,500 helpful links to national and local resources.

National Association for the Education of Young Children
http://www.naeyc.org

The NAEYC Web site is a valuable tool for anyone working with young children. Also see the National Education Association site: http://www.nea.org.

U.S. Department of Education
http://www.ed.gov/pubs/TeachersGuide/

Government goals, projects, grants, and other educational programs are listed here as well as many links to teacher services and resources.

Unit 1: Perspectives

Child Care and Early Education Research Connections
www.researchconnections.org

This site offers excellent help for anyone looking for research based data related to early childhood education. Full text articles and other reference materials are available.

Child Care Directory: Care Guide
http://www.care.com

Find licensed/registered child care by zip code at this site. See prescreened profiles and get free background checks on providers. Pages for parents along with additional links are also included.

Complementary Learning Approach to the Achievement Gap
http://www.gse.harvard.edu/hfrp/projects/complementary-learning.html

Complementary learning provides a variety of support services for all children to be successful. These supports reach beyond the school and work toward consistent learning and developmental outcomes for children.

Early Childhood Care and Development
http://www.ecdgroup.com

This site concerns international resources in support of children to age 8 and their families. It includes research and evaluation, policy matters, programming matters, and related Web sites.

Global SchoolNet Foundation
http://www.gsn.org

Access this site for multicultural education information. The site includes news for teachers, students, and parents as well as chat rooms, links to educational resources, programs, and contests and competitions.

Mid-Continent Research for Education and Learning
http://www.mcrel.org/standards-benchmarks

This site provides a listing of standards and benchmarks that include content descriptions from 112 significant subject areas and documents from across 14 content areas.

The National Association of State Boards of Education
http://www.nasbe.org/

Included on this site is an extensive overview of the No Child Left Behind Act. There are links to specific state's plans.

Unit 2: Young Children, Their Families and Communities

Administration for Children and Families
http://www.dhhs.gov

This site provides information on federally funded programs that promote the economic and social well-being of families, children, and communities.

The AARP Grandparent Information Center
http://www.aarp.org/grandparents

The center offers tips for raising grandchildren, activities, health and safety, visitations, and other resources to assist grandparents.

All About Asthma
http://pbskids.org/arthur/grownups/teacherguides/health/asthma_tips.html

This is a fact sheet/activity book featuring the popular TV character Arthur who has asthma. The site gives statistics and helps parents, teachers and children understand asthma. It gives tips on how to decrease asthma triggers. It has English, Spanish, Chinese, Vietnamese, and Tagalog versions of some of the materials.

Allergy Kids
http://allergykids.com

Developed by Robyn O'Brien, a mother committed to helping children and families everywhere deal with allergies, this site is extremely valuable for all families and school personnel. Tip sheets are provided that can be shared with teachers and families as well as items for purchase to support allergic children.

Changing the Scene on Nutrition
http://www.fns.usda.gov/tn/Healthy/changing.html

This is a free toolkit for parents, school administrators, and teachers to help change the attitudes toward health and nutrition in their schools.

Internet References

Children, Youth and Families Education and Research Network
www.cyfernet.org

This excellent site contains useful links to research from key universities and institutions. The categories include early childhood, school age, teens, parents and family, and community.

The National Academy for Child Development
http://www.nacd.org

The NACD, an international organization, is dedicated to helping children and adults reach their full potential. Its home page presents links to various programs, research, and resources into such topics as learning disabilities, ADD/ADHD, brain injuries, autism, accelerated and gifted, and other similar topic areas.

National Network for Child Care
www.nncc.org

This network brings together the expertise of many land grant universities through their cooperative extension programs. These are the programs taped back in early 1965 to train the 41,000 teachers needed for the first Head Start programs that summer. The site contains information on over 1,000 publications and resources related to child care. Resources for local conferences in early childhood education are included.

National Safe Kids Campaign
http://www.babycenter.com

This site includes an easy-to-follow milestone chart and advice on when to call the doctor.

Zero to Three
http://www.zerotothree.org

Find here developmental information on the first 3 years of life—an excellent site for both parents and professionals.

Unit 3: Diverse Learners

American Academy of Pediatrics
www.aap.org

Pediatricians provided trusted advice for parents and teachers. The AAP official site includes position statements on a variety of topics related to the health and safety of young children.

Child Welfare League of America (CWLA)
http://www.cwla.org

The CWLA is the United States' oldest and largest organization devoted entirely to the well-being of vulnerable children and their families. Its Web site provides links to information about issues related to morality and values in education.

Classroom Connect
http://www.classroom.com/login/home.jhtml

A major Web site for K-12 teachers and students, this site provides links to schools, teachers, and resources online. It includes discussion of the use of technology in the classroom.

The Council for Exceptional Children
http://www.cec.sped.org/index.html

Information on identifying and teaching children with a variety of disabilities. The Council for Exceptional Children is the largest professional organization for special educators.

Early Learning Standards: Full report
http://www.naeyc.org/resources/position_statements/positions_2003.asp

This site provides the full joint position statement by the National Association for the Education of Young Children (NAEYC) and The National Association of Early Childhood Specialists in the State Department of Education (NAECS/SDE) on early learning standards.

Early Learning Standards: Executive Summary
http://www.naeyc.org/resources/position_statements/creating_conditions.asp

This site provides the executive summary for the joint position statement by the National Association for the Education of Young Children (NAEYC) and The National Association of Early Childhood Specialists in the State Department of Education (NAECS/SDE) on early learning standards.

Make Your Own Web page
http://www.teacherweb.com

Easy step-by-step directions for teachers at all levels to construct their own web page. Parents can log on and check out what is going on in their child's classroom.

National Resource Center for Health and Safety in Child Care
http://nrc.uchsc.edu

Search through this site's extensive links to find information on health and safety in child care. Health and safety tips are provided, as are other child-care information resources.

Online Innovation Institute
http://oii.org

A collaborative project among Internet-using educators, proponents of systemic reform, content-area experts, and teachers who desire professional growth, this site provides a learning environment for integrating the Internet into educators' individual teaching styles.

Unit 4: Supporting Young Children's Development

Action for Healthy Kids
www.actionforhealthykids.org

This organization works to assist the ever increasing numbers of students who are overweight, undernourished, and sedentary. They feature a campaign for school wellness.

American Academy of Pediatrics
www.aap.org

Pediatricians provide trusted advice for parents and teachers. The AAP official site includes position statements on a variety of issues related to the health and safety of young children.

Unit 5: Educational Practices

Association for Childhood Education International (ACEI)
http://www.acei.org/

This site, established by the oldest professional early childhood education organization, describes the association, its programs, and the services it offers to both teachers and families.

Early Childhood Education Online
http://www.umaine.edu/eceol/

This site gives information on developmental guidelines and issues in the field, presents tips for observation and assessment, and gives information on advocacy.

Reggio Emilia
http://www.ericdigests.org/2001-3/reggio.htm

Through ERIC, link to publications related to the Reggio Emilia approach and to resources, videos, and contact information.

Internet References

Unit 6: Helping Children to Thrive in School

Future of Children
http://www.futureofchildren.org

Produced by the David and Lucille Packard Foundation, the primary purpose of this page is to disseminate timely information on major issues related to children's well-being.

Busy Teacher's Cafe
http://www.busyteacherscafe.com

This is a Web site for early childhood educators with resource pages for everything from worksheets to classroom management.

Tips for Teachers
http://www.counselorandteachertips.com

This site includes links for various topics of interest to teachers such as behavior management, peer mediation, and new teacher resources.

You Can Handle Them All
http://www.disciplinehelp.com

This site describes different types of behavioral problems and offers suggestions for managing these problems.

Unit 7: Curricular Issues

Action for Healthy Kids
www.actionforhealthykids.org

This organization works to assist the ever increasing numbers of students who are overweight, undernourished and sedentary. They feature a campaign for school wellness.

Awesome Library for Teachers
http://www.neat-schoolhouse.org/teacher.html

Open this page for links and access to teacher information on everything from educational assessment to general child development topics.

The Educators' Network
http://www.theeducatorsnetwork.com

A very useful site for teachers at every level in every subject area. Includes lesson plans, theme units, teacher tools, rubrics, books, educational news, and much more.

The Family Involvement Storybook Corner
http://www.gse.harvard.edu/hfrp/projects/fine.html

In partnership with Reading is Fundamental (RIF) the Family Involvement Storybook Corner is a place to find compilations of family involvement, children's storybooks, and related tools and information.

Grade Level Reading Lists
http://www.gradelevelreadinglists.org

Recommended reading lists for grades kindergarten–eight can be downloaded through this site.

Idea Box
http://theideabox.com

This site is geared toward parents and has many good activities for creating, playing, and singing. The activities are creative and educational and can be done at home or in a classroom.

International Reading Association
http://www.reading.org

This organization for professionals who are interested in literacy contains information about the reading process and assists teachers in dealing with literacy issues.

PE Central
http://www.pecentral.org

Included in this site are developmentally appropriate physical activities for children, also containing one section dedicated to preschool physical education. It also includes resources and research in physical education.

The Perpetual Preschool
http://www.ecewebguide.com

This site provides teachers with possibilities for learning activities, offers chats with other teachers and resources on a variety of topics. The theme ideas are a list of possibilities and should not be used in whole, but used as a starting point for building areas of investigation that are relevant and offer firsthand experiences for young children.

Phi Delta Kappa
http://www.pdkintl.org

This important organization publishes articles about all facets of education. By clicking on the links in this site, for example, you can check out the journal's online archive, which has resources such as articles having to do with assessment.

Teacher Quick Source
http://www.teacherquicksource.com

Originally designed to help Head Start teachers meet the child outcomes, this site can be useful to all preschool teachers. Domains can be linked to developmentally appropriate activities for classroom use.

Teachers Helping Teachers
http://www.pacificnet.net/~mandel/

Basic teaching tips, new teaching methodologies, and forums for teachers to share experiences are provided on this site. Download software and participate in chats. It features educational resources on the Web, with new ones added each week.

Tech Learning
http://www.techlearning.com

An award-winning K-12 educational technology resource, this site offers thousands of classroom and administrative tools, case studies, curricular resources, and solutions.

Technology Help
http://www.apples4theteacher.com

This site helps teachers incorporate technology into the classroom. Full of interactive activities children can do alone, with a partner, or for full group instruction in all subject areas.

UNIT 1
Perspectives

Unit Selections

1. **Early Education, Later Success,** Susan Black
2. **The Changing Culture of Childhood: A Perfect Storm,** Joe L. Frost
3. **Joy in School,** Steven Wolk
4. **Accountability Comes to Preschool: Can We Make It Work for Young Children?,** Deborah Stipek
5. **No Child Left Behind: Who's Accountable?,** Lisa A. DuBois
6. **Preschool Comes of Age: The National Debate on Education for Young Children Intensifies,** Michael Lester

Key Points to Consider

- What are some of the key challenges affecting the early care and education profession?

- If our nation wants to make high-quality preschool education a priority, then what are some of the challenges we face?

- How much emphasis should be placed on academics in a preschool program?

- What are the long-term benefits of attending a quality preschool program?

- How are social disadvantage and poverty related to low achievement of young children?

- How can teachers become more involved in advocacy issues related to the care and education of young children?

- How has the introduction of early learning standards affected the profession?

Student Web Site
www.mhcls.com

Internet References

Child Care and Early Education Research Connections
www.researchconnections.org

Child Care Directory: Care Guide
http://www.care.com

Complementary Learning Approach to the Achievement Gap
http://www.gse.harvard.edu/hfrp/projects/complementary-learning.html

Early Childhood Care and Development
http://www.ecdgroup.com

Global SchoolNet Foundation
http://www.gsn.org

Mid-Continent Research for Education and Learning
http://www.mcrel.org/standards-benchmarks

The National Association of State Boards of Education
http://www.nasbe.org/

President Obama repeatedly calls for a focus on early childhood education when addressing questions about his plan for improving education in America. He recognizes that no improvement in educational achievement can be reached without starting with our youngest learners. This does not mean that early childhood education is viewed as a panacea or a solution to all problems, but it does mean that early childhood educators, and the work they do, are an integral part of the team that will work to improve learning experiences for all children while working to help students meet standards in all areas.

This unit starts with Susan Black's article "Early Education, Later Success," which is aimed at leaders in school districts seeking a way to improve their K-12 education. Black encourages school leaders to look down, to the preschool years, where a strong pre-K foundation can translate to significant learning gains down the road.

Generations of adults have reflected back on their own childhood experiences and schooling, and made comparisons to those of current children. Except for childhoods affected by war or the Great Depression, there has not been a greater change in one generation than is occurring now. In his article, "The Changing Culture of Childhood: A Perfect Storm," Joe L. Frost outlines the dramatic changes children are experiencing today on all fronts. The pressure for high-stakes achievement at an early age, the decreasing time allocated for spontaneous creative play, and the deep and lasting impact of poverty are all discussed by Frost.

The increasing high-stakes pressure of the past few years on accountability has caused many educators to suck the joy and passion out of learning. The prize has become higher test scores instead of learning for life long benefits. Many teachers are afraid that children are becoming turned off to school at a young age, and classrooms where children are required to sit all day in desks and complete endless piles of worksheets and work books are commonplace in many parts of the country. These types of joyless learning places are especially prevalent in inner cities and charter schools where high test scores translates into higher enrollment. Steven Wolk shares many ways joyful learning can flourish in school alongside high achievement and provides suggestions for educators of all levels of learners in his article, "Joy in School."

I always feel good when I realize that others outside of the field of early childhood education recognize that quality care and education for young children can have tremendous financial benefits as well as educational benefits for society. Of course I would always welcome the interest from more people outside of the profession, but the field is receiving increased attention from others for a number of reasons. The nation is learning that high quality programs are beneficial for young children's long-term development. Much of this interest is in part due to

© Imagemore/Getty Images

some state legislators allocating resources for state-operated preschool programs. Coupled with the knowledge of the importance of ECE programs is a realization that the quality of these programs should be of utmost importance. Another reason is the compelling evidence from brain research that children are born learning. Yet, despite new information on the importance of early childhood, we still tend to hold onto cultural traditions about who young children are and how to care for them. This dichotomy between information and tradition results in an impasse when it comes to creating national policy related to young children.

Two of the articles in this unit have the word accountable in the title. "Accountability Comes to Preschool: Can We Make It Work for Young Children?" and "No Child Left Behind: Who's Accountable?" send a powerful message about the way others view our profession and what we do. I am reminded of one of the more popular perceptions of early care and education held by those outside of the profession. For the past fifty years, "early childhood education was viewed as a panacea, the solution to all social ills in society." (Paciorek, 2008, p. xvii). This is huge pressure to put on one profession; especially one that is grossly underpaid. Early childhood is viewed by many as the cure for all social problems. We do have outside forces carefully watching how early education practices affect long-term development and learning. Early childhood professionals must be accountable for practices they implement in their classrooms and how children spend their time interacting with materials. Appropriate early learning standards are the norm in the profession and knowledgeable caregivers and teachers must be informed of the importance of developing quality experiences that align with the standards. Teachers can no longer plan cute activities that fill the child's days and backpacks with pictures to hang on the refrigerator. Teachers must be intentional in their planning to adapt learning experiences so that all children can achieve standards that are based on knowledge of developmental abilities.

For over 125 years, Peabody College of Vanderbilt University has been recognized as a leader in preparing future teachers, administrators, and professors for the field of education. The article "No Child Left Behind: Who's Accountable?" provides insight from key researchers and policymakers at this Nashville, TN institution. They examine how the No Child Left Behind (NCLB) law signed in 2001, and expected to show full results in 2014, has affected our education system. The next five years will be critical for NCLB and what will come for the future of this, at times, controversial law. As the editor, I hope you benefit from reading the articles and reflecting on the important issues facing early childhood education today.

Early Education, Later Success

How do you sustain the momentum generated by your prekindergarten and full-day kindergarten programs? Start by considering an aligned and unified PK-3 unit.

SUSAN BLACK

D oes your district offer high-quality prekindergarten and full-day kindergarten programs? If so, your youngest students are off to a good start.

Research confirms that children in good prekindergartens are eager and successful learners in kindergarten. And children who attend good full-day kindergartens stand a better chance of succeeding in first grade. That's the encouraging news.

But there's a worrisome downside. Prekindergarten children's gains in language, literacy, and math often fade out by the end of first grade. The gains children make in kindergarten, whether they attend half-day or full-day, often fade out by third grade.

Don't give up hope. There are steps you can take to ensure that prekindergarten and kindergarten pay off in the long run.

What's Needed?

PK-3 units are a "promising solution" to the fade-out problem, says Kristie Kaurez, director of early learning at the Education Commission of the States.

In an issue brief for the New America Foundation, a nonprofit public policy institute, Kaurez says success requires more than high-quality programs at each grade. The first five grades, she says, must provide similar instruction, curriculum alignment, well-managed transitions between grades, smaller class sizes, parent involvement, and top-quality teaching.

Kaurez envisions a five-step ladder—a "succession of sturdy rungs"—that children climb with confidence during their first five years of schooling. At each rung, children gain and maintain a "strong foothold" in language, literacy, and math.

Studies show it can be done, and children can profit immeasurably.

An evaluation of New Jersey's Union City School District's PK-3 "base camp," a program which links standards, curriculum, and assessments, showed significant gains: When the youngsters reached fourth grade, they nearly doubled their proficiency on state tests in language arts and math.

Multi-year studies of the Chicago Child-Parent Centers, a PK-3 program established by the Chicago Board of Education, show long-lasting effects. Students had higher achievement and, in later years, were less involved in juvenile crime.

Arthur Reynolds, with the University of Minnesota's Institute for Child Development, reports two "striking effects" for children in high-quality PK-3 units: By third grade, they're far less likely to be retained or to be placed in special education. While it's unproven that PK-3 units alone cause higher achievement, Reynolds stands by the "wisdom of high quality PK-3 programs."

Taking a Long View

Well-planned PK-3 programs help children master reading and math, according to researchers with the University of Michigan's Inter-University Consortium for Political and Social Research (ICPSR). Equally important, five-grade units help children develop "social, self-regulating, and motivating traits," attributes considered essential to learning.

PK-3 programs take a long view of children's learning and development, and they give children more time to succeed, ICPSR points out. Compared to school readiness programs, PK-3 programs provide a "richer, more detailed understanding and a better prediction of children's development outcomes," ICPSR says.

Success depends on getting PK-3 units right, and that can take time and effort.

Success depends on getting PK-3 units right, and that can take time and effort. ICPSR says these components are essential:

- School organization that supports PK-3 units
- Strong principal leadership
- Qualified teacher
- Classrooms designed as learning centers
- Curriculum and instruction that is aligned and coordinated across five grades
- Assessment and accountability systems for teachers and administrators
- Family and community engagement and support

An even longer view, beginning with infants and toddlers, adds to the benefits of PK-3.

A 2006 study in *Pediatrics* describes a 36-month health and educational program of home visits and parent support groups provided to families with low birth weight and premature infants. A follow-up study shows that, as teens, the children had higher achievement in math and reading; less tobacco, marijuana, and alcohol use; and less antisocial behavior and suicidal tendencies or attempts.

Citing such effects, some states have expanded early childhood education to include the years preceeding prekindergarten.

New York State's Board of Regents' early childhood education policy covers birth through fourth grade. It begins with prenatal care and extends to health services and educational programs for infants and toddlers. School districts are expected to "ensure that families have access to needed services," particularly families at or below the poverty level and those with children who speak limited English and whose children have disabilities.

Georgia's Department of Early Care and Learning oversees a statewide system that coordinates services for children from birth through age 4. Washington State's Department of Early Learning coordinates Head Start, child care, early reading programs, and prekindergarten.

All in the Family

How important are families? Linda Espinosa, with the University of Missouri-Columbia, says social-emotional development during an infant's first year contributes to learning language. By age 5, a child should have a large vocabulary, narrative skills, and the ability to verbalize thoughts, ideas, emotions, and observations.

Espinosa says children are more likely to succeed in school if they have these experiences during their first five years:

* Close, supportive relationships at home, in day care, and in nursery school
* Opportunities to describe and express feelings
* Opportunities to make choices and to develop self-control and self-regulated learning
* Enrichment, such as field trips to zoos, parks, and museums
* Playtime that includes role play and opportunities to be expressive and imaginative

A child's first relationships are the "prism through which they learn about the world," says Ross Thompson with the University of Nebraska. Social interactions during a child's early years have a greater effect on learning than educational toys, brain-stimulating activities, and nursery school lessons, he claims.

Thompson says infants and toddlers are more likely to succeed if they develop three types of skills: intellectual, including using simple numbers and clearly expressing ideas; motivational, including curiosity and confidence in learning; and social-emotional, including participating in groups, cooperating with others, and exerting self-discipline.

Family engagement is essential to "develop and sustain effective PK-3 programs," says Richard Weissbourd, co-chair of Pre-K to 3 Education: Promoting Early Success, Harvard University's

new institute for school leaders. Superintendents, principals, and teachers enrolled in the institute study early childhood literacy, and they learn the importance of helping parents provide reading, math, and rich conversations during daily home activities; involving parents in literacy activities at school; and strengthening teacher-parent partnerships through home visits.

Creating a Good Program

A suburban school district administrator told me it takes "perseverance and pushiness" to create a high-quality PK-3 unit. She's been at it for three years, but progress is slow-going.

So far she's secured board approval for PK-3, found space for new prekindergarten classrooms, and provided teachers with training and supplies. But problems persist. An elementary principal is half-hearted about the PK-3 concept, and some teachers refuse to try new strategies, plan as a team, or conduct home visits.

Still, I'm pinning my hopes on this dedicated administrator and the teachers who have stepped forward and are willing to do all they can to help their youngest students.

Here's why.

A *Washington Post* story describes Johnny, a 5-year-old child of immigrants who entered kindergarten in Maryland's Montgomery County Public Schools. Education writer Jay Mathews says Johnny is part of an "unnerving language gap" that contributes to a wide achievement gap. (Most children from affluent families enter school knowing 13,000 English words, a sharp contrast to many children from poor and immigrant families who know a meager 500 English words.)

Operation Johnny began soon after the school year started. Working as a team, the little boy's kindergarten teacher, his parents, an interpreter, a speech pathologist, a special education consultant, and a social worker designed a year-long plan to help Johnny learn. The teacher was pivotal to the plan, agreeing to sit close to the boy, teach him new vocabulary through games and activities, and videotape classroom lessons for Johnny's parents to reinforce at home.

The district is determined to rescue Johnny and others like him. MCPS's board of education authorized Superintendent Jerry Weast to spend more than $21 million for an Early Success Performance Plan that's reduced class sizes and created full-day kindergartens in all 123 primary schools. The plan is paying off: In three years, the percentage of low-income 5-year-olds attaining grade-level goals has risen from 44 percent to 70 percent. Their fourth-grade passing rate on state tests is 86 percent.

Johnny is off to a good start. He's eager to learn, due in part to the district's plan and in part to his kindergarten teacher's determination and extra effort. Operation Johnny illustrates what all school leaders and teachers can and should do to help struggling students succeed at every step on the five-step ladder.

Susan Black, an *ASBJ* contributing editor, is an education researcher and writer in Hammondsport, N.Y.

The Changing Culture of Childhood

A Perfect Storm

Joe L. Frost

A kind of "perfect storm" is now brewing in the education and development of children in the United States. Those who have not lived or explored the history of education in the United States; have not experienced both poverty and abundance; have lived lives sheltered from the barrios, slums, homeless shelters, and epidemics; or those unfamiliar with the rich legacy of history and child development scholarship on the nature of learning and relevance of culture are repeating the mistakes to be found in the history of U.S. education.

A combination of interrelated elements is currently changing the face of the civilizing traditions of U.S. education and forming a new culture of childhood. These include: 1) the standardization of education; 2) the dissolution of traditional spontaneous play; and 3) the growing specter of poverty in the United States and around the world.

The Standardization of Schooling

The standardization of schooling began as a state effort to improve achievement and reduce drop-outs by implementing the high-stakes testing movement, later known as No Child Left Behind. From the beginning, a fundamental fault of ignoring individual differences in all dimensions of education and child development spelled failure for this program. Well before the advent of the testing mania, educators learned the lessons of such folly from the scholarly research of the child study movement in the early 1900s, which was influenced by such philosophers as Rousseau, Pestalozzi, Froebel, Hall, and Dewey, and later Piaget and Vygotsky. Throughout the first half of the 20th century, U.S. educators and child development professionals framed their work around conclusions from extensive research at major universities throughout the nation and refined their work through ever-growing research during the second half of the 20th century. I search in vain for the scholarly underpinnings for high-stakes testing.

Historically, scholarship led to emphasis on individuality, creativity, cooperative learning, community involvement, and balancing academics, arts, and outdoor play. Assessment of young children became an ongoing process, involving intensive study of children, testing for diagnostic purposes, individualized assessment, and teacher observation and judgment. A mechanized model of education focuses on one-size-fits all testing and instruction and was never accepted or recommended by national professional organizations, never supported by research, and never embraced by educators and child development professionals.

In the No Child Left Behind program, high-stakes testing was to be the motor driving the standardization movement. Widely implemented in Texas, this movement was called the "Texas Miracle," because of early reported dramatic improvement in test scores—a promise to be dashed as evidence showed that the "improvements" were confounded by cheating and political deals with publishing companies (CNN, 2005). In 2004, the Dallas Morning News (*Austin American-Statesman*, 2004) found evidence of cheating in Houston and Dallas, and suspicious scores in dozens of other Texas cities. For example, 4th-graders in one large city elementary school scored in the bottom 2 percent in the state while the 5th-graders in that school ended up with the highest math scores in the state, with more than 90 percent of the students getting perfect or near-perfect scores. No other school ever came close to that performance. The U.S. Department of Education named this school a Blue Ribbon School and the superintendent of the district was named U.S. secretary of Education.

In September 2005, the Education Policy Studies Laboratory of Arizona State University (Nichols, Glass, & Berliner, 2005) published yet another study concluding that "pressure created by high-stakes testing has had almost no important influence on student academic performance" (p. 4). This study, conducted in 25 states, found a negative effect on minority students and illuminated the performance gap between white and minority students and between students from middle- and upper-income families and those from low-income homes. Such gaps come as no surprise to those who have studied the research on class, race, and educational achievement over the past half-century.

The prominent Latino authors in Angela Valenzuela's book *Leaving Children Behind: How "Texas-style" Accountability Fails Latino Youth* (2005) reveal the same kind of creeping, hidden discrimination that led to the civil rights struggle in the United States and the recent riots by disenfranchised minority youth in France and other European countries. The state's methods of collecting and reporting high-stakes test scores "hide as much as they reveal. . . . When skyrocketing dropout and projected retention rates are factored in, the state's 'miracle' looks more like a mirage" (p. 1). These Latino scholars contend that high-stakes testing is harmful to all children, but especially poor, minority, non English-speaking children; they state that children have a right to be assessed in a fair, impartial manner, using multiple assessment criteria.

Daily teaching and practicing the test has become the norm. Recess, arts, physical education, and creative inquiry are replaced with pizza parties, pep rallies, mock test practice, and teaching the test. Teachers, administrators, children, and parents face ever-growing pressure from threats of failure, retention, and demotion. As the schools focus ever more on bringing low-performing students up to grade-level standards, the most brilliant, most creative students, already performing well beyond their grade level, are left to languish in mediocrity and sameness. "In recent years the percentage of California students scoring in the 'advanced' math range has declined by as much as half between second and fifth grade" (Goodkin, 2005, p. A-15). It makes little difference in this draconian system whether a child merely meets the grade level standard or far exceeds it.

Politicians, not educators, are framing the U.S. education system and radically changing the culture of education, and standardized tests are becoming the curriculum of the schools. As the testing movement spreads across the nation, the Texas miracle is recognized by educators, professional organizations, and a growing number of politicians as bureaucratic bungling.

High-stakes testing is damaging to children and teachers—emotionally, physically, and intellectually. Around the country, children are wetting their pants, crying, acting out, becoming depressed, and taking their parents' pills on the day of testing to help them cope. In 2005, several children doped out and were taken to hospitals on the day of testing. In this same city, a high school that received a "School for Excellence Award" in 2002 was declared "low performing" in 2004 because a small group of children with disabilities did not perform well on a test designed for typical children.

Creative approaches to teaching value the souls and intellects of children and reveal and complement the wonderful creative powers of the best teachers. While teaching to the test may falsely guide the poorest teachers who struggle for direction, the best teachers are bound to a humdrum existence, divorced from teaching to interests, talents, and abilities; bound to endless regimented paperwork, meaningless workshops and repetition; and reduced to stress and mediocrity. Standardized tests tell good teachers what they already know and take an awesome toll on their teaching effectiveness, health, and creative powers.

In many states around the country, kindergartens and preschools are no longer a place for play, singing, and art; no longer a place for lessons on cooperation and sharing, or learning to love compelling literature and telling stories. They are no longer a place of fun and joy. Now, 3- to 5-year-olds, some still wetting their pants, not knowing how to stand in line, sit in a circle, or follow simple instructions, spend much of their time drilling skills and prepping for tests. We teach little kids to walk and talk and play together, then we tell them to sit down, shut up, and take the test. Yet learning by rote—by memory without thought of meaning—has never been a sound educational process.

The Dissolution of Traditional Spontaneous Children's Play

The early 20th century was a period of unparalleled interest in children's play and playgrounds. The U.S. play movement saw the promotion of spontaneous play and playgrounds in schools nationwide. The report of the 1940 White House Conference on Children and Youth (U.S. Superintendent of Documents, 1940, p. 191) stated, "All persons require types of experiences through which the elemental desire for friendship, recognition, adventure, creative expression, and group acceptance may be realized. . . . Favorable conditions of play . . . contribute much toward meeting these basic emotional needs." Play, the report stated, also supplies the growth and development of the child, and promotes motor, manual, and artistic skills—all conclusions supported by research and experience throughout the latter half of the 20th century.

Traditional spontaneous play is declining in U.S. neighborhoods and schools, and school recess is declining (Pica, 2003, 2005). The Atlanta school system built schools without playgrounds to demonstrate their devotion to high academic standards (Ohanian, 2002). Across the United States, school districts are abolishing recess or denying recess to children who score poorly on tests (Ohanian, 2002, p. 12). The International Play Association reports that 40 percent of U.S. elementary schools are deleting recess or reducing recess time to prepare for tests. *Psychology Today* reports that 40,000 schools no longer have play times.

Spontaneous play is also disappearing from the streets of cities throughout the industrialized world. In 1979, Keiki Haginoya began his intended life's work of preparing photo documentaries of children at play on the streets of Tokyo. In 1996, he wrote a sad conclusion to his career. Children's laughter and spontaneous play, which once filled the streets, alleys, and vacant lots of the city, had vanished. His photos show the rapid loss of play space, the separation of children from natural outdoor activities, traditional games, and creative play—indeed, the transformation of children's culture.

Haginoya's photos represent a sociological/psychological history of the cultural transformation—the construction of buildings and fences, the increase in cars, mass-produced toys, video game machines, and school entrance examinations. He mourns the demise of children's play and the end of his work:

> If I look back over the past seventeen years, it appears that I have taken the last record of children at play in the city, and that makes me deeply sad. . . . Children have learned enormous things through play. . . . The mere thought of

6

growing into a social person without the experience of outdoor play makes me shudder. (Haginoya, 1996, p. 4)

Kid pagers, instant messaging, video games, and chat rooms are replacing free, natural play in the fields and forests, a phenomenon Louv (2005) describes as "nature-deficit disorder." Even summer camps, only recently places for hiking in the woods, learning about plants and animals, and telling firelight stories, are now becoming computer camps, weight loss camps, and places where nature is something to watch, wear, consume, or ignore—places where attendance is linked to comfort and entertainment. If the present trends continue, summer camps may well become places to ditch children for tutoring on testing (Louv, 2005). In response, we have been transforming the playgrounds at our research site of three decades—Redeemer Lutheran School in Austin, Texas—into an integrated outdoor learning environment of playgrounds, natural habitats, and gardens. We see such work growing in acceptance, especially at child care centers where NCLB has only limited impact.

What is it like to bond with the wilderness? Having managed to survive the hazards of a childhood in the hillside farms and wilderness of the Ouachita Mountains of Arkansas more than half a century ago, I offer a personal glimpse of a childhood among the creeks and rivers, hills and valleys, and among domesticated and wild animals on the farm and in the wilderness. I never understood why kinfolk visiting from cities would ask, "Don't you get lonely down here?" The word "lonely "was not in my vocabulary or experience, because the days were filled with plowing and digging in the earth, wondering about the arrowheads found there; drinking from cool springs on hot days; swimming in the creeks and rivers at the end of long, sweaty days; riding horses and playing rodeo in the barn lots on weekends; feeding the cows, pigs, and chickens; building tree houses and hideouts in the woods; hunting raccoons at night and squirrels and deer in the daytime; cutting trees and chopping wood; taking pride in baling hay with the grown men; exploring fields and woods while eating watermelon and muscadines; building fires and cooking fish on the river bank; scanning the forest ahead for thorn bushes, snakes, and wild game; lying on the creek bank in the springtime, watching the creative movements of clouds; and all the while reveling in a sense of deep satisfaction and appreciation of the ever-changing natural wilderness.

We gathered along the gravel road before daylight during the winter to ride the back of a pick-up truck to school, stopping every half-mile or so to pick up other children who forded the river in boats or walked down out of the hills and valleys. We sat on sacks of mail, for the driver was also our mail carrier. We had five recess periods—before school and after school while waiting for the old truck to make runs over muddy road, and mid-morning, noon, and mid-afternoon. There was a level area in front of the school for organized games, most created by the children themselves, a creek along the back of the school for hunting frogs and building dams, and beyond that a pine-covered hillside. Here, we played war, built forts, and attacked the enemy with dead tree limb projectiles created by hitting the limb across a tree, breaking off the ends, which would fly

through the air, creating disarray and, sometimes, a bloody arm or nose. All of this constituted, as it turned out, a rather complete yet formidable playground. Play was truly free, for teachers stayed indoors. We stationed a kid at the edge of the woods to alert the group when the teacher rang the bell and it was time for "books." The ragged army then trooped indoors barefoot, muddy, and winded, but ready to sit down and pay attention. ADHD and obesity were unknown in that school and I never saw an injury that led to long-term consequences. What a difference six decades makes in the work and play of children!

The standardization of U.S. education extends well beyond the classroom curriculum into the playgrounds. Since the inception of national playground safety standards in 1981, constant revision has led to a 55-page standard of growing complexity, internal inconsistency, and estrangement from creativity. The "modern playground" is, in the main, an assemblage of steel and plastic structures, differing little from place to place, and devoid of natural habitats. Litigation replaces common sense and personal responsibility, and competition from testing and technology and careless parenting are producing a generation of obese kids with growing health and behavior problems. Safety standards are needed, but they should be consistent across state and national agencies, simple and clear in their expectations, and addressed to hazards in consumer products that threaten disability and death. Living is fraught with risks—emotional risks, financial risks, physical risks. Risk is essential for physical development. Overweight children with limited physical skills are unsafe on any playground. The issue is not merely how to make playgrounds safe for children, but how to make children safe for playgrounds.

In failing to cultivate the inherent play tendencies of children in the outdoor world, we fail to plant the early seeds of passionate exploration, artistic vision, creative reflection, and good health. Childhood is the time when, and playgrounds and natural habitats are the special places where, the culture, arising from tradition, knowledge, and skills, is readily and rapidly assimilated into the growing brain and psyche.

The Impact of Poverty on the Culture of Childhood

Poverty has powerful associations with school performance and exerts severe limits on what high-stakes testing can accomplish. Thousands of studies show positive correlations between poverty and achievement for children of all ethnic groups (Berliner, 2005). We don't need No Child Left Behind to tell us where failing schools are located—we have known for over a half century. The childhood poverty rate in the United States is greater than that of 25 wealthy countries, and poverty in the United States is clustered among minorities (UNICEF, 2005). As a group, African American and Hispanic American 15-year-olds rank 26th among 27 developed countries in reading, mathematics, and science literacy (Lemke et al., 2001).

More than half of all children born during this decade in developing countries will live their childhoods in urban slums. A quarter of those living in the United States will start their lives in urban slums (Nabhan & Trimble, 1996). Such children will have precious little opportunity to smell the flowers, sift clean dirt between their fingers, build a private hut in the wilds, walk in the morning dew, hear the quiet sounds of small animals at dusk, or see the heavens and the Milky Way in their full glory. Such seemingly insignificant experiences are the stuff that bond children to the natural world, introduce them to beauty and belonging, and surround them with opportunities to sharpen their growing minds with emerging concepts of geology, botany, physics, mathematics, and language.

For two decades, Annette Lareau (2003) and her team of researchers studied the differences in child rearing in upper middle-class versus working-class homes. The parenting styles and the results are dramatic, not good versus bad, but radically different in ways that prepare children to be successful in school. Upper middle-class families are more deeply involved in all aspects of their children's lives—providing a wide range of learning experiences, engaging in a lot of talk, reasoning with them, scheduling activities and getting them there, fighting over homework. In working-class homes, play is seen as inconsequential—a child's activity, not for adults. There was less talk, orders were brusque but whining was less. Parents offered fewer explanations and children, like their parents, were more likely to be intimidated by teachers and others in positions of authority. Working-class children had more intimate contact with extended families, they were taught right from wrong, and in many respects they were raised in the healthier environment. However, as adults, the working-class children are not doing well. They were not prepared for a world valuing verbal skills and an ability to thrive in organizations. They are picking up the same menial jobs their parents held, while the upper middle-class children are attending good colleges and preparing for professional careers.

The first White House Conference on Children in a Democracy was called by President Franklin D. Roosevelt in 1940, just after the onset of world war and during a time of exploitation of minorities and political patronage threatening the democratic process. The conference report (U.S. Superintendent of Documents, 1940, pp. 192–193) concluded that families of low-income children, minority children, slum children, and children with disabilities were deprived of toys, books, recreational areas, artistic events, and community recreation and playgrounds—in many respects, mirror images of what we see today.

The 2003 Census Report shows a steady rise in the number of families in poverty each year since 1999. When power and wealth rule a political structure, education itself is discriminatory (Wallis, 2005). We have known for decades that poverty is a key factor in school failure, yet both state and national governing bodies accommodate lobbyists and corporations while neglecting health care, housing, and living standards for the poor. Promises that the federal No Child Left Behind program would be accompanied by funds to make it work have gone unfulfilled, and children of the poor, especially minorities, are again stuffed into poverty-area schools rated "low performing" and "unacceptable." Now, public schools are threatened as students failing the tests are shifted to charter schools of questionable credentials and results, thus depriving public schools of desperately needed funds.

We see a growing storm for America's poorest children, with shrinking resources for school books, health insurance, affordable housing, health care, and food stamps. One in six U.S. children is poor; four million Americans are hungry and skipping meals; 45 million have no health insurance; 14 million have critical housing needs (Wallis, 2005, p. 223). With funding cuts in education and social services, the growing cost of war, tax cuts for the wealthy, natural disasters, and political cronyism, we now have a crisis among the poorest children.

The plight of the poor and minorities is nowhere more apparent than in the inequity of concern for the residents of New Orleans, both before and after Hurricane Katrina. Even before Katrina, the New Orleans schools were a failing system (Gray, 2005): already $45 million in debt; plagued by leadership crises (four superintendents in four years), scandals, and a squabbling school board; and strapped for resources. A majority of the students failed mandatory tests. After Katrina, we see a crisis of major proportions among displaced people striving to put their lives back together and a school system $300 million in debt.

Poverty-plagued and overlooked schools exist through the United States, especially in the slums and barrios of the cities. In Chicago, students from poor neighborhoods fail to receive their fair share of school funding and attend schools with tattered textbooks, decrepit buildings, overcrowded classrooms, and poorly qualified teachers (Loftus, 2005). Frustrated, stressed-out teachers desert the profession or pray for the day they can retire. Teachers in a growing number of schools must teach only one way. Policymakers must decide whether they want skillful, creative teachers or robots. If they want the former, they must put their money into supporting educators in developing curricula and sharpening their teaching skills.

Kozol (2005) tells stories about the dedication of teachers and the generosity in spirit of the children in the South Bronx; yet, in one school, only 65 of the 1,200 ninth-graders are likely to graduate. He points out that Mississippi spends $4,000 per pupil, inner-city Philadelphia schools get $6,000 per pupil, New York middle-class suburbs get $12,000 per pupil, and some very wealthy suburbs get $24,000 per pupil. Yet all are held to the same standards and all students take the same standardized exams. What history and research have always shown, but what policymakers ignore, is that poverty and hopelessness are fundamental causes of illiteracy and school failure in the United States. Regimented schooling does not address the problem of poverty.

Countering the Growing Storm

Author and poet Robert Louis Stevenson, sickly and in bed as a child, once watched the lamplighter move from place to place lighting the oil street lamps. He commented to his mother, "A man is coming down the street making holes in the darkness." We can all make little holes in the darkness and these holes can grow to illuminate entire neighborhoods, towns, and cities. Peaceful, informed dissent is a cornerstone of democracy and Americans are stepping up to protest the growing storm of elements that are eroding the culture of childhood. In April 2005, the Associated Press reported that the National Education Association (NEA) and school districts in Vermont, Michigan, and Texas, along with NEA chapters, were suing the federal administration for failing to provide support for the No Child Left Behind Act. In 2005, the Utah state legislature filed a lawsuit challenging the No Child Left Behind law, arguing that it is illegal to require expensive standardized testing for which it does not pay (Gillespie, 2005, p. A-10). Also in 2005, the NEA filed a lawsuit on behalf of local school districts and 20 state union chapters. A glimmer of hope emerged in November 2005, when the U.S. Secretary of Education, under fire from governors of several states, proposed allowing schools in some states to use children's progress on tests as evidence of success.

Who opposes high-stakes testing? Is it merely a handful of disgruntled parents, teachers, school boards, and professional organizations? Hardly. More than 70, and counting, professional organizations are in opposition, including such groups as the International Reading Association, the National Association for the Education of Young Children, American Educational Research Association, the American Psychiatric Association, the National Parent Teacher Association, the National Association for Elementary School Principals, the American Association of School Administrators, Students Against Testing, the National Association of School Psychologists, the American School Counselor Association, the National Council of Teachers of Mathematics, and the Association for Childhood Education International.

None of these organizations opposes meaningful testing or high academic expectations, nor do they hold that accountability is unnecessary. They simply contend that the system is deeply flawed. They promote assessments based on decades of research and experience; both formative and summative assessment, making decisions from multiple forms of assessment, not on a single test, adjusted for special needs and culturally different children; involving classroom teachers in assessment; and rejecting the use of test scores for punishing or rewarding administrators, teachers, and children.

Fortunately, private preschools remain relatively untouched by NCLB, although Head Start and other tax-supported early programs are under pressure to conform. Yes, professional standards and guidelines are essential, but look to those developed by such century-old organizations as NAEYC and ACEI-standards built by top researchers and successful practitioners worldwide, tied to the voluminous research of the past century, and refined by decades of experience.

High-stakes testing is not only wrong—it doesn't work. We are cultivating a culture of mediocrity and sameness and abandoning traditional ideas of creativity, ingenuity, ethical behavior, and imagination that make cultures and countries great. The most powerful policy for improving school achievement is reducing poverty. Focusing public policy on neighborhoods and families is an infinitely better strategy than focusing on testing to determine what we already know.

A reasonable substitute for the ill-founded emphasis on drill and testing for the very young would be to focus on encouraging parents to turn off the televisions, video games, and cell phones, and instead engage their children in conversation, take them to places of educational interest, read to them, teach them about the world beyond cartoons and video games, and teach them the value of giving over taking. Public policy should be directed toward rebuilding poverty-stricken neighborhoods, ensuring good jobs, medical care, and superior schools for all children, but especially for the very poor.

The impact of poverty, the demise of play, and high-stakes testing collectively are like the perfect storm. Each element contributes its destructive force, creating enormous potential for failure and damage to children—a sociopolitical system out of control. We must replace reactive, standardized learning with creative, thoughtful, introspective, interactive learning. We cannot allow the present generation of children to be the last to taste the joy of creative teaching and learning or to experience the delights of living with nature; the last children to know the collective inspiration of free, spontaneous play, and the separate peace of nature with all its fantasy, beauty, and freedom; the last to know the teachers and classrooms that molded people from all over the world into a fruitful, generous, and creative society. The engine that drives high-stakes testing, dismisses the value of children's play, and ignores the poor is a political engine. If we speak out, we can prevail; the storm will pass and good sense and a confluence of cultural creativity will return to the classrooms.

References

Austin American-Statesman. (2004, December 20). Signs of fraud found in study of TAKS results.

Berliner, D. C. (2005, August 2). *Teachers College Record*, www.tcrecord.org ID Number 12106.

CNN. (2005, May 8). *CNN Presents—High Stakes: No Child Left Behind*. Available on videotape.

Gillespie, N. (2005, August 23). Connecticut sues over No Child Left Behind. Associated Press in *Austin American-Statesman*, p. A-10.

Goodkin, S. (2005, December 28). We should leave no gifted child behind. *Austin American-Statesman* from *Washington Post*, p. A-15.

Gray, C. (2005). Even before the hurricane: A failed system. *Philadelphia Inquirer,* www.parentdirectededucation.org

Haginoya, K. (1996). Children's play has disappeared from the city. *PlayRights, 18*(1). Raleigh, NC: International Association for the Child's Right to Play.

Kozol, J. (2005). *Hypocrisy in testing craze*. Retrieved August 17, 2005, from www.weac.rg/news/2000-01/kozol.htm

Lareau, A. (2003). *Unequal childhoods: Class, race, and family life*. Berkeley, CA: University of California Press.

Lemke, M., Lippman, C., Jocelyn, L., Kastberg, D., Liu, Y. Y., Roey, S., Williams, T., Kruger, T., & Bairu, G. (2001). *Outcomes of learning: Results from the 2000 program for international student assessment of 15-year-olds in reading, mathematics, and science literacy*. Washington, DC: U.S. Department of Education, National Center for Education Statistics.

Loftus, K. P. (2005). *Katrina inequities already a reality for poor kids*. Retrieved March 23, 2006, from www.parentdirectededucation .org

Louv, R. (2005). *Last child in the woods: Saving our children from nature-deficit disorder*. Chapel Hill, NC: Algonquin Books.

Nabhan, G. P., & Trimble, S. (1996). *The geography of childhood: Why children need wild places.* Boston: Beacon Press.

Nichols, S. L., Glass, G. V., & Berliner, D. C. (2005). *High stakes testing and student achievement: Problems for the No Child Left Behind Act.* Tempe, AZ: Arizona State University, Education Policy Studies Laboratory.

Ohanian, S. (2002). *What happened to recess and why are our children struggling in kindergarten?* New York: McGraw-Hill.

Pica, R. (2003). *Your active child: How to boost physical, emotional, and cognitive development through age-appropriate activity.* New York: McGraw-Hill.

Pica, R. (2005). Reading, writing, 'rithmetic—and recess! *Linkup Parents Newsletter.* Retrieved August 8, 2005, from www.linkup-parents.com/education.html

UNICEF. (2005). *Child poverty in rich countries, Innocenti Report Card No. 6.* Florence, Italy: UNICEF Innocenti Research Centre, www.unicef.org/irc

U.S. Superintendent of Documents. (1940). *White House conference on children in a democracy.* Washington, DC: Author.

Valenzuela, A. (Ed.). (2005). *Leaving children behind: How "Texas-style" accountability fails Latino youth.* Albany, NY: State University of New York Press.

Wallis, J. (2005). *God's politics.* San Francisco: HarperCollins.

JOE L. FROST is Parker Centennial Professor Emeritus, University of Texas, Austin.

Joy in School

Joyful learning can flourish in school—if you give joy a chance.

STEVEN WOLK

Two quotes about schooling particularly resonate with me. The first is from John Dewey's *Experience and Education* (1938): "What avail is it to win prescribed amounts of information about geography and history, to win the ability to read and write, if in the process the individual loses his own soul?" (p. 49). If the experience of "doing school" destroys children's spirit to learn, their sense of wonder, their curiosity about the world, and their willingness to care for the human condition, have we succeeded as educators, no matter how well our students do on standardized tests?

The second quote comes from John Goodlad's *A Place Called School* (1984). After finding an "extraordinary sameness" in our schools, Goodlad wrote, "Boredom is a disease of epidemic proportions. . . . Why are our schools not places of joy?" (p. 242). Now, a generation later, if you were to ask students for a list of adjectives that describe school, I doubt that *joyful* would make the list. The hearts and minds of children and young adults are wide open to the wonders of learning and the fascinating complexities of life. But school still manages to turn that into a joyless experience.

So what can schools and teachers do to bring some joy into children's formal education? Children typically spend from six to seven hours each day in school for nearly 10 months each year. During the school year, children generally spend more time interacting with their teachers than with their parents. What happens inside schools has a deep and lasting effect on the mind-sets that children develop toward lifelong learning.

Dewey's point about the destructive power of our schools should make us ask ourselves some fundamental questions: What is the purpose of school? What dispositions about learning, reading, school, the world, and the self do we want to cultivate? Ask young adults why they go to school. You will hear nothing about joy.

I am not using the word joy as a synonym for *fun*. For many children, having fun is hanging out at the mall, watching TV, text-messaging their friends, or zipping down a roller-coaster. Having fun certainly brings us joy, but students don't need to be having fun in school to experience joy. According to my Random House dictionary, *joy* means, "The emotion of great delight or happiness caused by something good or satisfying." Surely our schools can do some of that. Joy and learning—including school content—are not mutually exclusive. Many of our greatest joys in life are related to our learning. Unfortunately, most of that joyful learning takes place outside school.

As educators, we have the responsibility to educate and inspire the whole child—mind, heart, and soul.

As educators, we have the responsibility to educate and inspire the whole child—mind, heart, and soul. By focusing on the following essentials, we can put more joy into students' experience of going to school and get more joy out of working inside one.

JOY 1:
Find the Pleasure in Learning

Why do people learn? I don't mean inside school—I mean learning as a part of life. Surely a large part of our learning is necessary for survival and a basic quality of life.

But there is another, entirely different, reason to learn. Learning gives us pleasure. This kind of learning is often (but not always) motivated from within, and no outside forces or coercions are needed. We also don't mind the possible difficulties in this learning. We often expect the challenges we encounter; we tend to see them as a natural part of the learning process, so we are far more open to taking risks. Some love to learn about cars, others love to learn about history, and some find great joy in learning how to dance. According to Mihaly Csikszentmihalyi (1990), such learning is an example of *flow,* which he defines as

> the state in which people are so involved in an activity that nothing else seems to matter; the experience itself is so enjoyable that people will do it at even great cost, for the sheer sake of doing it. (p. 4)

By helping students find the pleasure in learning, we can make that learning infinitely more successful.

If we want students to experience more flow in school—if we want them to see school and learning as joyful—we need to rethink how and what we teach. No longer can schooling be primarily about creating workers and test takers, but rather about nurturing human beings (Wolk, 2007). By helping students find the pleasure in learning, we can make that learning infinitely more successful.

JOY 2:
Give Students Choice

Outside of school, children are free to pursue their interests, and they do so with gusto. They learn how to play baseball or the drums; they learn how to ice skate or play video games; they read comic books, graphic novels, skateboard magazines, and Harry Potter.

But during a typical six-hour school day, how much ownership do students have of their learning? Practically none. It's not surprising that their interest in learning dissipates and that teachers complain of unmotivated students.

Joy in learning usually requires some ownership on the part of the learner. Students can own some of their school learning in several ways. They can choose the books they want to read through independent reading. In writing workshop, we can inspire them to be real writers and choose for themselves what genres to write in. During units in math, science, art, and social studies, they can choose specific subtopics to study; then, as "experts," they cart share their learning with the class. Students can also choose which products they want to create to demonstrate their learning. What brings more joy—studying the civil rights movement in the United States through a textbook and lectures or creating comic books, writing and performing plays, interviewing people to create podcasts, and proposing your own ideas? Which would *you* rather do?

I advocate giving students one hour each day to study topics of their choice in what I call "Exploratory" (Wolk, 2001). In Exploratory, teachers collaborate with students to help shape student-initiated ideas into purposeful, inquiry-based investigations. During this time, students are scattered around the room, absorbed in an endless variety of topics that matter to them. While one student is studying the life of ants, a second is researching the workings of the FBI, and a third is exploring the life of Frida Kahlo. While two students work together to investigate the history of soccer, another is engrossed in surveying adults on their opinions of video games. Exploratory can teach students that school can be a place that nurtures curiosity, inspires them to ask questions, and helps them find the joy in learning.

JOY 3:
Let Students Create Things

People like to make stuff. Having control of our work and using our minds and hands to create something original give us a tremendous sense of agency. There is a special pride in bringing an original idea to fruition. It empowers us and encourages us; it helps us appreciate the demanding process of creating something from nothing.

The list of what students can create across the curriculum is virtually limitless: newspapers and magazines, brochures, stories, picture books, posters, murals, Web sites, podcasts, PowerPoint presentations, interviews, oral histories, models, diagrams, blueprints and floor plans, plays and role-plays, mock trials, photographs, paintings, songs, surveys, graphs, documentary videos—the list goes on and on. At its best, school should help and inspire students to bring their own ideas and creations to life.

JOY 4:
Show Off Student Work

Our schools and classrooms should be brimming with wonderful, original student work. School spaces that are devoid of student work perpetuate a sterile and joyless environment. I tell my teacher education students that the walls of their classrooms should speak to people; they should say exactly what goes on in that space throughout the school day. I can tell what teachers value by simply walking into their classrooms and looking at the walls.

The same is true for a school building. My son, Max, is in 4th grade, and his school, Augustus H. Burley School in Chicago, is a joyous place to visit. The hallways and classrooms are filled with remarkable student work, and there is rarely a worksheet in sight. The teachers also show off the students themselves. There are photographs of students next to their favorite books, above their posted work from writing workshop, and next to the doors of some classrooms.

JOY 5:
Take Time to Tinker

Gever Tulley has started a unique summer school in California called the Tinkering School. His blog describes it this way:

The Tinkering School offers an exploratory curriculum designed to help kids—ages 7 to 17—learn how to build things. By providing a collaborative environment in which to explore basic and advanced building techniques and principles, we strive to create a school where we all learn by fooling around. All activities are hands-on, supervised, and at least partly improvisational. Grand schemes, wild ideas, crazy notions, and intuitive leaps of imagination are, of course, encouraged and fertilized (Tulley, 2005).

At Tinkering School, students are allowed to dream. They come up with their own ideas for an object, and the faculty and staff help them sketch, design, and build it. When have you seen a public school that encouraged students to come up with "grand schemes, wild ideas, crazy notions, and intuitive leaps of imagination"? In fact, schools actually work to prevent this from happening.

Our school days are too planned, leaving no room for spontaneity and happenstance. Kindergarten is the last refuge in school for letting kids tinker. Once they enter 1st grade, students must banish the joy of "fooling around" with objects and ideas and, instead, sit at their desks most of the day listening to lectures, reading textbooks, and filling out worksheets.

Sometimes the best ideas come from tinkering—and teachers, not just students, should be doing more of it. We must push beyond the teacher-proof curriculum the textbook industry has created, which tries to plan every subject for every hour of the day. Far from being think tanks or workshops, our schools continue to be assembly lines. We need to free teachers to take risks, experiment, play with the art of pedagogy, and feel the joy that comes from tinkering with their teaching.

JOY 6:
Make School Spaces Inviting

Why do classrooms need to look so much like, well, *classrooms,* with desks in rows or arranged in groups, with a chalkboard or whiteboard at the front? When I walk into a classroom in my son's school, I usually see a space that looks a lot like a family room. There's a large rug, a class library with the best in children's and young adult literature, bean bags, couches, comfortable chairs, pillows, colorful curtains, fabric hung over the ceiling lights, and lamps scattered about the classroom. In fact, sometimes the ceiling lights are off, and the lamps warmly light the room.

And what about the public spaces inside and outside the school—the hallways, foyers, meeting areas, and school grounds? Anyone who has spent time at a university knows how integral these spaces are to the learning and social dynamics of the campus. The same can be true for a school. Why not transform these often unused and sterile spots into places for small groups of students to work or cozy nooks for kids to read or write? How about filling a foyer with plants and flowers? Why not give a large wall to the students to create and paint a mural? One colorful mural can transform a barren hallway or entrance into a vibrant and joyful sight. And schools can turn outdoor spaces into gardens, sculpture parks, walking paths, and quiet reading areas.

JOY 7:
Get Outside

I am bewildered by how much time students spend inside schools. I don't mean that the school day should be shorter; I mean that more of the school day should be outside. We adults know all too well how much we like to get outside for a respite during the workday, and the same applies to students and teachers in school. They need a break from being confined inside a classroom all day. Fresh air, trees, and a sunny day can do miracles for the human spirit.

Interacting with nature brings a unique joy. Gavin Pretor-Pinney (2006) writes, "I have always loved looking at clouds. Nothing in nature rivals their variety and drama; nothing matches their sublime, ephemeral beauty" (p. 9). Naturalist and artist David Carroll (2004) describes his childhood enthrallment of seeking out turtles as he walked the ponds and marshes:

> The sheer joy of being there, of simply bearing witness, continued to be paramount. I went out neither to heal my heartbreaks nor to celebrate my happiness, but to be in nature and outside myself. Turtles, spotted turtles most significantly, were a living text moving upon an endless turning of the pages of the natural world, (p. 27)

The easiest way to get students outside is simply to have recess. There is a special joy in standing amidst the students as they burst from the school and spread out like a swarm of hungry ants. Kids say that recess is their favorite time in school. Recess was also one of my favorite times of the day as a teacher because I was outside and surrounded by children having fun. Tragically, recess has become a rare sight, which may say more about our schools today than anything else. Why do so many schools find it so difficult to allow children 20 minutes each day to play?

As a teacher, I would often take my students outside to read, write, or have a class meeting. It is delightful for a student to sit under a tree and read or for a class to sit in a circle on the grass and talk. Much of our science curriculums could directly include the outdoors. A school does not have to be near a forest or the ocean for students and teachers to explore nature. Ecosystems are all around us. Have students dig a hole in a patch of dirt, and they will witness the flourishing life in the soil beneath their feet. Don't underestimate the power of sheer joy that children—and adults—can experience from tipping over a large rock and seeing the ground teeming with life.

JOY 8:
Read Good Books

Everyone loves a good story. We all know that if you have a 5-year-old sitting on your lap and a good book in your hands, you will soon experience the magic of stories. And what amazing stories there are! We are living in an astonishing time of children's and young adult literature. Immerse students in a culture of good books, and you surround them with joy.

For the past few years, I've been working on a grant with a Chicago public school, in part to help teachers make literature an important feature of their classrooms. I have brought loads of good books into the school. As I did book talks in 4th and 8th grade classrooms about dozens of new titles we ordered, the room was abuzz with students who could not wait to get their hands on the books. When I walk into a classroom now, I am met with the excited voices of the students telling me what books they're reading.

Of course, if we want joy in schools, then sometimes students should read books that aren't so "serious." I believe that books with important themes can make a better world, but we must also sometimes allow—even encourage—students to experience books for sheer pleasure. Have 3rd graders read Dav Pilkey's *Captain Underpants and the Perilous Plot of Professor Poopypants* (Scholastic, 2000). Have 5th graders read Jeff Kinney's *Diary of a Wimpy Kid* (Amulet, 2007). Have young adults read Sherman Alexie's very funny (and serious) *The Absolutely True Diary of a Part-Time Indian* (Little Brown, 2007). Encourage students to read thrillers; romance novels; action-adventure books; stories about sports, animals, and pop culture; graphic novels and manga; and nonfiction on topics they love. You will see plenty of joy.

JOY 9:
Offer More Gym and Arts Classes
In recent years, with our zeal for increasing test scores, "specials" in school have become nearly as rare as recess. It is not uncommon, especially in more impoverished schools, for students to have no art, music, and drama at all, and gym only once or twice a week. In my son's previous school in Chicago, he did not have gym until January.

With his work on multiple intelligences, Howard Gardner has helped us better appreciate the uniqueness of children and has spoken to the need to give students opportunities to use their varied strengths and interests in school. For the legions of children who have a special affinity for the visual arts, theater, music, or sports, classes in these subjects are golden times for them to experience joy in school. But how much joy can they experience when it's limited to 45 minutes each week?

JOY 10:
Transform Assessment
When I was a kid, I dreaded report card time. When I was a teacher, many of my students were anxious about their grades. For far too many students, assessment in its dominant forms— tests, quizzes, letter grades, number grades, and standardized tests—is a dark cloud that never seems to leave. Must it be this way?

The idea of assessment in school is not inherently bad; children assess themselves all the time. When they're busy doing something they love outside school, such as tae kwon do, baking, or playing the saxophone—when they're experiencing *flow*—they don't mind assessment at all. In fact, they see it as an important part of the process. But for most students, assessment in school is the enemy.

We can, however, make it a more positive experience. We need to help students understand the value of assessment. We also need to rethink "failure." Our schools see failure as a bad thing. But adults know that failure is a vital part of learning. Portraying failure as a bad thing teaches a child to avoid risk taking and bold ideas. Imagine if we graded toddlers on their walking skills. We would be living in a nation of crawlers.

We should limit how we use quantitative assessments and make more use of narrative assessments and report cards,

portfolios of authentic work, and student presentations and performances. In addition, parent conferences should not only include students, but also encourage the students to do much of the talking, using the conference as an opportunity to present their work and discuss their strengths and areas to focus on for growth.

As a teacher, I had my students regularly do self-assessments. This gave them some real power over the process. They assessed most of their schoolwork before I did my own assessment. And during report card time, I passed out photocopies of a blank report card and had my students complete it, for both grades and behavior, before I filled it out. I don't recall a student ever abusing this opportunity. At another school in which I taught, I redesigned our report card to include space for a photograph of the student inside; the cover was left blank so students could either draw a picture or write something meaningful there.

JOY 11:
Have Some Fun Together
Recently, when I was visiting a school, I was standing in the hallway talking to a teacher when a tall 8th grade boy from another classroom exuberantly walked up to that teacher. They began some good-natured ribbing. Back and forth it went for a few minutes with smiles and laughter. What was this about? The teacher-student basketball game held earlier that week. Here were two people—an 8th grader and his teacher—having a joyous good time.

Schools need to find ways for students, teachers, and administrators to take a break from the sometimes emotional, tense, and serious school day and have some fun together. Sporting events, outdoor field days, movie nights, school sleep-ins, potluck meals, visits to restaurants, schoolwide T-shirt days, and talent shows can help everyone get to know one another better, tear down the personal walls that often get built inside schools, form more caring relationships, and simply have a wonderful time together.

Teaching as a Joyful Experience
Recently, I visited a former graduate student in her classroom. It is her third year as a teacher, and I was excited to see her creative and thoughtful teaching. But she said to me, "I never imagined this job would be so hard. I'm tired all the time."

Yes, teaching is hard. John Dewey's quote—about school sapping our souls—can be as true for teachers as it is for students. Considering the staggering turnover of new teachers in urban schools, it is in everyone's interest to help teachers find joy in their work. So teachers must strive in whatever ways they can to *own their teaching* so that each morning they can enter their classrooms knowing there will be golden opportunities for them—as well as for their students—to experience the joy in school.

References

Carroll, D. (2004). *Self-portrait with turtles.* Boston: Houghton Mifflin.

Csikszentmihalyi, M. (1990). *Flow.* New York: Harper Perennial.

Dewey, J. (1938). *Experience and education.* New York: Collier.

Goodlad, J. (1984). *A place called school.* New York: McGraw-Hill.

Pretor-Pinney, G. (2006). *The cloudspotter's guide.* New York: Perigee.

Tulley, G. (2005, May 4). About. *Tinkering School.* Available: www .tinkeringschool.com/blog/?p= 11

Wolk, S. (2001). The benefits of exploratory time. *Educational Leadership, 59*(2), 56–59.

Wolk, S. (2007). Why go to school? *Phi Delta Kappan, 88*(9), 648–658.

STEVEN WOLK is Assistant Professor of Teacher Education at North-eastern Illinois University, 5500 N. St. Louis Ave., Chicago, IL 60625; s-wolk@neiu.edu.

Accountability Comes to Preschool

Can We Make It Work for Young Children?

Early childhood educators are justifiably concerned that demands for academic standards in preschool will result in developmentally inappropriate instruction that focuses on a narrow set of isolated skills. But Ms. Stipek believes that teaching preschoolers basic skills can give them a good foundation for their school careers, and she shows that it is possible to do this in ways that are both effective and enjoyable.

DEBORAH STIPEK

Pressures to raise academic achievement and to close the achievement gap have taken a firm hold on elementary and secondary schools. Now, preschools are beginning to feel the heat. Testing for No Child Left Behind isn't required until third grade. But as elementary schools ratchet up demands on children in the early grades and as kindergarten becomes more academic, children entering school without basic literacy and math skills are at an increasingly significant disadvantage.

Accountability is also beginning to enter the preschool arena. Both the House and Senate versions of the Head Start reauthorization bill require the development of educational performance standards based on recommendations of a National Academy of Sciences panel. Head Start programs would then be held accountable for making progress toward meeting these goals, and their funding would be withdrawn after some period of time if they failed. States and districts are likely to follow with initiatives designed to ensure that children in publicly funded early childhood education programs are being prepared academically to succeed in school.

There are good reasons for the increased attention to academic skills in preschool, especially in programs serving economically disadvantaged children. Children from low-income families enter kindergarten on average a year to a year and a half behind their middle-class peers in terms of school readiness. And the relatively poor cognitive skills of low-income children at school entry predict poor achievement in the long term. Meredith Phillips, James Crouse, and John Ralph estimated in a meta-analysis that about half of the total black/white gap in math and reading achievement at the end of high school is explained by the gap between blacks and whites at school entry.[1] Preschool education can give children from economically disadvantaged homes a better chance of succeeding in school by contributing to their cognitive skills. Moreover, all young children are capable of learning far more than is typically believed, and they enjoy the process.

Until recently, kindergarten was a time for children to *prepare* for school. Today, it *is* school.

This new focus on academic preparation will undoubtedly have significant implications for the nature of preschool programs, and it could have negative consequences. Until recently, kindergarten was a time for children to *prepare* for school. Today, it *is* school—in most places as focused on academic skill as first grade used to be. Will the same thing happen to preschool? We need to think hard about how we will balance the pressure to prepare young children academically with their social/emotional needs. How will we increase young children's academic skills without undermining their enthusiasm for learning or reducing the attention we give to the many other domains of development that are important for their success?

The early childhood education community has resisted a focus on academic skills primarily because experts are worried that it will come in the form of whole-group instruction, rigid pacing, and repetitive, decontextualized tasks—the kind of "drill and kill" that is becoming commonplace in the early elementary grades and that is well known to suffocate young children's natural enthusiasm for learning. My own recent observations in preschools suggest that these concerns are well founded.

I am seeing children in preschool classrooms counting by rote to 10 or 20 in a chorus. When I interview the children, many have no idea what an 8 or a 10 is. They can't tell me, for example, how many cookies they would have if they started with 7 and I gave them one more, or whether 8 is more or less than 9. I am seeing children recite the alphabet, call out letters shown on flashcards, and identify letter/sound connections on worksheets (e.g., by drawing a line from a *b* to a picture of a ball). Some can read the word *mop* but have no idea that they are referring to a tool for cleaning floors, and they are not able to retell in their own words a simple story that had been read to them.[2] I am seeing young children recite by rote the days of the week and the months of the year while the teacher points to the words written on the board—without any understanding of what a week or a month is and without even a clear understanding that the written words the teacher points to are connected to the words they are saying. In these classrooms every child in the class gets the same task or is involved in the same activity, despite huge variability in their current skill levels. Some children are bored because they already know what is being taught; others are clueless.

Alternatives to Drill and Kill

The good news is that young children can be taught basic skills in ways that engage rather than undermine their motivation to learn. Motivating instruction must be child-centered—adapted to the varying skills and interests of children.

Good teachers embed instruction in activities that make sense to young children. They teach vocabulary, for example, by systematically using and reinforcing the meaning of new words in the context of everyday activities. When children are blowing bubbles, the teacher might introduce different descriptive terms (e.g., "shimmer") or names of shapes (e.g., "oval" versus "round"). Teachers promote oral language by reading stories, encouraging story making, joining in role play, asking children to explain how things work, giving children opportunities to share experiences, helping them to expand what they say, and introducing and reinforcing more complex sentence structures. Comprehension and analytic skills can be developed by reading to children and asking them to predict what will happen next and to identify patterns and draw conclusions. Print awareness is promoted by creating a book area, having materials and other things in the classroom labeled, and pointing out features of books being read to children. Phonics can be taught through songs, rhyming games, and language play. Early writing skills can be encouraged and developed in the context of pretend play (e.g., running a restaurant or post office) and by having children dictate stories or feelings to an adult and gradually begin to write some of the words themselves.

Good teachers are busy asking questions, focusing children's attention, helping them document and interpret what they see, and providing scaffolds and suggestions.

Young children develop basic number concepts best by actively manipulating objects, not by rote counting.[3] Mathematics, like literacy, can be learned in the context of playful activities. A pretend restaurant can provide many opportunities for learning math. Children can match one straw for each glass for each person, count out amounts to pay for menu items (five poker chips for a plastic pizza, four chips for a glass of apple juice, and so on), tally the number of people who visit the restaurant, or split the pizza between two customers. Questions about relative quantities (less and more, bigger and smaller) can be embedded in restaurant activities and conversations. (Who has *fewer* crackers or *more* juice left in her glass?) Children can categorize and sort objects (e.g., put all the large plates on this shelf and the tall glasses on the shelf below). Measurement of weight and even a basic notion of fractions can be learned by cooking for the restaurant (a half cup of milk, a quarter cup of sugar); volume can be learned by pouring water from measuring cups into larger containers.

Effective teaching of young children cannot be delivered through a one-size-fits-all or scripted instructional program, in part because teachers need to be responsive to children's individual skills and interests. Good teachers know well what each child knows and understands, and they use that knowledge to plan appropriate and varied learning opportunities. For example, whereas one child may dictate a few sentences to the teacher for his journal each day, another might actually write some of the words herself. While some children are asked to count beans by ones, others are asked to count them by twos or by fives.

Teaching in the kinds of playful contexts mentioned above can be direct and explicit. Young children are not left to their own devices—to explore aimlessly or to invent while the teacher observes. To the contrary, effective and motivating teaching requires a great deal of active teacher involvement. Teachers need to have clear learning goals, plan activities carefully to achieve those goals, assess children's learning regularly, and make modifications when activities are not helping children learn.

Good teachers are busy asking questions, focusing children's attention, helping them document and interpret what they see, and providing scaffolds and suggestions. Which object do you think will float, the small metal ball or the block of wood? Why do you think the wood floated and the ball didn't, even though the wood block is bigger? On the paper, let's put an "F" for float after the pictures of the objects that float and an "S" after the pictures of the objects that sink. Then we can look at our summary of findings to figure out how the floating objects and the sinking objects are different from each other. Teachers need to assess children's understanding and skill levels both informally—as they listen to children's replies and comments during classroom activities—and more formally—interacting with each child individually for a few minutes every few weeks. And teachers need to use what they learn from their assessments to plan instructional interventions that will move *each child* from where he or she is to the next step.

Effective teachers also maintain children's enthusiasm for learning by being vigilant and seizing opportunities to use children's interests to teach. I once observed a brilliant teacher turn a child's comment about new shoes (which most teachers would have found distracting) into a multidisciplinary lesson. She asked the students to take off one shoe and use it to measure the length of their leg, from their waist to their ankle. Some had to learn how to find their waist and ankle to accomplish the task (physiology and vocabulary). They also had to count each time they turned the shoe and keep track of where they ended up (math). The teacher then led a conversation about who had the longest and the shortest leg (comparisons). Then they measured arms and talked about whether arms were shorter or longer than legs and by how much (introduction to subtraction and idea of averages). The conversation finally turned to other objects that could be used as measuring instruments.

This teacher didn't always rely on spontaneous teaching opportunities. She had a very well-planned instructional program. But she also took good advantage of children's interests and seized opportunities to build academic lessons out of them.

Beyond Academic Skills

Ironically, to achieve high academic standards, we need to be more, not less, concerned about the nonacademic aspects of children's development. Children's social skills and dispositions toward learning, as well as their emotional and physical well-being, directly affect their academic learning.

Fortunately, efforts to promote development on important nonacademic dimensions need not reduce the amount of time children spend learning academic skills. As I describe below, efforts to support positive social, emotional, and physical development can be embedded in the academic instructional program and the social climate of the classroom.

Social skills. Children who have good social skills—who are empathic, attentive to others' needs, helpful, respectful, and able to engage in sustained social interactions—achieve academically at a higher level than children who lack social skills or are aggressive.[4] The higher achievement results in part because children who are socially adept develop positive relationships with teachers and peers. They are motivated to work hard to please their teachers, and they feel more comfortable and secure in the classroom. Aggressive and disruptive children develop conflictual relationships with teachers and peers and spend more time being disciplined (and thus less time engaged in academic tasks).

Social skills can be taught in the context of classroom routines and activities designed to teach academic skills. Lessons about appropriate social behavior can be provided as stories that are read to children and discussed. Opportunities to develop skills in collaboration can be built into tasks and activities designed to teach literacy and math skills. Teachers can encourage children to develop social problem-solving skills when interpersonal conflicts arise by helping them solve the problem themselves—"Is there another way you could have let Sam know that you wanted to play with the airplane?"—rather than solving the problem for them—"Sam, give the airplane to Jim. It's his turn."

A program called "Cool Tools," designed to promote social and academic skills, begins with preschoolers at the UCLA lab-

oratory elementary school—the Corinne A. Seeds University Elementary School. Children create an alphabet that decorates the walls of their classroom: "S" is for "share," "K" is for "kindness," "H" is for "help," "C" is for "cooperation." Teachers also take advantage of events in the world and in the community. Following the tsunamis in Southeast Asia, the children made lists of what survivors might need. They donated the coins they had collected for their study of money in mathematics to a fund for survivors, and they made muffins and granola and sold them to parents and friends to raise additional funds. Thus literacy and math instruction, and a little geography, were embedded in activities designed to promote feelings of responsibility and generosity.

Dispositions toward learning. Children's beliefs about their ability to learn also affect their learning. Children who develop perceptions of themselves as academically incompetent and expect to fail don't exert much effort on school tasks, and they give up as soon as they encounter difficulty. Engagement in academic tasks is also affected by students' sense of personal control. Children enjoy schoolwork less and are less engaged when they feel they are working only because they have to, not because they want to.[5]

Luckily, much is known about practices that foster feelings of competence and expectations for success. These beliefs are not "taught" directly. Rather, they are influenced by the nature and difficulty level of the tasks children are asked to complete and by the kind of evaluation used and the nature of the feedback they receive. Children's self-confidence is maintained by working on tasks that require some effort (so that when they complete them they have a sense of satisfaction and achievement). However, the tasks must not be so difficult that the children cannot complete them even if they try. The huge variability in children's skill levels is why rigidly paced instruction is inappropriate; if all children are asked to do the same task, it will invariably be too easy (and thus boring) for some students or too difficult (and thus discouraging) for others.

Classroom climate is also important. Self-confidence is engendered better in classrooms in which all children's academic achievements are celebrated than in classrooms in which only the best performance is praised, rewarded, or displayed on bulletin boards. Effective teachers encourage and praise children for taking on challenges and persisting when they run into difficulty, and they invoke no negative consequences for failure. ("You didn't get it this time, but I bet if you keep working on these kinds of problems, by lunch, you'll have figured out how to do them.")

The nature of evaluation also matters. Evaluation that tells children what they have learned and mastered and what they need to do next, rather than how their performance compares to that of other children, fosters self-confidence and high expectations. ("You are really good at consonants, but it looks like you need to practice vowels a little more.") All children can learn and will stay motivated if they see their skills developing, but only a few can perform better than their peers, and many will become discouraged if they need to compete for rewards.

We also know how to foster a feeling of autonomy. Clearly children cannot be given carte blanche to engage in any activity they want and be expected to master a set of skills and understandings adults believe to be important. But children can be given choices in what they do and how and when they do it, within a constrained set of alternatives. Even modest choices (whether to use beans or chips for a counting activity; which puzzle to work on) promote interest and engagement in learning.[6]

Emotional well-being and mental health. Children's emotional well-being and mental health (a clear and positive sense of the self; a positive, optimistic mood; the ability to cope with novel and challenging situations) have an enormous impact on how well they learn. Students who are depressed, anxious, or angry are not effective learners. Feeling disrespected, disliked, or disconnected from the social context can also promote disengagement—from academic work in the short term and, eventually for many students, from school altogether. Paying close attention to the social and emotional needs of students and creating a socially supportive environment can go a long way toward promoting social/emotional and mental well-being. It can also reduce the need for special services.

Substantial research suggests that the school social climate is also critical to mental health. A respectful and caring social context that ensures close, personal relationships with adults, that is orderly and predictable, and that promotes feelings of self-determination and autonomy in students can contribute substantially to students' emotional well-being. Peers affect the social context as much as teachers, and thus they have to be taught the effects of their behavior on other children. The "Cool Tools" program, for example, teaches 4-year-olds about "put-ups" and "put-downs," noting that it takes five put-ups to repair one put-down. Children also play games that illustrate how the same comment can be heard differently, depending on the volume and tone of voice and body posture.

Physical development. Lack of exercise and consumption of too much sugar are two behaviors that have immediate negative effects on children's ability to focus on academic work. We need to provide children with opportunities—such as outdoor play time and healthy snacks—to engage in positive behavior while they are at school. And we need to help them develop healthy habits—such as brushing teeth, washing hands, and exercising—that will contribute to their well-being.

Teachers can talk to children about how exercise affects their bodies in the context of a science lesson on physiology. (Why do we need a heart? How are muscles different from fat?) And compelling and visible messages can be given through science experiments, such as observing what happens to two pieces of bread several days after one piece was touched with a dirty hand and the other with a clean one.

Programs serving children from low-income families should also make an effort to work with community agencies to ensure access to dentists and physicians. Even a trip to the doctor or dentist can be used to promote academic skills. Children can develop communication skills by being asked to describe their experience, they can learn vocabulary, and they can develop the cultural knowledge that we now know is necessary for becoming a proficient reader. (It's hard to make sense of a sentence with the word "stethoscope" in it if you've never seen one used.)

Educating Children

Educational leaders need to take seriously the accountability demands made on them. By paying more attention to academic skills in preschool, we can help close the achievement gap, and we can give all children a chance to expand their intellectual skills. But we need to avoid teaching strategies that take all the joy out of learning. This will not, in the end, help students achieve the high standards being set for them.

We also need to resist pressures to prepare children only to perform on tests that assess a very narrow set of academic outcomes. Attention to other domains of development is also important if we want children to be effective learners as well as effective citizens and human beings. Policy makers should demand that if assessments for accountability are to be used in early childhood programs, they measure genuine understanding and the nonacademic skills and dispositions that we want teachers to promote. We have learned from No Child Left Behind that, if the tools used for accountability focus on a narrow set of skills, so will the educational program.

Finally, teaching young children effectively takes a great deal of skill. If we want teachers to promote students' learning and motivation, we need to invest in their training. States vary considerably in their credentialing requirements for early childhood education teachers. Few require a sufficient level of training. On-the-job opportunities for collegial interactions focused on teaching and learning and professional development are also critical. Preschools that are good learning environments for adults are likely to be good learning environments for children.

An investment in preschool education could help us achieve the high academic standards to which we aspire. Let's make sure we provide it in a way that does more good than harm.

Notes

1. Meredith Phillips, James Crouse, and John Ralph, "Does the Black-White Test Score Gap Widen After Children Enter School?," in Christopher Jencks and Meredith Phillips, eds., *The Black-White Test Score Gap* (Washington, D.C.: Brookings Institution Press, 1998), pp. 229–72.

2. A story recounted to me by a researcher who was assessing a young child's reading skill illustrates what can happen if decoding is overemphasized. The child read a brief passage flawlessly but was unable to answer a simple question about what he had read. He complained to the researcher that he had asked him to read the passage, not to understand it. Clearly this child had learned that reading was synonymous with decoding sounds.

3. See, for example, Barbara Bowman, M. Suzanne Donovan, and M. Susan Burns, eds., *Eager to Learn: Educating Our Preschoolers* (Washington, D.C.: National Academy Press, 2001); and Douglas Clements, Julie Sarama, and Ann-Marie DiBiase, *Engaging Young Children in Mathematics: Standards*

for *Early Childhood Mathematics Education* (Mahwah, N.J.: Erlbaum, 2003).

4. See, for example, David Arnold, "Co-Occurrence of Externalizing Behavior Problems and Emergent Academic Difficulties in Young High-Risk Boys: A Preliminary Evaluation of Patterns and Mechanisms," *Journal of Applied Developmental Psychology*, vol. 18, 1997, pp. 317–30; Nancy Eisenberg and Richard A. Fabes, "Prosocial Development," in William Damon and Nancy Eisenberg, eds., *Handbook of Child Psychology,* 5th ed., vol. 3 (New York: Wiley, 1997), pp. 701–78.

5. For a review, see Deborah Stipek, *Motivation to Learn: Integrating Theory and Practice*, 4th ed. (Needham Heights, Mass.: Allyn & Bacon, 2002).

6. See, for example, Leslie Gutman and Elizabeth Sulzby, "The Role of Autonomy-Support Versus Control in the Emergent Writing Behaviors of African-American Kindergarten Children," *Reading Research & Instruction*, vol. 39, 2000, pp. 170–83; and Richard Ryan and Jennifer La Guardia, "Achievement Motivation Within a Pressured Society: Intrinsic and Extrinsic Motivations to Learn and the Politics of School Reform," in Timothy Urdan, ed., *Advances in Motivation and Achievement: A Research Annual*, vol. II (Greenwich, Conn.: JAI Press, 1999), pp. 45–85.

DEBORAH STIPEK is a professor of education and dean of the School of Education at Stanford University, Stanford, Calif.

From *Phi Delta Kappan*, June 2006, pp. 740–744, 747. Copyright © 2006 by Phi Delta Kappan. Reprinted by permission of Phi Delta Kappan and Deborah Stipek.

No Child Left Behind

Who's Accountable?

Lisa A. DuBois

To many federal legislators, No Child Left Behind is like the cavalry sent to rescue the American educational system. To many teachers, the federal mandate is simply another shackle, more paperwork and red tape, as they try to stimulate and expand the minds of the young. But to many involved in educational research, No Child Left Behind is akin to the leg of an elephant. The information they are gathering about that leg is helpful and important, but it is also becoming increasingly clear that the animal resting on the appendage is far more gargantuan and complex than originally imagined. Still, many look forward to embarking on a quest, albeit imperfect and unpredictable, to unravel the mysteries of the beast.

Certainly, experts and non-experts across the nation do not dispute that the American system of education is not where it needs to be. Right now, for example, the United States is tied with Zimbabwe for achievement in 8th grade mathematics. Today, over 80 percent of African American and Latino 8th graders say they plan to attend a two- or four-year college. Yet, once there, many are not prepared for a rigorous post-secondary education. Between 40 and 60 percent of college students need remedial work to catch up, and between 25 and 50 percent of these students drop out after their first year. These data imply that although the existing K–12 system is graduating students, it is not necessarily preparing them for life beyond high school.

The Bush Administration's answer to this conundrum has been to rigidly implement the No Child Left Behind (NCLB) law. Enacted during the president's first term and up for reauthorization in 2007, NCLB requires that 100 percent of American public school students reach set proficiency standards in reading and math (and as of 2008, in science, as well) by the year 2014. Individual states set their own standards and all students, regardless of family income, race, ethnicity, or disability must comply. Schools whose students fail to achieve these goals face increasingly onerous penalties and sanctions.

> "NCLB makes a lot of sense if it would work. It's saying to schools, you can't ignore some of your kids just because they're tough to teach." —Andrew Porter

Academicians are studying NCLB's impact on a number of fronts. Andrew Porter, Patricia and Rodes Hart Professor of Educational Leadership and Policy, believes that NCLB, while flawed, is in many ways "a beautiful thing," because it has beamed a spotlight on the need for equity, opportunity and accountability from all schools. "You can't just forget about your poor kids, or forget about your English language learners, or your special ed kids, or your black or Hispanic kids, or your boys. You've got to do well by everybody. . . . NCLB is better than anything we've ever had in the past on that score," he says. "Think about a kid from a low-income family. NCLB makes a lot of sense if it would work. It's saying to schools, you can't ignore some of your kids just because they're tough to teach."

Also, Porter adds, deliberations have now effectively shifted from input and process to what teachers are teaching (content) and what students are accomplishing (proficiency), which he considers a healthy change from past educational reform movements. NCLB approaches the problems of the education system from the perspective of the students matriculating through it. Every public school student must take a state-designed reading and math assessment every year in grades 3 to 8, and also during one high school year, usually grade 10. These assessments hold schools accountable for student proficiency by requiring them to reach the stated benchmarks, known as Adequate Yearly Progress (AYP). Students in those schools that fail to meet AYP goals for two consecutive years are given "an escape hatch," meaning they can choose to attend a different school. Schools that fail three years in a row are given a carrot in the form of supplemental services like funds for tutoring and enhanced teaching materials. After five years of a school's failing to meet targets, the measures become more punitive—that school can be taken over by the state, reconstituted, restructured or shut down.

As with any nationally mandated reform that imposes sanctions for noncompliance, NCLB has generated angst and hand-wringing among those in the trenches—teachers, principals, parents and superintendents—particularly concerning issues of accountability. In fact, accountability debates crop up at every turn: Is it fair to hold schools accountable? Are these standardized tests valid measures of content and proficiency? And are sanctions the best way to address accountability issues?

Is It Fair to Hold Schools Accountable?

Porter, for one, favors school accountability, because it addresses the educational framework on a very specific local level. However, he also is pressing for "symmetry in accountability," meaning that teachers and students should likewise be held responsible for achieving certain benchmarks. "If you're going to have accountability for schools, then you should also have accountability for students. You don't want schools to be left hanging out to dry for students who don't try," he says. "When education is successful, students, teachers and administrators roll up their sleeves and work together." NCLB does not currently address this existing accountability gap.

By the same token, Porter is bothered that NCLB was set into motion with an endpoint that guarantees failure. The goal of having 100 percent of students achieve 100 percent proficiency by 2014 is so unattainable that even countries with the most proficient educational systems in the world would not use that as a target.

"Demanding 100 percent proficiency is the only way we could have gotten started," counters Stephen Elliott, Peabody professor of special education and the Dunn Family Professor of Educational and Psychological Assessment. Elliott is an international expert on testing accommodations and alternate assessments for children with disabilities. When NCLB was being formed, disability advocacy groups wanted schools to be held accountable for the inclusion of their children, realizing that every disabled child certainly would not be able to meet the national standards. Yet they also didn't want disabled children to be given short shrift or for the bar to be set inappropriately low just so schools could slide into compliance. The resounding consensus, says Elliott, was that these groups had to advocate for 100 percent proficiency, pushing the limits so that disabled students can get the educational tools and services they need. NCLB opens a window for them to design a criterion, set expectations, see if students can reach them, and then readjust them as necessary.

"This is an experiment and we're learning as we go," Elliott says, acknowledging that some schools have failed to meet AYP goals because their special needs students were unable to pass the assessment tests.

Are Standardized Tests Valid Measures of Content and Proficiency?

Porter believes that the testing industry, which is making a mint from the explosion in demand for more standardized tests from pre-school through graduate school, is actually pretty good at what it does. The validity of the content of these tests is a less critical issue than our nation's tendency to water down curricula and have teachers in charge of courses they were never trained to teach. Teachers, meanwhile, complain that they have to "teach to the test."

"That's cheating," claims Elliott. "They should be teaching to the standards the tests are aligned to. Curriculum, testing and standards are all being aligned, which is the backbone of the accountability issue. The finger-wagging should be on the instruction. Our tests today are far better than they were a decade ago because of this legislation."

Ironically, two of the biggest drivers forcing the refinement of standardized testing are children with disabilities and low-income gifted students. Because special needs children are included in AYP, researchers have been studying which kinds of multiple-choice questions, for example, are best at illuminating a child's mastery of content without being skewed by that child's decision-making and reading challenges. Most standard multiple-choice tests give the taker four or five options; but according to Michael Rodriguez of the University of Minnesota (*Educational Measurement: Issues and Practice*, Summer 2005), the best format for truly gauging knowledge is one that presents three multiple-choice options. It turns out that this format is the best determinant of content mastery for non-disabled students, as well.

Elliott and his colleagues have also been examining testing accommodations and their influence on the scores of students with special needs. They discovered some unsettling data. As expected, children with Individualized Education Programs (IEPs) tested better when given special accommodations, such as private settings, reading support and extra time. However, children with no perceived special needs also scored higher on standardized tests when given these same accommodations. Surprisingly, the highest functioning children were the only ones who actually used the extra time they'd been given. But all groups of students reported feeling a psychological edge and believed they performed better with the opportunity to have extra time if they needed it.

Teachers, meanwhile, complain that they have to "teach to the test."

For low-income, minority and English-language learners, NCLB has yanked the veil off the ever pervasive "achievement gap" in American education. Simply put, affluent children are receiving a better public education than those whose families are struggling. After studying this dilemma for years, Porter and others have found that the achievement gap between preschoolers who come from wealthy families versus those from impoverished families is enormous, as big as it will ever be—before these children ever go to school.

Once they reach school age, the gap does not increase during the school year. Minority and poor youngsters make achievement gains parallel to their more affluent peers. Unfortunately, says Porter, "Minority and poor kids lose more achievement in the summer than do white and more affluent kids. All the spread in the achievement gap happens when they're not in school in the summer time."

These two factors—that the achievement gap is greatest among preschoolers and that the gap widens every summer while children are not in school—means that schools are being asked to fix a societal problem that extends beyond the confines of the classroom. Donna Y. Ford, Betts Professor of Education and Human Development in the department of special education, and Gilman W. Whiting, director of Vanderbilt African American Diaspora Studies, have initiated the Vanderbilt Achievement Gap Project to bring about large-scale change by addressing contributing factors on a local level. Ford believes that a major obstacle to closing the achievement gap is that schools that serve large numbers of underprivileged children are not offering them the kinds of rigorous curricula that will enable them to excel. In other words, expectations for disadvantaged populations have been set too low.

Ford says, "If we don't put more poor kids in gifted programs in K–6, how are we going to get them into AP classes in high school? They've had nine years of not being challenged, so how can they survive? The ability is there and the potential is there, if given the opportunity."

The data support her argument. Researchers from the private Center for Performance Assessment identified schools in which 90 percent of the students are poor, 90 percent are members of ethnic minority groups, and 90 percent also meet high academic standards. Some of the common characteristics these schools share include a strong focus on academic achievement and frequent assessment of student progress with multiple opportunities for improvement (*Challenge Journal: The Journal of the Annenberg Challenge*, Winter 2001/02).

One approach for more accurately evaluating achievement, again being driven by advocates of students with disabilities, is to offer more formative assessments. Rather than giving students a single "do-or-die" test at the end of the school year to measure their progress, Elliott and others are promoting the idea of delivering shorter, lower stakes assessments, delivered two or three times during the school year. They're finding that good formative tests are predictive of how proficient students will be by the end of the year.

Elliott explains, "The lowest functioning kids can make progress, even if they may never be proficient."

"Across the nation, one of the fastest spreading reforms is interim assessment," Porter says. "The upside to interim assessment is that teachers find out how well students are performing

all along. The downside is what do you do when you find out they're not doing so well? Nobody's answering that question."

In 2005, NCLB asked states to compete for the opportunity to replace AYP with improved performance plans, considered by some researchers to be a superior index of proficiency, but, out of all the submissions, only North Carolina and Tennessee had the models and infrastructure to execute such a plan. "One of the most fragile areas of NCLB is the ability of states to manage the data," Elliott says. "Many statistical experts are going to work in the lower pressure, higher paying testing industry. So we're leaving people in the states who don't have the technical skills to manage the information."

One solution to this conundrum is to completely nationalize NCLB assessments, both in terms of content and proficiency. Porter is an avid proponent of this idea. Right now, each state has invested in its own content standards for math and reading. Unfortunately, a child from, say, Colorado, who moves to a new school in Georgia, may suddenly face an entirely different curriculum in the same school year. Concentrating all the energy that is now being used to develop materials, standards and assessments for 50 different states into the creation of one voluntary national standard, says Porter, "would mean enormous efficiency and would undoubtedly result in tremendous improvements in quality. If you're sinking all your resources into building one really great test, you can do a great job."

One approach for more accurately evaluating achievement, again being driven by advocates of students with disabilities, is to offer more formative assessments.

While national content standards may receive some level of support, Porter is also advocating for voluntary national proficiency standards, considered a less popular option. Right now, there are far-flung variances between states in benchmarks for achievement, and in most cases, a larger percentage of students reach proficiency on the state tests than on a comparable nationwide instrument, the National Assessment of Educational Progress (NAEP).

"In some states, the difference is enormous," Porter says, "like the difference between 30 percent and 90 percent."

Are Sanctions the Best Way to Address Accountability Issues?

In its current form, one of NCLB's most glaring glitches is its inability to impose the kinds of sanctions that result in student achievement. After a school fails for three consecutive years, students are supposed to receive the benefits of tutoring and supplemental services.

"Supplemental services haven't worked as well as we hoped they would," Porter says. Some districts aren't receiving the funding for these services in time to help the students, but more crucially, schools don't know what services they need until after their students have taken and failed the AYP assessment. So, they are faced with constantly moving targets.

Once a school misses its benchmarks two years in a row, students are allowed to transfer to schools that have not been identified as needing improvement. This has not panned out for a variety of reasons, Porter says. First, the better performing schools don't want to risk their AYP status by accepting an influx of students who've failed to meet the benchmarks. Second, in some cases, every school in the district is failing to reach NCLB guidelines. The sanction becomes irrelevant, because students have no place to go. Finally, poor and non-English speaking parents may find the logistics of transferring their children out of a neighborhood school to be too overwhelming to be worth the ordeal.

According to Ford, the solution will not be a band-aid or a simple promise to move kids to a new school. Instead it will require an intrinsic, primordial transformation across the education network. "If you move a child from an economically disadvantaged background and from a school that isn't rigorous into a school with a more rigorous curriculum, that child is going to need a lot of support not just to catch up, but to keep up," she says. "That's an equity issue. You can't just put children in a new school to frustrate them and make them fail. You have to believe in them and support them."

Now that NCLB is entering its first phase of reconstituting low-performing schools, the Bush administration is pushing to have private school vouchers added to the law, a proposal opposed by the National Education Association and others involved in collective-bargaining agreements.

Today, the achievement gap between underserved children and children of privilege stands at a full standard deviation, which in raw terms means that vast numbers of kids are undereducated.

The Next Wave Will Be NCLB's Effect on Higher Education

Today, the achievement gap between underserved children and children of privilege stands at a full standard deviation, which in raw terms means that vast numbers of kids are undereducated. Closing that gap by one standard deviation would, for example, bring a child at the 50th percentile up to the 84th percentile, a phenomenal gain. Porter contends that such a jump can happen if America improves the quality of its teaching.

"If we could get every kid to have a good teacher every year and if the effects of having a good teacher had a shelf life and were cumulative, it wouldn't take much of a change per year to add up to a standard deviation," he says. "We've got 12 years. If students could move up a tenth of a standard deviation every year, we'd get up to 1.2 standard deviations."

The onus, says Ford, is on the nation's universities to step up and prepare highly qualified teachers with high expectations who will enter the field and teach our children. To accomplish that, she thinks universities should revamp their courses so that student teachers start their practica earlier in college and spend more of their training out in the field gaining experience in a range of educational settings.

For all its many flaws and pitfalls, Porter, Elliott and Ford agree that NCLB has served the public well by forcing the conversation about education in the U.S. It has sparked new energy and directed attention to equity issues that have long been swept under the rug. NCLB obligates Americans to acknowledge the inadequacies in our school systems.

"That's the best thing NCLB could have done," says Ford. "The numbers are so dismal that we couldn't ignore them any longer. NCLB showed us the numbers. That's why I appreciate it. I don't blame NCLB solely for the problems we're having. It could have been any other piece of education legislation, and we still would have had to face these numbers."

Preschool Comes of Age

The National Debate on Education for Young Children Intensifies

Educators rave about the benefits of early-childhood schooling. So, why don't we support it more?

Michael Lester

Early this year, two dissimilar governors delivered two similar messages.

"Effective preschool education can help make all children ready to learn the day they start school and, more importantly, help close the enormous gap facing children in poverty," announced New York's Eliot Spitzer. He boldly promised to make a high-quality prekindergarten program "available to every child who needs it within the next four years."

Across the continent, California governor Arnold Schwarzenegger signed legislation expanding preschool opportunities in low-performing school districts and providing additional state dollars for building and improving preschool facilities. "Preschool gives our kids the strong foundation they need to be successful in school and in life," said Schwarzenegger.

Spitzer (a Democrat) and Schwarzenegger (a Republican) may not agree about a lot of things, but here's one area where they concur: Preschool education can perform miracles. Children who attend prekindergarten programs have bigger vocabularies and increased math skills, know more letters and more letter-sound associations, and are more familiar with words and book concepts, according to a number of studies.

Nationwide, almost two-thirds (64 percent) of children attend a preschool center in the year prior to kindergarten, typically at age four. On any given day, more than 5 million American youngsters attend some prekindergarten program.

And a preschool day is not just advanced babysitting for busy parents. Kids also practice many key components of the school day, including the importance of routine. That's key for early learners. "They understand carpet time, clean-up procedures, how to share crayons, or even getting their pants on and off without the teacher's help; that's big," says Steve Malton, kindergarten and first-grade teacher at Parkmead Elementary School, in Walnut Creek, California. "Little kids have only a certain amount of what's called 'active working memory.' If a large portion of their brain is figuring out what they're going to do next, there's less room there to spend on learning." Result: Preschool has a huge impact on their ability to keep up in class.

Too Much, Too Soon?

So, what's not to love about preschool? Plenty, say critics. "Young children are better off at home," says Michael Smith, president of the Home School Legal Defense Association. "We are in danger of overinstitutionalizing them. A child will develop naturally if the parents give the child what he or she needs most in the formative years—plenty of love and attention. In this way, the brain can develop freely."

As soon as the subject of schooling before K-12 comes up, another concept quickly follows: testing. That gives some parents the jitters. "The only way for school programs, including preschool programs, to show accountability of public funding for education is through testing," says Diane Flynn Keith, founder of Universal Preschool. "The only way to prepare children for standardized testing is to teach a standardized curriculum. Standardized preschool curriculum includes reading, writing, math, science, and social sciences at a time when children are developmentally vulnerable and may be irreparably harmed by such a strategy."

That's part of a broader test-them-sooner move across many grades. One pushdown from No Child Left Behind, for instance, is that highstakes testing now begins as early as the second grade. "It's not the same kindergarten we went to," says Don Owens, director of public affairs for the National Association for the Education of Young Children (NAEYP). "It's not the same kindergarten it was ten years ago. Kindergarten used to be preparation for school, but now it *is* school. That's why school districts and boards of education are paying attention to what happens before the kids arrive at school."

America is forcing its parents to decide between paying for early education and saving for college.

The result is a desperate tug-of-war between prekindergarten advocates and critics, with the under-six set placed squarely in the middle. In 2006, for instance, the Massachusetts legislature passed, by unanimous vote, an increase in state-funded high-quality prekindergarten programs. Governor Mitt Romney promptly vetoed the bill, calling preschool an "expensive new entitlement."

On the national stage, Oklahoma is the only state to offer publicly funded preschool education to virtually all children (about 90 percent) at age four. But twelve states—Alaska, Hawaii, Idaho, Indiana, Mississippi, Montana, New Hampshire, North Dakota, Rhode Island, South Dakota, Utah, and Wyoming—provide no preschool services at all. "There is not enough support for preschool," explains David Kass, executive director of Fight Crime: Invest in Kids. "It's very expensive, and most parents cannot afford it."

The three costliest states for private preschool are Massachusetts (where preschool runs an average of $9,628 per year), New Jersey ($8,985), and Minnesota ($8,832). In Rhode Island, the average yearly tab for preschool ($7,800) represents 45 percent of the median single-parent-family income. In California, part-time private preschool and child-care programs cost families on average $4,022 statewide. By comparison, the average full-time tuition at a California State University campus was $3,164.

"America is forcing its parents to decide between paying for early education for their kids and saving for their college education," says the NAEYP's Don Owens.

That's when the subject of state-sponsored preschool comes up. Over the past two years, the total state prekindergarten funding increased by a billion dollars to exceed $4.2 billion. But those numbers are often inadequate. After Florida voters approved a preschool-for-all initiative similar to a voucher program, the state legislature appropriated about $390 million—or roughly $2,500 per child served. Reasonable budgeting for preschool, however, should parallel that for K-12 schools. "If you're a state like Florida spending $9,000 per student on a yearly full-day program of K-12, your costs for a half day of prekindergarten should be somewhere around $4,500, not $2,500," complains Steve Barnett, director of the National Institute for Early Education Research.

That pattern is true nationwide. In 2002, average state spending was at $4,171 per enrolled child, but that figure fell to $3,482 in 2006, according to the NIEER's 2006 *State Preschool Yearbook*. Some states spend even less: New Mexico provides $2,269 per child, and Ohio budgets just $2,345. Compare those amounts with the national average of $10,643 for each child enrolled in K-12 schools.

Barnett says Florida and other states are creating a dual system consisting of high-quality, expensive preschools in private settings and underfunded public schools for low-income families.

The Survey Says . . .

While the battle over funding continues, it's difficult to dispute the positive effects of preschool not only in better learning in kindergarten but also in long-term educational value. Furthermore, key research findings indicate that those who go through prekindergarten programs are more likely to graduate from high school and make higher wages as adults.

The research recited in support of preschool education usually comes from three long-term studies of low-income families. In the Abecedarian Project, launched in 1972 in rural North Carolina, 57 infants from low-income, African American, primarily single-mother families were randomly assigned to receive early intervention in a high-quality child-care setting; 54 children were assigned to a control group. Each child had an individualized prescription of educational activities, which consisted of "games" incorporated into the child's day and emphasized language skills. The child care and preschool were provided on a full-day, year-round basis.

Initially, all children tested comparably on mental and motor tests; however, as they moved through the child-care program, preschoolers had much higher scores on mental tests. Follow-up assessments completed at ages twelve, fifteen, and twenty-one showed that the preschoolers continued to have higher average scores on mental tests. More than one-third of the children who attended preschool went to a four-year college or university; only about 14 percent of the control group did.

Another important research effort was the High/Scope Perry Preschool study, which began in Ypsilanti, Michigan. From 1962 to 1967, 123 three- and four-year-olds—African American children born into poverty and at high risk of failing school—were randomly divided into one group that received a high-quality preschool program and a comparison group that received no preschool.

These children were evaluated every year, ages 3–11, and again three times during their teens and twice in adulthood. The latest results of this High/Scope study were released in 2004. By the time members of the preschool-provided group reached age forty, they had fewer criminal arrests, displayed higher levels of social functioning, and were more likely to have graduated from high school.

Meanwhile, Chicago's Child-Parent Centers (CPC) have been around for forty years, and more than 100,000 families have gone through the federally funded program, which still operates in twenty-four centers. Parents are drawn into the program with classes, activities, and their own resource room at each school site.

A longitudinal study by Arthur Reynolds, a researcher at the University of Wisconsin at Madison, looked at 1,539 Chicago students enrolled in CPCs in 1985 and 1986 and tracked their progress through 1999. He found they were much more likely to finish high school and less likely to be held back a grade, be placed in special education, or drop out than 389 youngsters who participated in alternative programs. Intervening early improves student achievement and has a cumulative effect: The longer students were in the CPC programs, the higher their level of school success.

Quantifying Quality

The National Institute for Early Education Research has compiled ten generally accepted benchmarks for what constitutes high-quality prekindergarten education. The list follows:

- Lead teacher has a bachelor's degree, or higher
- Teacher has specialized training in prekindergarten
- Teacher has at least fifteen in-service hours per year
- Assistant teacher has a child-development associate (CDA) degree, or equivalent
- Early-learning standards are comprehensive
- Maximum class size is twenty
- Staff/child ratio is one to ten, or lower
- Children are screened for vision, hearing, and health
- Meals are provided at least once a day
- Monitoring takes place through on-site visits

Unfortunately, almost half the states do not meet the degree benchmark for all lead teachers. Not one state meets all ten benchmarks.

Other shorter-term studies—and there are many—argue these kinds of benefits are not limited to at-risk children but extend to middle income kids as well. But when a family's budget is tight, preschool becomes unaffordable. Less than half of low-income toddlers attend preschool, but half of middle-class four-year-olds and three-quarters from high-income families (earning $75,000 or more) attend preschool.

That enrollment gap can have immediate academic consequences, say educators, who note that the lower the family income, the more pronounced the benefits of preschool. "I've worked with a lot of kids and know the achievement gap starts before kids are even in kindergarten," says Kimberly Oliver, a kindergarten teacher from Silver Springs, Maryland, and 2006 National Teacher of the Year.

Learning While Playing

Many educators appreciate the wide range of positive influences preschool seems to germinate. Debra King, a preschool teacher for thirty-five years, has run the Debra King School, in San Francisco, for nearly half that time. "There's been a big push lately to make preschoolers ready for academic learning, to teach children the alphabet and how to write their names," King says. "Many children are developmentally ready to learn these things, but I think socialization skills are more important. I believe that playing with blocks, dolls, and toys, scribbling with crayons, painting, communicating, storytelling, and music—that's readiness for school. There are a lot of different things to learn to be successful in the world."

That's an important insight. "The original preschool was a place for socialization, but, increasingly, today it has become necessary because of working and single parents," explains David Elkind, professor of child development at Tufts University and author of *The Hurried Child* and *The Power of Play*. "And that's muddied the waters, because people think it needs to be an educational thing. We got it turned around and are learning the academic things before we learn the social skills that are prerequisites for formal education."

Elkind believes phonics, math, and book reading are inappropriate for young children. "There is no research supporting the effectiveness of early academic training and a great deal of evidence that points against it," he says. "The age of six is called the age of reason because children actually develop those abilities to do *concrete* operations; brain research substantiates this. Take reading: A child needs to be at the age of reason to understand that one letter of the alphabet can sound different ways. That age might be four or it might be seven. They all get it; they just get it at different ages."

Elkind argues that toddlers need to learn only three things before entering kindergarten, and they're all socialization skills: listen to adults and follow instructions, complete simple tasks on their own, and work cooperatively with other children. "Children need to learn the language of things before they learn the language of words," he adds. "They are foreigners in a strange land, and they need to learn about the physical world, they need to explore colors, shape, and time, they need to find out about water and the sky and the stars, and they need to learn about human relations. Much of this learning comes from direct experience."

Sharon Bergen, senior vice president of Education and Training for the Knowledge Learning Corporation, counters that curriculum and fun are not mutually exclusive: "Children are capable of a lot of development earlier than we thought," she says. "But we don't want their time to be overly structured. We still want kids to have a good, fun, joyful childhood." With prekindergarten education, many people think, we can have it both ways.

MICHAEL LESTER is a writer and editor. He recently launched a site about fatherhood, *Dad Magazine Online,* at www.dadmagazineonline.com.

UNIT 2

Young Children, Their Families and Communities

Unit Selections

7. **Class Matters—In and Out of School,** Jayne Boyd-Zaharias and Helen Pate-Bain
8. **Meeting of the Minds,** Laura Pappano
9. **Making Long-Term Separations Easier for Children and Families,** Amy M. Kim and Julia Yeary
10. **Supporting Grandparents Who Raise Grandchildren,** Jennifer Birckmayer et al.
11. **Children of Teen Parents: Challenges and Hope,** Barbara A. White, Mimi Graham, and Seaton K. Bradford

Key Points to Consider

- How can teachers develop strong working relationships with parents of children in their class?

- What are the responsibilities for teachers related to working with children who are allergic to various substances?

- Are teenage parents able to effectively care for their children with support from educators?

- What do grandparents raising grandchildren need to be effective parents for the second time?

Student Web Site

www.mhcls.com

Internet References

Administration for Children and Families
http://www.dhhs.gov

The AARP Grandparent Information Center
http://www.aarp.org/grandparents

All About Asthma
http://pbskids.org/arthur/grownups/teacherguides/health/asthma_tips.html

Allergy Kids
http://allergykids.com

Changing the Scene on Nutrition
http://www.fns.usda.gov/tn/Healthy/changing.html

Children, Youth and Families Education and Research Network
www.cyfernet.org

The National Academy for Child Development
http://www.nacd.org

National Network for Child Care
www.nncc.org

National Safe Kids Campaign
http://www.babycenter.com

Zero to Three
http://www.zerotothree.org

Many of the articles read for possible inclusion in this edition focused on the effects of poverty on young children. There is increased attention to narrowing the achievement gap among minorities and children living in poverty. Some say the best way for children to achieve higher test scores is for teachers to teach better. Others say higher achievement among minorities and children living in poverty cannot be possible without attention to the living conditions and the support families receive. Jayne Boyd-Zaharias and Helen Pate-Bain discuss this most important issue in "Class Matters—In and Out of School." They focus on the needs of affordable housing, access to health care and early childhood education, along with improved instruction from teachers in class sizes that have proved to support education, especially for children in poverty. There is substantial research indicating that high-quality prekindergarten programs can help narrow the achievement gap. The research is so solid that thirty-nine states now provide publicly-funded preschool education of some form that serve more than one million preschoolers.

One of the benefits of working with young children is having opportunities to interact with family members and to get to know what life is like at home for the children in our classes. The chance to interact with family diminishes as the learner gets older until it is almost nonexistent at the secondary level. Laura Pappano's article, "Meeting of the Minds" provides strategies for moving from the traditional teacher-dominated conference to a two-way conference where sharing between the parents and teachers about the strengths and needs of the child are discussed.

As the United States continues to send soldiers on long deployments overseas, some for multiple tours of duty, there are ramifications for the over 700,000 children with a parent serving in the U.S. military. Educators are also finding that the challenging economic times mean families are separated for long periods of time while one parent works in a distant city just to have a secure job. Recognizing the child may go through various stages of separation is important for teachers to understand. Suggestions for teachers working with children living in a

© Medioimages/Photodisc

stressful family situation are included. Support from the teacher and consistent communication with family members can help to ease the separation anxiety that children face.

The next two articles examine the heads of families at two very different ends of the spectrum. "Supporting Grandparents Who Raise Grandchildren" and "Children of Teen Parents: Challenges and Hope" really are not that different in their advice. In each article, the authors stress the importance of individual support and integrated services that meet the needs of a particular family. Younger parents, as well as second time around parents, all need support and welcome the opportunity to have teachers for their children or grand children who are understanding of their particular situation.

Families can provide a wealth of information about their child, and teachers who develop strong relationships with families are beneficiaries of this knowledge. Get to know the families of your children. Share a bit about yourself and your interests, and you may be rewarded with information from families about the children in your class. Build on this information to provide learning experiences that are relevant and meaningful to your children.

Class Matters—
In and Out of School

Closing gaps requires attention to issues of race and poverty.

JAYNE BOYD-ZAHARIAS AND HELEN PATE-BAIN

L ow achievement and high dropout rates among poor and minority students continue to plague U.S. society. And we say "plague" purposefully, because these children are all our children, and our nation will profit by or pay for whatever they become. While much attention over the past quarter century has focused on reforming the schools these students attend, little or no progress has been made in actually closing the achievement gaps or reducing the number of dropouts.

Why? Aren't Americans a "can-do" people? We eradicated the childhood scourge of polio, built the best road system since the Romans, put men on the moon, outlasted the Soviet Union, and created universities that are the envy of the world.

But the problem of underachievement by poor and minority students has confounded us. High-level commissions issue warnings, governors hold summits, think tanks produce reports, scholars write books, and Congress passes laws. But the U.S. has failed to deliver on its promise to provide a high-quality education to every child.

In the 1960s, Martin Luther King, Jr., forced our nation to face the inequities of race, poverty, and war. But today, these three inequities still exist in this country.

Rethinking the Problem

Surely schools need to be improved, especially the schools that serve poor and minority children. But school improvement alone will not suffice. We believe in the power of good teaching, but educators alone cannot do a job so large. We can inspire individual students to break through the boundaries of social class, but we cannot lift a whole social class of students to a higher level of achievement. Low achievement and dropping out are problems rooted in social and economic inequality—a force more powerful than curricula, teaching practices,

standardized tests, or other school-related policies. Richard Rothstein summed it up best:

> For nearly half a century, the association of social and economic disadvantage with the student achievement gap has been well known to economists, sociologists, and educators. Most, however, have avoided the obvious implication of this understanding—raising the achievement of lower-class children requires amelioration of the social and economic conditions of their lives, not just school reform.[1]

Once acknowledged, this truth has profound implications for educators and policy makers alike.

If all efforts to close achievement gaps concentrate exclusively on schools and school reform, they will fail, leaving schools and teachers to shoulder the blame. In turn, good administrators and teachers, who are doing their best under difficult circumstances, will be driven *out* of the profession, a prospect that can only make matters worse. As Gary Orfield sums it up: "Doing educational reform while ignoring the fundamental cleavages in society is profoundly counterproductive."[2]

A useful way of visualizing the remedy for the chronic problem of low achievement of poor and minority students is to return to Abraham Maslow's 1954 hierarchy of needs for self-actualization. We have patterned a hierarchy of needs for a self-actualized society after Maslow's (see Figure 1).

Affordable Housing in Stable Neighborhoods

Nearly one-third of the nation's poorest children have attended three different schools by third grade. Such high mobility depresses achievement. One study found that reducing the mobility of low-income students to that of other students would eliminate 7% of the test-score gap by income and 14% of the

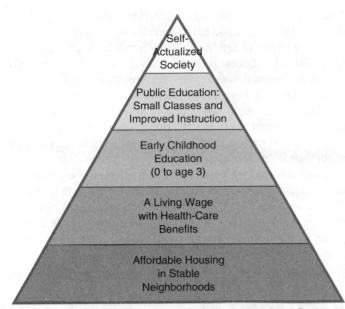

Figure 1 A Hierarchy of Needs for a Self-actualized Society.

black/white test score gap.[3] Other studies have shown that low-income families and children benefit when integrated into middle-class neighborhoods. This integration requires housing subsidies for poor families.[4]

After *Brown* v. *Board of Education,* "white flight" became common across the country. Middle-income white families moved to the suburbs, leaving only poor families in the inner cities. The challenge today is to integrate low- and middle-income families into stable neighborhoods. Margery Turner and Susan Popkin have identified several ways to afford this mix of income groups: 1) low-income housing tax credits, 2) housing choice vouchers, 3) HOPE VI (a public housing plan that has been successful in Seattle and Kansas City), 4) new communities, and 5) linking supportive services to affordable housing.[5] The most effective integrated communities will include:

- elected local committees to keep residents informed and active;
- public schools with small classes, teachers who make home visits, family resource centers with health-care services available to the community, active parent/teacher organizations, and after-school care and summer programs;
- support services: adult education, job training, and financial and budgeting classes.

A Living Wage with Health-care Benefits

One in four American workers today earns poverty-level hourly wages. What's more, 33% of black and 39.3% of Hispanic workers earn poverty-level hourly wages.[6] These are appalling numbers, and they have a profound impact on poor and minority

children. Poverty, especially long-term, chronic poverty, takes a terrible toll on children's health and their readiness for school.

In 1968, 12.8% of America's children lived in poverty. In 2006, that proportion had risen to 17.4%—an increase of 1.2 million children.[7] Raising the minimum wage, protecting workers' rights to organize and join unions, and implementing living wage ordinances will certainly benefit poor children and families.

Early Childhood Education

There is no question that those poor and minority children who participate in prekindergarten programs are better prepared for school, especially in terms of letter/word recognition, pattern recognition, and ability to work with others. As Clive Belfield has noted, "Model pre-K programs show extremely powerful effects over the long term. There are significant reductions in special educational placement and grade retention. Pre-K participation reduces high school dropout rates dramatically."[8]

Arthur Rolnick and Rob Grunewald conclude that the case in favor of investing in early childhood education is closed. "Now," they continue, "it is time to design and implement a system that will help society realize on a large scale the extraordinary returns that high-quality early childhood programs have shown they can deliver."[9]

Today, we are indebted to researchers in education and to economists for providing us with proof that early childhood education saves money and children. By acting on their findings, we can improve the lives of the 13 million children living in poverty.

Public Education: Small Classes

Teachers have long known intuitively that small classes allow them to devote more attention to individual students. Hence, class size has been one of the most researched topics in education. But studies prior to Tennessee's Project STAR, with which we have both been intimately involved, were found to be inconclusive because of weak methodologies. STAR was independently reviewed by Frederick Mosteller of Harvard University, and he declared it to be "one of the most important educational investigations ever carried out and illustrates the kind and magnitude of research needed in the field of education to strengthen schools."[10]

Because of STAR's strong research design, there is widespread confidence in its major finding that small classes in K-3 provide extraordinary academic benefits to students, especially low-income and minority students. STAR is where intuition met empirical proof. And since STAR, other studies (SAGE, Success Starts Small, Burke County, etc.) have shown the positive impact of small classes in the primary grades.[11]

Small classes in the early grades also provide long-term positive outcomes. STAR students have been followed through high school and beyond. Research from follow-up studies indicates that students who entered small classes in kindergarten or first grade and had three or more consecutive years of small classes showed gains in academic achievement through at least eighth grade.[12]

Attending small classes in K-3 reduces the black/white gap in the rate at which students take college entrance exams by an estimated 60%

In addition, Alan Krueger and Diane Whitmore found that attending small classes in K-3 reduces the black/white gap in the rate at which students take college entrance exams by an estimated 60%. Their research also showed that attending small classes raised the average score on the exams by 0.15–0.20 of a standard deviation for black students and by 0.04 of a standard deviation for white students.[13]

But cost is the bottom line when education budgets are developed. When the value of reducing class size was first introduced, the initial response of policy makers was that it would cost too much. However, recent research provides evidence that small classes produce long-term savings.

Follow-up data from STAR have shown that criminal conviction rates were 20% lower for black males assigned to small classes than for those assigned to regular size classes. Maximum sentence rates were also 25% lower for black males from small classes. Teen birth rates were shown to be one-third less for white females assigned to small classes than for their peers assigned to regular size classes, and the fatherhood rate for black teenage males from small classes was 40% lower than for those from regular size classes.[14]

Small K-3 classes have been identified as a cost-effective educational intervention that reduces high school dropout rates. They are a wise investment.

> From a societal perspective (incorporating earnings and health outcomes), class-size reduction would generate a net cost savings of approximately $168,000 and a net gain of 1.7 quality-adjusted life-years for each high school graduate produced by small classes. When targeted to low-income students, the estimated savings would increase to $196,000 per additional graduate.[15]

Although research related to small classes in later grades is somewhat scarce, new findings suggest that class size reduction at the middle-school level will also provide substantial benefits to students.[16] More studies need to be conducted to determine the impact of class size reduction beyond the primary grades.

Public Education: Improved Instruction

Most school improvement efforts don't focus sufficiently on instruction. It is time that policy makers recognize that teaching, which is at the very core of education, involves complex tasks that require specialized skills and knowledge. It is not enough, for example, for a teacher of mathematics to know mathematics.

Knowing math for teaching is different from knowing it for one's own use. The same holds for other subjects.

"Teachers can't learn for students," notes Deborah Ball, dean of the School of Education at the University of Michigan.[17] No matter the instructional format—lecture, small-group activity, or individualized assignment—students make their own sense of what they're taught. Ideas don't fly directly from teachers' minds into learners' minds. Effective teaching requires teachers to be able to assess what students are taking from instruction and adapt their instruction to meet the differing needs of students.

There is an old but wise saying in teaching, "If my students can't learn the way I teach, then I must teach the way they learn." This requires teachers to ask probing questions, listen carefully to student answers, and create assignments to provide appropriate help. Moreover, teachers today must do all of this with an ever-increasing variety of students, spanning gulfs of social class, language, and culture, to ensure that each student learns.

Confronting Three Inconvenient Truths

To achieve a high quality education for every child, policy makers in Washington, D.C., and in state capitals must confront three inconvenient truths.

Inconvenient truth #1. Our nation's social class inequalities are vast and growing. If we are serious about providing equal educational opportunity for every child, we must address these inequalities. They are not immutable. Barack Obama has addressed such inequalities directly and vowed:

> This time we want to talk about the crumbling schools that are stealing the future of black children and white children and Asian children and Hispanic children and Native American children. This time we want to reject the cynicism that tells us that these kids can't learn; that those kids who don't look like us are somebody else's problem. The children of Americans are not those kids, they are our kids, and we will not let them fall behind in a 21st century economy.[18]

Inconvenient truth #2. Schools alone cannot close the achievement gap or solve the dropout problem. The renowned sociologist James Coleman has written, "Inequalities imposed on children by their home, neighborhood, and peer environment are carried along to become the inequalities with which they confront adult life at the end of school."[19]

According to Thomas Bellamy and John Goodlad:

> Collaborative decision making and collective actions depend on leaders who can cross boundaries within and among various groups involved in setting school priorities. The ability to frame issues in ways that support broad participation, bridge communication gaps across groups, and facilitate local deliberation is critical, but often missing. Consequently one important way to support local renewal is by identifying individuals who are attempting such cross-sector leadership, connecting them with one another, and offering learning experiences related to local challenges.[20]

Inconvenient truth number #3. It is going to cost a lot of money to ameliorate the achievement-depressing social and economic conditions of lower-class children's lives and to improve the public schools they attend. But the costs of allowing another generation of children from lower-income groups to grow up undereducated, unhealthy, and unconnected with our economy or society will be even greater.

A black boy born in 2001 has one chance in three of going to prison in his lifetime. A Hispanic boy born in the same year has one chance in six of going to prison in his lifetime.[21] Faced with such stunning indicators of things gone wrong, one can only conclude that a serious course of correction is in order.

Advocating for Transformational Change

Educators have a special insight into the damage that deprivation does to children's learning. We and the organizations that represent us must speak up and keep the policy makers on task. It won't be easy. They are pushed and pulled in many different directions, so that even the more sympathetic ones are easily distracted. We will have to stop being so defensive and go on the offense. We will have to be bold without being belligerent. The stakes are high, but we must be heard.

In the words of David Labaree, "In a democratic society, everyone is affected by what schools accomplish as they educate the majority of each generation's voters, jurors, and taxpayers. So all have reasons to stay involved in the public conversation about school quality."[22]

As advocates for equal opportunity, we must insist on transformational change. Incremental change that merely nibbles around the edges of long-term problems will fall woefully short—again. When a swimmer is drowning 50 feet offshore, it does no good to throw a 10-foot rope. Yet that is precisely what we do, year after year, when it comes to poor and minority children.

The federal government can start by living up to its promises. It promised to cover 40% of the cost of educating disadvantaged students under Title I of the Elementary and Secondary Education Act (ESEA), and it has never done so. Since 2002, for example, when ESEA became No Child Left Behind, the federal government has shortchanged states and school districts by $54.7 billion.[23] School districts and states need fewer mandates and more monetary support.

We need a self-actualized society. We need massive public investments in our children, in their schools, and in our future. It has been more than half a century since *Brown* v. *Board of Education,* but if Linda Brown were a girl today, we still could not guarantee her a high-quality education. It's time we heed the words of Dr. Martin Luther King, Jr., "Save us from that patience that makes us patient with anything less than freedom and justice."[24]

Notes

1. Richard Rothstein, *Class and Schools: Using Social, Economic, and Educational Reform to Close the Black-White Achievement Gap,* Washington, D.C.: Economic Policy Institute, 2004, p. 11.

2. Gary Orfield, "Race and Schools: The Need for Action," *Visiting Scholars Series,* Spring 2008, National Education Association, Washington, D.C., www.nea.org/achievement/orfield08.html.

3. Eric A. Hanushek, John Kain, and Steven G. Rivkin, "Disruptions Versus Tiebout Improvement: The Costs and Benefits of Switching Schools," *Journal of Public Economics,* vol. 88, 2004, pp. 1721–46.

4. Rothstein, pp. 135–38.

5. Margery Austin Turner and Susan J. Popkin, "Affordable Housing in Healthy Neighborhoods: Critical Policy Challenges Facing the Greater New Orleans Region," statement before the Committee on Financial Services, U.S. House of Representatives, 6 February 2007.

6. *The State of Working America 2005–07,* Economic Policy Institute, Washington, D.C., www.epi.org/content.cfm/datazoneindex.

7. "CDF Examines Progress Made Since Dr. King's Death," Children's Defense Fund, 25 January 2008, www.childrensdefense.org.

8. Clive R. Belfield, "The Promise of Early Childhood Education Interventions," in Clive R. Belfield and Henry M. Levin, eds., *The Price We Pay: Economic and Social Consequences of Inadequate Education* (Washington, D.C.: Brookings Institution Press, 2007), p. 209.

9. Arthur J. Rolnick and Rob Grunewald, "Early Intervention on a Large Scale," Federal Reserve Bank of Minneapolis, 2007, http://woodrow.mpls.frb.fed.us/Research/studies/earlychild/earlyintervention.cfm.

10. Frederick Mosteller, "The Tennessee Study of Class Size in the Early School Grades," *The Future of Children: Critical Issues for Children and Youths,* Summer/Fall 1995, p. 113.

11. Student Achievement Guarantee in Education (SAGE), www.weac.org/sage; C. M. Achilles, "Financing Class-Size Reduction," SERVE, University of North Carolina, Greensboro, ERIC ED 419 288; and C. M. Achilles, Patrick Harman, and Paula Egelson, "Using Research Results on Class Size to Improve Pupil Achievement Outcomes," *Research in the Schools,* Fall 1995, pp. 23–31.

12. Jeremy D. Finn et al., "The Enduring Effects of Small Classes," *Teachers College Record,* April 2001, pp. 145–83.

13. Alan B. Krueger and Diane M. Whitmore, "The Effect of Attending a Small Class in the Early Grades on College-Test Taking and Middle School Test Results: Evidence from Project STAR," *Economic Journal,* January 2001, pp. 1–28.

14. Alan B. Krueger and Diane M. Whitmore, "Would Smaller Classes Help Close the Black-White Achievement Gap?" in John E. Chubb and Tom Loveless, *Bridging the Achievement Gap* (Washington, D.C.: Brookings Institution Press, 2002).

15. Peter Muennig and Steven H. Woolf, "Health and Economic Benefits of Reducing the Number of Students per Classroom in U.S. Primary Schools," *American Journal of Public Health,* November 2007, www.ajph.org/cgi/content/abstract/97/11/2020.

16. Christopher H. Tienken and C. M. Achilles, "Making Class Size Work in the Middle Grades," paper presented at the annual meeting of the American Educational Research Association, New York City, March 2008.

17. Deborah Loewenberg Ball, "Improving Mathematics Learning by All: A Problem of Instruction?" *Visiting Scholars Series,* Spring 2008, National Education Association, Washington, D.C., p. 5.

18. Remarks of Senator Barack Obama: "A More Perfect Union," Philadelphia, 18 March 2008, www.barackobama .com/2008/03/18/ remarks_of_senator_ barack_obam_53.php.

19. James S. Coleman et al., *Equal Educational Opportunity* (Washington, D.C.: United States Government Printing Office, 1966), p. 26.

20. G. Thomas Bellamy and John I. Goodlad, "Continuity and Change in the Pursuit of a Democratic Public Mission for Our Schools," *Phi Delta Kappan,* April 2008, p. 570.

21. "CDF Examines Progress Made Since Dr. King's Death."

22. David Labaree, quoted in Bellamy and Goodlad, p. 570.

23. "ESEA Title I-A Grants: Funding Promised in Law vs. Funding Actually Received, FY 2002–09, www.nea.org/lac/ funding/images/title1gap.pdf.

24. Martin Luther King, quoted in Michael J. Freedman, "U.S. Marks 50th Anniversary of Montgomery Bus Boycott," International Information Programs, www. america.gov/st/diversity-english/2005/November/ 20080225140519liameruoy0.664715.html.

JAYNE BOYD-ZAHARIAS began work on Project STAR in 1986 and was named director of Class Size Studies at Tennessee State University. She is currently executive director of Health & Education Research Operative Services, Inc. where she developed the National Class Size Database and continues her role as a co-principal investigator on STAR Follow-up Studies. **HELEN PATE-BAIN** was one of four original Project STAR principal investigators. She has been a classroom teacher, a professor of educational administration, and is a past president of the National Education Association. The authors wish to express their thanks to David Sheridan of the Human and Civil Rights Division of the National Education Association for his advice and input on this article.

From *Phi Delta Kappan,* September 2008, pp. 40–44. Copyright © 2008 by Phi Delta Kappan. Reprinted by permission of Phi Delta Kappan and Jayne Boyd-Zaharias and Helen Pate-Bain.

Meeting of the Minds

The parent-teacher conference is the cornerstone of school-home relations. How can it work for all families?

Laura Pappano

Agnes Jackson isn't proud to admit it, but last year she didn't attend a single parent-teacher conference for her youngest son, who just completed third grade at the Thomas O'Brien Academy of Science and Technology in Albany, New York.

It's not as if she didn't try. Jackson did respond when the school asked her to select a time for a face-to-face meeting. "They asked me what time could I be there and I told them, but they said, 'Oh, somebody already took that,'" says Jackson, a single mother of three who works nights as a certified nursing assistant. She made several impromptu visits to the school, whose website touts it as a "nationally recognized Blue Ribbon School of Excellence," but each time her son's teacher was unavailable. "They'd say, 'You need to wait until school is over,'" she recalls.

The parent-teacher conference may be the most critical, yet awkward, ritual in the school calendar. It is treated as a key barometer of parental involvement, so important that a Texas lawmaker earlier this year proposed fining parents $500 and charging them with a Class C misdemeanor for skipping one. New York City Mayor Michael R. Bloomberg wants to pay poor families up to $5,000 a year to meet goals, including attending parent-teacher conferences.

Yet, in practice, these conferences can be ill-defined encounters whose very high-pressure design—bringing together a child's two most powerful daily influences for sometimes super-brief meetings about academic and social progress—make them a volatile element in home-school relations. For schools, parent-teacher conferences can be a nightmare to organize and may leave teachers spinning after hours of quick encounters. For parents, sessions can feel more like speed-dating than team-building and may encourage snap judgments.

Surveys of K–8 parent involvement conducted by the National Center for Educational Statistics indicate that a majority of parents attended parent-teacher conferences in 2003. Yet, many are still absent. Those parents who might most need to show often don't or can't. The most involved can now, in a growing number of districts, access their child's homework, grades, and attendance online.

Given the weight that parents and teachers place on these once-or twice-a-year get-togethers, what can schools do to ensure that parent-teacher conferences are effective and productive—and meet the needs of all families?

The "Two-Way" Conference

Kathleen Hoover-Dempsey, associate professor and chair of the department of psychology and human development at Vanderbilt University, who studies home-school communication, says face-to-face conversations are more effective than written notes and e-mails, especially when the teacher has concerns or suggestions to make. For parents, "the heart just leaps a bit at the thought that something is wrong," she says. Conferences should include a chance for parents to share observations or concerns, specifics from the teacher about positive things a child is doing, and thoughts on how the teacher and parent might support a child's performance, Hoover-Dempsey says.

The conference is not for me to give you my judgment, but for us to share experiences and suggestions.

Many schools are rethinking conferences to make them less a complaint session and more a collaborative discussion, she says. "People are really starting to talk about the 'two-way parent-teacher conference' and the 'mutually respectful parent-teacher conference.' The conference is not for me to give you my judgment, but for us to share experiences and suggestions about things we can do to really support this child's education."

Collaborative conferences can be promoted by "bundling" them with other chances for parents and teachers to communicate, according to Karen Mapp, lecturer at the Harvard Graduate School of Education and a coauthor of *Beyond the Bake Sale: The Essential Guide to Family-School Partnerships.* Very effective schools may hold several face-to-face conferences each year, including some in which students present their schoolwork

Laying the Groundwork for Successful Parent-Teacher Conferences

To foster parent-teacher talk—formal or informal—Claire Crane, principal of the Robert L. Ford School in Lynn, Mass., has structured her school to get parents in the building as often as she can. Many are recent immigrants working two or three jobs, so she lures them to school by meeting *their* needs. School is open Monday and Tuesday until 9 p.m., when 250 parents attend English as a Second Language classes and a course on surviving in the U.S. Ford staff members teach the classes and provide babysitting and a chance to connect.

The school also operates like a community center. Parents perform in neighborhood talent shows, raise money, and plant trees to beautify the grounds. They have even volunteered alongside city health officials to try to halt a rat problem by putting out bait.

Crane says the intense level of involvement and communication enhances parent-teacher relationships and, in turn, both the formal and informal conferences that take place. So when it's time for formal parent-teacher conference nights three times a year, Crane says, "I can't handle the crowds."

As a result, when there are difficult conversations to have—and there are plenty in a school in which one-third of students attend summer school in order to be promoted— parents feel they are on the same team with the school.

"I feel so much confidence in the principal, I come and ask her, 'What can I do?'" says Beverly Ellis, a mother of five and Ford School parent for 22 years. Ellis, who has two children at the school now, recently had to speak with teachers when her daughter started throwing erasers in her sixth-grade class. "I like to hear they are doing good. But if things are not going right, you can talk to the teachers."

- In what ways is your child working up to his or her expectations?
- What things at school make your child happiest? Most upset?
- Think of a time when your child dealt with a difficult situation that made you very proud. What did you see as the strengths of your child in that situation?

Chrispeels, who trains teachers in conducting parent conferences, says such questions are important both for the information they provide teachers and because they position parents as partners in their child's schooling. The process also lets parents know that teachers realize children may be acting differently at school than at home.

Teachers should be prepared to show concrete examples of academic expectations, including student papers with names removed. "Teachers need to be able to explain to parents, 'Here is the range of work in this class,'" says Chrispeels. That way, she says, parents can have a better idea of what the teacher will be encouraging students to achieve in the future.

Chrispeels advocates ending conferences with what she calls a "one to grow on" message, to let parents know what the teacher intends to do to address any areas of weakness—and how the parent might help at home. Sometimes that can be as simple as explaining what skills they are working on in school and what resources are available to help students outside of school, like a before-school phonics help session.

Even parents of children who are doing well in school need reassurance that their child is developmentally, socially, and intellectually on track, says Chrispeels. Teachers also have experience and information to relay, for example, about planning high school course loads to meet graduation and college-entrance requirements. This helps parents anticipate a child's stresses and needs.

Facilitating Participation

More parent-teacher dialogue means schools must work harder to meet parents on their turf and tailor meetings to suit particular lifestyles and needs. Because their parent populations can vary significantly, school administrators are using different approaches to facilitate parent-teacher conferencing.

At Arlington (Mass.) High School, an upper-middle-class suburb of Boston where 72 percent of graduates go on to four-year colleges, parents can now sign up online for five-minute, face-to-face parent-teacher conferences. It's so popular that when administrators opened up the conference registration at midnight in the fall of 2004, 200 slots were booked in the first 10 minutes. Principal Charles Skidmore says online registration gives parents more choice and control and that, as a result, teachers are drawing more parents to conferences. "We are seeing some of the 'hard-to-reach' parents," Skidmore reports.

The situation is much different at the K–8 Robert L. Ford School in Lynn, Mass., where 90 percent of students are low-income and 58.5 percent speak English as a second language. Principal Claire Crane has created multiple ways for parents and teachers to talk, including holding parent-teacher conferences

and share responses to questions they have pondered in advance, says Mapp, former deputy superintendent for family and community engagement for the Boston Public Schools. Others may be times for parents and teachers to meet solo and discuss an agenda agreed upon in advance. The key, says Mapp, is that the school community should shape how conference time is used.

Shifting Dynamics: A Larger Role for Parents

Building a two-way exchange, says Janet Chrispeels, professor of education studies at the University of California at San Diego, also requires shifting the dynamic of the conference from *reporting on* a child to *eliciting from* parents a better understanding of a child's strengths at home, in order to provide clues to helping them at school. Questions that might reveal these clues include:

- What homework habits does your child have that make you proud?

Conference Dos and Don'ts

Some teachers dread parent-teacher conferences because no one has taught them what to do—or what not to do, says Todd Whitaker, professor of educational leadership at Indiana State University and author or coauthor of several books, including *Dealing with Difficult Parents*.

His advice for setting a positive tone and dealing with difficult parents:

- Hold the first parent-teacher conference early in the year, before children get into trouble or fall behind. Call parents in advance if there is a problem. Nothing in the conference should be a surprise.
- Sit next to the person. "We are on the same team," says Whitaker.
- Even if parents are angry, keep calm and treat them in a positive manner.
- Speak about "we" and not "you": "What can we do together so your son can be more successful?"
- Focus on the future. Do not treat conferences as a conclusion but as a step along a path.

as early as 7 A.M. and as late as 9 P.M. (see "Laying the Groundwork for Successful Parent-Teacher Conferences"). These conferences are sensitive to parents' needs. They are folded into family evenings that include displays of student work (no babysitters needed, and kids can show off learning). There is food. There are translators. The conferences are never held in the winter (easier for families with babies). Last year, Crane even held a conference in the street because a father with health problems couldn't easily get out of his car.

The formula appears to have worked. Crane, whose school has an attendance rate of 95.5 percent, had 92 percent of families come to an open house in November 2006 and attend parent-teacher conferences later that same night.

Other schools focus on welcoming parents during the school day. At Harriet Gibbons High School in Albany, New York, a new school serving ninth graders in a community in which 40 percent of students qualify for free or reduced-priced lunches, principal Anthony Clement built parent-teacher conference time into the daily school schedule. Team A teachers are available

from 12:40 P.M. to 1:40 P.M., and Team B teachers are available from 10:30 A.M. to 11:30 A.M. If parents are not free during the conference hour, teachers will meet at other times, or—as in the case of the mother of a child in math teacher George Benson's class who must pack up three young kids and take two city buses to attend a conference—plan regular phone calls. School social workers will even make home visits. Noting that many of his parents work at jobs with hourly wages, Clement says, "We know when a parent is here, we need to see them."

As a result, Clement says, 80 percent of parents have attended one or two daytime parent-teacher conferences *in addition* to the two districtwide conferences held on two school days in November and January. Clement credits the emphasis on conferencing with increasing school attendance from 63 percent last year to 85 percent this year, more parent involvement in school activities, and a dramatic up-tick in ninth graders earning five or more of the required credits for promotion to tenth grade, from 45 percent last year to almost 70 percent this year.

The school's approach has also helped parents like Agnes Jackson get involved in her middle son's education. Where Jackson has yet to attend a conference at her third grader's school, she sat down more than a dozen times with her ninth-grade son's teachers at Harriet Gibbons—and that doesn't count scores of informal conversations about her son's school progress.

The frequent conferences have given Jackson a better handle on how the school system works and what is expected of her children. "In the past, I was quick to say, 'These people are doing this to my child,'" she says. "Now I ask, 'But what is my child doing that causes this to happen?' I can hear good and bad. But it's all good because I know how to respond to help my child. It helps me to say, 'OK, bud, you've got to do this,'" says Jackson. "It's helped me to grow as a single parent."

The easy access to teachers at Harriet Gibbons has also colored her views about her son's schools. Her third grader's school, she says, "will call if there is a problem," whereas the constant conversation with her ninth grader's teachers has made her more of a partner. "They tell me about his potential; they tell me what he is capable of doing," she says.

LAURA PAPPANO writes about education and is coauthor, with Eileen McDonagh, of *Playing with the Boys: Why Separate Is Not Equal in Sports,* to be published in November 2007 by Oxford University Press.

Making Long-Term Separations Easier for Children and Families

Jenny, a teacher of young toddlers, notices that 18-month-old Kyle is very emotional this week. He cries and clings to his mother each morning, and Jenny has to hold him for quite a while after his mom leaves. Jenny sees that Kyle is eating less than normal, but he will let her spoon-feed him his lunch. Kyle's mom mentions that he is acting this way at home too. Since he has no fever or other symptom of illness, Jenny wonders if Kyle's mood change has to do with his dad leaving three weeks ago for a military deployment. Jenny decides she'll talk with Kyle's mom about this, and to see how she's coping as a "single parent."

Amy M. Kim and Julia Yeary

Jenny is very observant and tuned in to Kyle's emotional development. Often adult caregivers minimize or do not recognize the effects of long-term separation on young children. This may be due to a child's limited ability to express his discomfort or insecurity, coupled with the caregiver's assumption that the child is too young to be aware of his or her circumstances. Caregivers may attribute children's challenging behaviors or the return to previous developmental stages (such as wetting the bed after completing toilet training) to something other than a grief reaction to the separation from their parent.

The issues military families face when parents deploy, especially to combat zones, are quite complex; each family's circumstances, challenges, and stressors are unique.

In this article, we explore the importance of early attachments, the effects of separation on infants, toddlers, and 3-year-olds, and ways teachers can support children and families during separations. As difficult as a separation might be for an individual child and family, there are strategies to help them cope with this potentially challenging experience. The issues military families face when parents deploy, especially to combat zones, are quite complex; each family's circumstances, challenges, and stressors are unique. But all caregivers and teachers can learn from the methods used by military families who are very familiar with frequent extended parent-child separations.

Early childhood educators can explore the strategies that professionals supporting military families use to foster stronger parent-child relationships and, as appropriate, implement them in their own settings.

The Importance of Early Attachments

John Bowlby (1988) describes *attachment* as a lasting psychological connectedness between human beings. For young children, secure attachment develops when they know with certainty that a primary caregiver will respond to their emotional needs, such as by providing comfort or a calming presence if they are distressed or frightened, as well as their physical needs. Early relationships are critical, and the responsiveness of a parent is crucial to a child's healthy development. The benefits of a healthy attachment relationship may include the reduction of fear in challenging situations, an increase in self-efficacy, and the ability to build on skills to better manage stress (Shonkoff & Phillips 2000). These benefits extend into adulthood, supporting healthy adult relationships, the ability to maintain employment, and the capacity to care for one's own children (Edelstein et al. 2004; Onunaku 2005).

When a Caregiver Leaves

Bowlby, in referencing his work with researcher John Robertson, states that the effect of separation is considerable for the youngest children, who still rely on caregivers to help them regulate their emotions (Lieberman et al. 2003). Research shows that children who experience a prolonged separation may exhibit anxiety, withdrawal, hyper-vigilance, eating disorders, and possibly anger and aggression (Parke & Clarke-Stewart 2001). Young children may also have trouble sleeping, become clingy or withdrawn, and regress (for example, have a lapse in toilet learning).

It is important to remember that separation is not just a one-time event, but rather something experienced before, during, and after a departure.

It is important to remember that separation is not just a one-time event, but rather something experienced before, during, and after a departure. Often, the effects of separation continue after the reunion. One teacher offers an example from her classroom:

> Three-year-old Bailey had previously experienced separation when her father was deployed to Iraq for six months. For the first couple of weeks after his return, she continually asked, "Who will pick me up today?" Bailey also had difficulty at nap times, often waking up, looking for a teacher, and then closing her eyes as soon as she spotted one. Later, teachers learned that Bailey was afraid that her father would leave again while she was at school, without her knowing.

Offering Parents Support Impacts Family Resiliency

By understanding what military families do to foster resiliency in their children, caregivers and teachers can provide better support and information to the families of young children experiencing a lengthy separation from a parent. There are numerous factors that predict the level of resiliency a family coping with long-term separations will show. However, military families who use active coping styles, receive social and community support, are optimistic and self-reliant, and give meaning to the separation are shown to function more effectively than those who don't (APA 2007).

An active coping style can be as simple as the family planning to have a neighbor watch the children one afternoon a week so the caregiver at home can run errands. A family that participates in a neighborhood play group or attends family activities at their church is receiving support from their community. A parent who believes that he or she can get through the separation and that there will be support if problems arise is self-reliant and optimistic. The military family who feels their service member is deployed to help others or to defend the country is giving meaning to the separation. Adopting these attitudes or following similar actions will foster resiliency in a family, a key to successfully meeting the challenge of separation.

Understanding the Emotional Cycle of Long-term Separation

Pincus and colleagues (2005) developed the Emotional Cycle of Deployment as a model to explain the emotional responses many military families experience during a deployment. While every family will not react to separation in exactly the same way, there are some predictable stages. This model can offer insights into the emotions nonmilitary families may experience when one parent leaves for an extended period of time.

The first stage begins when the family is notified of the deployment. During this stage, families enter a period of anticipatory grief. Though the separation hasn't yet taken place, the thought of the separation can begin the grieving process. Anticipatory grief has been defined as a feeling of loss before a dreaded event occurs (Hodgson 2005). Symptoms can include denial, mood swings, forgetfulness, disorganized and confused behavior, anger, depression, and feeling disconnected and alone. Physical symptoms such as weight loss or gain, sleep problems, nervous behavior, and general fatigue may also be present. At this stage, families are working to strengthen their bonds while letting go at the same time.

The second stage occurs when the individual leaves. During this phase, family members left at home may go through a period of grief or mourning. They may have periods of tearfulness and experience a change in their appetite and sleep patterns. These depression-like symptoms are typical, and they usually lessen after two to four weeks. In some cases, the remaining family members may experience relief at the departure of the military member. This also is a typical reaction, as families have dealt with many of their emotions prior to the departure and are ready to move to the next stage.

About a month after departure, the family typically settles into the third stage: a new family routine that usually lasts until just before the absent parent returns home. Adults and children typically do best if the newly established family routine is similar to what they did prior to separation. Families who take advantage of neighborhood and community support systems report fewer difficulties during a separation.

The fourth stage occurs about four to six weeks prior to reunion, when the family begins anticipating the return of the absent family member. For many families, this reunion stage is more stressful than the other stages (National Military Family Association 2005). Not knowing how each partner in the relationship has changed, how those changes will be accepted, and how children will accept the returning family member can raise many questions and anxieties.

Upon the return of the member who has been away, the family enters the fifth stage, when they must renegotiate the family roles and reestablish their relationships. This stage may begin with a happy, almost honeymoon-like period but can turn stressful quickly if family members do not recognize the need to communicate and work together. Professionals working with military families identify this stage as one of great concern. This time of disequilibrium may contribute to heightened risks for child or spouse abuse due to the increased stress.

Ongoing Communication

Communication is one of the primary concerns of military families coping with family separation (National Military Family Association 2005), and it is the most important aid in minimizing negative effects during every stage experienced during the separation. Communication is important not only between the adults, but also with children (in developmentally appropriate ways). Parents and teachers can help by offering children words for the emotions they might be experiencing. Providing the child with needed vocabulary and simple, factual information will help them begin to make sense of the situation and will make them feel like what they are experiencing is validated (Parke & Clarke-Stewart 2001).

Working to Stay Connected: Co-parenting Alliance

Families who cope successfully with frequent separations are likely to work together as partners in raising their children. Such parents are likely to communicate regularly, using letters, e-mail, or phone calls to discuss *all* aspects of raising their child. One mother shared as much information as possible, so the father, who was in Iraq, was able to ask their 3-year-old son specific questions about his child care friends and activities. Another father, who had been away for 17 months, found resuming his role as father in the home was a great deal easier because he knew about his children's daily routine and accomplishments while he was away.

Military parents demonstrate this co-parenting alliance by working hard to keep the child and absent parent connected. Rather than simply letting an absence take its course, they work to keep the absent parent in the child's mind through a variety of interactive means, and include that parent in all major decisions regarding the child. A teacher can support families experiencing separation. For example, after sharing that a couple's 19-month-old daughter was biting other children in the class and displaying aggressive behaviors, her teacher arranged for her father, in Korea on military assignment, to participate in the parent-teacher conference via Webcam so everyone could strategize together about how to help the toddler learn more appropriate ways to express her frustration and cope with her strong feelings.

For the Classroom

Teachers of young children play an important role in supporting the strong connections between families and children. The strength of these connections begins with the teacher being aware of the circumstances of the children in the classroom and their families.

Support the at-home parent. Simply taking a moment to ask a parent how he or she is doing will help strengthen connections between the parent, caregiver, and child. It is difficult to parent without the support of a second adult in the home.

> **Simply taking a moment to ask a parent how he or she is doing will help strengthen connections between the parent, caregiver, and child.**

It is important that program directors and teachers know of community resources that can provide needed services. Mental health and financial concerns are two issues that may surface when a parent is faced with the long-term absence of his or her partner. It is helpful to have information or resources to discreetly give to parents should the need arise. These positive interactions may encourage parents to reach out to other agencies for assistance.

Maintain a consistent program environment. Although some change is inevitable, try to keep the classroom setting as consistent as possible, including maintaining a predictable daily routine. You may want to reconsider the timing of moving a child to a new class. Provide opportunities for a child to feel more in control of daily activities to help her feel more secure. Be aware of children's need to make choices whenever possible. For example, ask a child if he would like juice or water with his meal, or ask which center he would like to play in first.

Be aware of stages of child development. Separation anxiety is a normal part of development for infants and toddlers. Having a parent leave for an extended period of time adds another layer to the challenge of learning to separate from a parent. Children experiencing long separations from their parent are best supported in an environment that honors their need to stay connected to their parent.

Include parent-child photos. Place pictures of family members at children's eye level to help them feel closer to their parents, no matter the length of a separation. Teachers can have parents help create special memory books with laminated pictures for toddlers and young preschoolers to carry with them in the classroom.

Use video or audio tapes. Invite children's parents to create tape recordings of themselves singing or reading to their children. These tapes can bring the absent parent into the classroom while he or she is away. Such recordings help a child stay in touch with the parent and soothe the child when he or she is missing that parent. If video equipment is available, parents can record themselves playing with or reading to their children. Parents can take the videos home to watch with their child. Teachers can set up special viewing centers in the classroom. These ideas are extremely helpful to the child with an absent parent, but also are helpful for all young children as they learn to separate from their primary caregivers.

Use transitional objects. Transitional objects may help a child cope with strong feelings about a parent's absence. Programs can encourage parents to send their child's favorite cuddly toy to help the child feel more secure. These transitional objects, along with the voice recordings from parents, can be especially soothing for the older infant or young toddler.

To create a special transitional object for a young child, take a T-shirt the parent has worn and make it into a pillow. One mother made a pillow out of her nightgown because her young twins liked to feel the soft fabric while they rested. The scent of the parent adds an additional layer of comfort. Some military parents spray the pillow with the cologne or aftershave the absent parent uses to invoke memories of the parent for the child. Older infants and toddlers may hold onto the pillow and snuggle into it when they are missing their parent. (Note: Infants should not sleep with pillows.)

Teachers can establish a special place in the classroom for quiet reflection. Children can keep their transitional objects in that area and use them as needed.

Reinforce parent-child connections. Books can be a wonderful resource to connect a child with a caring adult. Some titles frequently used to emphasize the parent-child connection are *The Kissing Hand,* by Audrey Penn, *Owl Babies,* by Martine Waddell, and *Are You My Mother?* by P.D. Eastman. After reading books such as these, children can do follow-up activities. For example, after reading *The Kissing Hand* teachers can have young children trace their hands and place a kiss in the center to give to a parent. To extend this activity to home, ask parents to trace their hands and place a kiss in the palm. They can send the hands in with their children. This activity may also be done by a parent who is away.

If possible, mail items directly to the absent parent; this helps the parent know you are remembering to include him or her in the collaborative team caring for the child.

Review communication strategies. Ask yourself, "How can I share information with parents who are away?" Consider incorporating technology such as e-mail or Webcams to allow for conferences. Have the child make two different creations during a project; one to take home and one for the parent who is away. Teachers can make two copies of classroom reports or communications, so one can be mailed to the absent parent. If possible, mail items directly to the absent parent; this helps the parent know you are remembering to include him or her in the collaborative team caring for the child.

For More Resources on Separation

Many parents want to learn more ways to support their child through a period of separation and how to keep parent-child connections strong. The ZERO TO THREE Web site (www.zerotothree.org) has information to support families of young children and the professionals who work with them. Information specific to helping families cope with parental separation can be found in the Military Families section, under Key Topics. Links to organizations that support military families, including counseling and resource information, can also be found there.

Conclusion

As a teacher or caregiver, you play a very important role in a young child's life while a parent is away. You serve as a valuable resource by supporting the parent at home and helping to foster the relationship between the away parent and the child. Incorporating a few strategies may help families to develop coping skills, build resiliency, and maintain important relationships crucial to the well-being of children and families.

References

APA (American Psychological Association). 2007. *The psychological needs of U.S. military service members and their families: A preliminary report.* www.apa.org/releases/MilitaryDeploymentTaskForceReport.pdf

Bowlby, J. 1988. *A secure base: Parent-child attachment and healthy human development.* New York: Basic Books.

Edelstein, R.S., K.W. Alexander, P.R. Shaver, J.M. Schaaf, J.A. Quas, G.S. Lovas, & G.S. Goodman. 2004. Adult attachment style and parental responsiveness during a stressful event. *Attachment and Human Development* 6(1): 31–52.

Hodgson, H. 2005. Anticipatory grief symptoms: What's the big deal? www.americanhospice.org/index.php?option=com_content&task=view&id=80&Itemid=13

Lieberman, A.F., N.C. Compton, P. Van Horn, & C.G. Ippen. 2003. *Losing a parent to death in the early years: Guidelines for the treatment of traumatic bereavement in infancy and early childhood.* Washington, DC: ZERO TO THREE Press.

National Military Family Association. 2005. *Report on the Cycles of Deployment Survey: An analysis of survey responses from April through September, 2005.* www.nmfa.org/site/DocServer/NMFACyclesofDeployment9.pdf?docID=5401

Onunaku, N. 2005. *Improving maternal and infant mental health: Focus on maternal depression.* Los Angeles, CA: National

Center for Infant and Early Childhood Health Policy at UCLA. www.healthychild.ucla.edu/Publications/Maternal%20Depression%20Report%20Final.pdf

Parke, R., & K.A. Clarke-Stewart. 2001. Effects of parental incarceration on young children. Presented at the National Policy Conference: From Prison to Home: The Effect of Incarceration and Reentry on Children, Families, and Communities, Washington, D.C., January 2002. http://aspe.hhs.gov/HSP/prison2home02/parke&stewart.pdf

Pincus, S.H., R. House, J. Christenson, & L.E. Adler. 2005. *The emotional cycle of deployment: A military family perspective.* www.hooah4health.com/deployment/Familymatters/emotionalcycle.htm

Shonkoff, J., & D. Phillips, eds. 2000. *From neurons to neighborhoods: The science of early childhood development.* Washington, DC: National Academy Press.

AMY M. KIM, MEd, is a training and consultation specialist for military projects at ZERO TO THREE, the National Center for Infants, Toddlers, and Families. Amy works on material development and trainings for military professionals and families. akim@zerotothree.org **JULIA YEARY,** LCSW, is a senior training and consultation specialist with military projects at ZERO TO THREE, the National Center for Infants, Toddlers, and Families. Julia has worked extensively with military families; she is also a military spouse and mother. jyeary@zerotothree.org

Supporting Grandparents Who Raise Grandchildren

JENNIFER BIRCKMAYER ET AL.

Four-year-old Kyle enters the classroom slowly, clinging to the hand of his grandmother. His friend George runs toward him, shouting "Hey Kyle–wanna play?" Suddenly George stops short and stares. "Who's that?" he asks.

When Kyle's eyes begin to fill with tears, his teacher intervenes. "Hello," she says warmly. "Our director told me Kyle's grandma would be visiting today. George, maybe you and Kyle would like to show his grandma the seeds we are growing on the windowsill."

"OK," George says doubtfully, "but where's your mommy, Kyle?"

In the past 10 years the United States has seen a dramatic increase in the number of children who live without their parents in a household headed by a relative. More than 2.5 million grandparents now raise grandchildren without a biological parent present in the home (Simmons & Dye 2003).

Many other grandparents provide full- or part-time child care for working parents, often as a supplement to early childhood education programs such as Head Start or family child care. Because grandparents are often the ones who see teachers or caregivers at drop-off or pickup times or may be the only adults available, many become the logical family contact for a program.

Grandparents who assume responsibility for their grandchildren are unsung heroes and heroines of the twenty-first century. Without them, many children whose parents are unwilling or unable to care for them would be in the foster care system.

Circumstances and Challenges Differ

A popular image of grandparents portrays them as individuals who provide loving relationships and enriching experiences for grandchildren or give practical help with child care for working parents. But the circumstances under which many grandparents become the *primary* adults in the lives of grandchildren are often unfortunate, even tragic. The reasons include parental drug and/or alcohol use, divorce, mental and physical illness (including AIDS), child abuse and neglect, incarceration, even death. Some skipped-generation families (grandparents raising grandchildren) are temporary arrangements while parents are completing their education, on military or business assignment, recovering from illness, or serving a short jail term. Whether brief or permanent, almost all skipped-generation families begin with trauma for children, parents, and grandparents.

The challenges for these caregivers are unique and sometimes overwhelming. Few adults in their later years plan to be caring for children—especially children who may be traumatized, deeply unhappy, or suffering from chronic health conditions—while they themselves are experiencing some of the more difficult aspects of growing older. For grandparents, shortages of time and money, declining health, unfamiliarity with existing community resources (especially in the fields of medical care and education), and confusing legal problems often combine with grief and guilt about their child's inability to parent.

A common refrain among grandparents who are parenting again is "I just feel so tired all the time. It keeps me from being the kind of grandparent I would like to be."

Contrary to popular belief, not all of these grandparents are elderly. Some are in their thirties, with children still at home; some are of the so-called sandwich generation, caring for children and grandchildren in addition to aging parents. Many must continue to hold jobs to provide adequately for grandchildren. A common refrain among grandparents who are parenting again is "I just feel so tired all the time. It keeps me from being the kind of grandparent I would like to be."

Older grandparents fear that they will become ill, disabled, or die and no one will be available to care for their grandchildren. They also worry that they will not be able to afford appropriate medical care if their grandchildren become ill or disabled. One half of the children living in homes with two grandparents (no parent present) have no health insurance (Bryson & Casper 1999).

Exploring Grandparenting Issues in Workshops

Parenting the Second Time Around is a manual that explores grandparenting issues in a workshop series. The manual contains invaluable material for six two-hour workshops on the following topics:

1. **It Wasn't Supposed to Be Like This**—Identifying and reflecting on ambivalent feelings about changing roles, finding helpful community resources
2. **Getting to Know You**—Exploring child development, individual differences, journaling
3. **Rebuilding a Family**—Examining adult-child interactions, grief and loss, relating to your adult child, solution-based problem solving
4. **Discipline Is Not a Dirty Word, But It May Look Different Today**—Covering characteristics of effective discipline, establishing a discipline style, addressing high-risk behaviors
5. **Protecting and Planning for Your Grandchild's Future**—Dealing with legal issues, including custody, visitation, and child support
6. **Standing Up for Grandparents'/Grandchildren's Rights**—Encouraging advocacy, negotiating systems, connecting with community programs

The 300-page manual features workshop outlines with handouts and supplementary material for the leaders.

From J. Birckmayer, J. Cohen, I. Jensen, D. Variano, & G. Wallace, *Parenting the Second Time Around* (Ithaca, NY: Cornell University, 2001). Available from The Resource Center, Cornell University, P.O. Box 3884, Ithaca, NY 14852; telephone 607-255-2080; online: www.cce.cornell.edu/store/customer/home.php?cat=271&page=3.

immunization (especially flu) clinics, Al-Anon meetings, and recreational events and exercise. Let them know it is good for their grandchildren to see them as active participants in community life.

- **provide information about where to obtain good legal services.** Legal concerns of custody and guardianship are serious issues for grandparents raising grandchildren. Help keep children from losing the security their grandparents may provide because legal guardianship has not been established.
- **gather information about community organizations or resources for children with special needs.** It may be particularly difficult for grandparents to recognize that children suffering from attention deficit disorder (ADD) or attention deficit hyperactivity disorder (ADHD) are not deliberately "misbehaving." Refer grandparents to national support groups such as Children and Adults with Attention Deficit Disorders (ChADD) and the Attention Deficit Disorder Association (ADDA). Both organizations offer families good information and practical advice and are available online (www.chadd.org and www.add.org).

An early childhood program can address grandparents' needs for information and social support by offering workshops designed especially for them.

An early childhood program can address grandparents' needs for information and social support by offering workshops designed especially for them. The Cooperative Extension Service has developed manuals with suggested outlines for meetings around topics of particular interest for grandparents. Resources can be obtained from local county extension offices or often online (for example, at www.fcs.uga.edu/extension/cyf_pubs.php/parent#parent or http://parenting.wsu.edu/relative/links.htm). If information is not available locally, a manual for grandparenting workshops is available (see "Exploring Grandparenting Issues in Workshops").

Effective workshop sessions require a skilled and experienced leader who can keep discussion on track. It is also important to allow unstructured time for informal discussion and socializing. Grandparents can be invaluable resources for each other, and friendships often develop while sharing common concerns.

In addition to offering special workshops for grandparents, early childhood programs can take the following specific and helpful steps:

Raising grandchildren sometimes isolates grandparents, regardless of age, from their peers, often leaving them depressed and lonely. The situations that bring about a grandchild-grandparent household may also create physical or psychological problems for children. Helping children feel secure and loved, while simultaneously dealing with special needs and challenging behaviors, is an enormous task for parents and can be an overwhelming responsibility for grandparents.

Grandparents parenting the second time around need social support as well as up-to-date information about effective parenting and available community services. The early childhood program in which their grandchild is enrolled may be in the best position to offer help.

Early childhood educators can

- **listen empathically to grandparents.** Introduce them to others in similar situations, or suggest workshops and community meetings about common concerns.
- **encourage grandparents to avail themselves of community resources.** Introduce them to food banks and clinics. Help them to stay well. Notify them of

- **Use the word** *families* instead of *parents* on bulletin boards and in newsletters and notices.
- **Use black print** (initial capitals followed by lower case letters) on white paper or printed material for families. Choose fonts that are readable and at least a 12-point type. This is helpful to people with impaired vision.

- **Prepare for questions** like George's in our introductory example. Ask grandparents how they would like you to respond when children ask, "Where's Kyle's mommy?" Respect confidentiality. If Kyle's grandmother wants you to say, "His mommy is away on a trip," but you know she is in jail or in a substance abuse program, you can answer, "Kyle's grandma says his mommy is away, so she's taking care of Kyle right now."

- **Look for ways to include grandparents** by focusing on their special skills or strengths. Grandparents may feel out of place in a group of young families, even when the age difference may not be great. Reading, singing, storytelling, and cooking are obvious areas to explore, but grandparents may surprise you with expertise in puppetry, folk dancing, gardening, or bird watching.

- **Be sensitive to the comfort needs** of all adult visitors by providing adult-size chairs for classroom visits or meetings. Arthritis can develop at any age, and an adult with swollen hands can have difficulty engaging with a child using child-size puzzles, scissors, and games with small parts.

- **Plan holiday celebrations with care.** Perhaps Mothers Day and Fathers Day can become People We Love days.

- **Display pictures and posters** of various family constellations, including some with grandparents as primary caregivers.

- **Model roles other than Mommy and Daddy** in the dramatic play corner. Ask to join the children's play as a grandpa or an aunt or a cousin.

- **Introduce assistive devices,** such as walkers or canes, in the classroom for children to explore, use, and discuss.

- **Include figures of many adults** (including older people) in the block play accessories.

- **Examine puzzles and other games** to be sure they represent many different family structures.

- **Consider the language in poetry, songs, and books** you share with children. Be aware of the negative impact a nursery rhyme such as the following can have on a sensitive child who lives with a grandparent:

There was an old woman who lived in a shoe
She had so many children she didn't know what to do
She gave them some broth without any bread
And whipped them all soundly and sent them to bed.
There was an old lady who swallowed a fly...
Perhaps she'll die.

- **Include, read, and discuss books** dealing with all kinds of families and family issues. Many books about grandparents seem to emphasize pleasant, leisurely visits; gardening; or dealing with disability and death; but there are others to be found. See "Children's Books about Family Relationships for Grandparents and Grandchildren to Share" for a list of some of our favorite books. (A longer list appears online in Beyond the Journal at www.journal.naeyc.org/btj.)

Early childhood educators are in ideal positions to provide substantial support and assistance to grandparent-/relative-headed families. Teachers may be the first or only nonfamily adults to see that a child is exhibiting aggressive, withdrawn, or depressed behaviors after circumstances necessitate a move in with grandparents.

Clear communication and strong partnerships between teaching staff and grandparents can result in strategies to reduce a child's fears and foster healthy development and feelings of self-worth. Working as partners, all adults can think of specific words and phrases for explanations that meet a child's needs and level of understanding.

While books are no substitute for spontaneous, loving conversations, they do often provide openings for discussion. Consider establishing a lending library of children's books dealing with a wide variety of family issues, from divorce and the death of pets to coping with a parent's alcoholism (see "Good Books about Grandparents and Grandchildren").

Teachers can help grandparents choose and use books appropriately. They also can encourage grandparents to share children's reactions to books and discussions and together brainstorm further steps to provide reassurance and comfort. By developing partnerships with grandparents raising children, early childhood educators can support the growth of stronger families.

References

Bryson, K., & L.M. Casper. 1999. Coresident grandparents and grandchildren. Table 2. Current Population Reports, Special Studies (May). Washington, DC: U.S. Census Bureau.

Simmons, T., & J. Dye. 2003. Grandparents living with grandchildren: 2000. *Census 2000 Brief* (October). Online: www.census.gov/prod/2003pubs/c2kbr-31.pdf.

JENNIFER BIRCKMAYER, MA, has been a senior extension associate with the Department of Human Development at Cornell University in Ithaca, New York, for 40 years. During that time she has been a teacher, trainer, speaker, and author. **JAN COHEN, MEd,** is executive director of Cornell University Cooperative Extension of Otsego County, New York. She has worked in the field of education and human services for more than 20 years. She is the author of "Help for Grandparents of Children with Developmental Disabilities," a six-workshop curriculum published by the New York State Office for Aging. **ISABELLE DORAN JENSEN, MS,** is an extension resource educator for human development with Cornell Cooperative Extension of Ontario County, New York. She has worked with grandparent/caregiver relatives since 1991 and has been recognized with several awards from the National Extension Association of Family and Consumer Sciences. **DENYSE ALTMAN VARIANO, RN, MPS,** is the senior extension resource educator in charge of human development programming for Cornell Cooperative Extension of Orange County, New York. Denyse is the administrator for the Relatives as Parents Program in Orange County.

Children of Teen Parents

Challenges and Hope

BARBARA A. WHITE, MIMI GRAHAM, AND SEATON K. BRADFORD

Virtually every publicly funded early childhood program serves teen parents and their children. Some programs serve pregnant and parenting teens, and their infants and toddlers, exclusively. Yet all too often, health services, school-based programs, and home visiting initiatives focus primarily on outcomes for the teen mother (for example, repeat pregnancies) and place very little emphasis on outcomes for the child.

In this issue of *Zero to Three*, we hope to explore as thoroughly as possible the experience of infants and toddlers who have adolescent parents. What is it like, for example, for a baby and her mother to be in foster care together? To have the same pediatrician? How does a toddler feel when he spends the day in a child care classroom in his parent's high school? What happens when a toddler and his parent compete for a home visitor's attention?

The contributors to this issue report from the perspective of the child, but their larger goal is to describe the development of the dyad—the adolescent parent and the child. Taken together, the articles in this issue suggest that in health care settings, center-based services, and home-based programs, practitioners who effectively support the dual development of teen parents and their young children have a number of characteristics in common. They:

- understand the role of multiple risk factors in the lives of the children of teen parents;
- are comprehensive in approach, integrating services from a variety of community partners;
- appreciate the specialized knowledge and skills required to work effectively with teen parents and their children; and
- are committed to providing strength-based, relationship focused services to promote positive outcomes.

Risks Associated with Adolescent Parenthood

Any discussion of young families includes a discussion of risk factors. Teenagers who have had academic difficulty and mental health problems are more likely than their peers to give birth before graduating from high school. These young parents often bring to parenthood a history of poverty, abuse, violence, and unresolved grief and loss. Poverty is a risk factor for adolescent childbearing, which in turn compounds and perpetuates poverty. Children who

are born to teen mothers are 8 times as likely to grow up in poverty as are children of older mothers. Babies of teens are less likely than children of older parents to live with both a mother and father. The resulting inadequate financial support translates into poor housing, inferior child care, and limited health care options.

Teens who have been raised in poverty often feel that they have never "had enough." When they become parents, they have difficulty sharing limited resources with a child. Thus programs that serve the children of teen parents should be prepared to provide for babies' needs at two levels. Formula, diapers, and baby clothes ensure basic survival. At a second level, programs must compensate for the "poverty of experience" that is common to young families by offering front-pack carriers, board books, play materials, and, perhaps most important, learning opportunities and life experiences in the community that link to school readiness for the child.

Community-based Strategies to Support Young Families

High-quality services for teen parents and their children are integrated services. Effective program planners identify points of entry, unique to each community, where teen parents are most likely to seek help for themselves and their children. No single service program is likely to be able to address the multiple needs

At a Glance

Programs for teen parents and their children promote dual development by:

- Acknowledging the role of multiple risk factors in the lives of the children of teen parents;
- Integrating services from a variety of community partners;
- Employing specialized strategies and specially trained staff; and
- Providing strength-based, relationship-focused, high quality services.

of young families; partnerships among programs and agencies are essential. Community providers also have a responsibility to explore research evidence, recommended practices, and professional development resources that are likely to contribute to positive outcomes for teen parents and their young children.

In the context of well-designed programs for young families, competent practitioners individualize intervention strategies. Drawing on their understanding of adolescent development and early childhood, they find ways to give hope to teen parents and their children. Those professionals who are most successful in their work with young families constantly look for ways to capitalize on the motivation, resilience, and responsiveness of young parents. If skilled support is available, the rapid pace of development in the early years and the baby's powerful drive toward attachment can bring out the best in teen mothers and fathers.

In 2004, the Task Force on Teen Parents and Their Children, convened by the Miami-Dade School Readiness Coalition and the Florida State University's Center for Prevention and Early Intervention Policy, identified 14 components of a comprehensive service system for teen parents and their children. The Task Force recommended that service providers address these components when developing new programs or improving upon existing services for young families (White, Larsen, & Schilling, 2004). These components include:

1. A "medical home" (stable source of health care) for parent and child
2. Good-quality early care and education (child care)
3. Social work services
4. Prenatal and parenting education
5. Family planning counseling and services
6. Comprehensive educational programs/work force development
7. Family violence intervention/protection
8. Mental health/infant mental health services
9. Housing/shelter referrals
10. Legal services
11. Family literacy activities
12. Sexual abuse treatment
13. Substance abuse education and treatment
14. Early intervention

The Task Force further recommended that communities:

- Use co-located programs or carefully crafted interagency agreements to establish a network of service providers;
- Inform teen parents of service options;
- Assure developmental screening for each teen parent and child;
- Educate practitioners, community policy makers, and the general public about the developmental needs of teen parents and their children;
- Provide for the basic needs of young families;

- Identify risk factors for healthy development of young families and build protective factors into community institutions such as schools, the health care system, libraries, recreational programs, and the arts;
- Promote a relationship-based approach in all interventions;
- Use an infant mental health framework to understand the behavior of teen parents and their children;
- Establish multidisciplinary teams to assess the functioning of teen parents and their children, develop intervention plans with parents, and offer comprehensive services;
- Use a continuous improvement model to raise the quality of community services; and
- Integrate reflective practice into all levels of service for young families.

Changing Lives

Although they usually lack the skills, experience, and means to make it happen, most adolescent mothers are determined to make the lives of their children better than their own. Unlike many adult women who seem defeated by years of living in poverty, even the most challenged adolescent mothers have a reservoir of resilience and hope that their new baby will experience success and happiness.

Practitioners who work with young families will attest that most adolescent parents respond positively to caring adults who have an interest in their well-being and that of their baby. Even young parents who have lacked consistent relationships with loving, attentive, responsible, and trustworthy adults during much of their childhood will—eventually—respond to and deeply appreciate kindness that is offered to them.

Well-designed programs with skilled staff work to reduce risk factors and build protective factors—both internal and external—into the lives of teen parents and their children. Committed practitioners know that the children of teens are resilient and that most teen parents want a good life for their child. In the hopeful words of one young mother, "My main dream is to give my baby the life I didn't have . . . a home, a family that I didn't have when I was growing up." Using proven and promising practices, practitioners, programs, and communities can do far more than simply help the children of teen parents survive. As the contributors to this issue of *Zero to Three* demonstrate, systematic efforts to understand young families and thoughtfully designed, skillfully implemented interventions can overcome challenge and justify hope.

References

White, B. Larsen, R, & Schilling, M. (2004). *Interim report of the Task Force on Teen Parents and Their Children.* Tallahassee: Florida State University, Center for Prevention and Early Intervention Policy.

UNIT 3
Diverse Learners

Unit Selections

12. **Whose Problem Is Poverty?,** Richard Rothstein
13. **Learning in an Inclusive Community,** Mara Sapon-Shevin
14. **Including Children with Disabilities in Early Childhood Education Programs: Individualizing Developmentally Appropriate Practices,** John Filler and Yaoying Xu
15. **Creative Play: Building Connections with Children Who Are Learning English,** Sara J. Burton and Linda Carol Edwards

Key Points to Consider

- What are some strategies that teachers can use to assist English language learners and their families?

- Describe some of the ways in which teachers can include children with disabilities in their classroom.

- What are some ways through which children from other cultures can acquire English language skills?

Student Web Site
www.mhcls.com

Internet References

American Academy of Pediatrics
   www.aap.org
Child Welfare League of America (CWLA)
   http://www.cwla.org
Classroom Connect
   http://www.classroom.com/login/home.jhtml
The Council for Exceptional Children
   http://www.cec.sped.org/index.html
Early Learning Standards: Full report
   http://www.naeyc.org/resources/position_statements/positions_2003.asp
Early Learning Standards: Executive Summary
   http://www.naeyc.org/resources/position_statements/creating_conditions.asp
Make Your Own Web page
   http://www.teacherweb.com
National Resource Center for Health and Safety in Child Care
   http://nrc.uchsc.edu
Online Innovation Institute
   http://oii.org

This unit focuses on the many diverse learners who are in our early childhood programs and schools. This unit starts with a continuation of the issue of poverty that was prominent in the previous unit on working with families. "Whose Problem is Poverty?" by Richard Rothstein explores the need for collaboration between families, educators, and community members to counteract the effects of poverty. This issue is so important that I have included it in more than one unit so that students can revisit the issue and build on discussions as they read the various articles included in this edition.

Another issue with deep implications for the early childhood profession is how we care for and educate children in inclusive environments. Early childhood educators who are knowledgeable and comfortable working with children and families who come from a variety of cultures, speak world languages, or have a disability will be most successful in meeting the learning needs of the children. In Mara Sapon-Shevin's "Learning in an Inclusive Community," the reader will find ten strategies for creating positive, inclusive classrooms to meet the needs of all children. Preservice teachers need many experiences in settings serving diverse learners. This can be challenging for teacher-preparation institutions located in communities lacking diversity. Education students with limited experience traveling to other areas or interacting with children and families who are different from themselves must supplement their own experiences to be successful teachers who are able to meet the needs of all children and families.

Nationwide, college and university programs are adapting to new standards from the National Association for the Education of Young Children that requires programs educating teachers at two and four year institutions to include much more on working with special needs children, especially children with disabilities. As teacher preparation institutions adapt to meet the new standards, there will be teachers out in the field better equipped to meet the needs of special needs children and their families. "Including Children with Disabilities in Early Childhood Education Programs: Individualizing Developmentally Appropriate Practices" provides strategies that will help with a successful transition for schools planning for inclusion of all children.

© Dream Pictures/VStock

In "Creative Play: Building Connections with Children Who Are Learning English," Sara J. Burton and Linda Carol Edwards present ways teachers can help families and children as they work to learn the English language. In China, every child begins to learn a second language in the first grade. In the United States, it is not uncommon for languages other than English to begin in middle or high school. If world languages are taught in the elementary school, it is often an exploratory course only and not of sufficient time or content to really begin to learn the language.

There are more and more examples of teachers adjusting their image of diverse learners. Only when all educators are accepting of the wide diversity that exists in family structures and among individual children will all children feel welcomed and comfortable to learn at school. The collaboration of families, the community, and school personnel will enable children to benefit from the partnership these three groups bring to the educational setting. The articles in this unit represent many diverse families and children and the issues surrounding young children today.

Whose Problem Is Poverty?

It's no cop-out to acknowledge the effects of socioeconomic disparities on student learning. Rather, it's a vital step to closing the achievement gap.

RICHARD ROTHSTEIN

In my work, I've repeatedly stressed this logical claim: If you send two groups of students to equally high-quality schools, the group with greater socioeconomic disadvantage will necessarily have lower *average* achievement than the more fortunate group.[1]

Why is this so? Because low-income children often have no health insurance and therefore no routine preventive medical and dental care, leading to more school absences as a result of illness. Children in low-income families are more prone to asthma, resulting in more sleeplessness, irritability, and lack of exercise. They experience lower birth weight as well as more lead poisoning and iron-deficiency anemia, each of which leads to diminished cognitive ability and more behavior problems. Their families frequently fall behind in rent and move, so children switch schools more often, losing continuity of instruction.

Poor children are, in general, not read to aloud as often or exposed to complex language and large vocabularies. Their parents have low-wage jobs and are more frequently laid off, causing family stress and more arbitrary discipline. The neighborhoods through which these children walk to school and in which they play have more crime and drugs and fewer adult role models with professional careers. Such children are more often in single-parent families and so get less adult attention. They have fewer cross-country trips, visits to museums and zoos, music or dance lessons, and organized sports leagues to develop their ambition, cultural awareness, and self-confidence.

Each of these disadvantages makes only a small contribution to the achievement gap, but cumulatively, they explain a lot.

I've also noted that no matter how serious their problems, all disadvantaged students can expect to have higher achievement in better schools than in worse ones. And even in the same schools, natural human variability ensures a distribution of achievement in every group. Some high-achieving disadvantaged students always outperform typical middle class students, and some low-achieving middle class students fall behind typical disadvantaged students. The achievement gap is a difference in the *average* achievement of students from disadvantaged and middle class families.

I've drawn a policy conclusion from these observations: Closing or substantially narrowing achievement gaps requires combining school improvement with reforms that narrow the vast socioeconomic inequalities in the United States. Without such a combination, demands (like those of No Child Left Behind) that schools fully close achievement gaps not only will remain unfulfilled, but also will cause us to foolishly and unfairly condemn our schools and teachers.

Closing achievement gaps requires combining school improvement with reforms that narrow the vast socioeconomic inequalities in the United States.

Distorting Disadvantage

Most educators understand how socioeconomic disadvantage lowers average achievement. However, some have resisted this logic, throwing up a variety of defenses. Some find in my explanations the implication that disadvantaged children have a genetic disability, that poor and minority children can't learn. They say that a perspective that highlights the socioeconomic causes of low achievement "blames the victim" and legitimizes racism. Some find my analysis dangerous because it "makes excuses" for poor instruction or because demands for social and economic reform "let schools off the hook" for raising student achievement. And others say it's too difficult to address non-school problems like inadequate incomes, health, or housing, so we should only work on school reform. The way some of these critics see it, those of us who call attention to such non-school issues must want to wait until Utopian economic change (or "socialism") becomes a reality before we begin to improve schools.

Some critics cite schools that enroll disadvantaged students but still get high standardized test scores as proof that greater socioeconomic equality is not essential for closing achievement gaps—because good schools have shown they can do it on their own. And some critics are so single-mindedly committed to a schools-only approach that they can't believe anyone could seriously advocate pursuing *both* school and socioeconomic improvement simultaneously.

Seeing Through "No Excuses"

The commonplace "no excuses" ideology implies that educators—were they to realize that their efforts alone were insufficient to raise student achievement—would be too simple-minded then to bring themselves to exert their full effort. The ideology presumes that policymakers with an Olympian perspective can trick teachers into performing at a higher level by making them believe that unrealistically high degrees of success are within reach.

There's a lack of moral, political, and intellectual integrity in this suppression of awareness of how social and economic disadvantage lowers achievement. Our first obligation should be to analyze social problems accurately; only then can we design effective solutions. Presenting a deliberately flawed version of reality, fearing that the truth will lead to excuses, is not only corrupt but also self-defeating.

Mythology cannot, in the long run, inspire better instruction. Teachers see for themselves how poor health or family economic stress impedes students' learning. Teachers may nowadays be intimidated from acknowledging these realities aloud and may, in groupthink obedience, repeat the mantra that "all children can learn." But nobody is fooled. Teachers still know that although all children can learn, some learn less well because of poorer health or less-secure homes. Suppressing such truths leads only to teacher cynicism and disillusion. Talented teachers abandon the profession, willing to shoulder responsibility for their own instructional competence but not for failures beyond their control.

Mythology also prevents educators from properly diagnosing educational failure where it exists. If we expect all disadvantaged students to succeed at levels typical of affluent students, then even the best inner-city teachers seem like failures. If we pretend that achievement gaps are entirely within teachers' control, with claims to the contrary only "excuses," how can we distinguish better from worse classroom practice?

Who's Getting Off the Hook?

Promoters of the myth that schools alone can overcome social and economic causes of low achievement assert that claims to the contrary let schools "off the hook." But their myth itself lets political and corporate officials off a hook. We absolve these leaders from responsibility for narrowing the pervasive inequalities of American society by asserting that good schools alone can overcome these inequalities. Forget about health care gaps, racial segregation, inadequate housing, or income insecurity. If, after successful school reform, all adolescents regardless of background could leave high school fully prepared to earn middle class incomes, there would, indeed, be little reason

for concern about contemporary inequality. Opportunities of children from all races and ethnic groups, and of rich and poor, would equalize in the next generation solely as a result of improved schooling. This absurd conclusion follows from the "no excuses" approach.

Some critics urge that educators should not acknowledge socioeconomic disadvantage because their unique responsibility is to improve classroom practices, which they *can* control. According to such reasoning, we should leave to health, housing, and labor experts the challenge of worrying about inequalities in their respective fields. Yet we are all citizens in this democracy, and educators have a special and unique insight into the damage that deprivation does to children's learning potential.

If educators who face this unfortunate state of affairs daily don't speak up about it, who will? Educators and their professional organizations should insist to every politician who will listen (and to those who will not) that social and economic reforms are needed to create an environment in which the most effective teaching can take place.

And yes, we should also call on housing, health, and anti-poverty advocates to take a broader view that integrates school improvement into their advocacy of greater economic and social equality. Instead, however, critical voices for reform have been silenced, told they should stick to their knitting, fearing an accusation that denouncing inequality is tantamount to "making excuses."

What We Can Do

It's a canard that educators advocating socioeconomic reforms wish to postpone school improvement until we have created an impractical economic Utopia. Another canard is the idea that it's impractical to narrow socioeconomic inequalities, so school reform is the only reasonable lever. Modest social and economic reforms, well within our political reach, could have a palpable effect on student achievement. For example, we could

- Ensure good pediatric and dental care for all students, in school-based clinics.
- Expand existing low-income housing subsidy programs to reduce families' involuntary mobility.
- Provide higher-quality early childhood care so that low-income children are not parked before televisions while their parents are working.
- Increase the earned income tax credit, the minimum wage, and collective bargaining rights so that families of low-wage workers are less stressed.
- Promote mixed-income housing development in suburbs and in gentrifying cities to give more low-income students the benefits of integrated educations in neighborhood schools.
- Fund after-school programs so that inner-city children spend fewer nonschool hours in dangerous environments and, instead, develop their cultural, artistic, organizational, and athletic potential.

None of this is Utopian. All is worth doing in itself, with the added benefit of sending children to school more ready to learn. Educators who are unafraid to advocate such policies will finally call the hand of those politicians and business leaders who claim that universal health care is too expensive but simultaneously demand school reform so they can posture as defenders of minority children.

In some schools, disadvantaged students are effectively tracked by race, denied the most qualified teachers and the best curriculum. Failure is both expected and accepted. Unfortunately, some educators do use socioeconomic disadvantage as an excuse for failing to teach well under adverse conditions. But we exaggerate the frequency of this excuse. Some teachers excuse poor practice, but others work terribly hard to develop disadvantaged students' talents. Where incompetence does exist, we should insist that school administrators root it out.

But consider this: The National Assessment of Educational Progress (NAEP), administered to a national student sample by the federal government, is generally considered the most reliable measure of U.S. students' achievement. Since 1990, the achievement gap between minority and white students has barely changed, feeding accusations that educators simply ignore the needs of minority youth. Yet average math scores of black 4th graders in 2007 were higher than those of white 4th graders in 1990 (National Center for Education Statistics, 2007, p. 10). If white achievement had been stagnant, the gap would have fully closed. There were also big math gains for black 8th graders (National Center for Education Statistics, 2007, p. 26). The gap stagnated only because white students also gained.

In reading, scores have remained flat. Perhaps this is because math achievement is a more direct result of school instruction, whereas reading ability also reflects students' home literacy environment. Nonetheless, the dramatic gains in math do not suggest that most teachers of disadvantaged students are sitting around making excuses for failing to teach. Quite the contrary.

Reticent about Race

It is puzzling that some find racism implied in explanations of why disadvantaged students typically achieve at lower levels. But to understand that children who've been up at night, wheezing from untreated asthma, will be less attentive in school is not to blame those children for their lower scores. It is to explain that we can enhance those students' capacity to learn with policies that reduce the epidemic incidence of asthma in low-income communities—by enforcing prohibitions on the use of high-sulfur heating oil, for example, or requiring urban buses to substitute natural gas for diesel fuel—or provide pediatric care, including treatment for asthma symptoms. Denying the impact of poor health on learning leads to blaming teachers for circumstances completely beyond their control.

Denying the impact of poor health on learning leads to blaming teachers for circumstances completely beyond their control.

The fact that such conditions affect blacks more than whites reflects racism in the United States. Calling attention to such conditions is not racist. But ignoring them, insisting that they have no effect if teaching is competent, may be.

Some critics lump my analyses of social and economic obstacles with others' claims that "black culture" explains low achievement. Like other overly simplistic explanations of academic failure, cultural explanations can easily be exaggerated. There is, indeed, an apparent black-white test score gap, even when allegedly poor black and white students are compared with one another or even when middle class black and white students are compared with one another. But these deceptively large gaps mostly stem from too-broad definitions of "poor" and "middle class." Typically, low-income white students are compared with blacks who are much poorer, and middle class black students are compared with whites who are much more affluent. If we restricted comparisons to socioeconomically similar students, the residual test-score gap would mostly disappear (see Phillips, Grouse, & Ralph, 1998).

But probably not all of it. Responsible reformers are seeking to help low-income black parents improve child-rearing practices. Others attempt to reduce the influence of gang role models on black adolescents or to raise the status of academic success in black communities. Generally, these reformers are black; white experts avoid such discussions, fearing accusations of racism.

This is too bad. If we're afraid to discuss openly the small contribution that cultural factors make to achievement gaps, we suggest, falsely, that we're hiding something much bigger.

Dancing around the Issue

I am often asked to respond to claims that some schools with disadvantaged students have higher achievement, allegedly proving that schools alone *can* close achievement gaps. Certainly, some schools are superior and should be imitated. But no schools serving disadvantaged students have demonstrated consistent and sustained improvement that closes—not just narrows—achievement gaps. Claims to the contrary are often fraudulent, sometimes based on low-income schools whose parents are unusually well educated; whose admissions policies accept only the most talented disadvantaged students; or whose students, although eligible for subsidized lunches, come from stable working-class and not poor communities.

Some claims are based on schools that concentrate on passing standardized basic skills tests to the exclusion of teaching critical thinking, reasoning, the arts, social studies, or science, or of teaching the "whole child," as middle class schools are more wont to do. Increasingly, such claims are based on high proportions of students scoring above state proficiency standards, defined at a low level. Certainly, if we define proficiency down, we can more easily reduce achievement gaps without addressing social or economic inequality. But responsible analysts have always defined closing the achievement gap as achieving similar score distributions and average scale scores among subgroups. Even No Child Left Behind proclaims a goal of proficiency at "challenging" levels for each subgroup. Only achieving such goals will lead to more equal opportunity for all students in the United States.

Beyond Either/Or

Nobody should be forced to choose between advocating for better schools or speaking out for greater social and economic equality. Both are essential. Each depends on the other. Educators cannot be effective if they make excuses for poor student performance. But they will have little chance for success unless they also join with advocates of social and economic reform to improve the conditions from which children come to school.

Note

1. For further discussion of this issue, see my book *Class and Schools: Using Social, Economic, and Educational Reform to Close the Black-White Achievement Gap* (Economic Policy Institute, 2004) and "The Achievement Gap: A Broader Picture" (*Educational Leadership,* November 2004).

References

National Center for Education Statistics. (2007). *The nation's report card: Mathematics 2007.* Washington, DC: Author. Available: http://nces.ed.gov/nationsreportcard/pdf/main2007/2007494.pdf

Phillips, M., Grouse, J., & Ralph, J. (1998). Does the black-white test score gap widen after children enter school? In C. Jencks & M. Phillips (Eds.), *The black-white test score gap* (pp. 229–272). Washington, DC: Brookings Institution Press.

RICHARD ROTHSTEIN is Research Associate at the Economic Policy Institute; riroth@epi.org.

Author's note—For documentation of the specific critiques referenced in this article, readers can contact me at riroth@epi.org.

Richard Rothstein (riroth@epi.org) is a Research Associate at the Economic Policy Institute. He is the Richard Rothstein of *Class and Schools* (Teachers College Press 2004) and *Grading Education. Getting Accountability Right* (Teachers College Press 2008).

Learning in an Inclusive Community

Inclusive classrooms create students who are comfortable with differences, skilled at confronting challenging issues, and aware of their interconnectedness.

MARA SAPON-SHEVIN

Schools are increasingly acknowledging the heterogeneity of their student populations and the need to respond thoughtfully and responsibly to differences in the classroom. It's understandable that educators often feel overwhelmed by growing demands for inclusion, multi-cultural education, multiple intelligences, and differentiated instruction to deal with the growing diversity.

But what if including all students and attending thoughtfully to diversity were part of the solution rather than part of the task overload? What if we put community building and the emotional climate of the classroom back at the center of our organizing values? What if we realized that only inclusive classrooms can fully support the goal of creating thoughtful, engaged citizens for our democratic society?

Redefining the Inclusive Classroom

After years of struggle about the politics and practice of inclusion and multicultural education, it's time we understand that inclusive, diverse classrooms are here to stay. But inclusion is not about disability, and it's not only about schools. Inclusion is about creating a society in which all children and their families feel welcomed and valued.

Inclusion is about creating a society in which all children and their families feel welcomed and valued.

In truly inclusive classrooms, teachers acknowledge the myriad ways in which students differ from one another (class, gender, ethnicity, family background, sexual orientation, language, abilities, size, religion, and so on); value this diversity; and design and implement productive, sensitive responses. Defining inclusion in this way requires us to redefine other classroom practices. For example, *access* can mean, Is there a ramp? But it can also mean, Will letters home to parents be written in a language they can understand?

Differentiated instruction can mean allowing a non-reader to listen to a book on tape. But it can also mean organizing the language arts curriculum using principles of universal design, assuming and planning for diversity from the beginning rather than retrofitting accommodations after the initial design.

Positive behavior management can be a system of providing support to students with diagnosed emotional problems. But it can also mean ongoing community building, classroom meetings, cooperative games, and a culture of appreciation and celebration for all students.

What does it mean to think inclusively, and how can this framework enhance the learning of all children? There are many lessons that inclusive education settings can teach us. Here are just a few.

Comfort with Diversity

In our increasingly diverse world, all people need to be comfortable with diversity. Inclusion benefits all students by helping them understand and appreciate that the world is big, that people are different, and that we can work together to find solutions that work for everyone.

Inclusion teaches us to think about *we* rather than *I*—not to ask, Will there be anything for me to eat? but rather to wonder, How can we make sure there's a snack for everyone? Not, Will I have friends? but rather, How can I be aware of the children here who don't have anyone to play with? When we are surrounded by people who are different from us, we are forced to ask questions that go beyond the individual and address the community. When we have friends who use wheel-chairs, we notice that there are steep stairs and no ramps. When we have friends who wear hearing aids, we listen differently to comments like "What are you, deaf or something?" When we have friends with different skin colors, we become more alert to racist and exclusionary comments. When we have friends from different religious backgrounds, we are more aware that the decorations in the mall are about only one religion.

Inclusion teaches us to think about *we* rather than *I*.

In the absence of diversity, it's hard to learn to be comfortable with difference. The white college-age students I teach are often confounded about how to talk about people of color: "Is the right term *African American* or *black?* What if the person is from Jamaica or Haiti? How do I describe people?" Similarly, many adults are nervous about interacting with people with disabilities, unsure whether they should offer help or refrain, mention the person's disability or not.

The only way to gain fluency, comfort, and ease is through genuine relationships in which we learn how to talk to and about people whom we perceive as different, often learning that many of our initial assumptions or judgments were, in fact, erroneous. The goal is not to make differences invisible ("I don't see color"; "It's such a good inclusive classroom, you can't tell who the kids with disabilities are") but to develop the language and skill to negotiate diversity. Classrooms cannot feel safe to anyone if discussions of difference are avoided, discouraged, or considered inappropriate.

I am always delighted, and a bit stunned, when I see young people easily negotiating conversations about difference that would have been impossible a decade ago and that are still out of reach for many of us. I recently witnessed a discussion of different kinds of families during which children from ages 5 to 8 spoke of adoption, same-sex parents, known and unknown donors, and the many ways they had come to be members of their family.

These students, growing up in an inclusive, diverse community, will not need a book that says, "There are many kinds of families." That understanding is already part of their lived experience.

As a teacher, you can successfully facilitate discussions like this by doing the following:

- Familiarize yourself with the current terminology and debates about what people are called: Do Puerto Ricans call themselves *Latino?* Why is the term *hearing impaired* preferred by some but not all "deaf" people? If there are disagreements about terms—for example, some people prefer the term *Native American* and *some Indian*—find out what that conversation is about. Model appropriate language when discussing differences in the classroom.
- Provide multiple opportunities for talking about diversity. When a news story is about a hurricane in Haiti, pull down the map: Where is that country? What languages do the people there speak? Do we have anyone at our school from Haiti?
- If you hear teasing or inappropriate language being used to discuss differences, don't respond punitively ("I don't ever want to hear that word again!"), but don't let it go. As soon as possible, engage students in a discussion of the power of their language and their assumptions. Teach students the words *stereotype, prejudice,* and *discrimination* and encourage them to identify examples when they see them: "On the commercial on TV last night, I noticed that all the people they identified as 'beautiful' were white."

Inclusion is not a favor we do for students with disabilities, any more than a commitment to multicultural education benefits only students of color. Inclusion is a gift we give ourselves: the gift of understanding, the gift of knowing that we are all members of the human race and that joy comes in building genuine relationships with a wide range of other people.

Honesty about Hard Topics

Inclusion not only makes students better educated about individual differences, but also provides a place to learn about challenging topics. In inclusive classrooms, teachers and students learn to talk about the uncomfortable and the painful.

Often, as adults, we don't know what to do when we are confronted by people and situations that frighten, surprise, or confound us. Children, through their eagerness to engage with the world and seek answers to their questions, can learn important repertoires of communication and interaction in inclusive settings: How can I find out why Michelle wears that scarf on her head without hurting her feelings? How can I play with Jasper if he doesn't talk? Learning how to ask questions respectfully and how to listen well to the answers are skills that will provide a smoother entry into the complexities of adulthood.

In one school, a young boy who required tube feeding provided the opportunity for all the students to learn not only about the digestive system but also about ways to help people while preserving their dignity and autonomy. In another school, a child whose religion kept him from celebrating birthdays and holidays gave other students the opportunity to not only learn about different religions but also brainstorm ways of keeping Jonah a valued and supported member of the classroom. And when a young Muslim child was harassed on the way home from school in the months after the attack on the World Trade Center, the whole class was able to engage in an important discussion of racism and being allies to those experiencing prejudice and oppression.

A student in one classroom was dying of cancer. The teachers, rather than excluding the student and avoiding the subsequent questions, helped all the other students stay informed and involved in his life (and eventually, in his death). With close communication with parents, the teachers talked to students about what was happening to Trevor and how they could support him: "Of course we would miss you if you died." "Yes, it's very, very sad." "No, it's not fair for a 6-year-old to die; it doesn't happen very often." On days when Trevor was in school and feeling weak, the students took turns reading to him. On days when he was not able to come to school, they wrote him notes and made cards. When he died, many of them went to the funeral. Tears were welcomed and tissues were widely used; the teachers were able to show their sadness as well. Teachers had to be thoughtful about discussions of religious beliefs in order to be inclusive: "Yes, some people believe in heaven, and they think that's where Trevor is going."

Although no parents would want their children to have to deal with the death of a classmate, the sensitivity and tenderness of the experience helped bond the class and enabled students to connect to both the fragility and the sacredness of life. When they experience death again later in their lives, they will have some understanding of what it means to offer and receive support and will be able to seek the information and caring they need for their own journeys.

Ten Strategies for Creating a Positive, Inclusive Classroom

1. Make time for community building throughout the year. Time spent building community is never wasted.
2. Proactively teach positive social skills: how to make friends, how to give compliments, what to do if someone teases you or hurts your feelings. Don't wait for negative things to happen.
3. Be explicit in explaining to your students why treating one another well and building a community is important. Use key terms: *community, inclusion, friends, support, caring, kindness.* Don't let those words become empty slogans; give lots of examples of positive behaviors.
4. Adopt a zero-indifference policy. Don't ignore bullying in the hope that it will go away. Don't punish the participants, but be clear about what is acceptable. Say, "I don't want that word used in my classroom. It hurts people's feelings and it's not kind."
5. Share your own learning around issues of diversity and inclusion. When students see that you are also learning (and struggling), they can share their own journeys more easily. Tell them, "You know, when I was growing up, there were some words I heard and used that I don't use anymore, and here's why." "You know, sometimes I'm still a little uncomfortable when I see people with significant physical differences, but here's what I've been learning."
6. Think about what messages you're communicating about community and differences in everything you do, including the books you read to your students, the songs you sing, what you put on the walls, and how you talk about different families and world events.
7. Seize teachable moments for social justice. When students say, "That's so gay," talk about the power of words to hurt people and where such oppressive language can lead. When a student makes fun of another student, talk about different cultures, norms, and experiences.
8. Provide lots of opportunities for students to work together, and teach them how to help one another. End activities with appreciation circles: "What's something you did well today?" "How did Carlos help you today?"
9. Don't set students up to compete with one another. Create an atmosphere in which each student knows that he or she is valued for something.
10. Keep in mind that your students will remember only some of what you taught them but everything about how they felt in your classroom.

In inclusive classrooms, I have seen students learn to support a classmate with cerebral palsy, become allies in the face of homophobic bullying, and help a peer struggling with academic work. All of these were possible because the teachers were willing and able to talk to the students honestly about what was going on, creating a caring, supportive community for all students rather than marginalizing those who were experiencing difficulty.

Mutual Support

Sadly, teasing and exclusion are a typical part of many students' school experience. Bullying is so common that it can become virtually invisible. But inclusive classrooms foster a climate in which individual students know they will not be abandoned when they experience injustice. Inclusion means that we pay careful attention to issues of social justice and inequity, whether they appear at the individual, classroom, or school level or extend into the larger community.

I have used Peggy Moss's wonderful children's book *Say Something* (Tilbury House, 2004) to engage students and teachers in discussions about what we do when we see someone being picked on. In the book, a young girl goes from witnessing and lamenting the mistreatment of her classmates to taking action to change the patterns she observes.

This book and similar materials encourage students to talk about the concept of courage, about opportunities to be brave in both small and large ways, and about how they can make a difference.

Inclusive classrooms give us many opportunities to be our best selves, reaching across our personal borders to ask, Do you want to play? or Can I help you with that? Our lessons about how we treat one another extend beyond the specificity of rules (Don't tease children with disabilities) to broader, more inclusive discussions: How would you like to be treated? What do you think others feel when they're left out? How could we change this activity so more kids could play? How do you want others to deal with your challenges and triumphs, and what would that look like in our classroom?

Teachers in inclusive classrooms consider helping essential. The classroom becomes a more positive place for everyone when multiple forms of peer support—such as peer mentoring and collaborative learning—are ongoing, consistent, and valued. Rather than saying, "I want to know what you can do, not what your neighbor can do," inclusive teachers say, "Molly, why don't you ask Luis to show you how to do that," or "Make sure everyone at your table understands how to color the map code."

Inclusive settings provide multiple opportunities to explore what it means to help one another. By challenging the notion that there are two kinds of people in the world—those who need help and those who give help—we teach all students to see themselves as both givers and receivers. We recognize and honor multiple forms of intelligence and many gifts.

Courage to Change the World

When students develop fluency in addressing differences, are exposed to challenging issues, and view themselves as interconnected, teachers can more easily engage them in discussions about how to improve things.

Having a personal connection profoundly shifts one's perception about who has the problem and who should do something about it. When students have a classmate who comes from Mexico and is undocumented, discussions of immigration rights, border patrols, and fair employment practices become much more real. When students have learned to communicate with a classmate with autism, they understand at a deep level that being unable to talk is not the same as having nothing to say. When a classmate comes from a family with two mothers, reports of gay bashing or debates about marriage rights become more tangible.

A powerful way to combat political apathy is by helping young people make connections between their lives and those of others and giving them opportunities to make a difference in whatever ways they can. Although it's certainly possible to teach a social-justice curriculum in a fairly homogeneous school, inclusive classrooms give us the opportunity to put social-justice principles into action. In inclusive classrooms, students can *live* a social-justice curriculum rather than just study it.

A powerful way to combat political apathy is by helping young people make connections between their lives and those of others.

Inclusive classrooms that pay careful attention to issues of fairness and justice bring to the surface questions that have the potential to shift students' consciousness now and in the future: Who gets into the gifted program, and how are they chosen? How can we find a part in the school play for a classmate who doesn't talk? Why do people make fun of Brian because he likes art and doesn't like sports? How can we make sure everyone gets to go on the field trip that costs $20?

Inclusive classrooms put a premium on how people treat one another. Learning to live together in a democratic society is one of the most important goals and outcomes of inclusive classrooms. How could we want anything less for our children?

MARA SAPON-SHEVIN is Professor of Inclusive Education, Syracuse University, New York; msaponsh@syr.edu. She is the author of *Widening the Circle: The Power of Inclusive Classrooms* (Beacon Press, 2007).

From *Educational Leadership,* September 2008, pp. 49–53. Copyright © 2008 by Mara Sapon-Shevin. Reprinted by permission of the author.

Including Children with Disabilities in Early Childhood Education Programs
Individualizing Developmentally Appropriate Practices

JOHN FILLER AND YAOYING XU

Early childhood educators are facing the challenge of creating quality educational programs for young children from an increasingly diverse mix of racial and cultural backgrounds. Programs that, in the past, have largely ignored the diversity of their participants must now re-examine approaches that emphasize the universality of linear lists of developmental milestones; they must pursue practices that reflect a pluralistic approach to both content and methods of instruction. Too many educators assume that children reach developmental milestones at similar points, leading to rather simplistic attempts to justify singular content and approach. Yet a multicultural, multi-ethnic, and multi-ability student population demands a unique and nontraditional approach, characterized by individualization and sensitivity to unique expressions of group identity.

The realities of diversity do not mitigate the fact that all children do seem to exhibit a finite set of accomplishments (milestones) that build, one upon the other, and proceed in an age-related fashion. We recognize the relevance of a developmental approach that is based upon the work of such theorists as Rousseau, Locke, Pestalozzi, Froebel, Piaget, and Vygotsky, exemplified by Itard's techniques, the Montessori approach, and the Head Start movement in the 1960s, as well as numerous other, more recent, examples of successful early childhood education programs. However, some children acquire skills at an earlier age than their age-mates, while others acquire those same skills much later than their peers or not at all. For example, not all children begin walking up stairs by placing both feet on each step before they move to the next step. Some alternate, placing only one foot on each step—a skill that Brigance (2004) claims one should expect to see exhibited 6 to 12 months after the two-feet per step approach. Some children seem to skip steps in a developmental sequence while others do not. Such variations are viewed as part of the "normal" range of individual differences, defined as falling less than one to two standard deviations above or below the theoretical mean for a given developmental area (such as cognitive, gross and fine motor, or social or language skills). Most of our attempts to adapt curriculum and strategies to diversity have been based upon either sociocultural differences or ability differences that fall within the range of what might be termed "normal variation."

The realities of a multicultural, multi-ethnic, and multi-ability student population demand a unique and nontraditional approach, characterized by individualization and sensitivity to unique expressions of group identity.

Individually and Developmentally Appropriate Practices

Developmentally appropriate practice (DAP) is considered the foundation of early childhood education and serves as a guideline for curriculum development. The National Association of Education for Young Children (NAEYC) defined DAP in three dimensions (Bredekamp & Copple, 1997, p. 9):

- What is known about child development and learning— knowledge of age-related human characteristics that permits general predictions within an age range about what activities, materials, interactions, or experiences will be safe, healthy, interesting, achievable, and also challenging to children
- What is known about the strength, interests, and needs of each individual child in the group to be able to adapt for and be responsive to inevitable individual variations
- Knowledge of the social and cultural contexts in which children live to ensure that learning experiences are meaningful, relevant, and respectful for the participating children and their families.

On the one hand, this NAEYC statement views children as members of an overall group who follow similar predictable developmental patterns. Yet it also emphasizes the importance of valuing young children as individuals, with different personalities or temperaments and learning styles. Furthermore, children are considered part of a cultural group, members of the community in which children and their families live and by which they are influenced in every aspect of living. Additionally, the NAEYC statement encourages early childhood professionals to move from "either-or thinking" to "both-and thinking" (Gonzalez-Mena, 2000). As is often the case, what is developmentally appropriate is not always individually or culturally appropriate. Instead of having to make a falsely dichotomous choice, educators often need to combine all dimensions and know the child as a whole person with individual needs and cultural differences.

The nature of DAP encourages the placement of children, with and without disabilities, in the same setting. In fact, most professional organizations support the concept of inclusive programs for all children, regardless of the nature or severity of the disability. For example, the Division for Early Childhood of the Council for Exceptional Children issued its "Position Statement on Inclusion," which was endorsed that same year by NAEYC: "DEC supports and advocates that young children and their families have full and successful access to health, social, educational, and other support services that promote full participation in family and community life" (Sandall, McLean, & Smith, 2000, p. 150). The statement also proposed that young children participating in group settings (such as preschool, play groups, child care, or kindergarten) be guided by developmentally and individually appropriate curriculum. The Association for Childhood Education International published a brochure that discusses the benefits of inclusion for the children with disabilities, the children without disabilities, and the parents, school, and community (Kostell, 1997). The Association for Persons With Severe Handicaps (TASH) endorses the inclusion of children with severe disabilities in regular education settings and argues that inclusion implies more than just physical presence; it includes access to the curriculum that is taught in the regular education classroom (TASH, 2000).

Clearly, leading professional organizations endorse the concept of inclusive programming for children with disabilities; there also exists a strong legal basis for inclusion. The assumption of the universal relevance of the general education curriculum is readily apparent in the 2004 re-authorization of the Individuals With Disabilities Education Act (P.L. 108-446). This law requires that we reference the content of our curriculum for students with disabilities to that of their typically developing peers. For example, each student's individualized educational program (IEP), a written document that describes the needs of the child, must contain a statement of the child's present levels of educational performance, including how the child's disability affects his or her involvement and participation in appropriate activities. Furthermore, the IEP must include a statement of *measurable annual goals,* related to "meeting the child's needs that result from the child's disability to enable the child to be involved in and progress in the general curriculum" (Sec. 614; 20 USC 1414), and there must be a justification for non-participation in the regular class. Part C of P.L. 108-446 requires that

children from birth to 3 years of age receive early intervention services in environments that are *natural,* or normal for children the same age who have no disabilities (IDEA Rules and Regulations, 1998). This stipulation extends the requirements of the Americans With Disabilities Act (Public Law 101-336) by requiring each state to not only ensure reasonable access by infants with disabilities to child care/educare programs, but also deliver early intervention services in such settings.

Planning for Inclusion: Adapting Developmentally Appropriate Practices

While examples of curricula for young children can be found that do provide substantive suggestions for adapting to meet the needs of children with sensory, cognitive, motor, emotional, and/or learning disabilities (e.g., Bricker & Waddell, 2002a, 2002b; Hauser-Cram, Bronson, & Upshur, 1993), most do little by way of providing meaningful, practical suggestions to the early childhood teacher. This means that the task of planning to include these children will fall upon the shoulders of those whose formal training and experience may not have prepared them for such diversity (Gelfer, Filler, & Perkins, 1999; Heller, 1992). To be successful at what can, at first, appear to be a very daunting task, teachers will have to plan for modifications in both content and strategy. Numerous authors have recognized the importance of instructional flexibility and the need for an approach that includes the individual modifications that are often necessary in order to meet the needs of diverse groups of learners (Allen & Cowdery, 2004; Friend & Bursuck, 2002; Giangreco, Broer, & Edelman, 2002; Pretti-Frontczak & Bricker, 2004). Inclusion is not accomplished by simply placing a child with disabilities in a setting with his typically developing peers. It is realized only when we have succeeded in designing a set of activities that ensure the full participation of all children, including the child with disabilities. Participation and not mere geographical proximity is the necessary pre-condition for *achievement,* and so meaningful participation requires systematic planning.

Table 1 contains a description of the steps involved in planning for the inclusion of a child with disabilities in a typical early childhood program. The planning process begins with the selection of a team of knowledgeable individuals who will be responsible for developing the plan. Team planning is essential, because the success of efforts to include students with disabilities, especially those with severe disabilities, is not the sole responsibility of any single individual. This planning team should include the parents and/or any other family members who share in daily caregiving activities; the general education early childhood teacher and the early interventionist or early childhood special education teacher; and the program administrator and any related service personnel, such as speech or occupational therapists who may provide services to the child and family.

The second step in the planning process is to construct a simple schedule of the daily activities for the setting in which the target child with disabilities will be included from start to finish. When listing the activities, it is important to note the average length of time devoted to each activity and to include all activities in which the child will likely be included throughout the week, since activities may vary from day to day.

Step 3 involves a careful specification of the instructional goals for the target child, which are taken directly from the IEP or the Individualized Family Service Plan (IFSP). Since these documents contain goals and/or objectives that may cover six months to a year, only those that are currently being addressed are listed. Here, it is important to indicate the family's priorities for instruction. The family and the educators may feel differently about the relative importance of goals and objectives. For example, the family may not believe that the child learning a particular social behavior is as important as the child acquiring gross motor skills, while the teacher might think that more emphasis should be placed upon sharing and cooperative play than upon learning to throw and run. Such differences present opportunities to jointly discuss how both priorities can be addressed simultaneously in one or more activities. An important additional consideration is whether or not the child has a behavior support plan, the presence of which indicates the need to carefully and systematically pay attention to a recurring, potentially serious, form of inappropriate behavior.

Step 4 is, perhaps, the most important aspect of the planning process; it is the determination of exactly how many opportunities exist in the typical schedule to address the individual needs of the child with a disability and what program supports are needed to make an opportunity a successful reality. Each skill targeted in the IEP/IFSP must be referenced to the activities of the typical early childhood program. The team must ask (and answer) the question, "Does this activity provide an opportunity to address any of the skills in the IEP or IFSP?" and "If so, which ones?" In answering the questions, it becomes important to examine what the focus of the activity is for typically developing children. If it seems reasonable to the team that the activity may provide a context in which the needs of the child with disabilities can be addressed, *without completely altering the meaningfulness of the activity for typically developing children,* then the team can examine what adaptations may be needed. The effort to ensure that activities provide opportunities to address the needs of all children is central to what has been termed *activity-based instruction* (Pretti-Frontczak & Bricker, 2004).

As indicated in Table 1, adaptations may consist of two types. One involves individualizing the content of the activity by changing its focus or fundamental purpose for the target child. A modified content, or even a different content entirely, may be taught to the child with disabilities while the other children receive content appropriate for their needs. A second kind of adaptation involves changing the physical layout, modifying materials for the child, or even changing the way that staff conduct the activity. For example, while children with sensory disabilities, like blindness or low vision, may still function at age level and require no modification of content, they will require large print or Braille reading material. A child with cerebral palsy and an associated motor disability may require special equipment, such as a cut-out table and chairs with supports, wedges to facilitate upper body movement while in a prone play position, or a prone board to provide support in an upright

position (Campbell, 2006). In some situations, it may even be necessary to add staff during the activity to ensure adequate instructional support without sacrificing instructional time for the other children. This might be the case with a child who presents a significant challenging behavior that requires an involved support plan, the focus of which is to teach a positive incompatible replacement behavior (see Figure 2).

Step 5 involves determining what related services are required and how often and how long each related service session should be. Children with significant disabilities often require such services as occupational therapy and speech therapy, and may need to receive one-on-one instruction from an early childhood special educator. While the preference is to provide these services in the natural setting of the early childhood classroom, it may be necessary to remove the child to a different setting for the service. If that is the case, then the team must decide what classroom activity (or activities) is (are) least important and thus could be missed by the child. This is usually accomplished by viewing each activity in terms of the opportunities it provides for addressing skills from the IEP or IFSP, and then selecting times for the child to leave the classroom when activities are occurring that provide the fewest number of individually relevant instructional opportunities. Sometimes, however, the schedule of those professionals who are delivering the service may need to be taken into account when making the choice.

The final step, Step 6, is also an extremely important aspect of team planning. Parents and other family members have their own perspective on what, among all of the skills that may be included in the IEP or IFSP, is most important. It is critical that staff respect those priorities by making sure that, first, they are aware of parental priorities and, second, adequate opportunities exist to address high-priority skills during daily program activities. In addition, families may have concerns regarding skills or behaviors that are best addressed outside of the formal confines of the program setting. It is extremely important that the skills learned at the center also are taught and practiced in natural settings—those settings in which the skill or behavior is most likely to be demanded or exhibited. Natural settings are the environments where children with disabilities would participate or function if they did not have a disability. These environments may include the child's home, the neighborhood playground, community activity or child care centers, restaurants, Head Start programs, or other settings designed for children without disabilities (Cook, Klein, Tessier, & Daley, 2004). While it is unlikely that program staff will be able to provide continuous, direct instructional support at home or in the community, it still would be possible to make visits and provide occasional community-based instruction. Making suggestions to the family as to how to generalize procedures employed at the center is another important aspect of the child's program. These procedures need to be planned for as carefully as you would the daily activities.

The Activity Matrix

A good way to summarize and represent the results of this six-step planning process is to construct what has been referred to as an "Activity Matrix" (Fox & Williams, 1991). Figures 1 and 2

Table 1 Steps in Planning for Inclusion

STEP ONE: Form the inclusion planning team.	1.1 Invite the target child's parents and/or other significant caregivers to participate in planning for inclusion.
	1.2 Invite the EC program administrator to participate, along with the general early childhood education (EC) teacher and the special education (ECSE) teacher or early interventionist (EI).
	1.3 Determine if there are others who should be invited to participate on the planning team (e.g., speech or occupational or physical therapists who may be delivering related services).
STEP TWO: List each daily activity of the typical EC program	2.1 One member of the team (typically, the EC teacher) lists each activity from arrival to departure.
	2.2 If the daily activities vary from day to day, then care must be taken to include all activities.
	2.3 Note the typical length of time devoted to each daily activity.
STEP THREE: Determine the areas of instructional emphasis for the target child.	3.1 From the child's IEP or IFSP, list each current instructional target (these may be taken directly from the IEP objectives or child outcome statements that have not yet been met).
	3.2 Determine which of these objectives is a priority for the family.
	3.3 Note whether the child exhibits any particular behavior problems for which a support plan may have been developed.
	3.4 Inquire as to whether the family has any additional instructional concerns that may not have been noted in the IEP or IFSP. List these as well.
STEP FOUR: Determine what opportunities to address the needs of the target child may be provided by the daily EC program activities.	4.1 The team determines which of the activities in the typical program setting provide a reasonable opportunity to address the instructional needs of the target child.
	4.2 The team discusses and determines if an adaptation is required to address the instructional target.
	4.3 If an adaptation to the activity, as it is typically conducted, is needed to make a determination as to the nature of the adaptation; modification of content (changes in focus, rules, and/or materials); and/or modification in the way the activity is conducted (changes in physical setting, materials, and/or staffing).
STEP FIVE: Determine what modifications are necessary to meet the target child's possible need for related services.	5.1 From the IEP or IFSP, note the target child's need for a related service, the weekly schedule for each service, and the beginning date and length of time for each service visit.
	5.2 Discuss and determine whether the service can reasonably be delivered in the typical program setting by modifying an activity.
	5.3 If the service cannot reasonably be delivered in the natural setting of the classroom, then determine which activities the child will miss in order to receive the service in a different room or program setting.
STEP SIX: Determine what needs the family may see for addressing skills/ behavior at home or in the community.	6.1 Note any concerns of the family that are more appropriately addressed at home or in the community.
	6.2 Indicate which skills from the IEP/IFSP also can be addressed in these "other," more natural environments.

contain an example format for an activity matrix. Figure 1 is an Activity Matrix for Chu Chu, a Chinese American boy with moderate mental retardation. Figure 2 was developed for Nikki, an African American girl with autism spectrum disorder and moderate cognitive delay. Each of the daily activities of the typical early childhood program is written in one of the columns to the right of the box labeled "Activities" across the top of the form (planning Step 2). Directly below is a space for the "Length of Time," where the duration, in minutes, of each activity is entered. Since some children, particularly those with disabilities, may need to be involved in an alternative activity (e.g., speech therapy), space is provided to list those activities that could be substituted at an appropriate time for one of the regularly scheduled activities (planning Step 5). We have found it helpful to number each of these alternative activities directly above the activity

name and then refer to the activity by that number. Writing the number above one of the scheduled activities indicates that the alternative activity will occur instead of the scheduled activity. Down the left side of the matrix, room is provided for the individual instructional goals or objectives from the child's IEP or IFS (planning Step 3).

As suggested in Table 1, Step 4, the process continues by reading the first objective for the child and then looking at the first activity (arrival). You then ask yourself, "Does 'arrival' present an opportunity to address this objective?" Let's say, for the purpose of discussion, that the first objective for Chu Chu is from the "social skills/self-help" domain and it is "Chu Chu will greet his friends." Does "arrival" (i.e., coming into the room, hanging up his coat, putting his backpack away, and going to the table) present any opportunities for Chu Chu to

Child: Chu Chu Age: 4.2 years Setting: Rainbows Date: _____

Alternative Activities Listed by Number	1 Arrival	Free Choice Time	Outdoor Play	2 Large Group Time	Learning Centers	Closing Group Time	Outdoor Play	Departure	1 Speech Therapy	2 Special Ed. Resource (1:1)	Home/Family Eats at Restaurant
Length of Time for Activity	15 mins	30 mins	30 mins	15 mins	30 mins	15 mins	30 mins	15 mins	30 mins	30 mins	
Adaptation: Modified Content	X		X			X					
Adaptation: Modified arrangement / staffing	X		X			X	X				

☺ TARGET CHILD SKILL AREAS FROM CURRENT IEP or IFSP (√ indicates skill is a family priority)

	Arrival	Free Choice Time	Outdoor Play	Large Group Time	Learning Centers	Closing Group Time	Outdoor Play	Departure	Speech Therapy	Special Ed. Resource	Home/Family
Social Skill: Greets friends	√		√	√		√					√
Language: Expressive vocab.	X	X	X	X	X	X	X	X			X
Self Help: Washes hands					X						X
Fine Motor: Pincer grasp	X	X	X	X	X	X	X	X			X
Gross Motor: Kicks ball			X			X					
Self Help: Signals need for BR	√	√	√	√	√	√	√	√			√
BEHAVIOR SUPPORT PLAN?											

Figure 1 Early Childhood Activity Matrix.

Child: Nikki Age: 3.5 years Setting: Ladybugs Date: _____

Alternative Activities Listed by Number	1 Arrival	Opening Group	Outdoor Play	2 Snack	Learning Centers	Closing Group Time	Outdoor Play	Departure	1 Speech Therapy	2 Special Ed. Resource (1:1)	Home/Family Quietly occupies self during church service
Length of Time for Activity	15 mins	30 mins	30 mins	30 mins	30 mins	15 mins	30 mins	15 mins	30 mins	30 mins	
Adaptation: Modified Content	X		X			X					
Adaptation: Modified arrangement / staffing		X	X	X	X	X	X				X

☺ TARGET CHILD SKILL AREAS FROM CURRENT IEP or IFSP (√ indicates skill is a family priority)

	Arrival	Opening Group	Outdoor Play	Snack	Learning Centers	Closing Group Time	Outdoor Play	Departure	Speech Therapy	Special Ed. Resource	Home/Family
Social Skill: Plays and/or works cooperatively			√	√	√	√					√
Language: Expressive vocab.	X	X	X	X	X	X	X	X			X
Language: Receptive vocab.					X						X
Fine Motor: Pincer grasp	X	X	X	X	X	X	X	X			X
Self Help: Uses utensils					X						
Self Help: Signals need for BR	X	X	X	X	X	X	X	X			√
BEHAVIOR SUPPORT PLAN?	yes	yes	yes	yes	yes	yes	yes	yes			yes

Figure 2 Early Childhood Activity Matrix.

acknowledge the presence of the other children by saying "hello"? Of course, that is a natural sub-activity involved in "arrival," so an "X" is placed in the box out from it and under "arrival" to indicate that a naturally occurring opportunity exists to practice the skills involved in "greeting friends" during this activity. What of the next activity? Does free choice time provide an opportunity to work on "greeting friends"? Probably not, so leave that box blank and look across the page, still on the row for the first objective, to the next activity, which is "outdoor play." Does it present any natural opportunities to practice greeting friends? Do the same thing for the next objective, and the next, until you have examined each activity in terms of its potential for each of Chu Chu's current IEP objectives. Those with high potential will have more Xs in the boxes under them; those with less potential will have fewer Xs. Skills that are of high priority to parents are indicated by a ✓ instead of an X. The last row in the matrix is left blank so that additions can be made if, upon reflection, the team feels a certain skill or behavior not included in the IEP or IFSP would benefit from focused attention.

It is important to remember that while an activity presents an opportunity to address the needs of a student with disabilities, it does not necessarily require *adaptations*. As indicated in Table 1, Step 4.3, an *adaptation* refers to the need to either change the content or substantive purpose of an activity, or change the way in which the activity is conducted by changing the setting arrangements, staffing patterns and responsibilities, or materials. Again, to use Chu Chu as the example, we have suggested in Figure 1 that arrival provides an opportunity to address his need to learn to greet his friends, a social skill goal taken from his IEP. Since this is not typically a skill that is the focus of instruction during arrival time, an adaptation of the first type (change in focus or content) is indicated by placement of an "X" to indicate Adaptation: Modified content/focus. But in order to accomplish this goal, the teacher will have to change how she behaves during the arrival of all of her students by focusing her attention specifically upon Chu Chu, prompting him to say "hello" and acknowledge others' greetings. Since this focused structure is not a typical part of the teacher's behavior during arrival, it would constitute an *adaptation* of the second type (Adaptation: Modified arrangement/staffing) and may require additional staff to help out with the other children while the teacher concentrates her attention on Chu Chu. Or, perhaps a "special friend" can be designated to help.

As is evident from Figure 1, arrival also provides an opportunity to address three other goals from Chu Chu's IEP: expressive vocabulary, pincer grasp, and signaling to use the bathroom should he need to do so. Because teaching these skills is not a part of the arrival activity for the other children, it needs further adaptation. Later, while outside, Chu Chu can practice greeting friends and using his expressive language and fine motor pincer grasp, but the signs indicating the need for an adaptation suggest that Chu Chu's caregivers will need to more carefully structure his activities so that he has sufficient opportunities to practice these skills each time he goes outside.

As required by his IEP, Chu Chu also will receive two types of related services, outside of the classroom (planning Step 5). Looking at Figure 1, it is evident that his team believed that the best time for him to miss a class activity to receive these services was during free choice time and part of the time devoted to learning centers. Additionally, Chu Chu's Activity Matrix indicates two family priority skills (planning Step 3.2): the social skill of greeting friends and the self-help skill of signaling his need to use the bathroom. The family also had indicated that they very much want Chu Chu to exhibit age-appropriate skills at restaurants, since they enjoy eating out as a family (planning Step 6). Staff plan to help identify non-obtrusive strategies that the family may use to reinforce Chu Chu's use of appropriate social and communication skills in this community environment. Those that involve signaling his need to use the bathroom are of particular concern.

Figure 2 is similar to Figure 1. Activities of the early childhood (EC) program are listed in which Nikki, a 3-year-old with autism and moderate cognitive delay, is included. Skills that are the focus of instruction are taken directly from her IEP and are recorded down the left side of the matrix; an "X" is entered for each activity for each skill that may be addressed during that activity, and the need for adaptations is noted where necessary. As is the case with Chu Chu, Nikki's family's priorities are included. Attending church services is one of their top priorities. Therefore, their desire to have Nikki develop non-disruptive ways of occupying herself during the main service (so that they can all sit together as a family) is recorded in the matrix.

One major difference between Chu Chu's matrix and Nikki's is the indicated need for a behavior support plan for Nikki. She will often scream and hit when blocked from engaging in a behavior or if she is otherwise frustrated in an attempt to gain attention or access to a desired object. The support plan is the primary responsibility of those who are also responsible for the IEP, typically the ECSE teacher, behavior specialists with the public school district, and the family. However, since it will have to be implemented throughout the day in the regular early childhood setting, as well as in the community, it becomes essential that the EC program staff are involved in a determination of the adaptations that may be necessary to ensure success in the inclusive setting. Children with severe behavior problems often provide the greatest challenge to successful inclusion. We have found, however, that careful team planning with an eye toward modifications and supports, along with a willingness to try alternatives, will greatly reduce potential disruptions and go a long way toward creating an atmosphere of acceptance.

Conclusion

Developmentally appropriate practices in early childhood education programs must be implemented with a clear understanding of and appreciation for the extremes of individual variation that are likely to be encountered. Cultural, ethnic, and racial diversities are important and valued characteristics of the population of young children currently served by early childhood education programs. We now recognize the importance of curricula that celebrate different values and associated expressions of those values in both the content and strategy of instruction. As Noonan and McCormick (1993) noted, it is important to reference the early childhood curriculum to the child's social environment. However, recent social and legal imperatives have given additional meaning to "diversity." Children with a range of disabilities, including those with severe cognitive, motor, emotional, and behavioral disabilities, are a valuable aspect of the differences that we celebrate in our early childhood education programs. Their presence should cause us to pause and take a closer look at what we believe about how all children grow and learn and how we teach them.

If children are to benefit from the participation that inclusion brings, then educators, administrators, related service professionals, and parents must be ever-mindful that participation and achievement require that we emphasize the uniqueness of each child.

References

Allen, K. E., & Cowdery, G. E. (2004). *The exceptional child: Inclusion in early childhood education.* (5th ed.). Albany, NY: Thomson/Delmar Publishers.

Association for Persons with Severe Handicaps, The. (2000). *TASH Resolution on Quality Inclusive Education.* Baltimore: Author.

Bredekamp, S., & Copple, C. (Eds.). (1997). *Developmentally appropriate practice in early childhood programs* (Rev. ed.). Washington DC: National Association for the Education of Young Children.

Bricker, D., & Waddell, M. (2002a). *Assessment, evaluation and programming system (2nd ed.): Curriculum for birth to three years: Volume 3.* Baltimore: Paul H. Brookes.

Bricker, D., & Waddell, M. (2002b). *Assessment, evaluation and programming system (2nd ed.): Curriculum for three to six years: Volume 4.* Baltimore: Paul H. Brookes.

Brigance, A.H. (2004). *Brigance Diagnostic Inventory of Early Development* (2nd ed.). North Billerica, MA: Curriculum Associates.

Campbell, P. H. (2006). Addressing motor disabilities. In M. E. Snell & F. Brown (Eds.), *Instruction of students with severe disabilities* (6th ed., pp. 291–327). Upper Saddle River, NJ: Merrill.

Cook, R. E, Klein, M. D, Tessier, A., & Daley, S. (2004). *Adapting early childhood curricula for children in inclusive settings* (6th ed.). Upper Saddle River, NJ: Pearson Prentice Hall.

Fox, T. J., & Williams, W. (1991). *Implementing best practices for all students in their local school.* Burlington, VT: Center for Developmental Disabilities, The University of Vermont.

Friend, M., & Bursuck, W. D. (2002). *Including students with special needs: A practical guide for classroom teachers* (3rd ed.). Boston: Allyn and Bacon.

Gelfer, J., Filler, J., & Perkins, P. (1999). The development of a bachelor's degree in early childhood education: Preparation for teaching inclusive education. *Early Child Development and Care, 154,* 41–48.

Giangreco, M. F., Broer, S. M., & Edelman, W. (2002). "That was then, this is now!" Paraprofessional support for students with disabilities in general education classrooms. *Exceptionality, 10*(1), 47–64.

Gonzalez-Mena, J. (2000). *Foundations: Early childhood education in a diverse society.* Mountain View, CA: Mayfield.

Hauser-Cram, P., Bronson, M. B., & Upshur, C. C. (1993). The effects of the classroom environment on the social and mastery behavior of preshcool children with disabilities. *Early Childhood Research Quarterly, 8,* 479–497.

Heller, H.W. (1992). A rationale for departmentalization of special education. In W. Stainback & S. Stainback (Eds.), *Controversial issues confronting special education* (pp. 271–281). Needham Heights, MA: Allyn and Bacon.

Individuals with Disabilities Education Act (IDEA), §303.18 of Rules and Regulations (1998).

Individuals with Disabilities Education Improvement Act, 20 U.S.C. 1414, §614 (2004).

Kostell, P. H. (1997). *Inclusion.* (*ACEI Speaks* brochure.) Olney, MD: Association for Childhood Education International.

Noonan, M. J., & McCormick, L. (1993). *Early intervention in natural environments: Methods and procedures.* Belmont, CA: Brookes/Cole Publishing.

Pretti-Frontczak, K., & Bricker, D. (2004). *An activity-based approach to early intervention* (3rd ed.). Baltimore: Paul H. Brookes.

Sandall, S., McLean, M. E., & Smith, B.J. (2000). *DEC recommended practices in early intervention/early childhood special education.* Longmont, CO: Sopris West.

JOHN FILLER is Professor, Department of Education, University of Nevada, Las Vegas. **YAOYING XU** is Assistant Professor, Department of Special Education and Disability Policy, Virginia Commonwealth University, Richmond.

Creative Play
Building Connections with Children Who Are Learning English

How can teachers support young children, all of whom are English language learners? Play is a wonderful way to help all children gain the confidence and skills they need to succeed in school and life!

SARA J. BURTON, BA, MTA AND LINDA CAROL EDWARDS, EdD

> Six-year-old Ana Belen speaks Spanish. She is in the block center with an English-speaking friend named Malik. Ana Belen tries to get Malik's attention because she needs more blocks to complete her building. She calls out to Malik in Spanish, gesturing with her hands and asking for the blocks she needs. She looks at him with a confused look when he does not respond to her request. Ana Belen then walks around the block center and points toward the blocks for which she was asking. She then says, to Malik, "Tarugo" (block).
>
> Malik complains to their teacher that he cannot understand Ana Belen and cannot play with her. When the teacher approaches, she explains to Malik, "Ana Belen is asking you to get her the square block—tarugo. Look, she is making a block shape with her hands, too!"
>
> Immediately Malik understands how Ana Belen is communicating. His confused expression changes to a smile. Ana Belen smiles too, as Malik hands her a block. Both children understand that they can communicate, verbally and nonverbally. The teacher observes as the two children continue to play together.

Learning English: Opportunities for Everyone

English language learners (ELL) are learning to listen, speak, read, and write (Silvaggio, 2005). When speakers of other languages begin to acquire English, like all children, they develop at different rates. Teachers may encounter situations such as these with English language learners who already speak Spanish:

- Some children experience a silent period of 6 or more months.
- Other children practice learning by mixing or combining the two languages or use a form of "Spanglish."
- Some children may have the skills (appropriate accent, vocabulary, and vernacular) but they are not truly proficient.
- Other children quickly acquire English-language proficiency (National Association for the Education of Young Children, 1995).

Language acquisition is a very complex developmental process and it may take some students "a minimum of 12 years" to master a new language (Collier, 1989). Even when children seem to express themselves correctly, they may not have mastered the true complexity of the language.

Educators realize that children who are English language learners come to early childhood programs and schools with their own knowledge of the language used in their homes (NAEYC, 1995). Teachers of young children are encouraged to view the inclusion of children who are learning English as an enrichment opportunity for everyone: children who are learning English as a second language, the English-speaking students, and even themselves. Wise teachers embrace classroom diversity and create an atmosphere where all children can thrive and progress.

This article primarily considers children who come from homes where Spanish is spoken, but the premises and suggestions hold true for any of the "nearly 3 million ESL students" in the nation's schools (Shore, 2001). What better way to involve and encourage all children to learn than through play?

What Are the Benefits of Play for English Language Learners?

Play is the primary vehicle through which children learn about themselves and others and about the world in which they live and interact. Through play, children actively explore their world, build new skills, and use their imaginations. Best of all they do it for the simple *joy* of doing it.

Educators are well aware of the lasting benefits of play, but the idea of "playing with language, oral and especially written language, during dramatic play is not nearly as common as it ideally should be" (Korat, Bahar, & Snapir, 2002, p. 393).

Play is extremely beneficial in overcoming communication challenges between English speakers and speakers of other languages (Little, 2004–2005; Reeves, 2004–2005; Oliver & Klugman, 2002). For children who are learning English, self-directed play establishes an informal, non-threatening atmosphere that is one of the most valuable ways of learning.

When children are engaged in the process of play, they usually care very little about an end product. They are free to figure out what they want to do and when they want to do it. They engage in spontaneous activity. In other words, children are in control. Play is a hands-on activity in which children choose their own learning adventures. They learn while doing something they have decided to do. What are children learning through play?

- Children increase the size of their vocabularies and their ability to comprehend language.
- They develop skills in cooperation by sharing and taking turns.
- Play helps children to develop empathy and strengthens their ability to express emotions (Oliver & Klugman, 2002).
- Play enables children to develop patience and tolerance (Dorrell, 2000).
- During play, children feel comfortable enough to take risks. As they gain self-reliance and feel successful (Edwards, 2002) they begin to function more independently and eventually take more risks outside of the play environment.

Play is essential for the sound development of all children, but it is especially important in the growth and development of children who speak English as a second language. How did Ana Belen and Malik benefit from playing? They interacted in the block section, primarily with nonverbal communication, and both learned a new vocabulary word. After resolving their initial lack of knowledge about the Spanish and English words for *block,* they played together in such a way that both students felt comfortable.

Children who are learning a language benefit from play in several ways (Silver, 1999). Play helps establish bonds of friendship among children who do not communicate well in English (p. 67). During play, children who are learning English may exhibit independence and self-assurance that is not otherwise evident.

For example, Silver noted that children who were learning English tended to engage in solitary play when painting or doing cut-and-paste activities. As they got used to the routine, they became involved in play with rules and games. One child was very shy and used mostly telegraphic speech. After engaging in play, he gradually built up his confidence to volunteer to go first when playing a game. Silver concluded that only during periods of play was this child on "equal footing with the others in the class" (1999, p. 67).

Telegraphic speech: Use of only the words necessary to communicate. For example, "I want to be picked up," might be verbalized as "pick up."

How Can Teachers Support English Language Learners?

Teachers have a critical role in organizing their classrooms, structuring activities, and planning the use of materials in order to maximize all children's participation in play. Early childhood educators can celebrate children's strengths and allow them many ways to express their own interests and talents.

Many children born in the United States speak English at school, but speak their native language elsewhere. Speaking Spanish at home and among friends is one way that families cherish their ties to their home country. Silvaggio (2005) notes that children need adult help to negotiate this new world. It is not an easy task for teachers, who often lack resources to work with English language learners. As Shore (2001) explains, there are simple and practical ways that educators can help ESL children succeed. These are a few possibilities.

Assess needs. Find out where students' skill levels are, not only in English but in other areas of development as well. Families' perspectives, previous child care providers' insights, and regular observations are essential resources for understanding children.

Empathize. Imagine how overwhelming it is to walk into a classroom where you only understand part of what you hear. The first author of this article remembers studying in Spain during her college years and being truly scared during the first few months there. Even though she had studied the language for a number of years, she felt helpless, insecure, and disconnected. How much more difficult it must be for a young child!

Foster a sense of belonging. Make sure all children feel welcomed by being patient. Use body language and pictures to communicate while learning welcoming words in their languages. Take care to pronounce children's names correctly. Be aware of children's needs for personal space and privacy, too.

Assign buddies. All children yearn to feel important and included. English-speaking children can be terrific resources to those who speak other languages by making sure they can find the way around school, count money at lunchtime, understand directions, and more.

Keep track of language progress. Maintain a portfolio of each child. Save photographs, recordings, artwork, and writing samples. Review records with the child (and family) to see progress over time. This is an important way to acknowledge children's strengths and accomplishments.

Encourage family involvement. Encourage parents of children who are learning English to feel like they are a part of the community and classroom. If needed, arrange for an interpreter at meetings and conferences. Learn more about each family's culture so that interactions with each other are always respectful. Study the language and learn important words and phrases.

Learn key words. Make sure all staff and children quickly learn basic vocabulary words in both languages, such as restroom, clock, teacher, and bus. Picture cards and labels with words are an excellent tool to use with children who are beginning to learn about written language.

Foster an appreciation of cultural diversity. Diverse cultures are an asset for any classroom. Respect each culture's customs, make and taste a variety of foods, learn vocabulary words, create maps, talk with family members, and encourage all children to share their traditions.

Ask and observe to find out how children prefer to be encouraged and supported to succeed—these strategies vary by culture and custom. "Children with high motivation, self-confidence, and low levels of anxiety are more successful second language learners" (Szecsi & Giambo (2004/2005, p. 104)).

Find out how children prefer to be encouraged.

In an ideal environment, children play independently, at their own pace, in their own unique way, and have the necessary materials to facilitate their play. "We need to play in English, not just speak English at school," said one student (Reeves, 2004/2005). Learning centers provide unique opportunities for all children to participate in free play, and this puts children who are learning English on "a level playing field" with their peers (Silver, 1999).

Dramatic Play Enhances Language Development

A dramatic play center is especially useful for children who are English language learners. Pretend play enables them to communicate in an informal setting and gather information that will be helpful to them, even beyond the classroom.

For example, during pretend play, children explore activities and relationships important to them in the real world. They typically investigate the role of family members, community helpers, and health care professionals (Texas Workforce Commission, 2002). Children bring their own knowledge into their play as they cooperate with one another.

In the dramatic play center, children build language and literacy skills. English language learners soon begin to communicate in effective and appropriate ways with both children and adults. They have many opportunities to "practice their language skills with peers" (deAtiles & Allexsaht-Snider, 2002) in a "language-rich environment" (Szecsi & Giambo, 2004/2005).

A language-rich environment is essential in any early childhood classroom. Include props such as telephone books, magazines, and restaurant menus for dramatic play. By labeling items, teachers expose all children to print in both languages. This enables children who are learning English to encounter reading and speaking while they play and gives them a "multisensory approach" (Gasparro & Falletta, 1994) to language acquisition.

For example, Luis Jose and Sophie are pretending to go to the subway station. The props are labeled with text and pictures of a train, ticket, money, a caution sign in both languages, so each child knows each object in his or her language. Even though they speak different languages, they are able to recreate what happens at the subway station.

Unscripted role play is a valuable way for children to interact informally and gain the confidence they need to speak aloud. Similarly, playing restaurant is efficient and helpful for children as they read menus, practice ordering, interact with a waiter, and use table manners. For children, it seems less important that they can engage in English or Spanish conversations. What does appear to matter to them is that they can interact and understand each other.

Teachers can choose relevant, diverse themes for dramatic play and provide props for each theme. Stock the area with tickets, pretend money, many types of groceries, tools, and toy animals. By using mostly familiar items, children find creative ways to play. Playing with real-life materials helps children feel more comfortable.

Teachers can also create a Reader's Theater. Children perform dramatic representations of a story read to them in class or by a friend (Szecsi & Giambo, 2004/2005). The list in the box contains a sample of books that may be helpful in working with Spanish speakers. These books can be integrated into many themes. Some books are also available in English so that children can "read" together.

Teachers who want children to feel at ease in the classroom must "reach past psychological and cultural barriers that lead students to prefer the safety of silence to the danger of speaking" (Reeves, 2004/2005). When children feel comfortable and relaxed, they will speak up and show what they have learned. "Drama places learners in situations that seem real," (Gasparro & Falletta, 1994) so when students use the goal language (English) for a specific purpose, the language is more easily internalized and remembered.

How Families Help Children Adjust to a New Language and Culture

- Read aloud in both languages to your children. Many reading skills transfer between languages.
- Get involved in community activities with your children. Go on local history tours, visit nature centers, and attend library story times. Link up with groups with similar interests, such as recreation departments, faith communities, and heritage festivals.
- Play board games. This will enrich skills such as counting, using money, and learning new words.
- Watch a few English-language children's educational television programs together such as *Reading Rainbow* or *Zoom!* The language is easy to understand and the characters are real. Talk about children's ideas afterwards, too.
- Become active in sports. Choose sports suitable for children's ages. These welcoming social interactions enable children to learn new expressions and casual rules of the language. Families are likely to gain new friendships. (adapted from Giambo & Szecsi, 2005)

Through a variety of play experiences, children who are learning English become more prepared to engage in everyday interactions with English speakers. They eventually gain the confidence to participate in the community.

What Role Do Families Play?

Parents and extended family members play a large role in helping children learn a new language and successfully adapt to the culture in which they live. Many families who speak another language and value their own culture face a difficult challenge when it comes to maintaining that culture and wanting their children to learn English as quickly as possible (Giambo & Szecsi, 2005).

Celebrate children's strengths.

Keeping children's fluency and literacy (if already acquired) in the native language while developing new language skills is a tremendous benefit because people "who are bilingual have an advantage in our increasingly global economy" (Giambo & Szecsi, 2005). Share these suggestions with families, who can help their children thrive in two cultures and languages.

Many school-related skills that parents teach their children in their native language transfer to their new language and class-room. Translators and resources in other languages are increasingly available in many communities. Families and teachers are urged to work together to facilitate each child's growth in language and in life.

Outlook for the Future

"Young children are just beginning to learn about the world, and because they are still amateurs, they make mistakes, they get confused, and they do not always get things just right. They need a positive reaction from the adults around them, and they need to be recognized for their own individual value" (Edwards, 2005, p. 2).

This challenge is true for teachers and their interactions with all children, including those who are learning another language. Young children construct knowledge by building on familiar experiences. Educators provide young children with an extensive array of meaningful experiences.

When children learn new vocabulary words and practice pronunciation and language conventions, they are gaining skills for life. Taking the time to help children learn English as well as key words in other languages enables them to succeed in their learning environment. They will gain the confidence and abilities to succeed in the diverse culture in which they live.

Hispanics are the largest minority population in the United States, with 39.9 million people as of July 2003 (U.S. Census Bureau, 2005). Hispanic youth also have a high dropout rate: "Nearly one in three students fails to graduate from high school" (Clearinghouse on Urban Education, 2000). Solutions are urgently needed to help children who speak Spanish become fluent in the language and gain skills they need to become productive, healthy adults.

Young children construct knowledge by building on familiar experiences.

Almost every teacher works with one or more English language learners every year. The education challenge is to make every situation a truly beneficial "teachable moment." Partnerships with children (and their families) will benefit children's language and literacy skills and build the confidence they need to succeed. After all, "People who can communicate in at least two languages are a great asset to the communities in which they live and work" (Cutshall, 2004/2005, p. 23).

Summary

As leaders and mentors, teachers can best help culturally and linguistically diverse children and families by respecting the importance of each child's home language and culture. Educators who embrace, respect, and preserve the many ethnic and linguistic backgrounds of students will enable them to increasingly contribute to this diverse culture.

Put These Ideas into Practice!

Creative Play: Building Connections with Children Who Are Learning English

Sara J. Burton and Linda Carol Edwards

What Children Learn through Play

- Children's vocabularies increase.
- Sharing and taking turns improves cooperation.
- Children develop empathy and express emotions.
- They develop patience and tolerance.
- Children gain self-reliance and feel successful.
- They become more independent.

Ways Teachers Support English Language Learners

- Find out their skill levels in all areas. Ask parents and previous child care providers to share their insights.
- Imagine what it is like to be in a group where you only understand part of what you hear.
- Be patient.
- Make sure children and families feel welcome. Learn a few words of their languages.
- Ask classmates to help each other during classroom routines.
- Regularly observe children and record progress. Keep a portfolio of photos, recordings, art, and (for older children) writing samples.
- Help families feel part of the community and classroom.
- Appreciate diversity.

Enrichment Experiences for Young Children

Focus on the dramatic play area. Add familiar props such as clothing, flowers, restaurant menus, pretend money, foods and tools, toy animals, magazines, and real-life materials. Label items in both languages for older pre-schoolers and primary children. Encourage informal, language-rich play.

Create a Reader's Theater. Offer age-appropriate and culturally relevant books, puppets, and dress-up clothing. Encourage role play of the stories in both English and children's own languages.

Offer everyday opportunities to use English. Pair an English language learner with an English-speaking student. Ask older English-speakers to read to younger ELL students. Encourage ELL students to read to younger peers.

Enrich learning opportunities. Ask older ELL students to interview a teacher, another student, or a member of the community. Students create their own interview questions, take photos, record the answers, and share the experience with classmates.

Suggestions to Share with Children's Families

- Read aloud in both languages to your children.
- Get involved in community activities with your children. Go on local history tours, visit nature centers, and attend library story times.
- Play board games. This will enrich skills such as counting, using money, and learning new words.
- Watch a few English-language children's educational television programs together. Talk about children's ideas afterwards.
- Become active in sports. Choose sports suitable for children's ages.

Adult Learning Experiences That Build on These Ideas

- Start learning children's languages. Perhaps a child's family member would like to tutor YOU.
- Get to know children's cultures. Shop in ethnic stores their families frequent. Attend community events. Read about diverse families to gain a better understanding of their strengths and challenges.
- Engage staff in a cultural immersion experience. Find a meeting moderator who speaks the chosen language, such as Spanish. Show a clip from a Spanish-language film. Each teacher receives a handout, in Spanish, about the film. After viewing the film, small groups discuss feelings, thoughts, reactions, and realizations as a result of this cultural experience.
- Ask an ELL parent to attend a staff meeting, with a translator, to talk about issues within the school and broader community.
- Identify translators who can attend parent meetings, translate written materials, and otherwise facilitate communication with families.

Note: *Dimensions of Early Childhood* readers are encouraged to copy this material for early childhood students as well as teachers of young children as a professional development tool.

References

Clearinghouse on Urban Education. (2000). *School practices to promote the achievement of Hispanic students.* ERIC Digest Number 153.

Collier, V.P. (1989). How long? A synthesis of research on academic achievement in a second language. *TESOL Quarterly, 23*(3), 509–531.

Cutshall, S. (2004/2005). Why we need "The Year of Languages." *Educational Leadership, 62*(4), 20–23.

deAtiles, J.R., & Allexsaht-Snider, M. (2002). *Effective approaches to teaching young Mexican immigrant children.* ERIC Digest Number 20021201.

Dorrell, A. (2000, March/April). All they do is play? Play in preschool. Early *Childhood News*, pp. 18–22.

Edwards, L.C. (2002). *The creative arts: A process approach for children and teachers* (3rd Ed.). Columbus, OH: Merrill/Prentice-Hall.

Gasparro, M., & Falletta, B. (1994). *Creating drama with poetry: Teaching English as a second language through dramatization and improvisation.* ERIC Digest Number 19940401.

Giambo, D., & Szecsi, T. (2005, Spring). Parents can guide children through the world of two languages. *Childhood Education, 81*(3), 164–165.

Korat, O., Bahar, E., & Snapir, M. (2002). Sociodramatic play as an opportunity for literacy development: The teacher's role. *Reading Teacher, 56*(4), 386–394.

Little, C. (2004/2005). A journey toward belonging. *Educational Leadership, 62*(4), 82–83.

Oliver, S.J., & Klugman, E. (2002). Playing the day away. *Child Care Information Exchange, 66*–70.

National Association for the Education of Young Children. (1995). Position Statement. *Responding to linguistic and cultural diversity: Recommendations for effective early childhood education.* Retrieved February 22, 2005, from www.naeyc.org/about/positions/PSDIV98.asp.

Reeves, D.B. (2004/2005). "If I said something wrong, I was afraid." *Educational Leadership, 62*(4), 72–74.

Shore, K. (2001). Success for ESL students. *Instructor, 110*(6), 30–33.

Silvaggio, A.M. ESL demand challenge schools. Retrieved January 11, 2005, from greenvilleonline.com/news/2005/01/11/2005011156589.htm

Silver, A. (1999). Play: A fundamental equalizer for ESL children. *TESL Canada Journal, 16*(2), 62–69.

Szecsi, T., & Giambo, D. (2004/2005, Winter). ESOL in every minute of the school day. *Childhood Education, 81*(2), 104–106.

Texas Workforce Commission. (2002, Spring). Learning centers: Why and how. *Texas Childcare, 30*–42.

U.S. Census Bureau. *Hispanic Heritage Month 2004.* Retrieved January 24, 2005, from census.gov/Press-Release/www/releases/archives/facts_for_features_special_edition.

SARA J. BURTON, BA, MAT, is a third grade teacher at Goodwin Elementary School in North Charleston, South Carolina. She holds a B.A. degree in Spanish from Wofford College and has traveled extensively to Spanish-speaking countries around the world. She earned her M.A.T. degree from the College of Charleston in Charleston, South Carolina. **LINDA CAROL EDWARDS,** EdD, is Professor, Department of Elementary and Early Childhood Education, College of Charleston, Charleston, South Carolina. Before she began teaching at the college level, she taught kindergarten in the North Carolina public schools. Edwards is the author of two books on early childhood education.

From *Dimensions of Early Childhood*, Spring/Summer 2006, pp. 3–9. Copyright © 2006 by Southern Early Childhood Association (SECA). Reprinted by permission.

UNIT 4

Supporting Young Children's Development

Unit Selections

16. **Twelve Characteristics of Effective Early Childhood Teachers,** Laura J. Colker
17. **Health = Performance,** Ginny Ehrlich
18. **Which Hand?: Brains, Fine Motor Skills, and Holding a Pencil,** *Texas Child Care*
19. **What Can We Do to Prevent Childhood Obesity?,** Julie Lumeng
20. **When Girls and Boys Play: What Research Tells Us,** Jeanetta G. Riley and Rose B. Jones

Key Points to Consider

- Why has childhood obesity become such an epidemic in our country today?

- Have you thought about the way children develop handedness? What can teachers do to support development in that area?

- How would the elimination of play and recess from the school setting affect children?

Student Web Site

www.mhcls.com

Internet References

Action for Healthy Kids
 www.actionforhealthykids.org
American Academy of Pediatrics
 www.aap.org

This unit starts with Laura J. Colker's article, "Twelve Characteristics of Effective Early Childhood Teachers." If the readers of this book think back about the effectiveness of the many teachers they have had over the years, a pattern will begin to emerge. Historically, researchers have found knowledge of child development, enthusiasm, a caring attitude, and a child-centered approach to learning to be the characteristics of successful teachers. You may recognize a favorite teacher from your past just by seeing this list of characteristics or remember some of your best teachers as having other qualities. Colker wanted to directly ask teachers what makes an effective teacher, so she conducted extensive interviews which required the participants to reflect on why they work in the field, skills they need, the challenges they face along with the rewards. She found twelve consistent responses emerge, and expands on those in this article. How many of these twelve characteristics such as passion, patience, creativity, and high energy are a part of your repertoire of dispositions?

Issues related to the health of young children continued to emerge this year and two articles in this unit address that topic. "Health = Performance" and "What Can We Do to Prevent Childhood Obesity?" address the importance of a healthy body for optimal educational performance. Ginny Ehrlich shares suggestions for adults who want to provide an environment to support a healthy lifestyle in "Health = Performance." She states that adults are powerful role models for young children and should participate in healthy lifestyle choices. Childhood obesity is noticeable every time one enters a fast-food restaurant and hears a child order a meal by its number on the menu because they are so familiar with the selection at that particular restaurant. It is also evident on a playground where children just sit on the sideline not wanting to participate with their peers due to negative body image. In "What Can We Do to Prevent Childhood Obesity?," Julie Lumeng provides many suggestions for educators to follow which will help children develop appropriate eating habits and an active lifestyle. Parents and educators must work together to promote healthy living. Teachers should also participate in healthy-living activities. Only then will our society begin to realize that a lifestyle that includes good nutrition and exercise is one of the best ways to lead a long and healthy life.

Continuing with the theme of the importance of teachers carefully observing children to determine their preferences, strengths, and needs is the article, "Which Hand?: Brains, Fine Motor Skills, and Holding a Pencil." Parents and teachers worry about handedness of children and are confused about the best ways to help children feel confident with the hand that feels most comfortable to them. For every successful left-handed major

© Photodisc/Getty Images

league baseball pitcher with a multi-million dollar contract, there are thousands of left-handed children struggling to learn in a right-handed world. About ten to twelve percent of the population is left-handed. Strategies for helping all children strengthen motor skills that support learning are included.

The title of this unit, once again, must be stressed: Supporting Young Children's Development. Teachers who see their job of working with young children as finding the approach that best supports each child's individual development will be most successful. We are not to change children to meet some idealistic model, but become an investigator whose job it is to ferret out the individual strengths and learning styles of each child in our care. Enjoy each day and the many different experiences awaiting you when you work with young children and their families.

Twelve Characteristics of Effective Early Childhood Teachers

Laura J. Colker

What does it take to be an effective early childhood teacher? This is a question that has long gnawed at reflective teacher educators, idealistic teachers (especially those just beginning their careers), and worried families who place their young children in the care of another adult. Many educators feel that effectiveness as a teacher stems from a combination of knowledge, skills, and personal characteristics (Katz 1993).

While aspiring teachers can increase their knowledge and develop their skills, their personal characteristics—which involve the socioemotional and spiritual realms in addition to the cognitive—are likely to be more fixed. As Cantor (1990) notes, one can have both knowledge and skills, but without a disposition to make use of them, very little will happen. *Having* is not the same as *doing*.

Because personal characteristics are rooted in feelings and beliefs, we can neither observe them directly nor assess them through traditional methods (Ostorga 2003), which makes them difficult to identify. Nevertheless, teacher educators and administrators would benefit greatly from knowing the characteristics of an effective early childhood teacher, as they strive to improve the quality of the field. New teachers and those at a crossroads in their career would also benefit if they could confirm that the interpersonal and intrapersonal beliefs they possess are those demanded by the field.

Reviewing the Literature

With these goals in mind, this article summarizes an attempt to identify some of the key characteristics early childhood teachers need to excel in their job. This is by no means a novel idea. The literature cites numerous examples of positive teacher dispositions (Ebro 1977; Smith 1980; Glenn 2001; Usher 2003; Adams & Pierce 2004). These examples often include characteristics such as enthusiasm and a good attitude.

Although they serve a definite need, the existing examples have limitations. Characteristics, or *dispositions,* as they are sometimes called, are frequently used interchangeably with traits and skills in the literature, when in fact they are not the same. DaRos-Voseles and Fowler-Hughey (2007) make the point that traits, unlike dispositions, are unconscious behavioral habits.

Skills such as "being organized," "having command of the classroom," and "asking probing questions" are teacher abilities but not characteristics.

A second problem with the current literature on teacher characteristics is that most of the lists of characteristics were developed with teachers of students in grades beyond the primary years in mind. Indeed, the most common focus is on teachers in higher education; none of the lists of desired teacher characteristics apply exclusively to early childhood teachers. Such a list would certainly benefit the field. Because early childhood teachers need unique knowledge and skills, it is also likely that they need to have characteristics that are unique to them as a group.

A final limitation of the existing literature is that in most instances, teacher educators are the ones attempting to define characteristics of effective teachers. While there is value in this approach, dispositions compiled by experts working with practitioners do not necessarily represent characteristics that practitioners themselves consider important. Because characteristics involve personal perceptions, consulting the beliefs of those doing the job is essential when drawing up a master list of characteristics common among effective early childhood teachers.

In the literature, there are two exceptions in which researchers solicited practitioner perceptions. A study at Ball State University (Johnson 1980) surveyed 227 Indiana public school teachers and 14 school principals to determine the characteristics correlated with teacher effectiveness.

Teachers reported four key characteristics. According to these respondents, effective teachers

- Have a sound knowledge of subject matter.
- Take a personal interest in each student.
- Establish a caring/loving/warm atmosphere.
- Show enthusiasm with students.

Principals offered a slightly different list of characteristics they consider most important. They said effective teachers

- Conduct thorough instructional planning/organizing.
- Are child oriented.
- Show enthusiasm with students.

A more recent study (Taylor & Wash 2003) at Lander University surveyed 3,000 K–12 teachers and administrators in seven school districts. Participants completed a modified Delphi survey, ranking the priority of dispositions indispensable to K–12 teachers. Survey participants identified the following as the top 10 characteristics (in descending rank order) of an effective teacher: enthusiastic, an effective communicator, adaptable to change, a lifelong learner, competent, accepting of others, patient, organized, hardworking, and caring.

A New Survey

To begin to address the gaps in the literature, I interviewed 43 early childhood practitioners to obtain their perceptions about the personal characteristics of effective early childhood teachers. These participants represent a wide range of backgrounds in terms of ethnicity, gender, geographic location, and experience. Although some respondents are no longer classroom teachers (they are mentor teachers, supervisors, trainers, and the like), all were early childhood teachers for a number of years.

Because personal characteristics involve feelings and spirit as well as thought, I did not ask survey participants to simply compose a list of characteristics. Instead, I posed questions about what attracted them to the field of early childhood education, the skills they needed to do their jobs, the challenges they faced, and the rewards they reaped. By reflecting on their practice in this way, respondents described the characteristics of effective teachers.

While this is by no means a perfect approach, it provides insight into a construct that is difficult to define and describe. What follows is a qualitative analysis of the responses provided by the 43 participants. I have organized their responses into 12 themes. The content is entirely the respondents'; the analysis is mine.

What Draws Teachers to the Field of Early Childhood Education?

The reasons people choose a profession offer insight into the characteristics they need to do their job well. Common threads link the practitioners interviewed for this article. People do not enter the early childhood education field for monetary reward or occupational glamour.

I had a need to make a difference in children's lives and ensure they got all the opportunities and nurturing they needed and deserved.

The majority of respondents realized at a young age that they wanted to be early childhood teachers. Many, including Renee Hamilton-Jones, who taught preschool for 13 years, reported feeling that "destiny" led them to their career choice.

Donna Kirsch, a supervisor of early childhood teachers, termed teaching a *calling:* "I had a need to make a difference in children's lives and ensure they got all the opportunities and nurturing they needed and deserved. It was mostly a calling, much like the ministry—but I don't say that out loud to too many people."

The need to make a difference in children's lives was echoed by nearly every respondent, including longtime kindergarten teacher Joanna Phinney: "I entered the field of early childhood education because I wanted to make a difference in the world. I felt that the place to start was with young children because you can make the biggest difference when children are young."

If you ask early childhood educators who entered the field for idealistic reasons whether they made the right career choice, you'll find few regrets. In the group of 43 surveyed here, no one expressed regret. Here's what two prominent early childhood educators who were once classroom teachers said:

> At a certain point in my career I was offered a position that would have been a promotion, but it was not in early childhood. I debated the decision carefully because I was a single parent of two young children at the time and could have used the additional money that came with the promotion. I chose to stay in early childhood education primarily because I knew my heart was with children's programs. In the end, staying with children's programs was the best decision. Even at the time I did not regret the decision because knowing myself as I do, it was more important for me to believe in the cause than to make money.

—Linda Smith, Executive Director, National Association of Child Care Resource and Referral Agencies

> I can honestly say that I have never, not once, reconsidered my decision to be an early childhood educator. Quite the contrary, I have often marveled at my luck. This profession has never disappointed me. Sometimes it is hard and I am not always successful, but I have an abiding belief in the value of my contributions. Early childhood education has definitely been my "calling," and because of the good match, I have been able to apply my talents and skills in an arena that both needed and valued my insights.

—Linda Espinosa, Professor of Early Childhood Education, University of Missouri–Columbia

What Characteristics Make Early Childhood Teachers Effective?

All the survey participants felt strongly that the early childhood profession has been a good match for their personalities and life goals. What then are the personal characteristics that contributed to making early childhood education a good career match?

1. Passion. Probably more than anything else, teachers report that it's important to have a passion for what you do. In many of the studies referenced in the literature, participants singled out "enthusiasm for children" as a key attribute. For the teachers in this study, however, something stronger than enthusiasm makes a truly effective teacher; it is closer to *drive*.

Being an early childhood educator is not always easy. There may be physical and financial challenges, for example. But if you feel that what you are doing makes a difference, that sense of accomplishment can sustain and motivate you. John Varga, a Head Start site supervisor, counsels those who do not have a passion for early childhood to find a different career. "This is not a career for someone just looking for a job working with kids because they are cute and it looks like fun. This is a career that must ignite your passion."

2. Perseverance. This is another characteristic frequently cited. Some respondents referred to perseverance as "dedication;" others felt it was "tenacity." Whatever term they used, what participants described is the willingness to fight for one's beliefs, whether related to children's needs or education issues. Teachers have to be willing to be long-term advocates for improving the lives of children and their families. Respondents in this study believe children need and deserve teachers who can overcome bureaucracy and handle red tape.

3. Willingness to Take Risks. A third related characteristic is the willingness to take risks. Successful educators are willing to shake up the status quo to achieve their goals for children. Great teachers are willing to go against the norm. Taking a risk means not settling for a no answer if a yes will improve the quality of a child's education.

For example, one teacher reports wanting to team teach her preschool class with a self-contained special education program adjacent to her room. Integration of programs had never been done before at her school, and faculty and administration alike looked at the idea with skepticism. To secure administration approval, the teachers had to conduct research, do a parent survey, and bring in outside experts. They held parent meetings to convince both the families of children with disabilities and those of children without disabilities that their children would benefit. After much energy and effort, the program was initiated on a trial basis. Five years later, it is one of the most successful and popular programs at the school (Villa & Colker 2006).

4. Pragmatism. Pragmatism is the flip side of perseverance and willingness to take risks. Pragmatists are willing to compromise. They know which battles are winnable and when to apply their resources in support of children. The important point, respondents felt, is that effective teachers understand that by temporarily settling for small wins, they are still making progress toward their goals.

5. Patience. In line with pragmatism is the characteristic of patience. Respondents cite the need to have patience both when dealing with "the system" and when working with children and families. Not every child learns quickly. Some behaviors can challenge even the most effective teacher. Children need reminder after reminder. Good teachers have a long fuse for exasperation, frustration, and anger. They regard all such challenges as exactly that—challenges. Effective teaching requires patience.

6. Flexibility. This is the sixth characteristic linked by study participants to successful teaching. Indeed, any job in early childhood education demands that you be able to deal well with change and unexpected turns. Whether it's raining outside and you have to cancel outdoor play, or your funding agency has drastically reduced your operating budget, you need to be able to switch gears at a moment's notice and find an alternative that works.

Indeed, any job in early childhood education demands that you be able to deal well with change and unexpected turns.

Sometimes the challenges are both drastic and sudden. Fresh out of college, Ashley Freiberg—one of the study respondents—had been a kindergarten teacher for only a few weeks when she found herself welcoming evacuees from Hurricane Katrina into her Baton Rouge, Louisiana, classroom: "I have 28 kindergarten children in my classroom, and it is my job to work with each of my students and present them with information that will help them to become readers, to master basic math facts, to know about the world around them, and to follow the classroom and school rules. I must do this leaving no child behind, teaching each individual student in the classroom, *without* a classroom aide!" Despite the pressures, Ashley adapted, doing what she had to for each child. Her flexibility exemplifies a vital character trait that respondents felt effective teachers must have.

7. Respect. Surveyed teachers strongly believed that respect for children and families is basic to being a good early childhood teacher. Some identified this characteristic as an "appreciation of diversity." They described it as not only respecting children and families of all backgrounds, but also as maintaining the belief that everyone's life is enhanced by exposure to people of different backgrounds who speak a variety of languages. We know that children's self-concepts flourish in an environment of respect. Good teachers create this environment naturally.

8. Creativity. An eighth characteristic respondents cited was creativity. It takes creativity to teach in a physical environment that is less than ideal or when resources are limited. It takes creativity to teach children from diverse backgrounds who might not approach education in the same way. It takes creativity to teach children with differing learning styles who think and learn in different ways. And most of all, it takes creativity to make learning fun. Creativity is a hallmark of an effective early childhood teacher.

9. Authenticity. This is another frequently cited characteristic of effective teaching. Some respondents referred to this attribute as "self-awareness." Being authentic means knowing who you are and what you stand for. It is what gives you integrity and conviction.

Young children are shrewd judges of character; they know whether a teacher is authentic, and they respond accordingly.

Young children are shrewd judges of character; they know whether a teacher is authentic, and they respond accordingly.

10. Love of Learning. Respondents also singled out love of learning. To inspire children with a love of learning, they said, teachers themselves ought to exhibit this characteristic. Teachers who are lifelong learners send children the message that learning is an important part of life. Several participants felt that being an effective teacher involves seeking out knowledge about recent research on teaching. Respondents in this study regard both teaching and learning as dynamic processes.

11. High Energy. Though it may have more to do with temperament than disposition, many teachers felt it important that teachers display high energy. Most children respond positively to teachers with high energy levels, valuing their enthusiasm. As Linda Espinosa observed, "The energy it takes to get up every day and work on behalf of young children and families is enormous."

12. Sense of Humor. A final vital characteristic of effective teaching pinpointed by respondents in the study was having a sense of humor. Learning should be fun; nothing conveys this message more than a room that is filled with spontaneous laughter. John Varga summarizes the importance of this characteristic in teaching: "All children ask is that we love them and respect them and be willing to laugh when it's funny . . . even when the joke's on us."

Conclusion

Reflecting on their practice, 43 early childhood educators identified characteristics they believe are integral to effective teaching. The resulting 12 characteristics include: (1) passion about children and teaching, (2) perseverance, (3) risk taking, (4) pragmatism, (5) patience, (6) flexibility, (7) respect, (8) creativity, (9) authenticity, (10) love of learning, (11) high energy, and (12) sense of humor.

Interestingly—and not surprisingly—some of the identified characteristics parallel those already identified in the literature (patience, authenticity, and a love of learning, for example.) In other instances, practitioners identified characteristics not typically seen in the literature (perseverance, risk taking, and pragmatism, for example). A future research study could compare the findings; perhaps practitioners have identified trends not yet picked up on by teacher educators.

As acknowledged, data reported in this article were not scientifically collected nor are they meant to represent the view of the entire field. The article does, however, report what selected early childhood educators themselves believe are important characteristics for doing their work effectively. It is the difference between an expert telling a parent how to be a good parent and a parent giving his perspective on parenting. Thus, it is not a question of which is better. Rather, it is an attempt to honor the practitioner's own views about this hard to define but important component of teaching.

References

Adams, C.M., & R.L. Pierce. 2004. Characteristics of effective teaching. In *Traditions and innovations: Teaching at Ball State University.* Muncie, IN: Ball State University. www.bsu.edu/gradschool/media/pdf/chapter12.pdf

Cantor, N. 1990. From thought to behavior: "Having" and "doing" in the study of personality and cognition. *American Psychologist* 45 (6): 735–50.

Da Ros-Voseles, D., & S. Fowler-Haughey. 2007. The role of dispositions in the education of future teachers. *Young Children* 62 (5): 90–98.

Ebro, L.L. 1977. Instructional behavior patterns of distinguished university teachers. Doctoral dissertation, Ohio State University.

Glenn, R.E. 2001. Admirable teaching traits. *Teaching for excellence.* Spartansburg, SC: Author. www.education-world.com/a_curr/curr387.shtml

Johnson, M. 1980. Effective teaching as perceived by teachers and principals in selected Indiana school corporations. *Ball State University doctoral dissertations.* Abstract. Muncie, IN: Ball State University. www.bsu.edu/libraries/virtualpress/student/dissertations/author_list.asp

Katz, L.G. 1993. *Dispositions: Definitions and implications for early childhood practices.* Champaign-Urbana, IL: ERIC Clearinghouse on Elementary and Early Childhood Education. http://ceep.crc.uiuc.edu/eecearchive/books/disposit.html

Ostorga, A.N. 2003. The role of values in the development of dispositions. Paper presented at the Second Annual Symposium on Educator Dispositions, November 20–21, in Richmond, Kentucky.

Smith, R. 1980. A checklist for good teaching. Montreal, Quebec, Canada: Teaching and Learning Centre, Concordia University.

Taylor, B., & P. Wash. 2003. 3,000 educators respond to preferred dispositions. Paper presented at the Second Annual Symposium on Educator Dispositions, November 20–21, in Richmond, Kentucky.

Usher, D. 2003. Arthur Combs' five dimensions of helper belief reformulated as five dispositions of teacher effectiveness. Paper presented at the Second Annual Symposium on Educator Dispositions, November 20–21, in Richmond, Kentucky.

Villa, K., with L.J. Colker. 2006. A personal story: Making inclusion work. *Young Children* 61 (1): 96–100.

LAURA J. COLKER, EdD, is a curriculum developer and teacher trainer in Washington, D.C. She is a contributing editor to NAEYC's new publication, *Teaching Young Children.* The information in this article was collected for a project Laura collaborated on with NAEYC's Carol Copple and Sue Bredekamp of the Council for Professional Recognition. ljcolker@aol.com

Health = Performance

Efforts to increase student achievement also should address physical activity and a good diet.

GINNY EHRLICH

L ooking to improve student achievement? Consider this: How healthy are your students?

Healthy children learn better—few statements in education are as unequivocal. We know this on a common-sense level, and the data backs it up. Research suggests that students' health and learning are inextricably linked. Studies also have shown that school health programs can boost students' academic performance and improve behavior and attendance.

So, efforts to increase student achievement should include a focus on health. School health programs and board policies can address physical activity and healthy eating—two areas that are particularly important in light of the obesity epidemic in the U.S. One in three children and adolescents is already overweight or obese, the Centers for Disease Control and Prevention (CDC) reports. Extra weight can cause a host of health problems in children, including asthma and Type 2 diabetes.

Perhaps the most established relationship of health and achievement is between eating breakfast at school and academic performance, no matter what the student's socioeconomic status. Studies have linked eating breakfast at school with improved performance on standardized tests and better math grades, as well as with improved student attendance.

Though research suggests that school breakfast has a positive impact on all students' performance, impact is greatest for students from food-insecure households.

Qualitative studies also cited the relationship between healthy eating and better student behavior. In a longitudinal child health study, teachers consistently cited the link between students' eating habits and their behaviors.

Some teachers said that students who participated in the school meals programs or who had consumed less sugar were less likely to display aggressive behavior and less likely to be referred out of the classroom. Both factors increase learning time for students who arguably need it the most.

Studies also show that there are correlations between students' physical activity and academic performance. A statewide study of students in California found a positive relationship between students' physical fitness levels and their standardized math and reading scores.

Further, students who were physically active every day were more likely to report getting mostly As and Bs in school than their more sedentary peers, according to a 2003 CDC study.

One obvious way to increase students' physical fitness is to offer quality physical education programs. Though several districts around the country have cut physical education programs to make room for more reading, math, and science instruction, the evidence suggests that spending more time in physical education class did not have a negative effect on students' standardized test scores, even though less time was available for other academic subjects.

Taking the Leap

Most school leaders and educators acknowledge the importance of these links between health and achievement, but given the stakes of meeting No Child Left Behind measures, there is little action taken. However, some districts have taken the leap to address the whole child, and they have reaped the benefits.

Most school leaders and educators acknowledge the importance of these links between health and achievement.

In McComb, Miss., former Superintendent Pat Cooper made a commitment to concentrate on the health needs of students. McComb is a small district that serves a vulnerable student population, most of whom live in poverty. Cooper implemented a coordinated school health approach to address the physical, social, and emotional barriers to learning.

McComb's program includes the eight components of the coordinated school health approach: school employee wellness, physical education, health education, nutrition services, parent and family involvement, school health services, mental health counseling, and environmental health.

The district has seen improvement in its students' academic achievement. Between 1996 and 2005, dropout rates decreased from 31 percent to 11 percent, and graduation rates increased to 95 percent. The district's ranking rose from 59th to 14th in the state.

Not only did students stay in school, but they also performed better. Standardized test scores improved in reading, writing, language arts, and math in every grade (except eighth, which remained the same). These scores now exceed state averages in several areas and all McComb schools qualify as "successful" (Level 3), as measured by the Mississippi state standards.

Tennessee has made a statewide commitment to addressing physical, social, and emotional barriers to learning that also has yielded positive returns. In 2002, Tennessee implemented a coordinated school health pilot program in 11 school districts throughout the state.

An independent evaluation conducted between 2002 and 2006 found that this initiative helped raise student achievement along with improving their health. Specifically, there is a substantial difference in dropout rates and graduation rates between the pilot districts and the state norm. Dropout rates in pilot districts were lower than the state norm in 2006 in nine of 11 systems and the high school graduation rates were higher than the state norm in 2006 in nine of 11 systems.

Additionally, competency rates in reading, writing, and language in kindergarten through eighth grade revealed that the majority of pilot sites exceeded the state norm for 2006. All of the school systems saw steady improvement from the baseline of 2003. Competency in mathematics and reading in kindergarten through eighth grade improved in all 11 school systems from 2003 to 2006, and all systems had higher mean scores on writing assessments in 2006 than in 2002.

What You Can Do

The Alliance for a Healthier Generation's Healthy Schools Program supports districts and schools in the implementation of a coordinated school health approach to promoting physical activity and healthy eating among students and school staff.

The Healthy Schools Program provides no-cost support to any school in the country through training, online tools, and phone consultation focused on district-wide promotion of physical activity and healthy eating for students and staff. Within the Healthy Schools Program Best Practice Framework, there are specific policy recommendations for supporting a healthier school environment. They include:

- Offering a healthy breakfast for every student every day. Consider extending a common practice, providing breakfast for all students during testing periods, to an everyday practice. The learning benefits can only increase gains in test scores. It is also important to ensure that the breakfast includes a healthy balance of lean proteins, whole fruits, and whole grains to fuel students for learning.

- Allocating adequate time for quality physical education. Given that evidence suggests that physical education time does not detract from student performance, it makes sense to maintain it within the curriculum. Quality physical education, based on state and national standards, offers many other benefits, such as keeping students active and building their skills to maintain lifelong physical activity.

- Providing access to healthier foods and beverages before, during, and after the school day. A consistent message about, and access to, healthier options across the school, in hallways, classrooms, cafeterias, and canteens, helps students to see these options as the norm and to establish their healthy eating patterns. Studies have shown a 1 percent increase in students' body mass index for every 10 percent increase in less healthy foods available at school.

- Dedicating time to quality health education. Health education not only contributes to building the knowledge and skills students need to build healthy habits, it also has been linked to improved reading scores in elementary-age students.

- Supporting school staff to be healthy role models. Parents are the primary role models for their kids, but given that the vast majority of school-age youth spend at least six hours a day in school, it is important that school staff communicate consistent messages. School employee wellness programs can help motivate staff to be more active and make healthier food choices. Their enhanced awareness of the benefits of wellness often results in them modeling and promoting healthier behaviors.

- It is important to consider the program and policy implications for establishing school environments that promote healthy eating and physical activity for all students as a critical part of education reform. The evidence clearly suggests a link between students' health behaviors and their educational performance.

- Healthy school environments support a better future for all of us by ensuring that students who are academically prepared are also healthy and live long enough to contribute their talents to the nation's future.

GINNY EHRLICH is the executive director of the Alliance for a Healthier Generation in New York, N.Y.

Which Hand?

Brains, Fine Motor Skills, and Holding a Pencil

- Right hand, left hand, or ambidextrous?
- What is handedness?
- How does handedness happen?
- Do left-handed people think any differently than right-handed ones?
- When should children begin to show a hand preference?
- How does handedness affect how we use tools—spoons, toothbrushes, and pencils?

At birth, parents and physicians make a quick check: 10 fingers, 10 toes—a symmetrical body. Both sides are the same. As babies grow, we expect reflexes, muscles, and movements to be fairly balanced on the two sides.

But it's not uncommon for infants to hold one hand more fisted than the other, to wave one arm more vigorously, or to turn the head to one side more often. Still, we can't say that a baby has a preference for the left or the right.

Though not an exact science, handedness can often be predicted by these early infantile movements. Why?

Handedness: Does It Start with the Brain?

Theorists speculate that handedness has to do with brain specialization. Different brain functions take place in different parts of the brain.

During prenatal development, while the brain and spinal cord are forming, nerves cross from one hemisphere or side of the brain, across the midline of the body, and connect to muscles on the opposite side of the body. The right hemisphere of the brain controls the muscles on the left side of the body, and the left hemisphere controls the right.

For right-handed people, the left side of the brain has a better developed nerve network that supports motor development and skills. For left-handed people, the opposite is true.

How We Develop Fine Motor Skills

Motor skills involve the movement of muscles throughout the body. Gross motor skills involve larger movements—swimming, walking, and dancing, for example. Fine motor skills describe the smaller actions of the hands, wrists, fingers, feet, toes, lips, and tongue. Fine and gross motor skills develop in tandem. Many activities depend on their coordination.

Infants. Newborns have little control over their hands. Typically the fist is closed. Hand movement results from reflex and not deliberate control. For example, if you place a rattle in an infant's hand, the infant may grasp it momentarily and then drop it as hand muscles relax. The infant has no awareness of the object or its absence. Typically, babies swipe at objects when they are 1 month old and discover and play with their hands at 2 months.

Between 2 and 4 months, babies begin to coordinate their eye and hand muscles. Babies see an object and try to grasp it—often unsuccessfully.

By 5 months, most infants can grasp an object within reach—without looking at their hands. This important milestone in fine motor development allows more prolonged but clumsy grasps. Eager to discover and learn, infants not only grasp objects but also taste them. Hand-to-mouth exploration is a standard and expected developmental leap.

By 9 months, most babies begin to show a preference for reaching with their right hand—even if the toy is placed on their left side. They will, however, continue to use the non-preferred hand much of the time.

By the end of the first year, babies will usually be able to grasp an object with the entire hand, swipe surfaces, and poke at an object with one finger. Significantly, the pincer grip—the ability to hold an object between the thumb and index finger—typically appears at about 12 months. The pincer grasp gives infants the ability to manipulate and grasp an object and to deliberately drop it. At 12 months, babies can usually hold an object in each hand, drop an object into a bucket, and perform stacking and nesting tasks.

Toddlers. Toddlers continue to strengthen hand and finger muscles. They develop the ability to use their fingers independently—twisting, pulling, poking, pushing—and with greater control. They are typically able to turn the page in a board book. They are also able to hold a fat crayon in a palmer grasp (all fingers wrapped around the crayon).

By 15 months, most toddlers can eat independently, first with fingers and then with a spoon. Toddlers can reach for objects smoothly and with minimal effort. They can hold two objects in one hand, fit objects together (puzzles and snap toys, for example), and stack a few blocks into a tower.

By 30 months, most toddlers can draw using a finger grasp (holding a crayon with four fingers pushing in opposition to the thumb). They can pour liquids from one container to another, take off socks and shoes independently, and turn the faucet on and off when hand washing.

It's during this period that children start to display a preference for one side—that is, they use the preferred side more consistently than the non-preferred. This is clear not only when they grasp objects with the hand, hold a spoon, and turn pages in a book but also when they kick a ball, roll play clay into a snake, and push a wheel toy along a path.

Preschoolers. The preschool child's central nervous system is still developing and maturing, a process that enables the brain to send complex messages to the fingers.

By age 3 or 4, most children are able to complete complex fine motor tasks. These include drawing deliberate shapes, stringing beads, cutting with scissors, spreading paint and paste with the index finger, dressing and undressing dolls, opening and placing a clothespin to hang artwork, and folding paper in halves and quarters. Each of these tasks reinforces a child's hand preference.

As these preferences become evident, you can accommodate them to maximize a child's hand strength. For example, for a child who shows a left hand preference, you can provide left-handed scissors.

Because preschoolers are still developing small muscle strength and hand-eye coordination, it is inappropriate to expect handwriting skills. Children this age are generally not ready for precise handwriting instruction.

Instead, introduce writing activities slowly and gently, recognizing that each child will have a different skill set and a unique developmental level. For example, a 4-year-old who does not show a hand preference is likely to have less overall muscle control and coordination.

Some tools for writing are easier to use than others. Some teachers like to start with markers because they require little pressure and minimal muscle strength. Other teachers start with crayons because they require more focus and muscle strength. Make sure you provide many tool choices and encourage children to use the tools to draw and paint before you expect them to write.

As children indicate their interest in writing letters and words—and you have observed and documented readiness—make writing tools available for exploration. Generally, markers and felt-tipped pens are easiest for inexperienced fingers to control.

School age. By the age of 5, children will show better fine motor development and consistent hand preference for most tasks. Children can typically draw a complete human figure; cut out shapes with scissors; trace forms; manipulate buttons, zippers, and snaps; and copy letters. Some can play piano; build models; knit, crochet, and sew; use a computer keyboard and mouse; and help with basic household chores like sweeping, dusting, and washing dishes.

School-age children (as well as adolescents and adults) experiment with using the non-preferred side. And researchers hold that such experimentation can be useful in maintaining brain function and dexterity.

How Do We Develop Handedness?

From the developmental review, it's clear that handedness is not just about hands. Consider:

- Which foot do you kick with?
- Which eye do you use to peer through a magnifying glass?
- Which hand do you use to unscrew a jar, hold your toothbrush, or sign your name?

Many people are consistent—all left-sided functions or all right-sided. Some have a combination of left and right dominance, sometimes determined by the task. For example, a right-handed knitter may be able to make stitches more quickly using the left hand. Sometimes handedness is determined by efficiency. For example, a person may complete a jigsaw puzzle or cut flowers with the preferred hand because it's less frustrating.

Consider these historical facts and current investigations.

- The percentage of left-hand dominant people has remained consistent (10 to 12 percent) in the population for generations.
- In colonial America, left-handed people were considered witches and were executed. More recently, well-meaning teachers used harsh methods—slapping wrists or tying the left hand behind the child's back—to "cure" left-handedness.
- Some research suggests that left-handed children are more likely to be creative, with high verbal and math ability. Other research finds no difference between left- and right-handed children.
- Children with autism and other developmental disabilities, as shown by some research, have a higher percentage of left-handedness than the general population.
- Dorothy Bishop (1990) concluded there is no consistent link between IQ and handedness.
- Can openers, spiral notebooks, telephone keypads, and automobile consoles are built for the convenience of right-handed users.
- Left-handed people are more likely to have a left-handed relative, but researchers have not identified a left-handed gene.
- Most researchers believe that handedness preference is on a scale. Few people are strictly right- or left-handed. Most link a hand to a specific task: throw a ball with the left hand but stir a pot with the right, for example.
- Truly ambidextrous people—those indifferent to hand preference—are rare.
- In India and Indonesia, eating with the left hand is considered impolite.
- When necessary, such as after injury to the dominant hand or under cultural pressure, humans can learn to use the non-preferred hand.

About 1 person in 10 is left-hand dominant—a challenge in a right-hand dominant classroom and world. Some neurologists seek to explain the causes of handedness (likely a combination of genetics and environmental factors). Others explore whether left-handed people think differently. And teachers and parents strive to make left-handed children comfortable and successful in a right-handed world.

Hand to the Task

When children are ready to write, make sure tools and materials support the intense effort. Handwriting is more than forming symbols on a page. Writing effectively—and efficiently—includes the selection of writing tools, gripping the tool, positioning the tool on paper, and having fine muscle strength, coordination, and control in the hand doing the writing.

Use these tips for helping all children—left- and right-handed—develop fine motor control and fluid writing skills.

- Observe children's pencil grips. The pencil should be loosely held with the fingers above the shaved tip—about an inch up from the point—in a tripod grip. The index finger is on top of the pencil, the thumb and middle finger holding two sides. There should be equal pressure between the thumb, the side of the middle finger, and the tip of the index finger. The ring and pinky fingers are relaxed and in line with the middle finger. See diagram at right.

  Watch for excessive pressure on the index finger and all fingers pulled into a fist with knuckles flexed. When a child holds a pencil too tightly, fatigue and frustration will interfere with writing efficiency.

- Observe children's posture and body mechanics. When a child holds a pencil, the eraser end should point to the shoulder. The wrist should rest on the table surface. The arm from thumb to elbow should be in a straight line—the hand doesn't hook back toward the body.

  Position paper so that the sheet is angled—the right corner higher for right-handed writers, and the left corner higher for left-handed writers. The non-dominant hand should hold the paper in place.

- Provide child-sized chairs and writing table. Make sure the chair's height enables the child's feet to rest comfortably on the floor with hips and knees at a 90-degree angle. The table should be just above elbow height and support the arms without tensing and lifting or shrugging the shoulders.

- Help left-handed children discover that the best place at a table is not next to a right-handed friend. Bumping elbows while writing—or eating soup—is messy and frustrating.

- Help children relax. When a child has clenched teeth and a tense neck and makes deep indentations on paper from pressing too hard, it's wise to end the writing session and encourage general relaxation. Check the position of the pencil and the wrist.

- Schedule whole-body writing time with non-traditional materials. Invite children to write letters in the air with their hands or feet. Offer finger paint, shaving cream, and sand trays for finger writing. Invite children to write with water on the sidewalk or a brick wall.

- Explore print with tactile tools like Wikki-stix® and clay. Fill zipper-top bags with hair gel and invite children to form letters and shapes with one finger.

- Provide colored markers—felt-tipped and of varying thicknesses. Often children refine their grip—and relax muscles—when they are absorbed in color on unlined paper.

1-middle finger
2-thumb
3-index finger

- Offer a variety of writing implements—pencils, fat pencils, colored pencils, and markers—that have a triangular and not round shape.
- Explore pencil grips. Mechanical pencils and gel pens often have built-in grips. Encourage children with awkward to tight pencil grips to use them.
- Provide stencils, alphabet charts, and tracing grids for fun writing practice. Crossword puzzles give children practice in precise letter spacing.

Activities for Left and Right

Eric Chudler, University of Washington, has a Web site called "Neuroscience for Kids." It includes games, quizzes, and links to brain development and function. The following activities are adapted from his work.

Each activity offers school-agers opportunities for charting and graphing, surveying, and evaluating evidence. Have plenty of chart paper and markers on hand. Encourage children to make notes of their observations. If your classroom has Internet access, children can upload their data and exploration results.

Left Hand or Right Hand?

Rather than ask children which hand they use, set up observation experiments that rely on more than self-reporting. Prepare observation charts with three columns: Left Hand, Right Hand, Either Hand. Have observers chart peers in tasks such as using a fork, painting at an easel, turning a door knob, and throwing a ball.

Left Foot or Right Foot?

Set up the same observation system as in the previous activity. Have observers chart their peers in tasks such as kicking a ball, walking up stairs (Which foot steps first?), time spent balanced on each foot, and stepping on a picture of a cockroach.

Left Eye or Right Eye?

Check for eyedness. Chart these tasks: looking through a paper tube, looking through a magnifying glass, and winking (Which eye winks more easily?).

You can chart eye dominance too. Cut a coin-sized hole in a sheet of construction paper. Ask the subject to hold the paper and look through the hole at a distant object using both eyes. Ask the subject to bring the paper closer and closer to the face while still looking at the object. As the paper comes close to the face, only one eye will be looking through the hole. Which one?

Left Ear or Right Ear?

Chart which ear is preferred in different tests. Which ear does the subject cup to help make a whisper louder? Which ear does the subject hold against a small box when trying to determine what's inside? Which ear does the subject hold against a door to hear what's going on outside?

References

Chudler, Eric. *Neuroscience for Kids.* http://faculty.washington.edu/chudler/experi.html.

Encyclopedia of Children's Health. 2006. "Fine motor skills." www.answers.com/topic/fine-motor-skills.

Liddle, Tara Losquadro and Laura Yorke. 2003. *Why Motor Skills Matter: Improving Your Child's Physical Development to Enhance Learning and Self-Esteem.* New York: McGraw-Hill.

LiveScience. 2006. "What Makes a Lefty? Myths and Mysteries Persist." www.livescience.com/humanbiology/060321_left_hand.html.

Needlman, Robert. 2001. "What is 'Handedness'?" www.drspock.com/article/0,1510,5812,00.html.

Smith, Jodene Lynn. 2003. *Activities for Fine Motor Skills Development.* Westminster, Calif.: Teacher Created Materials.

What Can We Do to Prevent Childhood Obesity?

JULIE LUMENG

Childhood obesity is a real and pressing public health problem in the United States. Moreover, the obesity epidemic is accelerating—even among babies and toddlers. Contrary to popular opinion, all the information available to date indicates that a child less than 3 years old who is overweight is no more likely to be overweight as a young adult than is a toddler who is not overweight. However, the same research indicates that an overweight 3-year-old child is nearly 8 times as likely to become an overweight young adult as is a typically developing 3-year-old (Whitaker, Wright, Pepe, Seidel, & Dietz, 1997). In other words, by the time a child is 3, she may be on the path to obesity in adulthood. If we assume that the weight status of a 3-year-old has taken some time to develop, we must conclude that factors predisposing children to overweight begin operating in children in the first 3 years of life.

What factors in the experience of infants and toddlers seem likely to account for childhood overweight? What evidence do we have to suggest that these factors do, in fact, influence obesity risk? If research findings are scarce (or shaky), what advice about preventing obesity can practitioners offer to parents and caregivers of babies and toddlers? What can we do at a public health and policy level to change our obesigenic (obesity producing) environment? This article is an effort to answer these questions as fully as reliable research findings will allow. We will also define some terms that are used in medical discussions about childhood obesity; attempt to dispel some common misunderstandings about the causes of childhood obesity; and suggest some promising approaches for practice, research, and policy.

Definitions and Data

What is obesity in early childhood? *Obesity* is a term for excessive body fat. We measure body fat in anyone older than 24 months by calculating body mass index (BMI; weight in kilograms divided by the square of height in meters). Clinicians can plot a child's BMI on gender-specific charts provided by the National Center for Health Statistics (NCHS) of the Centers for Disease Control (CDC) (http://www.cdc .gov/growthcharts/). There are no BMI-for-age references or consistent definitions for overweight for children younger than 2 years. However, nutrition programs such as the Special Supplemental Nutrition Program for Women, Infants and Children have used weight-for-length recommendations to determine overweight and thus program eligibility. Consequently, overweight in this age group is defined as at or above the 95th percentile of weight for length (Ogden, Flegal, Carroll, & Johnson, 2002). Thus, for the remainder of this discussion, we will use the term "overweight" to describe children aged 2 years to 18 years whose BMI falls at the 95th percentile or above.

> **An overweight 3-year-old child is nearly 8 times as likely to become an overweight young adult as is a typically developing 3-year-old.**

Why does BMI mean something different for adults than for children? Adults have stopped growing. Because an adult's height remains the same, one can look at the weight and height of an adult and calculate BMI in a straightforward fashion. But think about children. Who appears to be naturally "chubbier"—a healthy 3-year-old or a 5-year-old? The 3-year-old—because she is still losing her "baby fat." *All* children are naturally at their "skinniest" when they are between 4 and 6 years old. Then their BMI slowly increases. Compare a 10-year-old girl about to enter puberty to a 5-year-old girl. The 10-year-old's BMI is higher, but that is as it should be given her stage of development. In other words, different degrees of "adiposity" (fatness) are normal at different ages during childhood. Babies *should* be "fat"—but fat within the normal range on the NCHS weight-for-length

At a Glance

- Rates of childhood obesity are increasing.
- Children less than 3 years old who are overweight are no more likely to be overweight in adulthood than are children who are not overweight, but 3-year-olds who are overweight are likely to be overweight in adulthood.
- Children learn many of their food preferences from their peers and from advertisements—not from their parents.
- Researchers have studied many possible factors in childhood obesity, such as genetics; the family's access to supermarkets and fresh, healthy foods; parents' attempts to limit when a child eats; and parents' attempts to make children eat more vegetables.

charts. The 3-year-olds who are in the top 5% of the weight-for-length bell curve are much more likely to continue to be overweight into adulthood. And adults who are at the top end of the BMI bell curve are at increased risk for serious health problems.

Terminology aside, more of America's children are becoming overweight, and today's overweight children tend to be heavier than overweight children were in past years. These data are concerning for a number of reasons. First of all, the obesity epidemic is accelerating—even among our youngest children. For example, between 1976 and 2000, the prevalence of overweight in 6- to 23-month-old children increased from 7% to nearly 12%. Most of this increase occurred from 1990 to 2000. Among 2- to 5-year-old children, the prevalence of overweight more than doubled (from 5% to more than 10%), again with most of the increase between 1990 and 2000 (Ogden et al., 2002).

Even among very young children, we are seeing significant—and growing—racial disparities in the prevalence of overweight. The greatest increases in the prevalence of overweight between 1971 and 1994 occurred in children of black and Hispanic race/ethnicity (Ogden et al., 1997). Racial disparities with respect to overweight appear to grow and interact with socioeconomic status as children grow older. For example, in 1986, the prevalence of overweight among 12-year-old upper-income White girls and low-income African American and Hispanic boys of the same age was nearly identical—6.5%. By 1998, the prevalence of overweight in upper-income White girls was essentially unchanged at 8.7%, but had more than quadrupled among low-income African American and Hispanic boys, at 27.4% (Strauss & Pollack, 2001). Unfortunately, we do not yet understand the causes underlying these alarming racial and socioeconomic disparities in the prevalence of overweight among children.

Chubby Babies, Fat Adults?

As noted above, all of the information available to date indicates that a child who is overweight at less than 3 years of age is no more likely to be overweight as a young adult than is a child who is not overweight. However, a child who is overweight at 3 years or older is nearly 8 times as likely to be overweight as a young adult than is a 3-year-old who is not overweight (Whitaker et al., 1997). Why and how is overweight in early childhood tied to adult obesity? Not surprisingly, current hypotheses focus on genes and the environment.

Genetic factors that predispose to obesity in a family may already be expressing themselves in early childhood. Genetic factors related to obesity may include: metabolism rates, behavioral predispositions to food preferences, eating behavior, and patterns of physical activity. Even among children younger than 3 years, a child with one parent who is obese is 3 times as likely to become an obese adult as is a child with two parents of normal weight. A child with two obese parents is more than 13 times as likely to become an obese adult as is a child with parents of normal weight (Whitaker et al., 1997). This phenomenon undoubtedly reflects a complex interplay of biology and behavior. In other words, as we have come to recognize that with respect to most aspects of child development, the old dichotomy of nature versus nurture represents an oversimplification of a complex issue.

We do know that the dramatic increase in the prevalence of overweight in the general population and among children since 1990 absolutely cannot be accounted for by genetic shifts in the population. Genetic changes simply do not occur this quickly. It *is* possible, however, that genetic predispositions toward certain behaviors (e.g., preferences for sweet or high-fat foods) vary within the population. When the environment changes, these genetic predispositions may be more apt to express themselves than formerly; the result is overweight or obesity. The overarching message? Our genes have not changed recently; our environment has. What does this conclusion tell us about the strong transmission of overweight risk from parent to child?

Parents' modeling of behavior and their shaping of a child's relationship to food have been areas of active research in child development for quite some time. Accounts in the lay press do not hesitate to hold parents responsible for childhood overweight. For example, recent articles in national newspapers have been headlined, "Overweight kids? You might deserve a big slice of the blame" (Lee, 2004), or "If parents can't say no, then their children won't learn to either" (Hart, 2003). Blaming parents for a problem that is growing more quickly—and at epidemic proportions—in disadvantaged minority populations than in the population as a whole immediately raises concerns about the validity of this conceptualization of the problem. If parents are generally and primarily to blame for the increased prevalence of child overweight since 1990, one or both of the following statements would have to be true: (a) Parenting practices as a whole have shifted dramatically in the last 15 years, and (b) low-income parents (especially mothers) have a reasonable chance of overcoming the influence of both food advertising that is targeted at their children and the economic conditions in which they live.

Who Influences Children's Eating Behavior?

If poor parenting is to blame for the growing prevalence of childhood obesity, then something must have changed since 1990 in the ways in which parents teach their children about food, set limits around food, and promote healthy eating habits. This assertion is difficult to support, for a variety of reasons. For example, if parents have a powerful influence over children's eating behavior and development of food preferences, then family members' food preferences should be very much alike. In fact, very little correlation exists between parent and child food preferences (even when the children have grown to be adults; Rozin, 1991). Parents are not very effective at transmitting preferences for foods to their children (a finding that will not surprise any parent or caregiver who has struggled to encourage a child to sample a new food!).

Today's overweight children tend to be heavier than overweight children were in past years.

Although parents have limited control over what children are willing to eat while sitting at the dinner table parents *do* control what food is in the cupboards. Given that obesity is more common in low-income minority populations, perhaps efforts should focus on encouraging low-income mothers with young children to stock the house with a range of healthy food options for their children. Unfortunately, this recommendation is problematic from a public health perspective. Consider, for example, the research finding that families who live closer to supermarkets are more likely to consume a healthier diet than are families who live further away, presumably because those living closer have readier access to a range of fresh and healthy foods (Morland, Wing, & Roux, 2002). However, the number of supermarkets per capita is nearly 6 times greater in White neighborhoods than it is in neighborhoods of primarily minority race/ethnicity (Morland, Wing, Roux, & Poole, 2002). The reasons for these stark disparities are undoubtedly complex, and not fully understood. These differences, however, would potentially be amenable to public policy intervention.

Where *do* children learn their food preferences? The bulk of the evidence suggests that even children as young as 2 years learn food preferences from their peer group. In one study, researchers in a preschool setting seated children who didn't like broccoli next to children who did. The broccoli eaters ate their green vegetable in full view of their broccoli-averse classmates. Over time, the children who hadn't liked broccoli began to eat it (Birch, 1980). In a more recent experiment, teachers in a preschool setting and peer models were put head-to-head to determine who was more likely to influence a child's food preferences. The children were significantly more powerful influences than the adults were (Hendy & Raudenbush, 2000).

Evolutionary biology suggests two principal reasons why peers may be more powerful than adults in shaping children's food preferences:

- *Young children's reluctance to sample new foods is biologically wired.* Reluctance to try new foods begins to emerge at around age 2 years and lessens as children approach school age. The unfamiliar foods that children are most reluctant to try are vegetables (Cooke, Wardle, & Gibson, 2003). That children become reluctant to sample new foods just as they are becoming mobile, independent explorers seems to be more than mere coincidence. It would be to the human species' survival advantage for its young to be reluctant to eat unfamiliar plant life (e.g., vegetables): Plants can be poisonous. Instead of tasting any new item that they encounter, human children (in fact, nearly all mammals) determine what to eat by observing others around them.

- *Modeling eating behavior after peers may provide young children with some survival advantage.* A biological perspective suggests that the nutritional needs of the young human are more similar to those of other young humans than to those of full-grown adults. For example, because children's bodies are smaller than those of adults and to some extent less able to protect against infection, foods that adults can eat or drink safely in reasonable quantities could prove toxic to a young child (e.g., sushi, steak tartar, unpasteurized apple cider, and alcohol).

In brief, if nature had tried to equip children's brains with a preset system for recognizing which foods are safe to eat, a system that led children to imitate the behavior of the organisms most like themselves (i.e., other children), would clearly be the best design. This appears to be, indeed, the food-selection system that children use.

Unfortunately, advertisers seem to have recognized the power of peers to influence children's food preferences long before the rest of us. Anyone who has ever watched television recognizes that to sell food to children, advertisers use other children (e.g., "Mikey") or characters designed to appeal to and resonate with children. No cereal or candy company would ever attempt to sell a product to a child with a commercial featuring a firm (yet kind and gentle) adult model eating the product while enthusiastically explaining to the child how "yummy" it is. Paradoxically, this is exactly the method by which parents try to get children to eat healthy foods. Perhaps reframing our efforts at changing childhood eating behavior is in order. Food advertisements on television are powerful. Children's consumption of specific foods correlates with their having viewed advertisements for these foods. Obese children are more likely than are children of normal weight to recognize food advertisements on television (Halford, Gillespie, Brown, Pontin, & Dovey, 2004). Even children as young as 2 years are more likely to select a food that they recently saw advertised in a 30-second commercial embedded in a cartoon than are children who have watched the cartoon without the commercial (Borzekowski & Robinson, 2001). Unless the government can be convinced to provide sufficient funding to advertise vegetables, whole grains, and milk on television with the same vigor and enormous advertising budget of the junk-food industry, hawking healthy food to children through television may be an unreachable goal. However, children who attend preschool and child care are exposed to peers in eating situations every day. These interactions may be prime opportunities for promoting the transmission of healthy food preferences between and among children.

What Is the Right Way to Parent to Prevent Obesity?

Parents do exert some control over how their children learn to prefer healthy foods and regulate food intake. Therefore, professionals who work with the parents of young children should base their recommendations about nutrition and feeding on solid scientific evidence. Unfortunately, although professionals frequently give families advice on these topics, we have little data to back up our suggestions.

Although parents have limited control over what children are willing to eat . . . parents do control what food is in the cupboards.

For example, early childhood professionals and clinicians generally believe that young infants should be fed "on demand." (Whether or not parents actually accept and implement this advice is an unanswered question.) But although feeding an infant on demand may certainly promote a sense of security and help the infant to calm and self-regulate, we have no evidence to suggest that feeding a baby on demand has anything to do with her eventual ability to regulate appetite. Interestingly, at some point in the early childhood years, however, general professional opinion and advice seem to shift from feeding "on demand" to feeding at scheduled snack and mealtimes. We encourage parents to have a child wait until dinner for food, even if he or she is clearly hungry. The theory is that the child will then "have a good appetite" and will "eat a good dinner." On the other hand, some professionals advise parents to allow young children to "graze" on healthy foods all day long. They counsel parents to allow

their child to eat a snack when they ask for one, with the thought that the child is learning to respond to his hunger cues accurately. Feeding children when they say that they are hungry, these professionals and parents believe, will teach children that "we eat when we are hungry," not that "we eat because it is dinnertime."

Evidence to support either method of regulating food intake is scanty. Some data suggest that restricting children's access to palatable foods makes children like and want these foods even more over time (Birch, Zimmerman, & Hind, 1980) and promotes overeating when the restricted foods are actually available (Fisher & Birch, 1999). The more that mothers control how much, what, and when children eat at age 5 years (regardless of the child's weight status at that age), the more likely the child is to eat without being hungry (i.e., to be insensitive to hunger cues and therefore apt to overeat) by age 9 years (Birch, Fisher, & Davison, 2003). These data suggest that parents who set strict limits on their young children's eating may actually promote obesity. This information might, therefore, prompt professionals to instruct mothers *not* to restrict the amount, timing, or content of children's meals. However, such advice runs directly counter to how much of the general public views the cause of today's childhood obesity epidemic—lax, inconsistent parenting with little limit-setting.

Similar confusion exists concerning strategies to get children to eat more vegetables. Simply encouraging parents to put vegetables on the dinner table each evening does not result in children's becoming more familiar with a food and therefore more likely to eat it. Children must actually taste a vegetable repeatedly before they begin to like it (Birch, McPhee, Shoba, Pirok, & Steinberg, 1987). If simply prompting a child to "take one bite" could make a typical child easily and pleasantly take a bite of a disliked vegetable, parenting (and obesity prevention) would certainly be a much simpler endeavor than it is. Unfortunately, as we have seen, children have an inherent reluctance to sample new vegetables, and parental modeling, as described above, has limited power to overcome this reluctance. If these methods fail, parents often then resort to rewarding the child for trying one bite of the vegetable. Most commonly, parents will tell a child that she may not leave the table, or may not have dessert, or may not have any more servings of a preferred food until the target vegetable is sampled. Unfortunately, it seems that these methods of reward actually result in a decreased preference for the target vegetable over time—certainly not the desired outcome (Birch, Marlin, & Rotter, 1984).

Synthesis of the Research to Date

Do we have evidence that any feeding practices in the first few years of life influence obesity risk? It is relatively well-accepted among researchers that breast-feeding reduces the risk of obesity (Hediger, Overpeck, Kuczmarski, & Ruan, 2001), although questions remain concerning whether this correlation is simply due to the presence of confounders, such as the general health consciousness of mothers who breast-feed (Parsons, Power, & Manor, 2003). If one accepts that a relationship exists between breast-feeding and low-ered risk of obesity, one should note that breast-feeding in infancy has not been found to be associated with protection against overweight among children of preschool age in all populations. Among low-income children, for example, the relationship between breast-feeding and protection against overweight is present only in white children—not in black or Hispanic children (Grummer-Strawn & Mei, 2004). The reason for this discrepancy remains unclear. Researchers are also debating whether or not the timing of a baby's intro-duction to solid foods is associated with an increased risk of child overweight. Most recent research seems to indicate that introduction of solid foods before 4–6 months does not seem to be associated with infant weight status, at least at 12 months of age. We have no data about timing of solid food introduction and weight status at age 3 years or later. The use of food as a reward (for example, to avert a tantrum) has been associated with children's increased preference for the food that has been used as a reward (Birch et al., 1980). However, the children of mothers who report that they use food as a reward do not seem, as a group, to be particularly obese (Baughcum et al., 2001).

Because of the high prevalence of obesity among chil-dren living in poverty, several researchers have studied the feeding practices of low-income mothers of young children. However, efforts to relate children's weight status at 11 to 24 months of age to self-reported maternal feeding practices in low-income populations have not uncovered any clear associations. Baughcum and her colleagues (2001) found that low-income mothers of children who were overweight did not report being more concerned about their infant's hunger, being less aware of their infant's hunger and satiety cues, feeding their infant more on a schedule, being more likely to use food to calm their infant, or having less social interaction during feeding than did low-income mothers of children of normal weight. However, low-income obese mothers in this study were more likely to be concerned about their baby's being underweight than other mothers. Given their concern, obese mothers may have been more apt to overfeed their babies, and thereby place them at greater risk for overweight. Regardless of the weight status of child or mother, low-income mothers are more likely to be con-cerned about their child's hunger than are higher-income mothers (Baughcum et al., 2001). Low-income mothers said that they found it difficult to withhold food from a child who said he or she was hungry, even if the child had just finished a meal.

Results from the same authors for children 23 to 60 months of age provide equally confusing information for the practitioner who wants to provide straightforward advice to a family. The researchers found that obese mothers and low-income mothers were more likely to engage in what professionals consider age-inappropriate feeding practices

than were non-obese or upper-income mothers (Baugh-cum et al., 2001). For example, low-income toddlers and preschoolers were more likely than upper-income young children to eat in front of the TV or walking around the liv-ing room rather than having a meal at a table with a place setting. Lower-income mothers said that they had less dif-ficulty feeding their children than did higher-income moth-ers, but low-income mothers reported a tendency to push their children to eat more. However, none of these frowned-upon feeding practices were associated with increased risk of overweight at age 5 years.

Some data suggest that restricting children's access to palatable foods makes children like and want these foods even more over time.

In summary, we find no evidence from mothers' reports that overweight children experience a different feeding style from their mothers than do non-overweight children. Although lower-income mothers do feed their young children differ-ently than do upper-income mothers, we have no evidence that these different feeding practices are actually related to an increased risk of child overweight. In other words, the fact that a low-income mother chooses to have unstructured mealtimes, encourages her child to eat more, allows her child to have a bottle during the day, or will feed the child herself if the child does not want to eat, may reflect sociocultural differences between lower-income and upper-income parents in their beliefs about feeding practices. Professionals have no basis on which to make a value judgment about these practices as they pertain to child overweight outcomes.

What *Should* Professionals Recommend to Parents?

We have reviewed the research on young children's eating behavior and parental feeding practices (with a particular focus on low-income minority children) and their relation-ship to childhood overweight. We have found an absence of robust research to guide us in advising parents about how to prevent childhood overweight. What advice *should* profes-sionals give to parents of young children about feeding prac-tices? Research suggests four guidelines for practice:

1. *Acknowledge the limits of parental influence in the face of an obesigenic environment.*

Especially when working with disadvantaged parents, acknowledge that, although parents influence their children's eating and will do the best job they can to prevent obesity in their child, individual parents are constantly battling a myriad of societal and biological influences on their child's eating behavior.

2. *Empower parents to advocate for systemic change.*

Parents are in a prime position to advocate for change in their children's child-care and preschool settings with regard to the foods served and the mealtime atmosphere. Parents are also important voices in advocating for more and safer playgrounds in their neighborhoods so that children can get exercise outdoors.

3. *Refrain from urging parents to change their feeding practices when we have little scientific evidence to suggest that these are actually "wrong."*

Although allowing a child to walk around all day with a bottle of juice is certainly problematic from an oral health perspective, professionals tend to frown on other feeding practices without compelling evidence that these practices increase children's risk of poor health outcomes. For example, telling a mother to have structured mealtimes rather than allowing her young child to "graze" has little basis in science, and may only serve to alienate a mother from the health care provider. She is likely to be feeding her child as her mother fed her, and as her cultural and socioeconomic peers feed their children.

4. *Advocate, advocate, advocate.*

Although working with individual families to reduce their child's risk for overweight is important, advocating for change on a public health and policy level is critical. Providing low-income families in both urban and rural areas with ready access to fresh and palatable fruits and vegetables would be an important change for the better. Increasing the availability of healthy, tasty, and inexpensive fast food could also make a big difference in children's health. Although an upper-income working family can find palatable (albeit expensive) rather healthy take-out food in some communities, cost and availability preclude this option for most low-income families. Yet few low-income mothers have the time or energy after a long day at work to take public transportation (which doesn't exist in many communities) with several children in tow to buy fresh food at a supermarket (which may not exist in the vicinity of many low-income families' homes), and then cook while the children vie for her attention. Because many low-income families do not feel safe allowing their children to play outside in their home neighborhoods, it is important to ensure that, along with healthy meals and snacks, children get adequate opportunity for physical activity in child-care, preschool, school, and after-school programs. Of course our long-term goal should be safe child- and family-friendly communities with ample sources of affordable, healthy food to purchase and accessible resources for information and physical exercise (including community gardening).

In Conclusion

The early childhood professional can play a critical role in stemming the tide of childhood overweight. However, this role may not play out in the home of the individual family as much as it may in the Early Head Start or Head Start classroom or the community meeting hall. Preventing childhood overweight will, as the saying goes, take a village.

References

Baughcum, A., Powers, S., Johnson, S., Chamberlin, L., Deeks, C., Jain, A., et al. (2001). Maternal feeding practices and beliefs and their relationships to overweight in early childhood. *Journal of Developmental & Behavioral Pediatrics, 22*(6), 391–408.

Birch, L. (1980). Effects of peer models' food choices and eating behaviors on preschoolers' food preferences. *Child Development, 51,* 489–496.

Birch, L., Fisher, J., & Davison, K. (2003). Learning to overeat: Maternal use of restrictive feeding practices promotes girls' eating in the absence of hunger. *American Journal of Clinical Nutrition, 78*(2), 215–220.

Birch, L., Marlin, D., & Rotter, J. (1984). Eating as the "means" activity in a contingency: Effects on young children's food preference. *Child Development, 55,* 432–439.

Birch, L., McPhee, L., Shoba, B., Pirok, E., & Steinberg, L. (1987). What kind of exposure reduces children's food neophobia? *Appetite, 3,* 353–360.

Birch, L., Zimmerman, S., & Hind, H. (1980). The influence of social affective context on the formation of children's food preferences. *Child Development, 51*(3), 856–861.

Borzekowski, D., & Robinson, T. (2001). The 30-second effect: An experiment revealing the impact of television commercials on food preferences of preschoolers. *Journal of the American Dietetic Association, 101*(1), 42–46.

Cooke, L., Wardle, J., & Gibson, E. (2003). Relationship between parental report of food neophobia and everyday food consumption in 2–6-year-old children. *Appetite, 41*(2), 205–206.

Fisher, J., & Birch, L. (1999). Restricting access to palatable foods affects children's behavioral response, food selection, and intake. *American Journal of Clinical Nutrition, 69,* 1264–1272.

Grummer-Strawn, L., & Mei, Z. (2004). Does breastfeeding protect against pediatric overweight? Analysis of longitudinal data from the Centers for Disease Control and Prevention Nutrition Surveillance System. *Pediatrics, 113*(2), e81–e86.

Halford, J., Gillespie, J., Brown, V., Pontin, E., & Dovey, T. (2004). Effect of television advertisements for foods on consumption in children. *Appetite, 42*(2), 221–225.

Hart, B. (2003, November 16). If parents can't say no, then their children won't learn to either. *Chicago Sun-Times,* p. 36.

Hediger, M., Overpeck, M., Kuczmarski, R., & Ruan, W. (2001). Association between infant breastfeeding and overweight in young children. *Journal of the American Medical Association, 285,* 2453–2460.

Hendy, H., & Raudenbush, B. (2000). Effectiveness of teacher modeling to encourage food acceptance in preschool children. *Appetite, 34,* 61–76.

Lee, E. (2004, May 30). Overweight kids? You might deserve a big slice of the blame. *Atlanta Journal-Constitution,* p. 1A.

Morland, K., Wing, S., & Roux, A. D. (2002). The contextual effect of the local food environment on residents' diets: The atherosclerosis risk in communities study. *American Journal of Public Health, 92*(11), 1761–1768.

Morland, K., Wing, S., Roux, A. D., & Poole, C. (2002). Neighborhood characteristics associated with the location of food stores and food service places. *American Journal of Preventive Medicine, 22,* 23–29.

Ogden, C., Flegal, K., Carroll, M., & Johnson, C. (2002). Prevalence and trends in overweight among US children and adolescents, 1999–2000. *Journal of the American Medical Association, 288,* 1728–1732.

Ogden, C., Troiano, R., Briefel, R., Kuczmarski, R., Flegal, K., & Johnson, C. (1997). Prevalence of overweight among preschool children in the United States, 1971 through 1994. *Pediatrics, 99*(4), e1.

Parsons, T., Power, C., & Manor, O. (2003). Infant feeding and obesity through the life-course. *Archives of Disease in Childhood, 88*(9), 793–794.

Rozin, P. (1991). Family resemblance in food and other domains: The family paradox and the role of parental congruence. *Appetite, 16,* 93–102.

Strauss, R., & Pollack, H. (2001). Epidemic increase in childhood overweight. *Journal of the American Medical Association, 286*(22), 2845–2848.

Whitaker, R., Wright, J., Pepe, M., Seidel, K., & Dietz, W. (1997). Predicting obesity in young adulthood from childhood and parental obesity. *New England Journal of Medicine, 337,* 869–873.

From *Zero to Three,* January 2005, pp. 13–19. Copyright © 2005 by National Center for Infants, Toddlers and Families. Reprinted by permission.

When Girls and Boys Play: What Research Tells Us

JEANETTA G. RILEY AND ROSE B. JONES

Research on play suggests that children of all ages benefit from engaging in play activities (Bergen, 2004). With the recent emphasis on standards and testing, however, many teachers have felt the increased pressure to spend time on structured learning events, leaving few moments of relaxation in a child's day (Chenfeld, 2006). Many elementary schools have even reduced or eliminated recess times in an effort to give children more time to work on academics (Clements, 2000). That is unfortunate, as findings from studies of play indicate that play helps children to develop social, language, and physical skills.

While beneficial for both, play often differs for girls and boys (see Gallas, 1998; Gurian & Stevens, 2005). This article reviews research related to the differences found between the genders as they play and the benefits that elementary children can gain from play. In addition, the authors include suggestions for educators regarding children's play at school.

Social Development

Girls and Boys Sharing Social Interactions during Play

Researchers have found differences in the way the genders socialize during play. In an early study examining gender and play, Lever (1978) found several differences in how 5th-grade girls and boys play. For example, boys played more competitive, rule-oriented, group games than did girls; girls interacted in smaller groups, had conversations, and walked and talked with friends more often than did boys. Lever concluded that the nature of boys' team games and their experiences with rule-dictated play: 1) allowed for the development of cooperation skills between peers with differing ideas, 2) afforded them opportunities to work independently to accomplish a common task, and 3) provided motivation to abide by established rules.

Other recent studies have found results similar to those of Lever (1978). A study of elementary students at recess conducted by Butcher (1999) indicated that boys more often participated in competitive games, and girls chose activities that allowed them to have conversations. Likewise, Lewis and Phillipsen (1998) found that elementary-age boys at recess played physically active group games with rules more often than did girls. However, in contrast to Lever's (1978) findings on groupings during recess, Lewis and Phillipsen (1998) noted that while girls tended to play in small groups, boys tended to play in groups of various sizes, from dyads to more than five children.

Also consistent with Lever's (1978) findings, a study of 4th-graders by Goodwin (2001) indicated that boys tended to form social structures, wherein the boys who were more skilled at the activity took the lead and directed the players. Boys with less skill were allowed to play but were not allowed a leadership role. In contrast, girls' leadership roles during games of jump rope did not depend on their ability to carry out the physical tasks of the game. Instead of one girl taking the lead, several girls directed the games; however, Goodwin (2001) found that the girls were more likely to exclude others from their play than were the boys.

Even very young children tend to be socially influenced by playing with same-sex peers. For example, Martin and Fabes' (2001) investigation of preschool and kindergarten children at play indicated that playing with same-gender peers affects play behaviors. Their research findings added to the evidence (e.g., Boyatzis, Mallis, & Leon, 1999; Thorne, 1993) that children often choose to play with same-sex peers. Additionally, Martin and Fabes found gender-typical behaviors for children who more often played with same-sex peers. For instance, the girls who most often played with other girls were generally less active during play and chose to play in areas close to adults. Boys who played with other boys more often engaged in play that was more aggressive and farther from adult supervision. This stereotypical play was found less often in children who tended to play with the opposite sex.

Not all students have positive social experiences during play activities. Some students may have difficulty developing the appropriate skills necessary for positive peer interactions. Children with inadequate social skills may tend to behave inappropriately during times of free play, such as recess (Blatchford, 1998). Rather than limit free play due to inappropriate behavior, however, these times can provide opportunities for conflict resolution interventions. In one study by Butcher (1999), the researchers trained college students to use conflict resolution strategies when interacting with 1st- through 6th-graders during recess times. The volunteers provided positive feedback, modeled appropriate social skills, and implemented strategies to increase cooperation among the children. As a result, when the numbers were analyzed, combining all grade levels, the means for the number of incidents of inappropriate targeted behaviors (i.e., violent behavior, verbal abuse, and inappropriate equipment use) declined during interventions. However, it is important to note that when the results were analyzed according to gender, significant differences were found in the reduction of targeted behaviors for boys only. No significant differences were found for girls' behavior. The researchers suggested that this lack of difference for the girls was due to the limited number of negative behaviors the girls initially exhibited (Butcher, 1999).

Overall Play and the Social Development of Children

By the time children reach school age, play typically becomes a social activity (Jarrett & Maxwell, 2000). As children play with others, they begin to learn what behaviors are expected and acceptable in their society. Playing with peers permits children to adjust to the expected norms (Fromberg, 1998).

Opportunities for free play with limited adult intervention provide time for children to explore which behaviors are accepted among their peers (Wortham, 2002). As younger children associate in play situations, they begin to realize that play ends if they do not negotiate behaviors and cooperate; therefore, play helps children learn to regulate their behaviors in order to continue playing together (Heidemann & Hewitt, 1992; Poole, Miller, & Church, 2004).

For older children, recess can be a time for learning about and adjusting to peer expectations. Pellegrini and Blatchford's (2002) findings suggest that recess play provides children with time to enter into social relationships early in the school year, which, in turn, helps them in social situations throughout the year. Pellegrini, Blatchford, Kato, and Baines (2004) also found that recess allowed opportunities for children to increase positive social experiences. For the 7- and 8-year-old participants in their study, basic games played at the beginning of the school year permitted the children time to get acquainted with peers, leading to more advanced play once the children became more familiar with each other. Additionally, Jarrett et al. (1998) speculated that children who move from one school to another find recess times helpful in adjusting and making new friends.

Language Development
Girls and Boys Expressing Language during Play

Research indicates that the types of games in which girls often engage may support language development differently than the types of games boys typically play. Blatchford, Baines, and

Pellegrini (2003) studied playground activities of children in England during the year the children turned 8 years old. The researchers found that girls held significantly more conversations and played significantly more verbal games than did boys. Goodwin (2002) also found that 4th- through 6th-grade girls spent most of their playtime talking with one another. Their games tended to require close proximity to one another, thus allowing for extended conversations. Conversely, some studies found that the games boys tended to choose often involved language usage that was more instruction-oriented, with boys verbally directing the play actions of one another (Boyle, Marshall, & Robeson, 2003; Goodwin, 2001).

Overall Play and Language Skill Development of Children

Play is a natural environment for children's language development (Perlmutter & Burrell, 1995). Children use language during their solitary play as well as in social play encounters (Piaget, 1962). Both expressive and receptive language skills are needed to plan, explain, and execute play activities. Language skills give children the ability to cooperate in creating and prolonging their play episodes (Van Hoorn, Monighan-Nourot, Scales, & Alward, 2003).

Developing language skills facilitates peer relationships. Piaget (1962) theorized that the talk of preschool-age children is egocentric (i.e., talk that is not for the sake of communicating with others). Very young children verbalize without a need for others to enter into the conversation; however, as older children begin to interact more often with adults and peers, the need to communicate arises. Egocentric speech gradually subsides and social speech takes over as children practice using language (Ginsburg & Opper, 1979).

Language in the context of play provides children with the ability to develop strategies for cooperation, engage in varied and complex play themes, and share perspectives about their world.

Language is a major factor in social play scenarios, such as sociodramatic play in which children create pretend play episodes and take on the roles of others. Language in the context of play provides children with the ability to develop strategies for cooperation, engage in varied and complex play themes, and share perspectives about their world (Van Hoorn et al., 2003). Children's language guides their play and provides the communication needed for the continuation of the play (Guddemi, 2000; Heidemann & Hewitt, 1992).

Language usage during play allows children to develop and test their verbal skills. Children experiment with language by telling jokes and riddles, reciting chants and poems, and making up words. As children use language during play, they create meaning for themselves concerning the nature of language and communication (Frost, 1992). Additionally, playing with language develops children's phonological awareness by allowing for experimentation with the sounds of words. Children learn that sounds can be manipulated as they rhyme words and create nonsense words (Johnson, Christie, & Wardle, 2005).

A more complicated form of play, games with rules, also requires children to expand their language skills. Once the egocentrism of earlier childhood diminishes, children can become more proficient at working together to negotiate the rules of games (Van Hoorn et al., 2003). Games with rules provide practice in cooperation, as well as opportunities to build language skills, as children create new games or discuss rules of known games.

Physical Development
Girls and Boys Engaging in Physical Activity during Play

Research indicates gender differences in physical activity during play. Studies have noted that boys, from infancy through adolescence, tend to participate in more physically active play than do girls (Campbell & Eaton, 1999; Frost, 1992; Lindsey & Colwell, 2003). For example, Lindsey and Colwell (2003) observed young children and found that boys playing with one other child engage in more physical play than girls playing with one other child. Additionally, a study by Sarkin, McKenzie, and Sallis (1997) compared gender differences in play levels of 5th-graders during physical education classes and recess. They found no significant differences between the boys' and the girls' activity levels during physical education classes. However, during recess times, boys more often played games requiring higher levels of physical activity than did girls. Girls played less strenuous games or held conversations as they walked around the playground. These results suggested that during times of unstructured activity, such as recess, boys tend to choose more active play than girls do.

Likewise, other researchers also concluded that the physical play of girls and boys often differs. Boys and girls tend to divide into gendered groups during outdoor play, and they often choose different types of activities (Thorne, 1993). Studies suggest that boys engage in play that involves more physical activity (Boyle, Marshall, & Robeson, 2003), more competition (Lever, 1978), and more space (Martin & Fabes, 2001) than do girls. Pellegrini and Smith (1993) suggested that boys tend to prefer playing outdoors, due to the need for open space to participate in their active games. One type of active play in which boys tend to engage in more frequently than girls is rough and tumble play (Martin & Fabes, 2001; Pellegrini, 1989; Thorne, 1993). Rough and tumble play involves such activities as grabbing and wrestling and may be a socially acceptable way for boys to physically demonstrate their feelings of friendship (Reed, 2000).

Overall Active Play and Physical Development in Children

The human body needs movement to stay healthy and well. Findings by the Centers for Disease Control and Prevention (2005) indicate that the incidence of childhood obesity is increasing. In today's world, many children spend most of their time in sedentary activities that do not enhance physical fitness. Active play encourages movement, thereby helping children's fitness. According to Huettig, Sanborn, DiMarco, Popejoy, and Rich (2004), young children need at least "thirty to sixty minutes of physical activity a day" (p. 54). Physical advantages that children gain from active play are increased motor control and flexibility (Brewer, 2001). Furthermore, with the added body control that develops as they play, children often become more competent in their skills and gain the self-confidence to play games with peers (Wortham, 2002).

Physical movement is necessary for the growth and development of the mind as well as the body. The brain needs movement in order to function properly.

Physical movement is necessary for the growth and development of the mind as well as the body. The brain needs movement in order to function properly (Gurian, 2001). Although indoor play encourages creativity and socialization, it provides only a limited amount of space for the type of physical movement children need each day. Time in outdoor play encourages physical activity, which, in turn, increases children's physical fitness. Consequently, outdoor recess periods provide the time and space for children to engage in the physically vigorous active play that is limited indoors (Sutterby & Frost, 2002).

Further Research Needs

Understanding more about how play benefits the social, language, and physical development of children can help teachers as they create learning environments; however, more research is needed to gain a clearer picture of how play enhances children's learning. For example, studies examining the influence of recess on classroom behaviors, such as concentration and amount of work produced, have yielded conflicting results (Jarrett et al, 1998; Pellegrini & Davis, 1993). Therefore, more work is necessary to determine how unstructured play correlates with behavior as well as academic achievement. Additionally, more research needs to be conducted about social interventions during play. Children who have been targeted as requiring assistance in developing positive social behaviors may have more difficulty during times of unstructured activity (Blatchford, 1998). Research to determine how to best assist these children, particularly during recess periods, is needed.

Finally, some researchers have included such variables as race and gender within the framework of their study of play; however, less often has the researcher's main purpose been to examine the educational implications based on the different ways girls and boys play. This aspect of play needs further examination if educators are to gain a better understanding of how to best structure learning environments for both genders.

Implications for Educators

Knowing the research about how children play and what they learn as they play can help educators and parents make sound decisions about how to provide appropriate play opportunities. To create learning environments in which children can thrive, adults must observe children's needs and try to accommodate those needs. The following are some suggestions for educators and parents.

- **Importance of Observations of Play Experiences:** Teachers can use playtimes to observe and assess children's social, emotional, physical, and cognitive development. Observing children's play can provide teachers with information about how to create appropriate learning environments. In some settings, recess may be a prime time to do this.

- **Girls' Play:** Girls have been found to engage in more sedentary, language-oriented activities during recess play than boys. Although this type of activity is important, girls also need to be encouraged to be physically active. While many boys may participate in physical movement through rough and tumble play, educators may need to help girls create activities in which they become more active. Providing areas and equipment for active play is the first step; additionally, ensuring that girls have the opportunity to engage in this type of physical play is necessary.

- **Boys' Play:** Rough and tumble play may provide an outlet for boys' physical, social, emotional, and verbal expression. Schools where all physical contact during play has been banned may need to consider how to reduce aggressive behaviors while allowing for this type of physical contact between boys. Recess monitors may need to be trained to recognize differences between acts of aggression and rough and tumble play. Additionally, the exploration of language that girls enjoy during play may need to be encouraged for boys by creating play environments that support language development. For example, teachers can lead boys in discussing their play activities.

- **Accommodations for Differences:** Children have various interests and styles of play; therefore, schools can provide a variety of play materials and equipment to accommodate the differences. Additionally, an assortment of resources can encourage children to expand and extend their play. Children with special needs should be considered in this process.

- **Parental Awareness:** Parents may be concerned that their young children are "only playing" at school. During Open House, at PTA meetings, and through newsletters, educators can make parents aware of growth and development that takes place as children play, both in classrooms and at recess. It is necessary to make adults aware that natural outdoor play environments are important for girls and boys and that these areas do not always require equipment. Rustic, wooded settings can provide children with many opportunities for creative movement, imaginative growth, and cognitive learning as they participate in such activities as nature walks with adult supervision.

- **Cooperative Activities:** Although research indicates that girls tend to enjoy cooperative activities while boys pursue competitive games, children need to learn about both cooperation and competition. Teachers can incorporate each type of activity into classroom lessons.

Conclusion

While some adults dismiss play as mere fun, much growth and development occurs during playtimes. As children play, they gain knowledge of the world and an understanding of their place in it. Although play may differ generally for girls and boys, it offers both genders opportunities to test and refine their developing social, language, and physical skills, which leads not only to academic achievement but also to a lifetime of success. Thus, play does benefit children.

References

Bergen, D. (2004). *ACEI speaks: Play's role in brain development* [Brochure]. Olney, MD: Association for Childhood Education International.

Blatchford, P. (1998). The state of play in schools. *Child Psychology and Psychiatry Review,* 3(2), 58–67.

Blatchford, P., Baines, E., & Pellegrini, A. (2003). The social context of school playground games: Sex and ethnic differences, and changes over time after entry to junior high school. *British Journal of Developmental Psychology,* 21(4), 481–505.

Boyatzis, C. J., Mallis, M., & Leon, I. (1999). Effects of game type on children's gender-based peer preferences: A naturalistic observational study. *Sex Roles: A Journal of Research,* 40(1–2), 93–105.

Boyle, D. E., Marshall, N. L., & Robeson, W. W. (2003). Gender at play: Fourth-grade girls and boys on the playground. *American Behavioral Scientist,* 46(10), 1326–1345.

Brewer, J. A. (2001). *Introduction to early childhood education: Preschool through primary grades* (4th ed.). Boston: Allyn and Bacon.

Butcher, D. A. (1999). Enhancing social skills through school social work interventions during recess: Gender differences. *Social Work in Education,* 21(4), 249–262.

Campbell, D. W., & Eaton, W. O. (1999). Sex differences in the activity level of infants. *Infant and Child Development,* 8(1), 1–17.

Centers for Disease Control and Prevention. (2005). *Preventing chronic diseases through good nutrition and physical activity.* Retrieved July 18, 2006, from www.cdc.gov/nccdphp/publications/factsheets/Prevention/obesity.htm

Chenfeld, M. B. (2006). Handcuff me, too! *Phi Delta Kappan,* 87(10), 745–747.

Clements, R. L. (Ed.). (2000). *Elementary school recess: Selected readings, games, and activities for teachers and parents.* Boston: American Press.

Fromberg, D. P. (1998). Play issues in early childhood education. In C. Seefeldt & A. Galper (Eds.), *Continuing issues in early childhood education* (2nd ed.)(pp. 190–212). UpperSaddle River, NJ: Merrill Prentice-Hall.

Frost, J. L. (1992). *Play and playscapes.* Albany, NY: Delmar.

Gallas, K. (1998). *Sometimes I can be anything: Power, gender, and identity in a primary classroom.* New York: Teachers College Press.

Ginsburg, H., & Opper, S. (1979). *Piaget's theory of intellectual development* (2nd ed.). Englewood Cliffs, NJ: Prentice-Hall.

Goodwin, M. H. (2001). Organizing participation in cross-sex jump rope: Situating gender differences within longitudinal studies of activities. *Research on Language & Social Interaction,* 34(1), 75–106.

Goodwin, M. H. (2002). Exclusion in girls' peer groups: Ethnographic analysis of language practices on the playground. *Human Development,* 45(6), 392–415.

Guddemi, M. P. (2000). Recess: A time to learn, a time to grow. In R. L. Clements (Ed.), *Elementary school recess: Selected readings, games, and activities for teachers and parents* (pp. 2–8). Boston: American Press.

Gurian, M. (2001). *Boys and girls learn differently! A guide for teachers and parents.* San Francisco: Jossey-Bass.

Gurian, M., & Stevens, K. (2005). *The minds of boys: Saving our sons from falling behind in school and life.* San Francisco: Jossey-Bass.

Heidemann, S., & Hewitt, D. (1992). *Pathways to play: Developing play skills in young children.* St. Paul, MN: Redleaf Press.

Huettig, C. I., Sanborn, C. R, DiMarco, N., Popejoy, A., & Rich, S. (2004). The O generation: Our youngest children are at risk for obesity. *Young Children,* 59(2), 50–55.

Jarrett, O. S., & Maxwell, D. M. (2000). What research says about the need for recess. In R. L. Clements (Ed.), *Elementary school recess: Selected readings, games, and activities for teachers and parents* (pp. 12–20). Boston: American Press.

Jarrett, O. S., Maxwell, D. M., Dickerson, C., Hoge, P., Davies, G., & Yetley, A. (1998). Impact of recess on classroom behavior: Group effects and individual differences. *The Journal of Educational Research,* 92(2), 121–126.

Johnson, J. E., Christie, J. R, & Wardle, F. (2005). *Play, development, and early education.* Boston: Pearson Education.

Lever, J. (1978). Sex differences in the complexity of children's play and games. *American Sociological Review,* 43(4), 471–483.

Lewis, T. E., & Phillipsen, L. C. (1998). Interactions on an elementary school playground: Variations by age, gender, race, group size, and playground area. *Child Study Journal,* 2S(4), 309–320.

Lindsey, E. W., & Colwell, M. J. (2003). Preschoolers' emotional competence links to pretend and physical play. *Child Study Journal,* 33(1), 39–52.

Martin, C. L., & Fabes, R. A. (2001). The stability and consequences of young children's same-sex peer interactions. *Developmental Psychology,* 37(3), 431–446.

Pellegrini, A. D. (1989). Elementary school children's rough-and-tumble play. *Early Childhood Research Quarterly,* 4(2), 245–260.

Pellegrini, A. D., & Blatchford, P. (2002). The developmental and educational significance of recess in schools. *Early Report,* 29(1). Retrieved March 16, 2004, from www.education.umn.edu/ceed/publications/earlyreport/spring02.htm.

Pellegrini, A. D., Blatchford, P., Kato, K., & Baines, E. (2004). A short-term longitudinal study of children's playground games in primary school: Implications for adjustment to school and social adjustment in the USA and the UK. *Social/ Development,* 13(1), 107–123.

Pellegrini, A. D., & Davis, P. (1993). Relations between children's playground and classroom behaviour. *British Journal of Educational Psychology,* 63(1), 88–95.

Pellegrini, A. D., & Smith, P. K. (1993). School recess: Implications for education and development. *Review of Educational Research,* 63(1), 51–67.

Perlmutter, J. C, & Burrell, L. (1995). Learning through 'play' as well as 'work' in the primary grades. *Young Children,* 50(5), 14–21.

Piaget, J. (1962). *Play, dreams, and imitation in childhood* (G. Gattegno & F. M. Hodgson, Trans.). New York: W.W. Norton & Company.

Poole, C., Miller, S., & Church, E. B. (2004). Working through that "It's Mine" feeling. *Early Childhood Today,* 18(5), 28–32.

Reed, T. (2000). Rough and tumble play during recess: Pathways to successful social development. In R. L. Clements (Ed.), *Elementary school recess: Selected readings, games, and activities for teachers and parents* (pp. 45–48). Boston: American Press.

Sarkin, J. S., McKenzie, T. L., & Sallis, J. F. (1997). Gender differences in physical activity during fifth-grade physical education and recess periods. *Journal of Teaching in Physical Education,* 17(1), 99–106.

Sutterby, J. S., & Frost, J. L. (2002). Making playgrounds fit for children and children fit on playgrounds. *Young Children,* 57(3), 36–41.

Thorne, B. (1993). *Gender play: Girls and boys in school.* New Brunswick, NJ: Rutgers University Press.

Van Hoorn, J., Monighan-Nourot, P., Scales, B., & Alward, K. R. (2003). *Play at the center of the curriculum* (3rd ed.). Upper Saddle River, NJ: Merrill Prentice-Hall.

Wortham, S. C. (2002). *Early childhood curriculum: Developmental bases for learning and teaching* (3rd ed.). Upper Saddle River, NJ: Merrill PrenticeHall.

Jeanetta G. Riley is Assistant Professor, Department of Early Childhood and Elementary Education, Murray State University. **Rose B. Jones** is Assistant Professor of Early Childhood Education/Literacy, The University of Southern Mississippi.

From *Childhood Education,* Fall 2007, pp. 38–43. Copyright © 2007 by the Association for Childhood Education International. Reprinted by permission of Jeanetta G. Riley and Rose B. Jones and the Association for Childhood Education International, 17904 Georgia Avenue, Suite 215, Olney, MD 20832.

UNIT 5
Educational Practices

Unit Selections

21. **What Research Says about . . . Grade Retention,** Jane L. David
22. **Back to Basics: Play in Early Childhood,** Jill Englebright Fox
23. **Scripted Curriculum: Is It a Prescription for Success?,** Anita Ede
24. **Using Brain-Based Teaching Strategies to Create Supportive Early Childhood Environments That Address Learning Standards,** Pam Schiller and Clarissa A. Willis
25. **Successful Transition to Kindergarten: The Role of Teachers and Parents,** Pam Deyell-Gingold
26. *Rethinking* **Early Childhood Practices,** Francis Wardle
27. **The Looping Classroom: Benefits for Children, Families, and Teachers,** Mary M. Hitz, Mary Catherine Somers, and Christee L. Jenlink

Key Points to Consider

- What is causing the pressure to push the curriculum down from the primary grades into preschool? How can teachers of young children resist that pressure?

- Can you think of a few brain-based activities that teachers could incorporate into their daily plans?

- What caused the large increase in scripted curriculum programs on the market?

- Make a brief list of the components of developmentally appropriate practice that you believe are vital.

- How can teachers and parents assist young children as they move from preschool to kindergarten?

- What are some of the best design features of a preschool classroom where you have worked or observed?

- Why is the ability to make choices a crucial skill to learn in the early years?

Student Web Site
www.mhcls.com

Internet References

Association for Childhood Education International (ACEI)
http://www.acei.org/
Early Childhood Education Online
http://www.umaine.edu/eceol/
Reggio Emilia
http://www.ericdigests.org/2001-3/reggio.htm

Each spring, the issue of grade retention creeps into the vocabulary of teachers and parents as educators struggle to best address the needs of students who did not meet the standards or content expectations for that particular year. It is a challenge for teachers, parents, and the children who face another year in the same grade, which, research has consistently found is not the best approach. Many countries do not retain students at all, while the United States retains over two million children each year. Is spending another year in the same grade the solution or are there other ways educators can support struggling learners? Support for families, differentiated instruction, and outside services are successful strategies for children who do not achieve at the same level as their peers.

I am distressed with the increasing push to have young children do things at an earlier and earlier age as the life expectancy keeps increasing. Children born today have an excellent chance of living into their 90s and beyond. There is no great need to rush and acquire skills that can easily be learned when the child is a little older at the expense of valuable lifelong lessons that are best learned when they are young. How to get along with others, make choices, negotiate, develop a sense of compassion, and communicating needs are all skills that require introduction and practice during the preschool years. "Back to Basics: Play in Early Childhood" by Jill Englebright Fox focuses on the importance of developmentally appropriate play experiences for young children, and not on the basics of core academic skills as many would think. The basics to which Fox refers are a solid foundation in understanding how things work, many opportunities to explore and manipulate materials, and opportunities for creative expression. How all this can be accomplished in the new world of standards is the balancing act that many teachers now do.

The passage of the No Child Left Behind legislation has many implications for early childhood care and educational practices. As academic assessment and accountability measures are implemented, many publishers have rushed to develop scripted curriculum for teachers to use. Most of these programs are centered on teaching reading. In "Scripted Curriculum: Is It a Prescription for Success?," Anita Ede examines the politics behind the development of scripted curriculum and both positive and negative research findings.

© Getty Images

Teachers knowledgeable about best practices for brain-based learning can help their students succeed. In "Using Brain-Based Teaching Strategies to Create Supportive Early Childhood Environments That Address Learning Standards," Pam Schiller and Clarissa A. Willis share strategies for teachers to infuse inquiry-based learning experiences.

We now know teaching IS rocket science and does require committed individuals who are well prepared to deal with a variety of development levels and needs, as appropriate, intentional learning experiences are planned for all children. Good teaching does make a difference and children deserve no less than adults who truly are passionate about being with young children on a daily basis. Teaching cannot be viewed as a great profession for someone who wants their summers off. Teachers well prepared to provide exemplary learning experiences for their children can make a real difference in the lives of their students.

In "Successful Transition to Kindergarten: The Role of Teachers and Parents," the author provides ways in which teachers and parents can help young children make the major transition to kindergarten. For some children, kindergarten is their first experience with formal schooling. For many others, it means a different school, classroom, and teacher than they had during their preschool years. With this new experience comes many different expectations.

What Research Says about . . . Grade Retention

In this new column, Jane L. David shares with readers what research says about the effectiveness of current education reforms.

In the coming months, David will examine the research behind such approaches as incentives to attract teachers to high-poverty schools and small learning communities. In framing the issues and drawing conclusions, she will draw on articles from peer-reviewed journals and reports from research institutions as well as her own 35 years of experience studying schools and districts.

We welcome readers' comments at edleadership@ascd.org.

JANE L. DAVID

Today's expectation that all students will meet high standards has contributed to a backlash against "social promotion." In this environment, grade retention has been making a comeback.

What's the Idea?

Educators and policymakers have debated for decades whether struggling students benefit more from repeating a grade or from moving ahead with their same-age peers. The argument for retention is that students who have not met grade-level criteria will fall further and further behind as they move through the grades. A failing 2nd grader, retention advocates argue, would be better served by repeating 2nd grade than by moving on to 3rd grade. Surely a student who could not succeed in 2nd grade will have an even harder time succeeding in 3rd grade.

What's the Reality?

School systems cannot hold back every student who falls behind; too many would pile up in the lower grades. Moreover, it is expensive to add a year of schooling for a substantial number of students. Therefore, in practice, schools set passing criteria at a level that ensures that most students proceed through the grades at the expected rate.

Although solid statistics are hard to come by, estimates of the number of students retained at least once in their school career range from 10 to 20 percent. Black students are more than twice as likely to be held back as white students, and boys twice as likely as girls (National Center for Education Statistics, 2006).

Estimates of the number of students retained at least once in their school career range from 10 to 20 percent.

In the past, teacher judgment played a larger role in decisions about individual students. More recently, in the context of high-stakes testing, states and urban districts have begun formalizing and tightening requirements for promotion, often using a single test score. Drawing such a line in the sand aims to limit teacher discretion to promote students who are struggling academically; it also aims to motivate students to work harder to avoid retention. Policymakers believe that stricter requirements for promotion will increase the proportion of students likely to meet standards at higher grade levels.

What's the Research?

Published research on retention is vast. Hundreds of studies have been carried out during the last century, most focused on the elementary grades. As with any large body of research, the studies ask different questions, look at different consequences, and are fraught with methodological problems. It's tricky in most cases to determine whether the students in the study would have fared better if they had been promoted instead of retained.

Jackson (1975) reviewed 44 studies that met a minimal set of methodological criteria. Finding few with significant results or even compelling patterns, he concluded that the evidence was insufficient to support the claim that grade retention is more beneficial than grade promotion. About 10 years later, Holmes and Matthews (1984) reviewed an additional 44 studies that all included some type of comparison group of students. These researchers concluded that promoted students had higher academic achievement, better personal adjustment, and more positive attitudes toward school than retained students did.

Moving ahead another 17 years, Jimerson (2001) summarized the historical research and added a carefully culled set of studies conducted between 1990 and 1999, all of which included comparison groups of promoted students. Most of the comparisons showed no significant differences between promoted and retained students on measures of achievement or personal and social adjustment. In those studies that did show a difference, the results favored the promoted students, especially on measures of achievement.

Recent studies have investigated retention in the context of state and district policies to require students to achieve a certain score for promotion. For example, Roderick and Nagaoka (2005) studied the effects of the Chicago Public Schools policy that bases promotion in grades 3, 6, and 8 on standardized test scores. Using comparison groups of students who just missed the promotion cutoff, these researchers found that 3rd graders struggled during the repeated year, had higher rates of special education placement, and two years later showed no advantage over those who had been promoted. Retained 6th graders had lower achievement growth than similar students who were not retained.

Retention can increase the likelihood that a student will drop out of school. Students who drop out are five times more likely to have been retained than those who graduate (National Center for Education Statistics, 2006). Using data from Chicago, Jacob and Lefgren (2007) concluded that students retained in 8th grade were more likely to drop out than their peers, a finding that was not true for retained 6th graders. They speculated that the 6th graders had more opportunities to catch up.

Studies with the strongest research methods compare students who were retained with similar students who were not retained. They ask whether repeating a grade makes a difference in achievement as well as personal and social adjustment over the short run and the long run. Although individual studies can be cited to support any conclusion, overall the preponderance of evidence argues that students who repeat a grade are no better off, and are sometimes worse off, than if they had been promoted with their classmates.

A major weakness in the research on retention is documenting the educational experiences of students who are retained. Roderick & Nagaoka (2005) argue that retention under high-stakes testing presumes the problem lies with the student, not with the school. If the goal of retention is to provide an opportunity for students to catch up, the quality and appropriateness of their academic experiences is likely to be the determining factor. After all, why should repeating the same experience produce a different result?

What's One to Do?

For most students struggling to keep up, retention is not a satisfactory solution. Nor is promotion. Juxtaposing the two as if these are the only options casts the debate in the wrong terms.

The challenge is figuring out what it takes to help failing students catch up. Understanding why a particular student has fallen behind points to the best course of action.

> **Juxtaposing retention and promotion as if these are the only options casts the debate in the wrong terms.**

For many students, especially those who start school far behind their peers, intensive intervention, even prior to kindergarten, may be the best path to success. For students who are frequently absent, understanding and addressing the reasons for their absences might be the solution.

Retention usually duplicates an entire year of schooling. Other options—such as summer school, before-school and after-school programs, or extra help during the school day—could provide equivalent extra time in more instructionally effective ways. Without early diagnosis and targeted intervention, struggling students are unlikely to catch up whether they are promoted or retained.

References

Holmes, C. T., & Matthews, K. M. (1984). The effects of nonpromotion on elementary and junior high school pupils: A meta-analysis. *Review of Educational Research, 54*(2), 225–236.

Jackson, G. B. (1975). The research evidence on the effects of grade retention. *Review of Educational Research, 45*(4), 613–635.

Jacob, B., & Lefgren, L. (2007). *The effect of grade retention on high school completion* (Working Paper No. 13514). Cambridge, MA: National Bureau of Economic Research. Available: www.nber.org/papers/w13514.

Jimerson, S. R. (2001). Meta-analysis of grade retention research: Implications for practice in the 21st century. *School Psychology Review, 30*(3), 420–437.

National Center for Education Statistics. (2006). *The condition of education: Grade retention* [Online article]. Washington, DC: Author. Available: http://nces.ed.gov/programs/coe/2006/section3/indicator25.asp.

Roderick, M., & Nagaoka, J. (2005). Retention under Chicago's high-stakes testing program: Helpful, harmful, or harmless? *Educational Evaluation and Policy Analysis, 27*(4), 309–340.

JANE L. DAVID is Director of the Bay Area Research Group, Palo Alto, California; jld@bayarearesearch.org. She is the author, with Larry Cuban, of *Cutting Through the Hype: A Taxpayer's Guide to School Reform* (Education Week Press, 2006).

Back to Basics
Play in Early Childhood

Jill Englebright Fox, PhD

Kyle plays with blocks and builds a castle. Tony and Victoria play fire station and pretend to be firefighters. Kenzo and Carl play catch with a ball. Children playact with playmates in the playhouse. Playgroups on the playground choose players to play ball. As an early childhood professional, you probably use the word "play" a hundred times per day.

Research indicates that children learn best in an environment which allows them to explore, discover, and play. Play is an important part of a developmentally appropriate child care program. It is also closely tied to the development of cognitive, socio-emotional, and physical behaviors. But what exactly does it mean to play and why is play so important for young children?

What Is Play?

Although it is simple to compile a list of play activities, it is much more difficult to define play. Scales, et al., (1991) called play "that absorbing activity in which healthy young children participate with enthusiasm and abandon" (p. 15). Csikszentmihalyi (1981) described play as "a subset of life . . . an arrangement in which one can practice behavior without dreading its consequences" (p. 14). Garvey (1977) gave a useful description of play for teachers when she defined play as an activity which is: 1) positively valued by the player; 2) self-motivated; 3) freely chosen; 4) engaging; and 5) which "has certain systematic relations to what is not play" (p. 5). These characteristics are important for teachers to remember because imposing adult values, requirements, or motivations on children's activities may change the very nature of play.

According to *Webster's Desk Dictionary of the English Language,* the word play has 34 different meanings. In terms of young children and play, the following definitions from Webster's are useful:

- light, brisk, or changing movement (e.g., to pretend you're a butterfly)
- to act or imitate the part of a person or character (e.g., to play house)
- to employ a piece of equipment (e.g., to play blocks)
- exercise for amusement or recreation (e.g., to play tag)
- fun or jest, as opposed to seriousness (e.g., to play peek-a-boo or sing a silly song)
- the action of a game (e.g., to play duck-duck-goose)

Why Is Play Important?

According to Fromberg and Gullo (1992), play enhances language development, social competence, creativity, imagination, and thinking skills. Frost (1992) concurred, stating that "play is the chief vehicle for the development of imagination and intelligence, language, social skills, and perceptual-motor abilities in infants and young children" (p. 48).

Garvey (1977) states that play is most common during childhood when children's knowledge of self, comprehension of verbal and non-verbal communication, and understanding of the physical and social worlds are expanding dramatically.

Fromberg (1990) claims that play is the "ultimate integrator of human experience" (p. 223). This means that when children play, they draw upon their past experiences—things they have done, seen others do, read about, or seen on television—and they use these experiences to build games, play scenarios, and engage in activities.

Children use fine and gross motor skills in their play. They react to each other socially. They think about what they are doing or going to do. They use language to talk to each other or to themselves and they very often respond emotionally to the play activity. The integration of these different types of behaviors is key to the cognitive development of young children. According to Rogers and Sawyer (1988), "until at least the age of nine, children's cognitive structures function best in this unified mode" (p. 58). Because children's play draws upon all of these behaviors, it is a very effective vehicle for learning.

Play and Cognitive Development

The relationship between play and cognitive development is described differently in the two theories of cognitive development which dominate early childhood education—Piaget's and Vygotsky's.

Piaget (1962) defined play as assimilation, or the child's efforts to make environmental stimuli match his or her own concepts. Piagetian theory holds that play, in and of itself, does not necessarily result in the formation of new cognitive structures. Piaget claimed that play was just for pleasure, and while it allowed children to practice things they had previously learned, it did not necessarily result in the learning of new things. In other words, play reflects what the child has already learned but does not necessarily teach the child anything new. In this view, play is seen as a "process reflective of emerging symbolic development, but contributing little to it" (Johnsen & Christie, 1986, p. 51).

In contrast, Vygotskian theory states that play actually facilitates cognitive development. Children not only practice what they already know, they also learn new things. In discussing Vygotsky's theory, Vandenberg (1986) remarks that "play not so much reflects thought (as Piaget suggests) as it creates thought" (p. 21).

Observations of children at play yield examples to support both Piagetian and Vygotskian theories of play. A child who puts on a raincoat and a firefighter's hat and rushes to rescue his teddy bear from the pretend flames in his playhouse is practicing what he has previously learned about firefighters. This supports Piaget's theory. On the other hand, a child in the block center who announces to his teacher, "Look! When I put these two square blocks together, I get a rectangle!" has constructed new knowledge through her play. This supports Vygotsky's theory.

Whether children are practicing what they have learned in other settings or are constructing new knowledge, it is clear that play has a valuable role in the early childhood classroom.

Play—Indoors and Out

Early childhood teachers have long recognized the value of play in programs for young children. Unfortunately, teachers often fail to take advantage of the opportunities play provides for observing children's development and learning. Through such observations teachers can learn about children's social interactions, cognitive and language abilities, motor skills, and emotional development.

Frost (1992) recommends that observing children at play be a daily responsibility for early childhood professionals. Regular observations provide teachers with assessment information for identifying children with special needs, planning future play experiences, evaluating play materials, determining areas of strength and weakness for individual children, planning curriculum for individual children, reporting to parents, and checking on a child's on-going progress. The increased use of authentic assessment strategies is making observations of children's play more commonplace in early childhood classrooms.

Hymes (1981) recommends that children have two classrooms—one indoors and one outdoors. The outdoor play environment should be used as an extension of the indoor classroom. It should be a learning environment as carefully planned as the indoor activity centers and should encourage motor and social skills as well as help children refine existing cognitive structures and construct new ones. Used in this way, the outdoor play environment provides a basis for observational assessment in all areas of development.

Fox (1993) researched the practicality of observing young children's cognitive development during outdoor play. Her observations of four- and five-year-old children during outdoor play found examples of addition and subtraction, shape identification, patterning, one-to-one correspondence, number sense, sequencing of events, use of ordinal numbers, knowledge of prepositions, and identification of final and initial consonants. Fox's outdoor observations also found multiple examples of problem-solving, creative thinking, social competence, language use, and gross and fine motor skills. Although outdoor observations do not replace classroom assessment, they can provide valuable information for teachers of young children. As Fox stated, "These observations can be performed unobtrusively, without intruding upon the children's activities and without placing children in a stressful testing situation" (p. 131).

Parten's Five Types of Play

Play for young children assumes many different forms. Mildred Parten (1932) was one of the early researchers studying children at play. She focused on the social interactions between children during play activities. Parten's categories of play are not hierarchical. Depending on the circumstances, children may engage in any of the different types of play. Parten does note, however, that in her research with two- to five-year-olds, "participation in the most social types of groups occurs most frequently among the older children" (p. 259).

Extra playtime allows children to become involved in more complex and productive play activities.

- **Onlooker behavior**—Playing passively by watching or conversing with other children engaged in play activities.
- **Solitary independent**—Playing by oneself.
- **Parallel**—Playing, even in the middle of a group, while remaining engrossed in one's own activity. Children playing parallel to each other sometimes use each other's toys, but always maintain their independence.
- **Associative**—When children share materials and talk to each other, but do not coordinate play objectives or interests.
- **Cooperative**—When children organize themselves into roles with specific goals in mind (e.g., to assign the roles of doctor, nurse, and patient and play hospital).

How Much Should Children Play?

Indoors and outdoors, children need large blocks of time for play. According to Christie and Wardle (1992), short play periods may require children to abandon their group dramatizations or constructive play just when they begin to get involved. When this happens a number of times, children may give up on more sophisticated forms of play and settle for less advanced forms that can be completed in short periods of time. Shorter play periods reduce both the amount and the maturity of children's play, and many important benefits of play, such as persistence, negotiation, problem solving, planning, and cooperation are lost. Large blocks of time (30 to 60 minutes, or longer) should be scheduled for indoor and outdoor play periods. Christie and Wardle remind teachers that extra playtime does not result in children becoming bored. Instead, it prompts children to become involved in more complex, more productive play activities.

The Teacher's Role

The early childhood teacher is the facilitator of play in the classroom. The teacher facilitates play by providing appropriate indoor and outdoor play environments. Safety is, of course, the primary concern. Age and developmental levels must be carefully considered in the design and selection of materials. Guidelines for selecting safe and appropriate equipment for outdoor play environments are available through the U.S. Consumer Product Safety Commission's Handbook for Public Playground Safety and the Playground Safety Manual by Jambor and Palmer (1991). Similar guidelines are also available for indoor settings (Torelli & Durrett, 1996; Caples, 1996; Ard & Pitts, 1990). Once appropriate environments and materials are in place, regular safety checks and maintenance are needed to ensure that the equipment is sound and safe for continued play.

Teachers also facilitate play by working with children to develop rules for safe indoor and outdoor play. Discussion about the appropriate use of materials, the safe number of participants on each piece of equipment, taking turns, sharing, and cleaning up provides the children with information to begin their play activities. These discussions need to be ongoing because some children may need frequent reminders about rules and because new situations may arise (e.g., new equipment).

By providing play materials related to thematic instruction, early childhood teachers can establish links between the children's indoor and outdoor play and their program's curriculum. Thematic props for dramatic play can be placed in the dramatic play center or stored in prop boxes and taken outside to extend the dramatic play to a new setting. An art center in the outdoor play environment may encourage children to explore the possibilities of using leaves, twigs, pebbles, and sand in their three-dimensional art productions. Painting easels and water tables may also be moved outside periodically for children's use during outdoor play periods. Finally, a collection of books stored in a wagon to be taken outside during play time may offer some children a needed alternative to more active play.

As facilitators of children's play, teachers should closely observe children during play periods not only for assessment purposes, as stated earlier, but also to facilitate appropriate social interactions and motor behaviors. It is important that children be the decision-makers during play, choosing what and where to play, choosing roles for each player, and choosing how play will proceed. Occasionally, however, some children will need adult assistance in joining a play group, modifying behavior, or negotiating a disagreement. Careful observation will help the teacher to decide when to offer assistance and what form that assistance should take.

Conclusion

Although play is a difficult concept to define, it is very easy to recognize. Children actively involved in play may be engaged in a variety of activities, independently, with a partner, or in a group. Because play is closely tied to the cognitive, socio-emotional, and motor development of young children, it is an important part of developmentally appropriate early childhood programs.

JILL ENGLEBRIGHT FOX, PhD, is an assistant professor of early childhood education at Virginia Commonwealth University. She taught kindergarten and first grade in the Texas public schools for eight years, and is currently an active member of the International Play Association-USA. Her research interests focus on play and aesthetic development in young children, and professional development schools.

Scripted Curriculum
Is It a Prescription for Success?

ANITA EDE

I magine walking down the halls of your school and hearing the same sentences read, the same questions asked, and the same teacher comments coming from each classroom. "Impossible," you say to yourself. "This could not possibly be happening." But it is. This scenario is becoming more and more commonplace throughout schools in the United States as scripted curriculum materials are implemented more widely. In 2001, one in every eight schools in California used Open Court, a scripted reading program (Posnick-Goodwin, 2002). Nationwide, 1,551 elementary schools in 48 states use Success for All, another scripted reading program (Dudley-Marling & Murphy, 2001). Scripted curriculum materials are instructional materials that have been commercially prepared and require the teacher to read from a script while delivering the lesson (Moustafa & Land, 2002). Scripted materials reflect a focus on explicit, direct, systematic skills instruction and are touted as a method to boost sagging standardized test scores and narrow the achievement gap between children growing up in poverty and those who are more affluent (Coles, 2002).

Politics and the Scripted Curriculum

The goal of the education system in the United States has long been to provide an effective public education for all children in order that they may realize their full potential. Precisely how this is to be achieved, however, is the subject of a great deal of debate.

In April 1999, the National Reading Panel (NRP), based on its review of 100,000 studies of how children learn to read, provided a guide for scientifically based reading instruction (cited in Coles, 2002). Those numbers are a little misleading, however. The NRP began by looking at 100,000 studies on reading that had been conducted since 1966. It then established criteria that limited the studies to those relating to instructional material that the panel decided, ahead of time, represented key areas of good reading instruction. The field was further narrowed to studies that had been conducted "scientifically"; that is, using only quantitative data. When all was said and done,

the 100,000 studies had been pruned to 52 studies of phonemic awareness, 38 studies of phonics, 14 studies of reading fluency, and 203 studies related to comprehension instruction (Coles, 2002). After examination of the aforementioned 307 studies, the NRP concluded that the most effective course of reading instruction included explicit and systematic instruction in phonemic awareness and phonics (Metcalf, 2002)—that is, the scripted curriculum.

> **It is important for teachers to understand the politics of the scripted curriculum, as well as who profits, its basic structure, current research as to its effectiveness, and concerns about its effect on students as well as teachers.**

One week after becoming president, George W. Bush sent Congress an education reform bill that referred to the NRP's research findings; he promised to eliminate reading inequalities and ensure that all children would read at grade level by the time they reached the 3rd grade. This would be achieved through the use of scientifically based reading instruction. These education reforms became law when the No Child Left Behind Act (NCLB) was passed in 2002.

The Reading First initiative, the portion of NCLB that applies to reading instruction, provides funding to schools on the condition that they adopt "scientifically based" reading programs. The "scientifically based" (quantitative) research by the NRP that resulted in the funding for "scientifically based" reading programs by Reading First is the basis for the scripted reading curriculum. Programs qualifying as scientifically based are those that incorporate explicit and systematic instruction in phonemic awareness, phonics, fluency, vocabulary, and comprehension. Two such highly scripted and very profitable curriculum programs are Open Court and Success for All (SFA).

Profits and the Scripted Curriculum

The Reading First initiative provides an enormous amount of taxpayer dollars to states in the form of grants. States then dispense the money to individual school districts in the form of subgrants. For example, Oklahoma received a multi-year Reading First grant in 2003 that provided $12.5 million to schools implementing scientifically based reading programs (The National Right to Read Foundation, 2003) in its first year. Over the next six years, Oklahoma will receive a total of $82 million to further implement these programs. Taking into account that 49 other states will also receive federal funds to implement scientifically based reading programs, it stands to reason that the companies publishing these programs will make a resounding profit. In the third quarter of 2003, SRA/McGraw-Hill, which publishes Open Court, one of the most frequently used scripted reading programs, posted an increased net income of $14.1 million (5.1 percent) over the same period in the previous year (McGraw-Hill Newswire, 2003). Success for All (SFA), another highly scripted reading curriculum, published by a nonprofit foundation, has flourished into a $45 million-a-year business (Mathews, 2000).

Scripted curriculum materials are a costly solution for school districts that are having difficulty raising their students' academic achievement.

Socioeconomics and the Scripted Curriculum

Students in high poverty areas have a much higher likelihood of being taught in schools using a scripted curriculum than those living in more affluent school districts. Schools in which more than 50 percent of all students are on free or reduced-price lunches qualify for Title I funds from the federal government. Currently, Title I regulations specify that "all participating schools must use program funds to implement a comprehensive school reform program that employs proven methods and strategies based on scientifically based research" (Comprehensive School Reform Program, n.d., p. 2). In essence, these regulations prescribe the use of scripted curriculum materials because these are the only ones that qualify as being scientifically based. Schools that do not receive Title I funds (i.e., those located, in general, in more affluent areas) are free to spend their district's funds on the curriculum of their choice.

The Scripted Curriculum

As noted, two of the most widely used scripted reading curriculum programs are Open Court and Success for All. Both deliver explicit, systematic instruction by way of a script the teacher is required to follow in the areas of phonemic awareness, phonics, fluency, vocabulary, and comprehension. Open Court and SFA share certain characteristics. Both publishers advocate grouping students by reading level during the reading portion of the lesson. Both programs are available in English as well as Spanish and are available for a wide range of age and grade levels. Open Court is available for students ranging from Pre-K to 6th grade and SFA is available for students ranging from Pre-K to 8th grade.

Depending on the teacher's familiarity with either the Open Court or SFA material and the students' abilities, up to three hours of class time every day may be needed to cover the lesson script, thus leading to a significant narrowing of the curriculum. In a survey conducted in the fall of 2003 by the Council for Basic Education, principals reported that their schools currently spent 37 percent less time teaching civics and 35 percent less time teaching geography than they had previously (Perkins-Cough, 2004). Other principals surveyed for this study reported that their schools spent 29 percent less time teaching languages and 36 percent less time teaching the arts than they had in the past (Perkins-Cough, 2004). Given that many schools have already curtailed children's exposure to geography, civics, languages, and art, one must question if these subjects would be completely eliminated following the implementation of a scripted curriculum.

The diverse ethnic and cultural makeup of today's classrooms makes it unlikely that one single curriculum will meet the needs and interests of all students.

Reading Achievement and the Scripted Curriculum
Positive Research Findings

One study in an urban Title I school (no geographic information was given) compared the word recognition, reading comprehension, vocabulary growth, and spelling achievement of three groups of 1st- and 2nd-grade students. They were taught using one of three methods: Open Court, the district's standard curriculum, and less direct instruction embedded in a connected text (Foorman, Fletcher, Francis, Schatschneider, & Mehta, 1998). The latter approach emphasized the teacher-as-facilitator, children's active construction of meaning using learning centers, and portfolio assessment. Achievement test scores at the end of the year indicated that the children who had used Open Court approached the national average in their decoding skills (43rd percentile) and passage comprehension (45th percentile). The group using the district's standard curriculum scored in the 27th percentile for decoding skills and the 33rd percentile for passage comprehension. The group using less direct instruction embedded in the text scored in the 29th percentile for word decoding and the 35th percentile for passage comprehension. Spelling skills were not significantly different for any of the groups.

On first impression, it appears that the performance of students taught using Open Court clearly exceeded that of students taught using different methods. However, even though the

285 students in this study were randomly grouped by age, gender, and ethnicity, no mention is made of the students' ability levels prior to their assignment to a group. Without knowing the ability levels of the participants and ensuring that they were evenly distributed among all three groups, it would be difficult to attribute performance increases to a particular instructional method.

In a study conducted in Memphis, Tennessee, students from eight SFA schools were matched with students in statistically similar non-SFA schools. After two years of SFA instruction, the students in the SFA schools performed significantly better than their comparison groups on measurements of reading, language, science, and social studies (Slavin & Madden, 2001). In Baltimore, where SFA actually began, a longitudinal study conducted from 1987–93 comparing Comprehensive Test of Basic Skills (CTBS) scores of students in the five original SFA schools to students in five control schools indicated that SFA students' scores exceeded those of students in the control group at each grade level (Slavin & Madden, 2001).

It must be noted that subsequent researchers disagreed with these findings. Pogrow (2002) notes that only students who had been in the same school for five years were included in this study and that almost no special education students were included. In other words, the group of students that reflected the greatest gain from SFA was not representative of the population as a whole. He further notes that when the same data were reevaluated, this time including all students who were assessed, students' reading levels ranked, on average, three years below grade level by the time they got to 6th grade. SFA has since been dropped by the Baltimore city school district.

Negative Research Findings

A study of 2nd- through 5th-grade students in California comparing the Stanford Achievement Test, Ninth Edition (SAT 9) scores of children in urban schools using Open Court to students in comparable schools using non-scripted materials found no evidence that Open Court fosters higher reading achievement (Moustafa & Land, 2002). In an all-grade comparison study of SAT 9 scores, 28 percent of the students in non-scripted programs were in the bottom quartile, compared to 57 percent of the students using Open Court. The researchers found that 72 percent of the students from non-scripted programs scored above the bottom quartile, compared to only 43 percent of the students taught using Open Court.

A study comparing the standardized test scores of Title I elementary school students using SFA to the scores of students in comparable Title I schools using a different reading program found that, over a three-year period, students in non-SFA schools experienced an average gain of 17 percent in the reading proficiency section, compared to an average gain of 8.5 percent in the reading proficiency of students in schools using the SFA reading curriculum (Greenlee & Bruner, 2001).

English Language Learners

Both Open Court and SRA offer program adaptations in Spanish that may be used in Spanish-only, Spanish-English, and English-only classrooms. Literature compiled by Open Court states that the English scores of 2nd-grade students rose in all but four of Sacramento's 60 elementary schools in 1998 (Open Court, 2002). Slavin and Madden (2001), the founders of SFA, cite studies in California and Arizona in which English language learners using SFA scored higher on English reading measures than did comparable students who were using a different curriculum. In contrast, a three-year study of Miami-Dade County schools in Florida found that English language learners who attended SFA schools actually made smaller gains in English language proficiency than did comparable students at schools not using SFA (Pogrow, 2002).

Concerns

As scripted curriculum materials become more and more commonplace, certain concerns must be addressed. The diverse ethnic and cultural makeup of today's classrooms makes it unlikely that one single curriculum will meet the needs and interests of all students. Curriculum must be flexible so that teachers are able to construct lessons that will be of high interest to their unique group of students, and actively engage them in creating knowledge. Reading aloud scripted lessons that have been created for a generic group is unlikely to accomplish this goal.

Another concern is whether scripted curriculum challenges gifted learners as well as supports those who are struggling. A typical classroom consists of students with a wide spectrum of learning strengths and needs. Classroom teachers are in the best position to identify individual strengths and needs and adjust a curriculum to address them. Again, reading aloud scripted lessons that have been created for a generic group is unlikely to accomplish this goal.

What about the long-term success of students who are read aloud scripted lessons? If the focus of curriculum is on test-driven instruction and rote memorization, will critical-thinking skills and comprehension be overlooked? Students learn when curriculum is relevant to their lives, when it is of personal interest to them, and when they are actively engaged in the pursuit of knowledge.

What about time? If it takes between two to three hours to deliver a script, will science, social studies, art, music, and physical education be eliminated? All of these subject areas contribute to children's overall learning, and their elimination would result in a watered-down educational experience.

What about the teacher? Will teachers be willing to spend their days reading from a script, rather than planning and facilitating lessons that further their students' construction of knowledge? Perhaps teachers with the most experience and education would transfer to school districts that do not use a scripted curriculum, leaving the least experienced teachers to read the script to students with the greatest needs.

These concerns must be addressed in order to determine whether or not the use of a scripted curriculum is truly a prescription for success or a one-size-fits-all approach that does not reflect sound pedagogical practice.

References

Coles, G. (2002). Learning to read scientifically. *Rethinking Schools Online.* Retrieved February 2, 2005, from www.rethinkingschools.org/special_reports/bushplan/Read154.shtml

Comprehensive School Reform Program. (n.d.) Guide to U.S. Department of Education Programs. Retrieved April 3, 2005, http://wdcrobcolp01.ed.gov/CFAPPS/GTEP_PUBLIC/index

Dudley-Marling, C., & Murphy, S. (2001). Changing the way we think about language arts. *Language Arts, 78*(6), 574–578.

Foorman, B. R., Fletcher, J. M., Francis, D. J., Schatschneider, C., & Mehta, P. (1998). The role of instruction in learning to read: Preventing reading failure in at-risk children. *Journal of Educational Psychology, 90*(1), 37–55.

Greenlee, B. J. & Bruner, D. Y. (2001). Effects of Success for All reading programs on reading achievement in Title I schools. *Education, 122*(1), 177–188.

Mathews, J. (2000, January). Prepackaged school reform. *The School Administrator.* Retrieved April 2, 2005, from www.aasa.org/publications/sa/2000_/mathews.htm

McGraw-Hill Companies. (2003, October). *Investors: News releases.* Retrieved April 2, 2005, from http://investor.mcgraw-hill.com

Metcalf, R. (2002, January). Reading between the lines. *The Nation.* Retrieved April 2, 2005, from www.thenation.com/docprint.mhtml?i=20020128&s=metcalf

Moustafa, M., & Land, R. E. (2002). The reading achievement of economically disadvantaged children in urban schools using Open Court vs. comparably disadvantaged children using non-scripted reading programs. 2002 Yearbook of the *Urban Learning, Teaching, and Research Special Interest Group of the American Educational Research Association,* 44–53.

National Right to Read Foundation, The. (2003, February). Paige announces $12.5 million Reading First grant for Oklahoma children. Retrieved February 6, 2005, from www.nrrf.org/pr_OK-RF_2-6-03.htm

Open Court. (2002). *Programs & Practices.* Retrieved on April 3, 2005, from www.sra4kids.com

Perkins-Gough, D. (2004). The eroding curriculum. *Educational Leadership, 62*(1), 84–85.

Pogrow, S. (2002, February). Success for All is a failure. *Phi Delta Kappan, 83*(6), 463–468.

Posnick-Goodwin, (2002). Scripted learning: A slap in the face? *California Educator, 6*(7), 6–16.

Slavin, R. E., & Madden, N. (2001). Research on achievement outcomes of Success for All. *Phi Delta Kappan, 82*(1), 38–66.

ANITA EDE is a doctoral student, College of Education, Oklahoma State University, Stillwater.

From *Childhood Education*, Fall 2006, pp. 29–32. Copyright © 2006 by the Association for Childhood Education International. Reprinted by permission of Anita Ede and the Association for Childhood Education International, 17904 Georgia Avenue, Suite 215, Olney, MD 20832.

Using Brain-Based Teaching Strategies to Create Supportive Early Childhood Environments That Address Learning Standards

PAM SCHILLER AND CLARISSA A. WILLIS

Learning (or content) standards are intended to set the bar for student achievement. They can help create equity among learners by ensuring that all children are prepared to meet the challenges of an increasingly complex, demanding world. Although standards vary state by state, they generally have similar broad goals for children in the primary grades (National Institute for Early Education Research 2008). As they mature and develop from ages 5 to 8, young children are expected to achieve the following:

1. develop as effective readers;
2. expand their abilities to use complex mathematical applications;
3. deepen their understandings of science concepts; and
4. broaden their social studies skills and learn the concepts necessary to be responsible citizens.

Many learning standards also address a wider range of skills children can master in technology, art, music, theater, health education, and physical education. The Early Childhood Education Assessment Consortium of the Council of Chief State School Officers defines early learning standards as

> Statements that describe expectations for the learning and development of young children across the domains of: health and physical well-being; social and emotional well-being; approaches to learning; language development and symbol systems; and general knowledge about the world around them. (CCSSO 2008)

This definition is broad in nature, specific to domains, yet consistent with nurturing the whole child. It is also compatible with brain research timetables for neurological wiring.

It's important to understand that standards are *not* intended to fence in creative teachers or to become obstacles for learners with special needs. Instead, they can guide, support, and encourage enterprising and knowledgeable primary teachers to create intriguing and motivating educational environments and experiences that are developmentally appropriate for each child and optimize learning for all (NAEYC & NAECS/SDE 2002).

Creating Conditions for Success

Enormous potential exists in applying early brain development research findings to the implementation of learning standards. Here are three research findings that can be used with learning standards to optimize learning.

Experiences impact the architecture of the brain. At birth the human brain is in an amazingly unfinished state. The hardware is present but the connections are yet to be made. The child's experiences in the larger world result in connections that are reinforced as the experiences are repeated. This becomes the neural circuitry that lays the foundation for the child's lifelong learning (Shonkoff & Phillips 2000).

A predictable process assists the brain in channeling stimuli into long-term learning. When teachers present information in a sequence that supports this process, it is much

---

The National Association of Early Childhood Specialists in State Departments of Education (NAECS/SDE) works to improve instruction, curriculum, and administration in education programs for young children and their families. Of Primary Interest is written by members of NAECS/SDE for kindergarten and primary teachers. The column appears in March, July, and November issues of *Young Children* and Beyond the Journal (online at www.journal.naeyc.org/btj).

easier for children to learn (Sousa 2006). To help children focus on a lesson, begin by asking them a relevant question or showing them intriguing photos. When presenting the actual content (learning standard) of the lesson, show children how the new information is similar to other information familiar to them. Point out any patterns that occur in the new information. Allow children to practice using new information, through hands-on activities when possible. Finally, encourage children to think about how they will use the new information and to ask themselves, How is this information relevant to my life?

Environmental influences—such as safety, emotions, novelty, humor, music, choices, physical movement, and hands-on activities—**can contribute to increased alertness and memory** (Jensen 2001). Keeping these influences in mind when implementing learning standards sets the stage for success.

Applying Brain Research in Implementing Learning Standards

Standards guidelines and brain research findings are the tools needed to implement standards. Then the following brain-based strategies become a means to optimize learning for all children.

1. Safe Environments Matter

Safety and well-being come before anything else. The brain attends to these needs first. A child who comes to school hungry, ill, or frightened by something that happened on the way will find it difficult, if not impossible, to focus on what is going on in the classroom. Children will struggle with learning if they feel afraid because a classroom setting is too restrictive, a home environment is very demanding, or a classmate's behavior is aggressive. To evaluate what changes are needed, take these steps:

- **Make sure the physical classroom is free of anything that could scare a child.** For example, some kindergarten children (ages 5 and 6) may be afraid of certain classroom pets or science specimens, such as snakes or spiders. What have you included in your science center? Are children spending the day checking on the snake in the aquarium to make sure it has not escaped?
- **Start the children's day with a safety ritual.** For example, try a greeting such as, "We are safe when we are at school" or "We are a community of learners who take care of one another." Positive affirmations help to reduce fears. For children with special needs, such as autism or anxiety disorders, create a symbolic representation of a safe haven. Have the child place his name or photo in a classroom box with a lid, then close it to represent his being safe inside.
- **Remind children they are in your safekeeping.** Reassure children who have emotional challenges or who have difficulty separating from a parent. Explain that your job is to keep them safe while they are at school. Listen to a timid child and acknowledge her

fears. Then redirect her attention to an engaging activity or invite another child to be her peer buddy. Encourage the buddies to do an activity together. Never dismiss a child's fear, even if it seems irrational to you.

2. Emotions Are Effective Tools

Emotions affect memory and brain function. When a person feels content, the brain releases endorphins that enhance memory skills (Jensen 2005).

- **Start the day with humor.** Tell a funny story or share a silly picture. Laughing makes children feel secure and content.
- **Sing a few songs together.** Incorporate dance and movement with singing whenever possible. Children can draw, paint, or do other creative projects while listening to various types of music.
- **Sequence and pace daily activities.** Children can feel overwhelmed by too much new information and unfamiliar materials. After presenting new information, give children time to practice and reflect on what they are learning.
- **Help learners feel in control of their learning.** Researchers tell us that keeping lessons short and relative to the topic is more compatible with the brain's processing ability (Sousa 2006). You can use several strategies to help children master large amounts of information over time. For example, break down activities or routines into steps. Display pictures of each step to teach and remind children of what to do next. This works particularly well for children with special needs, such as a child with cognitive delays, autism, or a language delay.
- **Be proactive.** Use guidance strategies that reflect the natural or logical consequences for inappropriate behavior rather than threats and punishment. Negative emotions can impede learning. For example, if you know that a child has difficulty transitioning from indoor to outdoor play, alert him before the transition so he knows what is going to happen next.
- **Nurture social and emotional intelligence.** Children must learn to follow directions, work with others, stay on task, finish their work, and take initiative to master new information. They also must learn to control their verbal and behavioral impulses, solve problems, and take responsibility for their own actions (Bilmes 2008). Nurture these skills by providing time for cooperative learning, collaboration, and teamwork.

3. Multisensory Practices Make Sense

The more senses involved during learning, the more likely the brain will receive and process information. By using multiple senses to learn, children find it easier to match new information to their existing knowledge (Schiller 1999; Willis in press).

- **Use real materials.** Familiar and tangible objects demonstrating concepts can help make ideas concrete. For example, rather than talking about birds with 5- and

6-year-olds, go outside to observe them, then make a graph of all the different birds the children see and hear. Seven- and 8-year-olds might begin classifying birds by common characteristics or migration patterns.

- **Use chants and rhymes.** Rhythmic patterns stick in the brain. For kindergarten, use *Chicka Chicka Boom Boom,* by Bill Martin Jr. and John Archambault, to teach the alphabet. For first and second grade, use a chant like the one below to practice spelling words.

It's time to spell!
Let's show what we know.
It's time to spell!
Ready, set, go!

Shhh, shhh, shhh, shhh, shhh, shhh
Spell bear.
Bear. B-e-a-r.

Shhh, shhh, shhh, shhh, shhh, shhh
Spell chair.
Chair. C-h-a-i-r. [*Continue the chant with more words.*]

(Schiller unpublished; for other chants and rhymes, see Schiller & Willis [2008], pp. 262–65)

- **Make it fun!** Sing, dance, play games, and laugh. These activities use multiple senses and at the same time increase memory (Jensen 2005).
- **Provide natural environments.** Use places where an activity would ordinarily occur—home, school, outdoors, the zoo, or anyplace where learning is more meaningful than sitting at a desk. For example, when studying nature, go outdoors for a nature hunt rather than show children pictures of trees. Teach a child with special needs, such as Down syndrome, how to brush his teeth in the bathroom instead of the classroom.

4. Differentiated Teaching Practice Is Supportive

The term *differentiated* once meant that teachers planned ways to address children's differences in age, development, and learning styles. Now, this term encompasses everything that makes a child unique, such as culture, family, temperament, multiple intelligences profile, personality style, and special needs or developmental delays. These differences are even greater in the primary years because young children develop on individual timetables that often vary greatly. Primary teachers may wonder if it is even possible to teach every child as an individual. They can begin by first looking at how learning is consistent.

- **Provide a focus to hold children's attention.** This might be a photograph, a finger play, a song, or a provocative question. For example, in the primary grades, play a song in French before starting a discussion about France.
- **Break teaching into small parts.** Children are better able to focus on important information when they

receive less, rather than more, information. When first-graders are learning about animals, focus on one species at a time. Teach the two critical attributes of mammals: they nurse their young and they have hair. Have the children sort animals into mammals and nonmammals. When they are successful, use the same process to add reptiles and eventually amphibians and birds.

- **Provide hands-on practice.** Hands-on manipulation increases the chance by 75 percent that new information will be stored in long-term memory (Hannaford 1995; Sousa 2006). Hands-on investigation increases sensory input, which helps learners focus. It allows for experimentation by letting children use trial and error, which increases the chance that learners will make sense of and establish relevancy for what they are learning (Sousa 2006).
- **Use an integrated approach.** Combine math, reading, spelling, and writing to teach children about plants. To extend learning, have the class plant a butterfly garden together. Offer the children feedback on their progress, and build in time for their reflection.

Application of these strategies and commitment to the concept that all children learn based on their development and experience level make differentiated teaching possible in every classroom.

5. Special Needs Are Met Through Planning

In today's blended or fully inclusive classrooms, children with special needs (visual or hearing impairments, cognitive challenges, motor or speech/language delays, or emotional/behavioral issues) learn in the same environment along with their peers (see Schiller & Willis 2008). This can be a positive experience for all children when teachers shape their practices to do the following:

- **Present concepts in simple steps.** Provide materials that enable a child who cannot fully participate in an activity to be engaged with his peers and to participate in his own way. For example, a child with language delays might work with a peer to write a journal entry together.
- **Look for ways to modify tools and materials.** Provide pencil or crayon grips for a child with motor challenges or picture schedules for a child with communication issues.
- **Recognize signs of developmental delay.** Be alert to a child whose development appears to be delayed, and provide extra opportunities for the child to practice using new information. Try several methods to introduce learning concepts.
- **Set appropriate goals.** Goals for learning should fit a child's age and stage of development. For example, most of the class may work on identifying letters, while a child with special needs, such as a cognitive or general developmental delay, learns the first letter of her name.

6. Sense and Meaning Are Essential

The brain processes new information by making sense and meaning of it (Sousa 2006). The process of sense making requires finding the patterns. One way to do this is by having children ask themselves questions, such as, How is this new information like the information I already have? How is it different? What parts of this information do I understand? Which parts are confusing?

For information to have meaning children must find its relevance. Teachers can help children when they

- **Tap into prior knowledge.** Review what the children already know before introducing new information. Point out any patterns in children's prior knowledge that overlap with new information. For example, "Remember last week, when we talked about the days of the week and we found them on a calendar? Today we are going to talk about the months of the year, which are also found on a calendar."
- **Use organizers.** Graphic organizers help children to see relationships between several pieces of information. Story maps, word wheels, and K-W-L (a chart or graphic representation that reflects "What I know, What I want to know, and What I just learned") work well with kindergarten children and first-graders.
- **Provide hands-on practice.** Offer Wikki Sticks and magnetic, sandpaper, and three-dimensional letters to help children learn alphabet letters.
- **Give the children time to reflect.** After a group activity or discussion, teachers can ask questions such as, How will you use this new information? How would what we learned today be different if ———? How do you feel about ———?

Conclusion

With careful planning, knowledge of brain research findings, and a little creativity, primary teachers can offer engaging, brain-based activities that encourage exploration and learning and support learning standards. Teachers and children can build a strong community of learners who see learning as an opportunity to be successful problem solvers while anticipating each new challenge as another exciting adventure.

References

Bilmes, J. 2008. Beyond behavior management. St. Paul, MN: Redleaf. CCSSO (Council of Chief State School Officers), Early Childhood Education Assessment Consortium. 2008. Glossary. Washington, DC: Author. www.ccsso.org/projects/SCASS/projects/early_childhood_education_assessment_consortium/publications_and_products/2892.cfm

Hannaford, C. 1995. *Smart moves: Why learning is not all in your head.* Arlington, Va: Great Ocean Publishers.

Jensen, E. 2001. Fragile brains—Damage to the brain and environmental influences can account for certain learning problems. *Educational Leadership* 59 (3): 32.

Jensen, E. 2005. *Teaching with the brain in mind.* 2nd ed. Alexandria, VA: Association for Supervision and Curriculum Development.

NAEYC & NAECS/SDE (National Association of Early Childhood Specialists in State Departments of Education). 2002. Early learning standards: Creating the conditions for success. Joint position statement. www.naeyc.org/about/positions/pdf/position_statement.pdf

National Institute for Early Education Research (NIEER). 2008. State standards database. http://nieer.org/standards/statelist.php

Schiller, P. 1999. *Start smart: Building brain power in the early years.* Beltsville, MD. Gryphon House.

Schiller, P., & C. Willis. 2008. *Inclusive literacy lessons for early childhood.* Beltsville, MD: Gryphon House.

Shonkoff, J.P., & D.A. Phillips, eds. 2000. *From neurons to neighborhoods: The science of early childhood development.* Report of the National Research Council and Institute of Medicine. Washington, DC: National Academies Press.

Sousa, D. 2006. *How the brain learns.* 3rd ed. Thousand Oaks, CA: Corwin.

Willis, C. In press. *Creating inclusive learning environments for young children.* Thousand Oaks, CA: Corwin Press.

PAM SCHILLER, PhD, is a curriculum specialist and freelance author and speaker. She has worked as a child care administrator and taught in public schools. Pam served as head of the Early Childhood Department at the University of Houston and directed its Lab School. She is the author of five early childhood curriculums and more than 30 teacher resource books. **CLARISSA A. WILLIS,** PhD, is a full-time author, speaker, and consultant, and former associate director of the Center of Excellence in Early Childhood Learning and Development at East Tennessee State University. As a consultant, she has provided workshops and keynote addresses for schools and organizations across the country and abroad. Clarissa@clarissawillis.com

From *Young Children*, July 2008, pp. 52–55. Copyright © 2008 by National Association for the Education of Young Children. Reprinted by permission.

Successful Transition to Kindergarten
The Role of Teachers and Parents

Pam Deyell-Gingold

W hile new kindergartners are worrying about whether or not anyone will be their friend and if they'll be able to find the bathroom, their preschool teachers are wondering if they've succeeded at preparing their small students for this big transition. In recent years the role of kindergarten has changed from an extension of preschool to a much more academic environment because of new standards in the public schools that "push back" academic skills to earlier grades.

How can we ensure that our students make a smooth transition? Are our students mature enough? What can we do to make them "more" ready? This article will explore the skills that constitute kindergarten "readiness," how preschool teachers can collaborate with parents and kindergarten teachers to make the process more rewarding for all, and activities to help prepare children for what will be expected of them in kindergarten.

The Transition Process

Children go through many transitions throughout their lives, but one of the most important transitions is the one from a preschool program to kindergarten. "During this period behavior is shaped and attitudes are formed that will influence children throughout their education" (PTA and Head Start, 1999). Children's transitions are most strongly influenced by their home environment, the preschool program they attend, and the continuity between preschool and kindergarten (Riedinger, 1997).

In 1995, Head Start and the Parent Teacher Association (PTA) began a plan to create a partnership between the two organizations in order to create effective transition practices and to promote continuity in parent and family involvement in the schools. Three pilot programs were studied to determine "best practice" in kindergarten transition, and to foster the continued strong involvement of families in their children's education. They worked with elementary schools to create parent-friendly environments and to develop strategies that lessen the barriers to involvement (Head Start & PTA, 1999). Even Start, a federal program for low-income families implemented to improve educational opportunities for children and adults, also helps parents to work with the school system to help their children

succeed. Their research found that parents felt that the way in which Even Start focuses on the family strengths rather than weaknesses and allows the families to identify their own needs, empowered them more than anything else to help them to support their children in school (Riedinger, 1997).

Kindergarten Readiness

A 1998 study by the National Center for Early Development & Learning of nearly 3,600 kindergarten teachers nationwide indicated that 48 percent of children have moderate to serious problems transitioning to kindergarten. Teachers are most often concerned about children's skills in following directions, academics, and working independently. There seems to be a discrepancy between the expectations of teachers and the actual skills of kindergarten children. Therefore, a need for kindergarten teachers to collaborate with both parents and preschool teachers exists (Pianta & Cox, 1998). School readiness is more than a matter of academics, though. As reported in a National Education Goals Panel in 1998; "The prevailing view today, however, is that readiness reflects a range of dimensions, such as a child's health and physical development, social and emotional development, approaches to learning, language and communication skills, and cognitive and general knowledge" (California Department of Education, 2000).

Historically, kindergarten was a "children's garden": a place to interact for the first time with a group of agemates, and to learn basic skills through play. Today, because of increasing numbers of working mothers, single-parent families, and strict welfare regulations, many children begin having group experiences in a child care program or family child care home at a much earlier age. Together with the concern that America's children are not getting adequate education to compete in a global market, our schools began to make the transition from the children's garden to "curriculum escalation" (Shepard & Smith, 1988) and "academic trickle-down" (Cunningham, 1988). While the trend towards focusing on academic skills continues at a fast pace, early childhood professionals argue for a more integrated curriculum that addresses the developmental needs of each child.

Social Adjustment

Although academics may be becoming increasingly more important, research shows that social skills are what most affect school adjustment (Ladd & Price, 1987; Ladd, 1990). Preschool teachers should not feel pressured into teaching academics beyond what is developmentally "best practice" (Bredekamp & Copple, 1997) but should continue to focus on social and emotional development. Children who have been rejected by their peers in kindergarten tend to have poor school performance, more absences, and negative attitudes towards school that last throughout their school years. "Three particular social skills that are known to influence children's peer acceptance: play behavior, ability to enter play groups, and communication skills" (Maxwell & Eller, 1994).

Play Behavior and Communication Skills

Specific behaviors that cause rejection by fellow students include things like rough play, arguing, upsetting things in class, trying to get their own way, and not sharing. Children who exhibit these behaviors also tend to be less independent and less cooperative than their peers. Most children prefer playing with others who are polite, caring, and attentive. Preschool teachers and parents need to teach young children social skills, especially how to enter social groups. For example, children who say, "Looks like that's a fun game, can I play?" are more likely to be accepted than those who shove others aside and whine, "I want a turn!"

Another important social skill is the ability to participate in complicated fantasy games and take part in making up and extending the story. Children who lack sufficient experience playing with agemates may feel frustrated at not being able to keep up with the capabilities of their classmates. "A generous amount of guided social experience with peers prior to kindergarten helps children do well in this new world" (Maxwell & Eller, 1994). Some children need assistance to learn how to play make-believe. A teacher can help model this by giving verbal cues like, "You be the mommy, and I'll be your little girl. Can I help you make dinner, Mommy?" Some children need reminders to keep them focused on their roles. Others may need help to read the emotions on people's faces. "Look at Nick's face. He is sad because you pulled the hat away from him." Because young children do not have a large enough vocabulary to express themselves, teachers can help them find words to express their feelings such as, "You're feeling frustrated. Let's go find a puzzle with fewer pieces."

Communication skills, such as being able to take part in a conversation, listen to others, and negotiate are also important. For example, children who speak directly to peers, are attentive to others in the group, and respond to the initiations of others tend to be liked by the other children. Disliked children are more likely to make irrelevant comments, reject the initiations of other children without reasons or explanations, and often make comments without directing them to anyone (Maxwell & Eller, 1994). Part of a teacher's task is to quietly remind children to look at the person they're talking to, and listen to what another child is saying.

Immaturity and Redshirting

A common practice when dealing with children who are not socially mature is to keep them out of school for a year, in the hope that "readiness will emerge." In academic circles this is referred to as "redshirting," a term borrowed from college athletics. However, "Research shows that redshirts are not gaining an academic advantage, and the extra year does not solve the social development problems that caused initial concern" (Graue, 1994). Parents who are told that their children need to stay home for a year should ask for the reasons.

"Developmentally appropriate practice is less common in kindergarten, and primary teachers face many constraints and pressures that teachers of younger children are not yet experiencing in the same intensity [although preschool appears to be next in line for "pushdown" curriculum]." (Jones, Evans, & Rencken, 2001). "If we think inclusively we have to problem-solve in ways to accommodate the incredible diversity presented by the characteristics of kindergartners.... Redshirting and retention are outmoded tools that should be replaced by more appropriate practices. One step in the right direction is collaboration between preschool and elementary school educators" (Graue, 1994). A second step is to have parents understand what experiences can help their child have a successful transition.

Learning about Classroom Styles

In collaborating with kindergarten teachers, preschool teachers and parents need to visit the school and pay close attention to details that may affect their students in kindergarten. "When teachers and parents agree on a philosophy of education, children usually adjust more easily" (Maxwell & Eller, 1994). Children feel more secure in their new environment if they feel that their parents support the teacher and the school.

The first step may be either a meeting with the kindergarten teacher or a class field trip to the elementary school. "Observe kindergarten classrooms to identify teaching styles, classroom management techniques, and routines. Also try to identify skills that are needed to be successful in participating in the kindergarten classroom" (Karr-Jelinek, 1994).

In her research, Karr-Jelinek used a checklist of what parents (and teachers) should look for in a kindergarten classroom, to see if their children—both normally developing and with special needs—are ready for the classroom they visit (Karr-Jelineck, 1994):

- How many steps are given at a time in directions?
- What types of words are children expected to understand?
- How does each individual child compare to the other children?
- How long are children expected to sit still in a group?
- How often do children speak out of turn or move around when they should be sitting?
- How much independence is expected?
- What type of work is being done? (small groups, seatwork, etc.)
- Where might my special needs students need extra help?
- What kind of special information can I pass along to the teacher about each child?

Although expectations vary by teacher and school district, by the time children reach kindergarten they should be able to listen to a story in a group, follow two or three oral directions, take turns and share, follow rules, respect the property of others, and work within time and space constraints. They need to learn the difference between work and play, knowing when and where each is appropriate. "Most five-year-olds can express themselves fluently with a variety of words and can understand an even larger variety of words used in conversations and stories" (Nurss, 1987).

Many kindergartens make use of learning centers, small group instruction, and whole group language activities. However, others use "structured, whole group paper-and-pencil activities oriented to academic subjects, such as reading and mathematics. The curriculum in these kindergartens often constitutes a downward extension of the primary grade curriculum and may call for the use of workbooks, which are part of a primary level textbook series. Many early childhood professionals have spoken out on the inappropriateness of such a curriculum" (Nurss, 1987).

Preparing Parents for the Transition

High-quality preschool programs encourage parent involvement in the home and in the classroom. Volunteering to read during story time, to share cultural traditions, or to be a lunch guest are all ways for parents to feel that they are a part of their child's school life. According to the National PTA, parent and family involvement increases student achievement and success. If preschool teachers can make parents feel welcome helping in the classroom, they will be more likely to remain involved in their child's future education.

Many parents worry about their children entering elementary school because of their own negative school experiences. They may feel intimidated by teachers and uncomfortable showing up at school events—even for orientation and enrolling their children in school (Reidinger, 1997). Parents' expectations of how well children will do in school influence children's performance. It appears that parents who expect success may provide more support, encouragement and praise, which may give their children more self-esteem and confidence. The most important thing is that children who believe in their own abilities have been found to be more successful in school (Dweck, 1991).

To assist parents, preschool teachers can arrange visits to the school and take parents along on the kindergarten field trip. They can ask for children to be paired with a kindergarten "buddy" who can take them around, while parents meet with the teacher or go to the office to register their child. A study done by Rathbun and Hauskin (2001) showed that the more low-income students that were enrolled in a school, the less parental involvement there was. Involving low-income families in the schools may help to break the cycle of poverty of future generations.

One way to really help the family with transition is to empower the parents to act as advocates for their children. Parent

Kindergarten Readiness Is . . .

A Child Who Listens

To directions without interrupting
To stories and poems for five or ten minutes without restlessness

A Child Who Hears

Words that rhyme
Words that begin with the same sound or different sounds

A Child Who Sees

Likenesses and differences in pictures and designs
Letters and words that match

A Child Who Understands

The relationship inherent in such words as up and down, top and bottom, little and big
The classifications of words that represent people, places and things

A Child Who Speaks and Can

Stay on the topic in class discussions
Retell a story or poem in correct sequence
Tell a story or relate an experience of her own

A Child Who Thinks and Can

Give the main idea of a story
Give unique ideas and important details
Give reasons for his opinions

A Child Who Adjusts

To changes in routine and to new situations without becoming fearful
To opposition or defeat without crying or sulking
To necessity of asking for help when needed

A Child Who Plays

Cooperatively with other children
And shares, takes turns and assumes his share of group responsibility
And can run, jump, skip, and bounce a ball with comparative dexterity

A Child Who Works

Without being easily distracted
And follows directions
And completes each task
And takes pride in her work

*Adapted from Howlett, M.P. (1970, February 18). Teacher's edition: *My Weekly Reader Surprise*, Vol. 12, Issue 20.

meetings and newsletters can help parents learn how to work with school staff, learn about volunteer opportunities at school, as well as how to prepare their child at home for kindergarten. They may need some advice on how to help their children and themselves cope with anxieties related to transitions from preschool to kindergarten.

Preparing Children for Transition

In the last few weeks of summer, children start getting excited about going to kindergarten, and are apprehensive at the same time. It is important for parents to treat the child's entrance into kindergarten as a normal occurrence and not build up the event in children's minds. An important way to provide continuity for the child is to find preschool classmates or other children who will be in their kindergarten class. According to research, children who have a familiar peer in a new group setting have fewer problems adjusting to new environments (Howes, 1988).

Transition Activities for Parents and Children

The more you discuss this transition in a matter-of-fact way, the more comfortable children will become. Encourage parents to prepare their child for kindergarten with the following:

- Visit the school so the children can meet the kindergarten teacher and see what kindergarten is really like. Try to arrange for them to see more than one type of classroom activity, such as seatwork time and free choice time.
- Show them where the bathroom and cubbies are located.
- Find out what lunchtime will be like. If the children are going to be getting a school lunch, they may have to learn how to open new kinds of containers.
- Read books about kindergarten.
- Answer children's questions in a straight forward way about what they will do in kindergarten. Tell them they will listen to stories, do counting activities, have group time, and play outside.
- Explore how long the kindergarten day is and what the daily routine will be like. They will want to know what will be the same as preschool and what will be different.
- If the children are going to a school that presents more diversity than they are familiar with, talk honestly with them about racial and ethnic differences and disabilities.
- If children are going to be taking the schoolbus for the first time, you will need to discuss schoolbus safety rules.
- Reassure children that they will be picked up from school every day just as they are in preschool.
- Check to make sure your pre-kindergarten children are capable of basic kindergarten "readiness" skills. (See sidebar.)

Conclusion

The transition from preschool to kindergarten can be a stressful time for both children and parents. However, if preschool teachers can facilitate collaboration between parents and kindergarten and familiarize children with the workings of kindergarten, it will be a smoother process. Parents need to try to find a developmentally appropriate class for their child by observing different classrooms and talking to teachers about educational philosophies. Preschool teachers, with their knowledge of different learning styles and the temperaments of their students, can help everyone with this important transition.

References

Bredekamp, S. & Copple, C. (1997). *Developmentally appropriate practice for early childhood programs*. Revised edition. Washington, DC: NAEYC.

California Dept of Ed., (2000). *Prekindergarten learning and development guidelines*. Sacramento, CA.

Cunningham, A. 1988. Eeny, meeny, miny, moe: Testing policy and practice in early childhood. Berkeley, CA: National Commission on Testing and Public Policy In Graue, E (2001, May) What's going on in the children's garden today? *Young Children*.

Dweck, C.S. (1991). Self-theories and goals: their role in motivation, personality and development. In *Nebraska symposia on motivation*, Vol. 36, ed. by R. Dienstbier, 199–235, Lincoln: University of Nebraska Press. [In Maxwell, Eller, 1994]

Graue, E. (2001, May) What's going on in the children's garden today? *Young Children*, pp. 67–73.

Howes, C. (1988). Peer interaction of young children. Monographs of the Society for Research in Child Development 53 (2. Serial No. 217). In Maxwell, K. and Eller, C. (1994, September) Children's Transition to Kindergarten, *Young Children*.

Howlett, M.P. (1970, February 18). Teacher's edition: *My Weekly Reader Surprise*, Vol. 12, Issue 20.

Jones, E., Evans, K., & Rencken, K. (2001) *The Lively Kindergarten*, NAEYC publications.

Karr-Jelinek, C. (1994). *Transition to kindergarten: Parents and teachers working together*. Educational Resources Information Center.

Ladd, G.W., 1990. Having friends, keeping friends, making friends and being liked by peers in the classroom: Predictors of children's early school adjustment? *Child Development* (61) 1081–100.

Ladd, G.W., & J.M. Price. 1987. Predicting children's social and school adjustment following the transition from preschool to kindergarten. *Child Development*, (58) 1168–89.

Maxwell, K. & Eller, S. (1994, September). Children's transition to kindergarten. *Young Children*, pp. 56–63.

National PTA & National Head Start Association. (1999). *Continuity for success: Transition planning guide*. National PTA, Chicago, IL. National Head Start Association, Alexandria, VA.

Nurss, J. 1987, *Readiness for Kindergarten*, ERIC Clearinghouse on Elementary and Early Childhood Education, Urbana, IL; BBB16656.

Pianta, R. & Cox, M. (1998). Kindergarten Transitions. Teachers 48% of Children Have Transition Problems. *NCEDL Spotlights Series*, No. 1, National Center for Early Development & Learning: Chapel Hill, NC.

Rathbun, A. & Hauskin, E. (2001). How are transition-to-kindergarten activities associated with parent involvement during kindergarten? Paper presented at the Annual meeting of the American Educational Research Foundation: Seattle, WA.

Riedinger, S. (1997), *Even Start: Facilitating transitions to kindergarten*. Dept. of Education: Washington, DC: Planning and Evaluation Service.

Shepard, I.A. & M.I. Smith. (1988) Escalating academic demand in kindergarten: counterproductive policies. *The Elementary School Journal*, (89) 135–45. In Maxwell, K. and Eller, C. (1994, September) Children's Transition to Kindergarten, *Young Children*.

PAM DEYELL-GINGOLD is a graduate student in Human Development at Pacific Oaks College. She works as master teacher at Head Start, teaches child development classes for Merced Community College, and is a freelance writer and anti-bias curriculum enthusiast. Her home is in the Sierra foothills near Yosemite National Park, California.

From *Earlychildhood NEWS*, May/June 2006, pp. 14–19. Copyright © 2006 by Excelligence Learning Corporation. Reprinted by permission.

Rethinking Early Childhood Practices

Francis Wardle, PhD

All professions have a canon of beliefs and practices. Some of these come from research and best practices; many simply develop and are passed on without critical examination. The early childhood field is no exception. Not only should any "self-renewing" profession continually re-examine itself on a regular basis, but, in this period of postmodern thought, we have the opportunity to carefully evaluate many beliefs that our profession accepts as the truth.

Critical theory is one way to examine our common beliefs and practices. Critical theory is, "an umbrella term for a range of perspectives . . . (that) all assume knowledge is socially constructed . . . From a critical theory perceptive, therefore, no universal truths or set of laws or principals can be applied to everyone." (Ryan & Glieshaber, 2004, p. 45) However, this article does not suggest we simply deconstruct our profession from one specific point of view for several reasons. First, a critical theory critique presupposes our current early childhood practices come from some kind of logic and order—one of power and oppression. Secondly, the power orientation creates straw arguments: in early childhood education an attack on developmentally appropriate practice (DAP) (Hatch, Bowman, Jortlan, Morgan, Hart, Soto, Lubeck & Hyson, 2002; Lubeck, 1998.). As you will see in this article, many early childhood practices should be more DAP, not less (particularly because, in spite of the view of many critics, most of our early childhood programs are not DAP) (Dunn & Kontos, 1997). Finally, when I teach my qualitative methods graduate classes I strongly advise students against threats to theoretical validity—the temptation to force or morph all data into an existing and popular theoretical orientation (Burke, 1997). It's not hard to make 'the data fit'.

The question, of course, is where have our practices come from? Critical theorists say from research on white, middle class students, and from dead white men (Ryan & Grieshaber, 2004). I believe they have largely developed as a downward extension of school practices (Wardle, 2003). It seems to me, historically, that our approach to everything regarding young children—building design, playgrounds, health/safety, bus safety, scheduling, curriculum, etc., can be characterized as a reaction against the traditional home, farm and village upbringing, and a belief that school is better and early school is even better (Johnson, Christie & Wardle, 2005).

Same-Age Grouping

Part of the history of U.S. public schools is the one-room schoolhouse, which was characterized by vertical grouping of children, with older children assisting younger ones as they themselves learned about service and caring for others. But in 1843 Horace Mann returned from visiting the Prussian military, and decided the regimented, same-age grouping would be an improvement (Wiles & Bondi, 1998).

While same-age grouping has dominated K–12 schools, it is slowly becoming the norm in most early childhood programs. Many Head Start programs, for example, have children grouped by "older 4s" and "younger 4s". The pedagogical rationale for this approach is to target curricula content and instruction to specific age groups. However, the arguments against same-age grouping of children in early childhood programs are overwhelming:

The tremendous diversity within age groups, due to gender; race/ethnicity social-economic status, experience, and exceptionality (special needs and gifted) make curriculum targeting well neigh impossible.

The reduced size of most US families (Berger, 2005) requires that children have multiage experiences in their early childhood programs.

Vygotsky argues learning takes place when an 'expert' assists the learner to learn within his zone of proximal development; and the best expert is often a child who is slightly more advanced than the learner (Berk & Winsler, 1995).

Piaget argues that one of the best ways for a child to learn is when a child is 'forced' to expand his existing schemas to match overwhelming evidence from the environment. One of the best ways to expose a child to this evidence is by interacting with a child who is one level higher than the learner (Brainerd, 1978).

It would seem that, along with language, race/ethnicity and income, age differences are forms of diversity we should expose our children to.

Character education curricula in early childhood programs stress a sense of caring and responsibility (Wardle, 2004). One of the best ways to develop these values is to have children practice helping, caring for, and protecting younger, more vulnerable children. The result may be fewer issues with bullying and harassment in the later school years.

The Importance of a Daily Schedule

A regular, daily schedule teaches children a needed sense of security, especially children from low-income and minority homes. Almost all early childhood textbooks and research articulate this belief. For example, "Daily routines form the framework for a young child's day; some children depend on them for a sense of security. . . . But no matter what type of schedule the early childhood program follows, there are certain routines that should occur daily" (Gonzalez-Mena, 2001, p. 262). And, according to Gordon & Browne, (2004), "Children are more secure in a place that has a consistent schedule; they can begin to anticipate the regularity of what comes next and count on it" (p. 367). "Routines are the framework of programs for young children. A routine is a constant; each day certain events are repeated, providing continuity and a sense of order. Routines are reassuring to children, and they take pride in mastering them" (Gordon & Browne, 2004, p. 366).

The argument for this canon goes something like this: "Children need regular routines to enable them to develop a sense of security in a predictable environment". And, of course, the more "unstructured" their home life, the more they need structure and routine in a program. Argument against this fixation on routine include:

Research has shown time and again that the most important form of security for young children is a consistent, warm, responsive, long-term relationship with a caregiver (Bowlby, 1969; Honig, 2002; Lally, 1998). Yet there is an embarrassing dearth of suggestions in the literature about ways to achieve this important relationship, which requires providing caregivers with adequate salaries, benefits, and working conditions. Is our fixation on schedules and routines due to the inability to provide consistent and long-term care with one provider?

Children have no sense of time as adults' know it. Certainly the sequence of activities provides important mental scripts that children use in cognitive and language development (Berger, 2005). Many argue that one reason for schedules is to teach children about time, and the behaviors needed to function in an adult world fixated on schedules. Members of one of my early childhood classes argued vehemently that children who don't follow a strict timetable would not be able to function effectively in the adult world. After I pointed out that each of them were late for class, they dropped the argument!

Children from less structured, more chaotic environments desperately need time to fully complete important projects they are personally and socially invested in, without being interrupted by a more powerful adult. Research suggests that children who lack a sense of control over their learning eventually reduce commitment to on-task behavior (Johnson, Christie & Wardle, 2005). Thus it would seem to me that all children, but particularly children from unstructured environments, need programs that encourage them to pursue projects and interactions until they decide they are finished.

The new brain research has reinforced the need for stimulation, change, challenge, involvement, and meaningful learning (Shore, 1997), which is often much easier to achieve with a less

structured schedule, and more difficult to achieve with more structure. Structure begets bored children, frustrated teachers, and stressful transitions.

Learning is continuous. Young children learn in continuous ways, relating new learning to past experiences and accomplishments. Children learn best when a project, idea, or activity veers off into new and different directions, "emerging" into new and exciting learning (Dewey, 1938).

The American workplace is less and less structured by traditional routines, and more often organized by projects, flextime, team activities, and self-directed problem solving. Early childhood programs need to develop workers who can structure their own time, and who do not feel confused when work demands require varied and flexible schedules.

Meals Must Be Provided at Regular Intervals

One of the areas where early childhood programs insist on a schedule is eating. While this is often dictated by the reality of the kitchen schedule, catering service, and use of the cafeteria, we also seem to deeply believe that children should be fed "on schedule". However, it is fairly well established that infants should be fed, "on demand".

Most of us will stop off at a store to pick up a snack when we get hungry, and go to the refrigerator when we cannot last till the next full meal. Why not allow children to do the same? Does our meal schedule—and the accompanying need for children to clean off their plate before they get desert—contribute to our child obesity problem? After all, if a child thinks they won't get food until a specific time (or maybe, if they won't get it till very late at home), they might "stuff themselves" so they won't get hungry. Providing healthy snacks in a refrigerator in the classroom for children to eat when they are hungry might be a good idea.

Sleep-Time Should Be Scheduled

The biggest struggle my wife and I had with our children's child care was naptime. We insisted our children not have a nap because when they did they would not get tired until 11 at night. At the opposite end of the spectrum, some teachers complain that parents keep their children up so late that they fall asleep before naptime. Maybe early childhood programs should provide a quiet area away from the noise and activity of the classroom, where children can lie down when they get tired.

A Curriculum Is at the Center of All Good Educational Programs

According to Diane Trister Dodge and Toni Bickart (2003), "Curriculum and assessment drive our work with young children every day. If we do them well we achieve positive outcomes for children. Good input means good output" (p. 28). The No Child Left Behind Act and the Head Start outcomes have refueled this belief in the veracity of a curriculum. A curriculum is "a plan for learning" (Wiles & Bondi, 1998), and most are driven by specific outcomes—those that some expert has decided are needed to reach the next rung on the educational ladder (usually developmentally inappropriate kindergarten entry-level skills). Several questions, however, must be asked:

Does, in fact, input result in output? Is the educational model so simple, mechanical, linear, and businesslike? Doesn't this kind of model deny any sense of inner direction, child-center learning, and spirituality and soul? (Steiner, 1926).

Does following the prescribed rungs of the ladder develop the kind of people we want? There are many examples of famous people who did not follow these rungs: Einstein, Erikson, Bill Gates, home-schooled students, and the very successful graduates of the free schools in the 1960s and 1970s. A mother told me a story of her daughter who dropped out of high school. When she finally decided to go to college she negotiated with the college to take the first two semesters on a trial basis—without ever getting a high school diploma or GED. Not only did she pass with flying colors, she is now a pediatrician!

Who develops the plan, and how do they know what is best for our children? John Dewey (1938) talked a lot about basing curricula of children's own experiences, interests, and aspirations.

Why do we not trust children and teachers to collaborate with parents to develop their own curriculae? This reliance on a curriculum is a strong indictment against the professionalism of teachers; it's also obviously a deep belief that children will not learn what is needed without a curriculum-by-numbers approach.

What happens if the plan is wrong? More specifically, what happens if the plan misses important outcomes, such as teaching a second language beginning in preschool, focusing extensively on the epidemic of childhood obesity, spending more time and energy on emotional and social development and conflict resolution, and integrating effective diversity education? Are we developing a bunch of fat, asocial citizens who cannot relate to others, who are intolerant of differences, and who cannot compete in the global marketplace because they only speak English, but who can read, write, and work on a computer at home?

Minority Students Are Unsuccessful Due to a Eurocentric Approach to Education

Multiculturalists insist that the failure of minority children in our educational programs is because these programs are Eurocentric—developed to work only for the white children. Early childhood multiculturalists have fully embraced this cannon (Ramsey, 1998; York, 2003). Clearly, there is a tragic achievement gap between white and Asian students on the one hand, and Native American, Black and Hispanic students on the other hand. But is this gap due solely to an Eurocentric approach?

Asian children as a group, who are clearly a minority, not only do as well as white children, but in some cases do better (Thernstrom & Thernstrom, 2003).

Picture young Mayan children in their ragged clothes and bare feet writing on small slate tablets with stubs of chalk in a 'school'—a four-post structure with a laminar (corrugated iron) roof. These little children learned their lesson enthusiastically. The fact the building was primitive and lacked resources, the instructor white, and the material Eurocentric, did not bother them. They were motivated to learn because their parents were learning with them, and because they were starved for basic literacy instruction.

We must admit that, while we have children in this country from a variety of cultural backgrounds, all of them are American—especially African American, Native American, and Hispanic families that have been here for generations. As such, these children and their families generally subscribe to the American values of competition, individualism, legal justice, materialism, gender differences, the value of education, and religious freedom.

The fact a disproportionate number of minorities are placed in special education is, I believe, more of a function of the U.S. deficit approach to disabilities (IDEA), than a Eurocentric idea. After all, far fewer students in Europe are diagnosed with special needs than the U.S., and more boys, including white boys (the ultimate symbol of white privilege) are in special education (Berger, 2005).

The strongest statistical correlation with school success is income (Hout, 2002). The problem is that minority families are statistically more represented in the low-income category. Schools in low-income areas tend to have fewer resources, less experienced teachers, and more discipline problems (Hout, 2002).

School success is largely dependent on family support of education. I have proposed what I call a three-legged-stool model of school success: home, school and community. Each leg must provide the optimal stimulation, support, structure and expectations needed. The seat connects all 3 legs together, in a unified manner, much like Bronfenbrenner's mesosystem (1979). Without the seat the stool falls; without open, supportive two-way communication between home, school and community, the minority child will not succeed.

Is a Eurocentric approach really bad for our minority children? Many claim that because DAP is Eurocentric it is detrimental to minority children (Lubeck, 1998; Ramsey 1998; York, 2003). But a DAP approach calls for adjusting the curriculum to meet individual needs, working closely with families and the community, responding to "the whole child", and considering cultural and linguistic diversity (Bredekamp & Copple, 1997). How is this bad? As our population becomes more and more diverse we need a more DAP approach, and a less standards-based approach (Wardle & Cruz-Janzen, 2004).

Further, our very approach to special needs, linguistic diversity, and the right of each individual child to succeed in our schools is based on this country's Eurocentric belief in individual rights, educational opportunity, and legal justice. The academic divide is a tragedy in a society that depends heavily on its schools to provide equal opportunity. We must solve this dilemma. To do so, we must challenge our orthodoxies about the causes of the problem.

The Calendar Activity

In 1996 I was asked by Partners of the Americas to build a playground for a low income crèche in Brazil (Wardle, 1999). While I was checking out the site I toured the dingy classrooms. There were no books, building blocks, or paints. There was no housekeeping area or place for the children to nap, and the kitchen was very poorly equipped. But they did have a calendar proudly affixed to the wall (with names and numbers in Portuguese, of course). Recently in a graduate psychology class I discussed with my students that, according to Piaget, preoperational children cannot possibly do the calendar activity in a meaningful way (Wardle, 2001). Then a kindergarten teacher asked me the obvious question: why do we teach this activity? And it seems like we teach it all over the world!

I have already discussed that children's ideas of time are based on activity—what we do—not the passage of time. Further, in today's world it's extremely easy to know the date by checking a watch, computer or newspaper. Important concepts of such as past, present and future, sequence, repetition, can all be taught in much more effective ways.

Universal ECE Standards Will Improve the Image of Our Profession

Clearly our profession is not well regarded by much of the public: Many see us as "just babysitters"; the teaching profession still perpetuates the notion that school starts at kindergarten. I recently met a Head Start education manager who believes the new outcomes are very positive, "because now we are not just babysitters". And many colleges prefer to graduate teachers with an elementary education degree with a few ECE classes tacked on, rather than a full ECE degree (Silva & Johnson, 1999). Others deeply believe if it's something that any parent can do, then it can't be that difficult.

When the public's view of the counseling profession plummeted after the 'free love' approach of many therapists during the sixties, counseling organizations quickly established professional codes of ethics and developed training standards for their field. The early childhood profession is doing the same thing, creating codes of ethics (NAEYC, 1989, 1992, 1998), codifying a ladder of professional development, and professing the value of standards. Head Start now requires college degrees for teachers; the No Child Left Behind act requires degrees for public school paraprofessionals.

But this will not increase the status of the early childhood profession. First, professionals must be paid like professionals and get the kind of benefits professionals deserve. In France ECE teachers are paid the same as regular teachers, have the same professional requirements, are paid the same benefits, and have the same number of paid in-service and further education classes each year (and, of course, paid substitutes) (Hurless, 2004). Secondly, in my mind one of the things that perpetuate the public's low view of our profession is a total lack of ethical behavior. And I'm not talking about teachers. From my personal experience in Head Start, corporate child care, and early child-

hood leadership groups, I have come to realize that members at the top of our profession do not follow the ethical standards that we ask of our teachers.

And, as we are discovering with K-12 standards, the negatives of standards for the early childhood field far outweighs any positives. These include:

Children who cannot achieve the standards are viewed as failures or placed in special education.

All the schools resources—space, energy, professional support, money—are focused 100 percent toward the standards. Everything else is secondary: special education, emotional/mental health, school climate, diversity, anti-obesity efforts, working with parents, etc.

The standards are not DAP. A central component of DAP is individual differences (Bredekamp & Copple, 1997). Declaring that every child should be reading at a third grade level denies this individual difference.

The entire concept of standard implies lack of a standard. While we are trying to change the stigma of children with special needs, we are creating a stigma that children who cannot meet a standard are somewhat abnormal. In some states, for example, special education students are still required to take each of the standardized tests.

There are many instances where important learning activities are being withheld from children because they have performed poorly on a standardized test. This includes withholding recess, physical education, computers, and extra classes such as music and art. These activities are the very thing these children desperately need; yet they are being withheld to improve their scores in literacy, math, and science.

Since we teach to the standards and their tests, an area that is not tested is simply unimportant. Thus art, music, dance, social development, emotional development, character education, conflict resolution, and physical education are shortchanged.

Conclusion

All professions develop a canon of beliefs and practices that are passed from generation to generation. Unfortunately, if these canons are not carefully examined, we can end up perpetuating harmful practices in the name of professional behavior. This article highlighted areas important for careful examination, and most importantly areas where a change of approach might be beneficial to the children in early childhood programs.

References

Berger, K. (2005). *The developing person. Through the lifespan.* (6th ed.). New York, NY: Worth Publisher.

Berk, L.E. & Winsler, A. (1995). *Scaffolding children's learning: Vygotsky and early childhood education.* Washington, DC: NAEYC.

Bowlby, J. (1969). Attachment. *Vol.1 of attachment and loss.* New York: Basic Books.

Brainerd, C.J. (1978). *Piaget's theory of Intelligence.* Englewood Cliffs, NJ: Prentice-Hall.

Bredekamp, S., & Copple, C. (1997). *Developmentally appropriate practice* (rev. ed.). Washington, DC: NAEYC.

Bronfenbrenner, U. (1979). *The ecology of human development.* Cambridge, MA: Harvard University Press.

Burke, J. R. (1997). Examining the validity structure of qualitative research. *Education,* 118 (2), 282–293.

Dodge, D.T., & Bickart, T. (2003). Curriculum, assessment, and outcomes. Putting them all in perceptive. *Children and Families,* XVII (1), 28–31.

Dewey, J. (1938). *Education and experience.* New York, NY: McMillan.

Dunn, L., & Kontos, S. (1997). Research in review: What we have learned about developmentally appropriate practice. *Young Children,* 52(4), 4–13

Gonzalez-Mena, J. (2001). Foundations. *Early Childhood education in a diverse society.* (2nd ed.) Mountain View, CA: Mayfield.

Gordon, A.M. & Browne, K.W (2004). *Foundations in early childhood education.* (6th ed.) Clifton Park, NJ: Delmar Learning.

Hatch, A. Bowman, B., Jor'dna, J., Morgan, Hart, C., Soto, J, Lubeck, S., and Hyson, M. (2002). Developmentally appropriate practice: Continuing the dialogue. *Contemporary Issues in Early Childhood,* 3, 439–57.

Honig, A.S. (2002). The power of positive attachment. *Scholastics Early Childhood Today.* (April), 32–34.

Hout, M. (2002). Test scores, education, and poverty. In J.M. Fish (Ed.) *Race and Intelligence: Separating Science from Myth* (329–354). Mahwah, NJ: Lawrence Erlbaum Associates.

Hurless, B.R. (Sept, 2004). Early childhood education in France. A personal perspective. *Beyond the Journal: Young Children on the Web.* Retrieved, Oct, 2004.

Johnson, J., Christie, J., & Wardle, F. (2005). *Play, development, and early education.* Boston, MA: Allyn and Bacon.

Lally, J.R. (1998). Brain research, infant learning and child care curriculum. *Child Care Information Exchange* (May/June), 46–48.

Lubeck, S. (1998). Is developmentally appropriate practice for everyone? *Childhood Education,* 74 (5) 283–92.

National Association for the Education of Young Children (1989, 1992, 1998). *Code of ethical conduct and statement of commitment: Guidelines for responsible behavior in early childhood education.* (Rev. ed.). Brochure. Washington, DC: Author.

Ramsey, PG. (1998). *Teaching and learning in a diverse world: Multicultural education for young children.* (2nd ed). New York, NY: Teachers College Press.

Ryan, S., & Grieshaber, S. (2004). It's more than child development: Critical theories, research, and teaching young children. *Young Children,* 59 (6), 44–52.

Shore, R. (1997). *Rethinking the brain. New insights into early development.* New York, NY: Families and Work institute.

Silva, D.Y., & Johnson, J.E. (1999). Principals' preference for the N-3 certificate. *Pennsylvania Educational Leadership,* 18 (2), 71–81.

Steiner, R. (1926). *The essentials of education.* London: Anthroposophical Publishing Co.

Thernstrom, A., & Thernstrom, S. (2003). *No excuses: Closing the racial gap in learning.* New York, NY: Simon and Schuster.

Wardle, F. (1999). The story of a playground. *Child Care Information Exchange,* 128 (July/Aug), 28–30.

Wardle, F. (2001). Developmentally appropriate math: How children learn. *Children and Families. XVII (2),* 14–15.

Wardle, F. (2003). Introduction to early childhood education: A multidimensional approach to child-centered care and learning. Boston, MA: Allyn and Bacon.

Wardle, F. (2004). Character education: Seeing a bigger picture. *Child Care Information Exchange.* 160 (Nov/Dec.) 41–43.

Wardle, F., & Cruz-Janzen, M. I. (2004), *Meeting the needs of multiethnic and multiracial children in schools.* Boston, MA: Allyn and Bacon.

Wiles, J. & Bondi, J. (1998). *Curriculum development: A guide to practice* (5th ed.) Upper Saddle River, NJ: Merrill.

York, S. (2003). *Roots and Wings: Affirming culture in early childhood programs* (Rev. ed). St. Paul, MN: Redleaf Press.

Francis Wardle, PhD, teaches for the University of Phoenix (Colorado) and is the executive director for the Center for the Study of Biracial Children. He has just published the book with Marta Cruz Jansen, *Meeting the Needs of Multiethnic and Multiracial Children,* available from Allyn & Bacon, www.ablongman.com.

The Looping Classroom

Benefits for Children, Families, and Teachers

MARY M. HITZ, MARY CATHERINE SOMERS, AND CHRISTEE L. JENLINK

The second week of school, the second-graders work intently in small groups or individually. They require little direct teacher instruction and clearly understand their responsibilities and the teacher's expectations. How did this independence develop so early? What did the teacher do?

W elcome to a looping classroom! "Looping—which is sometimes called multiyear teaching or multiyear placement—occurs when a teacher is promoted with her students to the next grade level and stays with the same group of children for two or three years" (Rasmussen 1998, 1). What results is a continuity of relationship with their teacher that enables children to flourish (Wynne & Walberg 1994).

American's one room schoolhouse was a looping classroom, with the teacher teaching the same children over a period of several years.

Looping Origins

The practice of looping is not a new concept in education. America's one room schoolhouse was a looping classroom, with the teacher teaching the same children over a period of several years. In Germany in 1919 Rudolf Steiner developed the Waldorf School model. Oppenheimer suggests that one unusual aspect of education in the Waldorf School "Is a system called looping, whereby a homeroom teacher stays with a class for more than a year . . . from first through eighth grade" (1999, 82). Also in the early 1900s, Italian pediatrician Maria Montessori introduced the Montessori Method, characterized by relationship development over several years on the part of the teacher, child, and parents (Seldin n.d).

> ### The Multiage Classroom
>
> Two or more grade levels are intentionally placed in a single classroom. Children are taught as a class and regrouped as necessary for different activities based on interests and/or abilities rather than on chronological age or grade level. At the end of each year, the older students move to a new class, and a group of younger students joins the class. In a multiage grouping, children can experience being both younger and older among the students in their class.

Generally, in modern Germany, student groups formed in first grade remain together over the next four years (Zahorik & Dichanz 1994). In China, grouping is by grade level, with a homeroom teacher who stays with students two to three years in elementary school and for three years in both junior and senior high schools. Many subject area teachers also choose to teach the same students for two to three years (Liu 1997).

In 1974 Deborah Meier founded the Central Park East Elementary School in New York City. Because she believed it takes time to build relationships, in this school the children and teachers stayed together for two years (Meier 1995).

In other instances, U.S. schools developed looping classrooms to solve scheduling problems or manage the significant population shifts in enrollment numbers per grade. This led to teachers being assigned to different or combined grades especially in small rural schools where school populations fluctuate each year. The multiage model is another popular form of looping (see "The Multiage Classroom").

Introducing Looping Today

It is not expensive or difficult to begin a school looping program. Two teachers volunteer for the assignment on any two contiguous grade levels. For example, teacher A teaches first grade and teacher B teaches second grade. The next year, teacher A moves with her class to teach second grade, and teacher B cycles back to begin with a group of new first-graders. Prior to looping, the two teachers and their administrator thoughtfully plan for this structural change (see "Starting a Looping Program").

Benefits of Looping for Children

In today's rapidly altering world, many children's lives are filled with change: of residence, in family structure, in economic status. Numerous children come from single parent homes or have two parents both working full-time away from home. Children can benefit from the looping classroom's stability and teacher continuity (Nichols & Nichols 2002).

Children in typical settings. Because children typically attend school six or more hours a day, five days a week, the teacher is a significant adult in their lives. Staying together two years or longer enhances the bonding and trust established between children and teacher (Grant, Johnson, & Richardson 1996). Pianta and LaParo, in discussing how to improve early school success, conclude that "relationships that children have with adults and other children in families, child care, and school programs provide the foundation for their success in school" (2003, 27). When children form secure relationships with teachers and other caregivers, both social and cognitive competence show improvement (Kontos & Wilcox-Herzog 1997; Gallagher & Mayer 2006).

In the looping classroom children build relationships over time with an adult confidant. Grant and Johnson suggest, "For a lot of children today, their teacher is often the most stable, predictable adult in their life" (1995, 34). Several examples of benefits follow from two coauthors' (Hitz and Somers) primary grades looping classrooms.

> Makayla, an eight-year-old, was one of four children, including a sister who was very bright and two brothers with cognitive disabilities. She brought a great deal of pent-up anger to school. During the first year in the looping class, her many angry outbursts involved lashing out at anyone nearby. By her second year in the looping class, she trusted us enough to tell us what was happening. When necessary, Makayla could choose to move to a more isolated area to work alone or, with teacher permission, could go to the office to talk with the assistant principal. Makayla's aggressive expressions lessened, and she gained a sense of control over her emotions.

With additional time together, teachers can become more familiar with each child's learning style, interests, strengths, and needs and respond with individualized learning experiences (Seldin n.d.). In a looping classroom children are not apprehensive about their second or next years; they already know their teacher and classmates (Lacina-Gifford 2001). The familiar environment also allows a shy child to blossom. For example,

> At the beginning of his first looping year, Eric cried when called upon during any kind of discussion. Later in the year he would raise his hand to volunteer, only to shrink inside himself at being recognized. Once in a while he worked with another child.

> ## Starting a Looping Program
>
> - Form a proposal study group
> - Read about looping programs
> - Enlist and build support from administrators and other teachers
> - Involve parents in the planning
> - Design the program to allow for change
> - Provide time for staff development
> - Visit other looping programs
> - Invite teachers to volunteer for looping classrooms
> - Work with administrators on the careful selection of the teachers for looping

> Knowing we would have Eric for two years, we did not feel the pressure to force participation in the first year. We offered support and encouragement when he attempted to participate but also allowed him needed time to mature.
>
> Although Eric struggled in reading all that first year, during the second year he volunteered more often and answered questions. Eric was on grade level at the end of the year. His mother was glad he was in a looping classroom. He was still quiet, but he knew he could do well in a new third grade classroom.

In a looping classroom, the teacher and the children experience a sense of community. The bonds between children grow strong; they share achievements and disappointments, resolve problems, and learn to trust each other. Teachers personalize their teaching and talk about their individual interests and their families.

One of the most positive elements of looping is that it allows a child to grow at his or her own pace, not at an arbitrary fixed-grade rate. John Goodlad reminds us that children "don't fit into a nice, neat age-grade package, either collectively or individually. Each individual child differs in regard to the various areas of accomplishment" (Stone 1999, 265). An example from our classroom follows:

> Austin, a young first-grader, worked hard in class and at home with his parents. By the end of the year, however, he was barely able to read at the preprimary level. His mother asked if we should retain Austin in first grade. We suggested waiting, since as a looping class we could monitor Austin's progress in the coming year.
>
> Austin bloomed that second year. Reading became his favorite activity, and by the end of the year he was reading above grade level. In third grade he moved into the gifted program. Had Austin been in a nonlooping classroom, he might have been retained.

English-language learners. The looping classroom supports children and their families for whom English is a second language. As English-language learners (ELLs) adjust to a new school and become comfortable with their teacher, they develop confidence in practicing their new language. Eventually they may help others who are new to the class or have little knowledge of U.S. culture. When children who are ELLs are members of a class, the other children can learn firsthand from a peer about another culture and country. The experience results in respect and understanding among all the students (Haslinger, Kelly, & O'Lare 1996).

> Maritza uses both English and Spanish. One day, in her second year, she and three other Spanish-speaking friends chose a book to read to the class and designed follow-up activities. They read the story aloud—in Spanish. The other children gained an idea of what ELL students experience when learning a second language. Because Maritza and her friends felt safe and secure in their classroom, they could make this presentation to their peers.

Looping Pluses for Others

Looping provides time for teachers to get to know each child and family in a personal way, and it fosters stronger bonds between teachers and families.

Teachers. In nonlooping classrooms, each year teachers spend the first four to six weeks determining each child's skills, abilities, and interests. In contrast, in the second year of a looping classroom cycle, the teacher already knows the students and is able to immediately support their learning, thus making better use of instructional time (Little & Dacus 1999). Effective teaching and learning can begin on the first day of the second year after a brief review of rules and procedures (Burke 1996).

Many teachers provide summer learning packets to help children bridge from one year to the next. In looping classrooms the children are returning to the same classroom and teacher, and it is easy to design packets and follow up with them the second year. Children are excited to share journals kept over the summer, stories they wrote, or special books they read. The looping teacher can build on children's previous year's experiences and use the summer packets to lead into the second year's curriculum.

One of the most positive elements of looping is that it allows a child to grow at his or her own pace, not at an arbitrary fixed-grade rate.

Usually teachers choose to loop because they believe in developmentally appropriate practices, including the importance of encouraging emotional development (Dunn & Kontos 1997). Such teachers understand young children's need for stability and how the looping classroom addresses that need.

In looping classrooms, collaborating teachers learn new skills and curriculum (Albrecht et al. 2000) by sharing materials and ideas. They have a chance to know more about the children— where they live, who needs extra motivation, who works best

with whom (Burke 2000). Units of study can extend into the next year. Looping gives teachers an extra year to consider high-stakes decisions regarding retention or referral for testing for special services (Jacobson 1997; Liu 1997; Bracey 1999).

Families. Looping classrooms foster stronger bonds between families and teachers. "Because parents are the most significant people in a child's life, the relationship between the teacher and the parents is paramount" (Albrecht et al. 2000, 24). Parents tend to place more trust in a teacher the second year, with the development of a relaxed relationship conducive to a positive attitude toward the teacher (Nichols & Nichols 2002). Conversely, the teacher values input from the home, a direct result of the collaborative relationship that has been forged in this type of classroom setting.

Parents get to know the teacher's philosophy of education and how it relates to their child. Because a trusting relationship builds over the long span of a looping classroom, families may be more willing to accept a teacher's constructive suggestions (Chirichello & Chirichello 2001) and tend to be comfortable sharing the challenges they face with their child at home. Our looping classroom provides this example:

> Zach had difficulty completing classroom assignments on time. At home, his family reported he was never ready on time and every morning was a fight to get dressed for school. Zach's mother called one morning to say he would be at school on time, but in his pajamas. We were proud of the other children for not making fun of Zach or teasing him. But ever after, Zach was always ready for school.

For the families of children who are English-language learners, the stability of having the same teacher for a span of two years helps them gain confidence in talking with the teacher about their children's progress. The teacher can also smooth this transition by having materials translated as frequently as possible into the family's home language and arranging for translators to attend conferences.

A looping classroom favors both the child and the teacher and adds stability to children's lives.

What Concerns Might Arise in Looping?

While the advantages of a looping classroom are many, some concerns do arise. One issue parents express is a fear of their child being locked in for two years with a possibly ineffective teacher. Other potential problems include a teacher-child personality conflict, a child who simply does not get along with the other children, or a parent who does not get along with the teacher. Although looping teachers report that these occurrences are rare; each school needs to have procedures for reviewing class placements. The school principal plays an important role in identifying teacher-child personality conflicts as well as ensuring that teachers have the skills and work ethic necessary to create a successful looping classroom.

In our looping classroom two sets of parents came to us with concerns about their children. In both instances the issues reflected differences about teaching philosophy. After discussions, with both sets of parents, we jointly decided to place each child in a traditional classroom. Involvement of the school principal is essential in such situations to ensure making the best decision for the child.

Another challenge involves a new child entering the program, especially in the second year when children are already familiar with each other and the classroom. The looping teacher must prepare and encourage the children to welcome and accept the new student and help the child become part of the community.

Conclusion

At the end of the school year, it is always difficult to say goodbye, but when a teacher and children have been together for two years, it is doubly difficult. The class is a learning community that has shared joys as well as the sadness of departure. Some teachers plan special events to highlight their two years together. The children outline their advice to the incoming group of younger students and write letters to their future teachers to introduce themselves. Receiving teachers visit the looping class to be introduced to their new students when possible.

Good-bye is a bittersweet time. Sometimes it's harder for parents. Not only do looping teachers have to reassure the children that they will succeed, but also they have to reassure the families.

The concept of a looping classroom is being revisited by many teachers today. It favors both the child and the teacher and adds stability to children's lives. It provides time—time for children to grow and develop at their own rates and time for teachers to get to know each child and family in a personal way.

Looping may not be a good fit for everyone nor solve all the problems in education. But teacher proponents express it this way: Looping provides the most rewarding opportunity for helping children succeed (Rasmussen 1998).

References

Albrecht, K., M. Banks, G. Calhoun, L. Dziadul, C. Gwinn, B. Harrington, B. Kerr, M. Mizukami, A. Morris, C. Peterson, & R.R. Summers. 2000. The good, the bad and the wonderful! Keeping children and teachers together. *Child Care Information Exchange* (136): 24–28.

Bracey, G.W. 1999. Going loopy for looping. *Phi Delta Kappan* 81 (2): 169–70.

Burke, D.L. 1996. Multi-year teacher/student relationships are a long-overdue arrangement. *Phi Delta Kappan* 77 (5): 360–61.

Burke, D.L. 2000. Learning to loop and loving it. *The School Administrator Web Edition*. Online: www.aasa.org. publications/content.cfm?ItemNumber=3831

Chirichello, M., & C. Chirichello. 2001. A standing ovation for looping: The critics respond. *Childhood Education* 78 (1): 2–10.

Dunn, L., & S. Kontos. 1997. What have we learned about developmentally appropriate practice? *Young Children* 52 (5): 4–13.

Gallagher, K.C., & K. Mayer. 2006. Teacher-child relationships at the forefront of effective practice. *Young Children* 61 (6): 44–49.

Grant, J., & B. Johnson. 1995. *A common sense guide to multiage practices, primary level*. Columbus, OH: Teachers' Publishing Group.

Grant, J., B. Johnson, & I. Richardson. 1996. *Our best advice: The multiage problem solving handbook*. Petersborough, NH: Crystal Springs Books.

Haslinger, J., P. Kelley, & L. O'Lare. 1996. Countering absenteeism, anonymity, and apathy. *Educational Leadership* 54 (1): 47–49.

Jacobson, L. 1997. 'Looping' catches on as way to build strong ties. *Education Week* 17 (7): 1–3.

Kontos, S., & A. Wilcox-Herzog. 1997. Teachers' interactions with children: Why are they so important? *Young Children* 52 (2): 4–12.

Lacina-Gifford, L.J. 2001. The squeaky wheel gets the oil, but what about the shy student? *Education* 122 (2): 320–21.

Little, T.S., & N.B. Dacus. 1999. Looping: Moving up with the class. *Educational Leadership* 57 (1): 42–45.

Liu, J. 1997. The emotional bond between teachers and students: Multi-year relationships. *Phi Delta Kappan* 78 (2): 156–57.

Meier, D. 1995. *The power of their ideas: Lessons for America from a small school in Harlem*. Boston, MA: Beacon.

Nichols, J.D., & G.W. Nichols. 2002. The impact of looping classroom environments on parental attitudes. *Preventing School Failure* 47 (1): 18–25.

Oppenheimer, T. 1999. Schooling the imagination. *The Atlantic Monthly* 284 (2): 71–83.

Pianta, R.C., & K. LaParo. 2003. Improving early school success. *Educational Leadership* 60 (7): 24–29.

Rasmussen, K. 1998. Looping: Discovering the benefits of multiyear teaching. *Education Update* 40 (2): 41–44.

Selden, T. N.d. Montessori 101: Some basic information that every Montessori parent should know. Online: www.montessori.org/ sitefiles/Montessori_101_nonprintable.pdf.

Stone, S.J. 1999. A conversation with John Goodlad. *Childhood Education* 75 (5): 264–68.

Wynne, E.A., & H.J. Walberg. 1994. Persisting groups: An overlooked force for learning. *Phi Delta Kappan* 75 (7): 527–30.

Zahorik, J.A., & H. Dichanz. 1994. Teaching for understanding in German schools. *Educational Leadership* 51 (5): 75–77.

UNIT 6

Helping Children to Thrive in School

Unit Selections

28. **Play: Ten Power Boosts for Children's Early Learning,** Alice Sterling Honig
29. **Ready or Not, Here We Come: What It Means to Be a Ready School,** Paula M. Dowker, with Larry Schweinhart, and Marijata Daniel-Echols
30. **"Stop Picking On Me!": What You Need to Know about Bullying,** *Texas Child Care*
31. **"You Got It!": Teaching Social and Emotional Skills,** Lise Fox and Rochelle Harper Lentini
32. **Fostering Positive Transitions for School Success,** Jayma Ferguson McGann and Patricia Clark
33. **A Multinational Study Supports Child-Initiated Learning: Using the Findings in Your Classroom,** Jeanne E. Montie, Jill Claxton, and Shannon D. Lockhart
34. **The Power of Documentation in the Early Childhood Classroom,** Hilary Seitz

Key Points to Consider

- What does it mean to be a ready school?

- Why is emotional stability so important to develop during the preschool years?

- Is it possible to prevent disruptive behavior before it occurs?

- How can a teacher build positive relationships with children?

Student Web Site
www.mhcls.com

Internet References

Future of Children
http://www.futureofchildren.org
Busy Teacher's Cafe
http://www.busyteacherscafe.com
Tips for Teachers
http://www.counselorandteachertips.com
You Can Handle Them All
http://www.disciplinehelp.com

Early childhood teaching is all about being proactive and establishing policies that support young children's development and learning. Good teachers are problem solvers just as children work to solve problems. Every day, teachers make decisions about how to guide children socially and emotionally. In attempting to determine what could be causing a child's emotional distress, teachers must take into account a myriad of factors. They should consider the physical, social, environmental, and emotional factors, in addition to the surface behavior of a child. Whether it is an individual child's behavior or interpersonal relationships, the pressing problem involves complex issues that require careful reflection and analysis. Even the most mature teachers spend many hours thinking and talking about the best ways to guide and support young children's behavior: What should I do about the child who is out of bounds? What do I do to best prepare the learning environment to meet the needs of all children? How can I develop effective relationships with children and their families? These are some of the questions teachers ask as they interact with young children on a day-to-day basis.

Alice Sterling Honig shares ten strategies for supporting young children's learning in her article, "Play: Ten Power Boosts for Children's Early Learning." Dr. Honig has consistently been a reassuring voice for teachers struggling to meet the needs of all children.

When those outside of the education profession talk about getting children ready to learn, many early childhood professionals instinctively say to themselves, "Children come to us already learning. Our job is to make our schools and classrooms ready to accept all children." That is the theme of "Ready or Not, Here We Come: What It Means to Be a Ready School" by Dowker, Schweinhart and Daniel-Echols. It is our responsibility to accommodate the learning environment and provide the support for children and their families to successfully transfer to the next phase in their learning.

This unit addresses teachers who establish positive relationships with children. "'You Got It!'" supports the need for positive relationships as the cornerstone for building rapport. The other theme that is woven throughout the articles in this unit is the importance of social and emotional development on all areas of development. Teachers who rush to teach academic skills at the expense of fostering the children's social and emotion development will find there are many unexpected hurdles to jump. Children who are not secure or confident in their surroundings or comfortable with the adults in their life will not be strong learners. "Fostering Positive Transitions for School Success" highlights the importance of socioemotional development and sets a proactive tone by providing teachers with an overview of the importance of children feeling secure about themselves and their place in life. When I sent my two sons off to college, I thought about the many ways their universities prepared them, and their parents, for this major transition. First year orientation programs, welcome week activities and parents' weekend were all carefully planned to assist the new students adjusting to college. We do little to help five-year-olds who are also making a major transition in their life. It is time preschool teachers, kindergarten teachers, and families collaborate to ensure a smooth progression to the next learning experience.

© Tom Grill/Corbis

As educators across the country work to implement an antibullying environment, it is important for teachers to work diligently to establish an environment that is supportive of all children and discourages and stops any attempt at bullying. "'Stop Picking On Me!': What You Need to Know about Bullying" provides suggestions for teachers to establish a positive climate in their classrooms. Children who believe they are accepted and respected in the classroom feel confident and are able to develop genuine relationships with their peers and with their teacher. Teachers who have a limited number of disruptive children in their class are those teachers who take precautionary steps to establish firm rules, establish a supportive environment, and help children learn about the consequences of their behavior.

Determining strategies for guidance and discipline is an important work for an early childhood teacher. Because the teacher-child relationship is the foundation for emotional well-being and social competence, guidance is more than applying a single set of guidance techniques. Instead of one solitary model of classroom discipline strictly enforced, a broad range of techniques is more appropriate. It is only through careful analysis and reflection that teachers can look at children individually, assessing not only the child but the impact of family cultures as well, and determine appropriate and effective guidance.

Children crave fair and consistent guidelines from caring adults in their world. They want to know the consequences of their behavior and how to meet the expectations of others. When the expectations are clear and the students see a direct relation between their behavior and the consequences, they begin to develop the self control that will be so important as they move through life.

This unit ends with Hilary Seitz's "The Power of Documentation in the Early Childhood Classroom." Seitz describes the benefits of documentation and shares suggested ways to document learning. Teachers who take responsibility to educate others about the learning in their classroom will have successful partnerships with others, including family members and administrators.

Play: Ten Power Boosts for Children's Early Learning

ALICE STERLING HONIG

Many adults think of play and learning as separate domains. Indeed, some people believe that academic school work is learning but that play is just what young children do to get rid of lots of energy. The truth learned from research is that rich, varied play experiences strongly boost children's early learning (Kaplan 1978; Bergen 1998; Johnson, Christie, & Yawkey 1999).

Children gain powerful knowledge and useful social skills through play.

Children gain powerful knowledge and useful social skills through play. This article offers 10 ideas about what children learn through play.

Play Enhances Dexterity and Grace

Preschoolers learn eye-hand coordination and skillful toy manipulation through play. They spin a top, stack blocks, wind up a jack-in-the-box, and try out ways to solve the chain bolt or buttoning activity on a busy board. The variety of hand motions required to latch, lace, or twirl a top enhances hand dexterity. As they eat with a spoon, infants and toddlers are learning wrist coordination. Teachers support this control learning when they provide interesting activities, such as tossing a beanbag or throwing a soft yarn ball into baskets placed nearer or farther away. Babies adore filling and dumping games and will try to work a windup toy over and over again.

Place babies on their tummies on safe, warm surfaces. This gives them opportunities to stretch and reach for favorite chew toys. As they push up on their arms, infants practice coordination of their shoulder and chest muscles. Such body games are particularly important today because infants are habitually placed on their backs for safe sleeping in cribs.

Learning how to ride a tricycle or scooter enhances the coordination of muscles in legs and feet for toddlers and preschoolers.

Older children learn to play sports. They kick and throw basketballs, baseballs, and soccer balls. These games help children coordinate use of both sides of the body. Sports help children develop confidence and pride in their control over body movement in space.

"Hold-operate" skills in play are important for later learning. For example, a preschooler holds an eggbeater with one hand and turns the handle vigorously to make lots of bubbles during water play. A school-age child holds a book page open with one hand and writes notes with the other. Making a pop-it bead necklace is a challenging activity allowing toddlers to push and pull with their fingers. To promote whole body gracefulness, play soft, slow music, such as the "Skater's Waltz," and invite children to move their bodies.

Peer Play Promotes Social Skills

With admirable patience, teachers help children gradually learn how to take turns riding a tricycle, to share materials, and to work and build together. Soon they learn the pleasures of playing with peers (Smilansky & Shefatya 1990). As buddies, older infants giggle and take turns crawling or running into the cardboard house in the play area and popping their heads through the play-house window to shout "Hi" to a grinning peer peeking in. Toddlers might help put a train track together on the floor and play at being engineers. Preschoolers collaborate on lugging a wagon full of blocks or filling it with a heap of scooped up snow for building a snowman together.

Some children need a teacher's encouraging words to ask a peer for permission to join in a game (Honig & Thompson 1994). Henry pulls his wagon, and Jerry wants his pet cat to go for a ride too. Giving words to such longings boosts a child's ability to learn a variety of ways to get to play with a peer, instead of standing on the sidelines. In a warmly encouraging voice, the adult suggests, "Tell Jerry, 'I want to put my cat in the wagon.'"

Children sometimes need an adult's unobtrusive arrangement of props to encourage more advanced sociodramatic play. Others need innovative, adult suggestions to encourage more *inclusive* play. Overhearing some preschoolers tell Kao he cannot play house with them because they already have a mommy, a daddy, and children in their play scenario, the teacher comments, "Suppose there is going to be a birthday party. Kao can be the mail carrier delivering birthday presents to your home." The children take over from there.

In a tussle over a toy, an adult may need to model prosocial solutions for children who struggle to come up with social problem-solving ideas on their own. Shure's (1994) ICPS (I Can Problem Solve) techniques can be helpful. "Julio wants to play blocks, and you want him to play Batman dress-up. Can the two of you find a way to play what you want some of the time and what Julio wants the rest of the time? If you each get a turn choosing an activity, both of you can get your wish and have fun together." Getting children to think through the consequences of interactions is a daily challenge. Teachers can help boost children's ability to figure out how to make and keep a play pal by role-playing helpful scenarios: "Howie, if you go on the seesaw with me awhile, then we can play in the sandbox together." Children learn social skills combined with body coordination in games such as Hokey Pokey and London Bridge Is Falling Down.

Teaching social skills in play is crucially important for children with neurological or developmental disabilities.

Not excluding other children from play is a noble task for which Vivian Paley has instituted a classroom rule: You can't say you can't play. Her book (1992) by this name describes the day-to-day struggles of children to gain empathy and lessen the hurt others feel when they are excluded from peer play. Teaching social skills in play is crucially important for children with neurological or developmental disabilities such as autism spectrum disorders, who may need help decoding the emotions of others and responding in socially effective ways.

Children's Play Sharpens Cognitive and Language Skills

Teachers who carefully prepare materials for sensory motor activities are helping children learn tasks that involve what Piaget ([1951] 1962) calls "means-ends separations" and "causal relationships." When a baby pulls a toy on a string to move it closer or shakes a bell to hear it ring, she is delightedly learning that from certain actions, she gets a specific effect. The toddler banging a stick on a xylophone and miraculously producing musical notes also learns that those specific actions cause interesting results. Scientists use these same early life lessons in their laboratories every day.

Singing with young children creates a pleasurable form of play that enhances brain development and learning.

Infants who play with syllables in their cribs are practicing coordination of lips, tongue, palate, and vocal chords. Singing with young children creates a pleasurable form of play that enhances brain development and learning. Some young toddlers stretch their language abilities amazingly as they try to sing along with the words (Honig 1995). This learning counters theories that play is purely for sensory, personal, or social pleasure. Musical play involves lots of word learning; listen as an enthusiastic group of toddlers tries hard to copy the teacher's words as she sings "Frère Jacques."

Teachers can play rhyming games with toddlers and preschoolers. Start out with easy syllables: "I have a little gray mouse, and he lives in a little gray _____!" If children have trouble at first hearing the sounds, give them the answers and start the rhyming couplet game again. The ability to enjoy and participate in rhyming games is one predictor of success in learning to read.

Play promotes language mastery. Children talk together as they build houses with blocks, piece puzzles together, or construct a space tower using Legos. They talk excitedly as they pretend to get "hurt people" from a car crash scene into ambulances. Social play strengthens language interactions, and teachers may provide a word here and there as catalysts for language interchanges (Honig 1982). Housekeeping corners with dress-up clothes and workbenches and tables with safety goggles and woodworking tools promote feelings of efficacy and self-esteem as well as purposeful, harmonious peer interactions and accomplishments.

Preschoolers Acquire Number and Time Concepts

The Piagetian concept of *conservation of number* is difficult learning during the preschool years (Piaget [1951] 1962). By playing with toys with large, separate parts (that cannot be swallowed!), a preschooler begins to find out that whether he stacks the pieces, lays them out in a circle, or sets them out in one long row, he will still count the same number if he puts his finger carefully on each item while counting. Learning that the sum total does not depend on configuration may be easier if children feel encouraged to experiment with different arrangements of small animals, cars, or blocks.

Concepts such as *soon* or *later* and *before* or *after* are hard for young children to understand. To make the child's construction work, inserting one special piece *before* adding another piece may be the secret. Lego blocks that fit together into three-dimensional space require learning which parts to put together first and which ones to add on later to make the structure stable.

Using a digital camera helps children become more aware of different spatial aspects and directions and viewpoints in space. Will Giana's picture of a small ball rolling really fast (or even slowly) down a chute into a basin capture the ball's action? Preschoolers will enjoy taking real pictures of favorite activity areas. A child might take a photograph while peering down from a raised reading loft or one at eye level while lying on her tummy.

Cooking activities offer rich possibilities for math learning. Children learn varieties of colors and textures of foods and first-before-next scientific procedures, such as measuring just one-half teaspoon of oil for each muffin pan before filling it with three tablespoons of batter.

When music play is embedded in the daily curriculum, children learn "sequences of time" as rhymes and rhythms of chants and songs vary in their patterns and progressions. Even eight-month-old babies can bounce to the musical syllables you emphasize as you chant or sing songs, such as "Hickory dickory dock! The mouse ran up the clock!" Offer play experiences with wrist bells, maracas, tambourines, and keyboards, and sing the same songs over and over. As children move their bodies to musical syllables, especially if they clap out rhythms, they learn one-to-one correspondence between a syllable and a clap of the hands.

Play Areas Promote Children's Spatial Understanding

Learning space concepts occurs gradually through the early years. Toddlers gain understanding of spatial extents, boundaries, and pathways as they develop the surety to run, twirl, jump, careen around corners, or stop to bend down and pick up something with ease while galloping past an interesting toy. Preschoolers hop, jump, slide, swing from hanging bars, and climb up rope ladders—exploring spatial dimensions ever more bravely.

Some items, like a cardboard box tunnel, allow infants to crawl through and learn about *forward* and *backward.* Such toys as a car or truck with a front and back or a set of wooden toy trains connected by magnets at each end help babies and toddlers learn *front* and *back, longer* and *shorter, first* and *last.* As a toddler steers herself forward, cheerfully mindful of the wonderfully satisfying noise of the Corn Popper toy she pulls behind her, she is maneuvering and navigating through space, sometimes solving the problem of how to continue forward under the legs of a play table.

After three years of age, many children still have not learned to consider bounded space over their heads while getting out from under a table where they have crept to retrieve a toy. To promote spatial learning, a toy barn, house, or fire station is a fine prop. Children learn that the height of the door makes it easy or difficult to bring in a toy horse, stroller, or fire engine.

Play Prompts Children's Reasoning of Cause and Effect

From early infancy, play with various materials supports children's learning of *if-then* reasoning required for early experimentation and scientific thinking. Play with materials can introduce basic concepts in physics and in chemistry. Children learn how liquids mixed together form solutions with different properties, such as a change in color. A spinning gyroscope overcomes gravity, a lever lifts or moves something

heavy, balances measure weights, and an eyedropper sucks in a liquid. As the preschoolers enjoy seesaw (spring-loaded for safety) rides with friends, they learn how important weight and balance are in keeping the seesaw going.

Teachers' preparation of materials for science play arouses intense curiosity and leads to creative play experiments.

Water play is a particularly wondrous activity for experimenting. As children play with wooden and plastic cups, sifters and strainers, and eggbeaters at the water table, they learn that objects float or sink, pour or sprinkle. Teachers' preparation of materials for science play arouses intense curiosity and leads to creative play experiments. Block building is particularly fine for learning causal and space concepts. Smaller blocks seem to balance on bigger ones but not vice versa, no matter how many times a toddler determinedly tries. Toddlers often walk their toy animals down a slide and are not aware of how gravity could help. A preschooler easily depends on the awesome power of gravity as he launches himself down the playground slide. At play, children learn that things can roll if they have rounded sides but not if they have square sides or bumpy sides, like a not-quite-round potato!

Other science concepts learned in play are how to group objects together because of color, shape, size, or pattern design. Children learn too that things exist within larger groups: knives and forks are silverware, sofas and chairs are furniture.

Sociodramatic Play Clarifies the World of *Pretend* versus *Real*

Young children are not too certain what is *real.* For years, some children fervently believe in the tooth fairy and monsters under the bed. Remember the shepherd boy in Menotti's opera, *Amahl and the Night Visitors,* and the three kings on their way to Bethlehem? Amahl comes into the hut and exclaims excitedly to his mother that he has seen a "star with a tail as long as the sky!" A child may not be telling a lie; but imagination does fuel fantasy.

TV programs also encourage belief in fantasy and propel imaginative flights of pretense. After the Mars landing of an exploring robot, one preschooler gave his teacher a toy car, saying, "We are going to Mars, and we can drive our cars on Mars." His teacher nodded agreeably but was quiet. The child added reassuringly, "We just pretending!"

Imagination and pretend play are important giant steps forward in learning how to create dramatic scenarios in complex play with peers. Three-year-olds stirring pop-it beads in a pot pretend to make popcorn to eat. Play promotes the use of a rich imagination. An adult may be nonplussed when a preschooler objects to her sitting down on the couch, explaining that his imaginary playmate is already sitting there. When Talya proclaims she is a superhero and grabs Terry's toy, Terry's firm "My toy!" helps Talya learn the difference between the seemingly unlimited power of a TV fantasy character and the real needs and preferences of a playmate.

Play Enriches Children's Sensory and Aesthetic Appreciation

Listening to music of various genres or exploring color combinations with finger paints can arouse different feelings in children and their appreciation of beauty. Watch the glow on their faces as children carefully add drops of color to a small pan of water and then rejoice in the subtle color-patterned swirls they have created.

Teachers support aesthetic appreciation when they hang up colorful Kente cloth, tape large posters of Monet's *Water Lilies* on the wall, and play fast-paced salsa tunes for dancing. Providing squares of rainbow-colored nylon gauze adds aesthetic pleasure as well as bodily grace to children's dancing. Toddlers blowing and chasing bubbles to catch them in cupped hands is a game that combines aesthetic pleasure with increasing hand dexterity. It also enhances toddlers' abilities to estimate how far and how fast to run to catch a bubble before it pops.

Children delight in watching the unfolding of a fern's graceful fronds or the production of giant flowers by a big, brown amaryllis bulb they have planted. Their eyes widen in awe at the goldfish's graceful flick of its tail while swimming across the aquarium. Children seem primed early on to become lovers of beauty.

Play Extends Children's Attention Span, Persistence, and Sense of Mastery

Some children are cautious and slow in temperament, while others tend to be more impulsive. When children become absorbed in play, even children with shorter attention spans often stretch out their playtimes. Skillful, adult play partners can help children with short attention spans to extend their play. By providing intriguing toys and experiences and encouragement geared to the unique interests of each child, teachers help strengthen children's abilities to prolong play. This ability to focus attention and to persist at challenging learning tasks is a crucial component for later academic success in school.

When play is child initiated, children control the play themes and feel empowered. They come to realize their capabilities of mastering the roles, scenarios, and logistical problems that may arise in the course of sociodramatic play. No kennel for the stuffed puppy? OK, what can we use as a substitute kennel? As playmates arrange props and environments, teachers are superb helpers in facilitating child mastery of play themes.

Play Helps Children Release Emotions and Relieves Separation Anxiety

Learning to express and regulate emotions appropriately is a major challenge for young children. Sometimes they repetitively play out the central emotional concerns in their lives (Honig 1998).

Some children suffer anxious feelings from repeated separations and tearful parting from playmates who have become good friends. Children in military families may have already moved quite a few times, and if parents are deployed, the children may move again to stay with relatives they do not know. Hearing scary talk on the radio and TV may increase children's fears and lead to sadness and distress, bed-wetting, nail-biting, or fighting with peers instead of playing harmoniously. Caring teachers may notice a child's compulsive war play with toys and wisely give the child space, time, and acceptance to act out separation anxieties and fantasies in play, along with extra hugs, lap time, and soothing supportive actions.

Pretend play, even scary war play, provides a deep release for emotions. A toddler may soothingly feed a bottle to a baby doll or put a baby bear to bed in a toy crib. Teachers can build on this tender play to reassure the child how much an absent parent loves the child. Toddlers love telephone talk and gain opportunities to practice social interaction skills. Pretend telephone talk also comforts young children experiencing separation anxieties and lets them feel connected to their families, especially with ones far away.

Teachers need to be attuned to the sometimes worrisome messages that children's play can reveal. By observing how children express troubled feelings in play, teachers may better figure out ways to help young children feel nurtured and safe. After the events of 9/11, many preschoolers built block towers and crashed toy airplanes into them. Children's play provides a valuable window for tuning in to the worries, fears, angers, and happiness in their emotional lives.

Play deepens a child's sense of serenity and joy.

In Closing, play deepens a child's sense of serenity and joy. Children digging in the sand at a neighborhood pocket park resemble scruffy cherubs, their faces and arms covered with sand or dirt. Their bodies look so relaxed. One rarely hears them crying.

Tuned-in teachers can shape almost any play experience into an opportunity for children to learn more about the world and how it works. Water play, sand play, block play, ball play, searching for signs with different shapes and colors on a neighborhood walk—all become grist for early learning as well as early pleasure in play.

As teachers promote and encourage play, they enhance children's feelings of security, of being deeply acceptable, of being a welcomed friend. In carving out safe, leisurely, and generous times for children's play, teachers provide the cognitive and social groundwork for children's future learning.

References

Bergen, D., ed. 1998. *Play as a medium for learning and development: A handbook of theory and practice.* Portsmouth, NH: Heinemann.

Honig, A.S. 1982. *Playtime learning games for young children.* Syracuse, NY: Syracuse University Press.

Honig, A.S. 1995. Singing with infants and toddlers. *Young Children* 50(5): 72–78.

Honig, A.S. 1998. Sociocultural influences on sexual meanings embedded in playful experiences. In *Play from birth to twelve and beyond: Contents, perspectives, and meanings,* eds. P.Fromberg & D. Bergen, 338–47. New York: Garland Press.

Honig, A.S., & A. Thompson 1994. Helping toddlers with peer group entry skills. *Zero to Three* 14(5): 15–19.

Johnson, J.E., J.F. Christie, & T.D. Yawkey. 1999. *Play and early childhood development.* 2nd ed. Upper Saddle River, NJ: Allyn & Bacon/Longman/Pearson Education.

Kaplan, L. 1978. *Oneness and separateness.* New York: Simon & Schuster.

Paley, V. 1992. *You can't say you can't play.* Cambridge, MA: Harvard University Press.

Piaget, J. [1951] 1962. *play, dreams, and imitation in childhood.* New York: Norton.

Shure, M. 1994. *Raising a thinking child: Help your young child to resolve everyday conflicts and get along with others.* New York: Henry Holt.

Smilansky, S., & L. Shefatya. 1990. *Facilitating play: A medium for promoting cognitive, socio-emotional and academic development in young children.* Gaithersburg, MD: Psychosocial and Educational Publications.

ALICE STERLING HONIG, PhD, professor emerita of child development, Syracuse University, New York, has authored more than 450 chapters and articles and more than a dozen books. She teaches annually the National Quality Infant/Toddler Workshop and lectures widely on prosocial and language development and gender patterns in play.

Ready or Not, Here We Come
What It Means to Be a Ready School

Paula M. Dowker, with Larry Schweinhart, PhD and Marijata Daniel-Echols, PhD

In the game hide-and-seek, one player counts to 10 while the others run and hide. Now, depending on how fast the one who is "it" counts, some players may find they are not ready and hiding when that person comes looking for them. The problem of not being ready could stem from many causes: perhaps the player did not have the proper shoes, which made running difficult; maybe the player did not understand the rules and was not sure what to do; or perhaps the player had never played the game before. We educators of young children, prekindergarten through grade 3, encounter many of the same readiness issues when it comes to the children in our classrooms, because each child enters school with a completely different set of experiences and abilities.

Planning effectively for children with diverse backgrounds, learning styles, and school-readiness levels can be daunting. To better understand and respond to such challenges, early elementary educators need to become familiar with what it means to be a ready school, so they can assess and implement strategies to ensure success for all students. Those of us working with young children who will soon be entering school need to provide quality early childhood education and care that extends beyond preschool settings. When children move from high-quality early childhood experiences into ready schools, they benefit from having a strong foundation and access to superior tools with which to continue building upon that foundation.

We all have a stake in seeing that our children's schools are ready schools. A ready school is a comprehensive vision of what a school can do to ensure that all children who enter its doors will fulfill their potential as learners:

> The idea of a ready school broadens the definition of school readiness. Instead of only focusing on whether or not children arrive at school ready to learn, a more inclusive definition of readiness also considers whether or not school policies and practices support a commitment to the success of every child. The concept of school readiness must align the best of early childhood practices and elementary education in ways that build upon the strengths of each and locus equally on child outcomes, adult behaviors, and institutional characteristics. It is expected that children should come to school ready to learn and schools should open their doors able to serve all children. (High/Scope Educational Research Foundation 2006, 1)

Is your school, or the school that the young children you serve will attend, a ready school? Are its classrooms ready classrooms? Consider your answers to the following assessment, which will give you some idea of how to evaluate a school in terms of readiness:

- Does the principal communicate a clear vision for the school—a vision that is committed to the success of every child?
- Are parents of incoming children contacted about registration and school entry three or more months before school starts?
- Do kindergarten teachers communicate with preschool/child care staff about children and curriculum on an ongoing basis?
- Do classrooms have a variety of manipulative materials and supplies for art, building, and hands-on learning?
- Are procedures in place for monitoring the fidelity of implementation of all instructional materials/methods?
- Does the school promote community linkages by making and following up on appropriate referrals of children and families to social service and health agencies?
- Do classroom activities provide accurate, practical, and respectful information regarding peoples' cultural backgrounds and experiences?
- Does the school employ improvement strategies that are based on an assessment of the quality of the classroom as well as children's progress? (High/Scope Educational Research Foundation 2006)

Between 2003 and 2006 the High/Scope Educational Research Foundation, funded by a grant from the W.K. Kellogg Foundation, researched, designed, and developed the Ready School Assessment. The assessment focuses on eight key dimensions that teachers and schools should evaluate when asking, "Are we a ready school?" The work of the National Education Goals Panel (Shore 1998) was an important source in identifying these dimensions. The dimensions were developed after researchers conducted intensive research and reality testing with practitioners throughout the nation. Assessment using the dimensions, listed here, can assist educators in evaluating their individual school's state of readiness:

1. **Leaders and leadership.** The principal, with the assistance of the teachers, advocates for and leads the ready school. For example, the principal encourages teachers to take responsibility for and implement ready school strategies. The principal provides professional development and resources on these strategies.

2. **Transitions.** Teachers, staff, and parent groups work with families, children, and the preschool teachers and caregivers before kindergarten and with families and children during kindergarten to smooth the transition from home to school. For example, teachers and staff at feeder early childhood programs are informed about registration before school starts so they can pass on to families information about kindergarten roundup dates, orientation dates, and any other planned transition activities.

3. **Teacher supports.** Classrooms, schedules, teams, and activities are organized to maximize the support for all adults to work effectively with children during the school day. For example, teachers from feeder early childhood programs (including those not part of the school) are invited to participate in professional development programs along with K–3 staff. This allows *all* adults to work effectively with children in both teaching venues and it allows teachers to share curriculum goals and benchmarks with each other.

4. **Engaging environments.** The school's learning environments employ elements that make them warm and inviting and actively engage children in a variety of learning activities. For example, classrooms have a variety of manipulative materials and supplies for art, building, and hands-on learning.

5. **Effective curricula.** The teachers and school diligently employ educational materials and methods shown to be effective in helping children achieve objectives required for grade-level proficiency. For example, teachers and staff are well informed about and well trained in developmentally appropriate methods and strategies for early childhood learners.

6. **Family, school, and community partnerships.** The teachers and school take specific steps to enhance parents' capacities to foster their children's readiness and to support children's learning in and outside of school. For example, teachers use an open-door policy that allows for, welcomes, and involves families' participation in classroom activities at all times of the day.

7. **Respecting diversity.** The teachers and school help all children succeed by interacting with children and families in ways that are compatible with individual needs, family backgrounds, and life experiences. For example, classrooms include many materials that reflect a variety of cultural backgrounds and experiences. Teachers plan classroom activities that provide accurate, practical, and respectful information regarding peoples' cultural backgrounds, traditions, languages, and experiences.

8. **Assessing progress.** Teachers and staff engage in ongoing improvement based on information that rigorously and systematically assesses classroom experiences, school practices that influence them, and children's progress toward curricular goals. For example, teachers address clearly defined and clearly stated curricular goals for each group/subgroup of children. In addition, the quality of the classroom experiences is assessed using a standardized, systematic approach. This results in teachers taking a focused look at what they are doing and making changes to the classroom experience so all students can achieve success (High/Scope Educational Research Foundation 2006).

A ready school is many things. It is a place where instruction is gauged to meet the learning level of each student, where diversity is welcome, where teachers have the support they need to do their best work for every learner. In this place partnerships between school, families, and community reinforce the education process. Most important, a ready school is a place that builds on its strengths and addresses challenges through the process of focused, ongoing school improvement.

Is your school, or the school that the young children you serve will attend, a ready school? For more information about becoming a ready school or about the Ready School Assessment, please contact Paula Dowker (pdowker@highscope.org) at the High/Scope Educational Research Foundation.

References

High/Scope Educational Research Foundation. 2006. Ready School Assessment. Ypsilanti, MI: High/Scope Press. Online: www.readyschool assessment.org.

Shore R. 1998. *Ready Schools.* A report of the Goal 1 Ready Schools Resource Group. Washington, DC: National Education Goals Panel. Online:http://govinfo.library.unt.edu/negp/Reports/readysch.pdf.

PAULA DOWKER is education specialist at High/Scope Educational Research Foundation in Ypsilanti, Michigan. Paula has been involved in Michigan's public education system for 16 years. She has been a teacher, administrator, and curriculum director. Paula is responsible for the dissemination of information regarding the Ready School Assessment nationwide and also is the designer and facilitator of the Ready School Training modules. **LAWRENCE J. SCHWEINHART,** PhD, is president of High/Scope Educational Research Foundation. A former member of the NAEYC Governing Board, Larry served as chair of the NAEYC Program Panel on Quality, Compensation, and Affordability. **MARIJATA C. DANIEL-ECHOLS,** PhD, is chair of the research division at the High/Scope Educational Research Foundation. She has served as the project director for High/Scope's W.K. Kellogg Foundation-funded Ready School Assessment instrument development project.

"Stop Picking On Me!"

What You Need to Know about Bullying

"Hi, guys," says Robert, the after-school program specialist, greeting his first graders. "Anybody hungry?"

The children take off their backpacks and help themselves to granola bars, apples, and milk. Willie, the smallest boy, gets pushed aside by bigger boys but manages to grab a granola bar before they're all gone.

"Willie is a weenie. Willie is a weenie," chants Jake, a large blond youngster with red cheeks. Two boys behind him chuckle, and most of the other children settle down into eating their snack.

Willie, his chin quivering, turns to Robert in a silent plea for help. Jake sees the gesture and smirks, "Willie is a tattle tale."

If you were Robert, what would you do in this situation?

1. Ignore the teasing. After all, "Kids will be kids."
2. Say to Jake: "Cut it out. Words can hurt, and we don't allow teasing."
3. Take Willie aside. "Hey, if someone is bothering you, you need to learn to stand up for yourself." Brainstorm ways to respond to future taunts.
4. Plan a learning activity on how to stop hurtful behavior. As a group, read and discuss books on teasing and bullying. Empower all children to speak out against hurtful behavior when they see it happen.

Many of us can remember being in situations like the one above when we were children. Or perhaps we ourselves were the target of such behavior. Experts say teasing and bullying are commonplace in schools, not just in the United States but around the world.

Bullying in particular has gained increased attention in recent years. Hundreds of books and research articles have been published on the subject, and at least 30 states have passed anti-bullying legislation (National Conference of School Legislatures 2008).

Why the attention? Research in the aftermath of school shootings, including Columbine High School in Colorado, has found that the shooters had been severely bullied by classmates. A study of school violence by the U.S. Secret Service and U.S. Department of Education found that "almost three-quarters of the attackers felt persecuted, bullied, threatened, attacked or injured by others prior to the incident" (2002).

Among girls, bullying is more likely to take the form of emotional hurt.

Research indicates that boys do most of the bullying, and they target girls as well as other boys. Among girls, bullying is more likely to take the form of emotional hurt, such as spreading hurtful rumors about another girl or excluding her from a group.

Most bullying takes place at school, typically in places with little or no adult supervision, such as the playground, cafeteria, and restroom. According to research, when teachers and other adults see or hear about bullying, they generally do nothing to stop it.

Teasing and bullying begin in the early grades and peak in middle school. The timing is linked to development. By fourth grade, children are comparing themselves to each other and become self-conscious, especially about appearance and ability. Consequently, a perceived difference is sometimes—not always—a trigger for teasing and bullying behavior.

Research findings like these have spurred the call for improved disciplinary policies and prevention efforts in schools as well as after-school programs, youth clubs, and summer camps. The fact that teasing and bullying can show up in the primary grades suggests that the precursors of this behavior may be found in early childhood and that parents and child care professionals also play a role in prevention.

A Continuum of Hurtful Behavior

According to Barri Rosenbluth, director of school-based services at SafePlace, a domestic violence and sexual assault center in Austin, teasing and bullying can be viewed as part of a continuum of intentionally hurtful behavior. At one end of the continuum is hurtful teasing, which can include making fun of someone, name-calling, put-downs, insults, and negative gestures. At the other end is abuse and assault, which can include the use of weapons. Teasing becomes bullying when it is repeated over time. Like teasing, bullying can take many forms—name-calling, threats, hitting—but it usually involves an imbalance of power. The bully is often bigger, older, smarter, or more popular than the targeted child.

Sexual harassment may seem out of place in a discussion of preschool and primary school behavior, but all educators need to be aware of it. According to a study by the American Association of University Women Educational Foundation, one-third of students who experienced sexual harassment said it first occurred in sixth grade or earlier (2001).

Sexual harassment is teasing or bullying of a sexual nature using words, gestures, pictures, or actions. Boys as well as girls can be the targets, and the harassment can be about the body, boy-girl friendships, or speculation about homosexuality. Sexual harassment may occur once or many times.

In the public schools, sexual harassment is serious because it's a form of sex discrimination prohibited by Title IX of the Education Amendments of 1972. Under this law, school officials must take reasonable steps to prevent and eliminate sexual harassment because it "can interfere with a student's academic performance and emotional and physical well-being" (Office for Civil Rights 2001).

Tune in to Teasing

Because intent plays a part in defining whether a behavior is hurtful, child development experts might argue that teasing and bullying don't occur until children can understand the feelings of others.

"Preschoolers say funny and absurd things that are not necessarily targeted at anyone," says Judy Freedman, an elementary school social worker, in her book *Easing the Teasing* (2002). "They are often experimenting with words they have recently learned."

Teasing becomes sharper as children expand their vocabulary and improve their verbal skills. "They think it's funny to rhyme a word with someone's name, as in the case of a second-grader who was called 'Fartin' Martin,'" says Freedman. But as children develop empathy, they are less likely to ridicule someone for a name or other qualities beyond a person's control.

Experienced teachers also recognize that much teasing is good-natured and friendly.

Experienced teachers also recognize that much teasing is good-natured and friendly. Best friends may josh each other for fun, and children might tease another child as a sign of welcome into a group.

What's harder to discern is teasing that's iffy, as though the teaser is testing for a reaction. If the targeted child cringes or punches back, the teaser may continue, delighted at finding a hot button. But if the targeted child tosses it off, the two may continue joking around, or the teaser may look for another target.

Experts say teasing becomes hurtful if the teaser intends to be cruel or if the targeted child feels upset, angry, or afraid as a result, regardless of the intent.

How's a teacher to know? "Talk to the targeted child privately," advises Rosenbluth. "Don't just assume the child will come to you." Ask: "What did you feel after Marianne's comment about your freckles?" or "How did you feel when Aaron shoved you?"

Why It Matters

For children targeted by teasers and bullies, school is miserable and frightening. They may experience headaches, stomachaches, bedwetting, and restless sleep. They can feel depressed,

inadequate, and lonely. Other children may avoid them, fearing they may also become targets, leaving the targeted child with no friends.

Targeted children may resist going to school out of fear for their safety. They may develop a dislike for school and fall behind their peers in learning. In extreme cases, if the bullying continues into the teen years, students can react by harming themselves or seeking revenge.

Children who do the teasing and bullying are usually popular and confident. But experts say they lack empathy and believe that such behavior is OK, even desirable. They need positive role models and help in learning social skills. Without that, they become at risk for other problem behaviors.

Bullying also affects bystanders. Non-targeted children can feel afraid and vulnerable at school. Their learning may falter as well.

Why It Happens

Many authorities say teasing and bullying are part of the larger issue of aggressive behavior in much of modern life. Studies attribute aggression to media violence, poverty, poor child-rearing practices, abusive home environments, and other factors.

Researchers Pamela Orpinas and Arthur Horne (2006) say the roots of hurtful behavior are better described as *risk factors,* not *causes.* Risk factors refer to personal or environmental characteristics that indicate a greater likelihood of behaving a certain way. For example, harsh parental punishment by itself does not make a child tease and bully others. But several risk factors taken together may indicate a greater tendency to hurt other children.

Orpinas and Horne argue that in addition to risk factors, educators must also consider protective factors—that is, characteristics that help diminish the likelihood of teasing and bullying.

Teachers and caregivers can do a great deal to prevent hurtful behavior, but no one can do it alone. The most effective prevention, says Rosenbluth, is a "caring community."

Assess the Environment

Survey teachers and parents about their perceptions of the climate in your program. Do children enjoy being there? Have they bonded with staff? Do they have friends? Are teasing and bullying an issue? Invite an expert on the subject to speak at a parents meeting and distribute handouts to provide more information. (For free, downloadable tip sheets, see http://stopbullyingnow.hrsa.gov/index.asp)

Talk with officials in public and private schools in your neighborhood. What are they doing about bullying prevention? Consult with leaders of nearby libraries, parks, and youth clubs about the programs they offer. Look for ways to collaborate in prevention efforts.

Examine your policies that deal with child guidance and supervision, particularly in your after-school program. According to the authors of *Quit it!* (1998), a teacher's guide for teasing and bullying prevention, a clearly stated, consistent school-wide policy is "an effective tool in combating teasing and bullying."

Rosenbluth, who has trained public school administrators and teachers in bullying prevention, says the ideal school policy specifically prohibits hurtful teasing and bullying. The policy also provides a way to document students' and parents' complaints, outlines an investigation process, and provides a stay-away agreement to separate the bully and the targeted child.

As you review policies, inform everyone in your school community—board members, teachers, staff, volunteers, and parents. Provide training so teachers and staff recognize and respond appropriately to hurtful behavior. Offer a workshop for parents to help them talk with their children about the subject.

Set Clear Rules and Consequences

As children learn social skills, they are influenced by many factors. Perhaps the most powerful is the behavior they see in adults and other children. If they see adults and playmates acting with kindness and respect, children are likely to develop kind and respectful behavior.

Another powerful influence is culture. Children learn how they are expected to behave from home life, their racial or ethnic group, church, and community life. They get messages from stories, television, toys, games, sports, clothing, advertising, and store displays. Research has shown that boys are often encouraged to take risks, seek adventure, and be aggressive. Girls, on the other hand, are encouraged to be nurturing, show their emotions, and seek protection.

When boys ridicule or shove someone and get away with it, children learn that boys are behaving in a normal and accepted way. The same is true when girls whisper hurtful things about another girl and exclude her from their play.

Counteract these influences by modeling desired behavior and challenging gender stereotypes. Address gender put-downs just as you would address racial or ethnic slurs. Encourage boys to express their feelings and be nurturing, and urge girls to take reasonable risks and stand up for themselves.

Rethink areas or times when supervision may be lacking, such as nap time and outdoor play. Train staff to improve the way they monitor areas, and consider involving other staff or volunteers as extra eyes and ears.

Review with children the rules for appropriate behavior and the consequences for breaking rules. Younger children often need reminders. About age 4 or 5, you can engage children in discussing the reasons behind rules and get their input on setting rules for the classroom.

An emphasis on rules may bring an increase in tattling. Experienced teachers know that some children use tattling to get attention or get another child in trouble. They handle it by having children write their complaints and drop them in a tattle box, which the teacher later reads. It may also help to consider the tattle-versus-tell guideline: Is the child trying to get someone in trouble (tattling) or get someone out of trouble (telling)?

Tattling may also be a way for children to test what a rule is and how you will enforce it. You can confirm (or deny) the rule and assure the child that you will handle it. If the information indicates a child is at risk of physical or emotional harm, you need to deal with the situation immediately.

Teach Positive Social Skills

Review your curriculum unit on friends. Help children learn effective ways of joining a play group, making conversation, and sharing interests. When children squabble, teach problem-solving techniques.

Offer cooperative games and learning opportunities. Call attention to children's positive behaviors such as sharing, listening, and helping when you see them happening.

Encourage teachers and after-school caregivers to learn about each child in the group as an individual.

Encourage teachers and after-school caregivers to learn about each child in the group as an individual. Knowing every child's personality, friendships, and behavior patterns will help you distinguish between friendly and hurtful teasing, and between rough play and bullying.

In group time, read books on teasing and bullying. Engage children in discussion: How did the targeted child feel? How did the bully feel? How did the bystanders feel? What happened to stop the hurtful behavior? What might you do if you saw the same thing happen to a classmate?

Brainstorm with children about what they might do to help someone being teased or bullied. If they feel safe, they might tell the bully to stop or invite the targeted child to play with them. If they don't feel safe, they might tell an adult.

Emphasize that they should not just stand and watch. Explain that speaking up takes courage and that telling an adult about hurtful behavior is not tattling. Children can ask a friend to help befriend the targeted child or go with them to tell an adult. Explain that the adult will listen and do something.

Intervene in Hurtful Behavior

When hurtful teasing and bullying occur, adults have a responsibility to stop it. Ignoring hurtful behavior can inadvertently promote it and all its negative effects. Some tips:

- Stand between the teasers or bullies and the targeted child. Do not send any participants or bystanders away. Using a moderate tone of voice, state what you heard or saw happening. State that teasing and bullying are against school rules.

- Reassure the targeted child. Don't force the child to answer questions in front of the other children. If the child is upset, talk in private. Increase supervision of the child to make sure bullying does not happen again. Give the child time to express anger or sadness. Help the child find classmates who can offer support.

- Speak to the bystanders. If they did nothing, say, "Maybe you didn't know what to do." Explain that teasing and bullying are "not cool." Suggest that next time they could tell the bully to stop, involve the targeted child in play, or go to an adult for help. If they acted appropriately, acknowledge the behavior without lavish, public praise.

- Impose consequences on the teasers or bullies, as outlined in your policy. Make sure the consequences are reasonable and related to the behavior.

  Be prepared to hear defenses such as, "I didn't mean to hurt him," or "I just called him a name." Respond by restating what happened: "It did hurt" or "Name-calling is hurtful."

- Allow children time to cool off. Don't force an apology. Watch the children closely for possible future hurtful behavior. Help them learn to take responsibility for their actions and offer activities to help them develop empathy.

- If appropriate, notify parents of children who are involved. Set up a parent-teacher conference and discuss social skills. For the targeted child: "How can we help Willie make friends and develop more self-confidence?" For the teaser: "How can we help Jake understand that name-calling is hurtful?"

It's Not a One-Shot Solution

It should be clear that in the opening example about Willie and Jake, ignoring hurtful behavior is not the answer. It should also be clear that stopping hurtful behavior is not a one-person, one-time fix.

What NOT to Do

- Many people believe the solution to bullying is to urge the targeted child to fight back. It's not uncommon to hear stories about this method's success: "I hit Joey in the mouth, and he never bothered me again."

  While fighting back may work on occasion, it has drawbacks. The targeted child may suffer injury, or the incident may set in motion a cycle of revenge attacks. Most important, urging children to fight back reinforces the message that some problems can best be solved with violence.

- Well-meaning adults may suggest having the bully and targeted child sit down together and work out their "conflict." This suggestion is misguided for three reasons.

  First, having the bully sit face-to-face with the targeted child may put the child at further risk of humiliation and harm.

  Second, the behavior is not about conflict any more than child abuse is about disagreement. The teaser or bully intends to inflict harm. Calling it a conflict sends the message that both children are partly responsible.

  Third, there is no evidence that conflict resolution or peer mediation is effective in stopping bullying.

U.S. Department of Health and Human Services, Health Resources and Services Administration. Stop Bullying Now campaign. "Misdirections in Bullying Prevention and Intervention," http://stopbullyingnow.hrsa.gov/index.asp

---

> **Reducing aggressive behavior in school is everyone's problem and requires a long-term solution.**

Reducing aggressive behavior in school is everyone's problem and requires a long-term solution. After-school caregivers can help children learn positive social skills and intervene in hurtful behaviors. Early childhood educators can work with parents to create a caring environment at home and at school that builds a foundation for learning.

Everyone agrees children should feel safe in school. They need to feel at ease and free to play and learn. They cannot learn if they feel threatened or afraid of their peers.

Books for Children

Ludwig, Trudy. 2003. *My Secret Bully.* Ashland, Ore.: Riverbend Books.

Monica is having headaches and stomachaches. Under questioning from her mother, Monica starts crying and reveals that a longtime friend has been saying bad things about her to other girls. Mom teaches Monica how to stand up for herself.

McCain, Becky Ray. 2001. *Nobody Knew What To Do: A Story About Bullying.* Morton Grove, Ill.: Albert Whitman & Co.

Children observe bullying at recess. The next day when the targeted child doesn't come to school, one boy reports the incident to his teacher. Both the teacher and the principal take action.

Romain, Trevor. 1997. *Bullies Are a Pain in the Brain.* Minneapolis, Minn.: Free Spirit Publishing.

This popular children's book author explains in simple words and black-and-white cartoons what bullying is and how to avoid it. He addresses most of the book to targeted children but devotes a few pages to bullies and ends with a message to teachers and parents.

Thomas, Pat. 2000. *Stop Picking on Me: A First Look at Bullying.* Hauppauge, N.Y.: Barron's Educational Series, Inc.

Using compassionate words and aided by vivid watercolor illustrations, author Pat Thomas explains what bullying is and how to stop it.

Books for Teachers and Parents

Bott, C.J. 2004. *The Bully in the Book and in the Classroom.* Lanham, Md.: Scarecrow Press.

This book contains annotated bibliographies in four sections: grades K-3, 4-6, 7-8 and 9-12. In addition, the author spotlights 8-10 books in each section with a brief summary and cover photo as well as discussion questions to use with children.

Froscshl, Merle; Barbara Sprung, and Nancy Mullin-Rindler. 1998. *Quit it! A Teacher's Guide on Teasing and Bullying for Use with Students in Grades K-3.* A joint publication of Educational Equity Concepts Inc., New York; Wellesley College Center for Research on Women, Wellesley, Mass.; and the National Education Association, Washington, D.C.

Lee, Chris. 2004. *Preventing Bullying in Schools: A Guide for Teachers and Other Professionals.* Thousand Oaks, Calif.: SAGE Publications, Inc.

Mullin, Nancy. 2003. *Selected Bibliography About Teasing and Bullying for Grades K-8: Revised and Expanded Edition.* Wellesley, Mass.: Wellesley College Center for Research on Women.

For more than three decades, the Wellesley Centers for Research on Women have studied issues such as gender equity in education, sexual harassment, and child care, resulting in changes in practices and policies. This bibliography can be ordered for $15 at http://www.wcwonline.org.

References

American Association of University Women Education Foundation. 2001. *Hostile Hallways: Bullying, Teasing, and Sexual Harassment in School* (p.25). http://www.aauw.org/research/upload/hostilehallways.pdf.

Freedman, Judy S. 2002. *Easing the Teasing: Helping Your Child Cope with Name-Calling, Ridicule, and Verbal Bullying.* New York: Contemporary Books.

National Conference of State Legislatures. 2008. *School Bullying.* http://www.ncsl.org/programs/educ/bullyingoverview.htm.

Office for Civil Rights, U.S. Department of Education. 2001. "Revised Sexual Harassment Guidance," http://www.ed.gov/about/offices/list/ocr/docs/shguide.html.

Orpinas, Pamela, and Arthur Horne. 2006. *Bullying Prevention: Creating a Positive School Climate and Developing Social Competence.* Washington, D.C.: American Psychological Association.

U.S. Department of Health and Human Services, Health Resources and Services Administration. Stop Bullying Now campaign. http://stopbullyingnow.hrsa.gov/index.asp.

"You Got It!"

Teaching Social and Emotional Skills

Lise Fox, PhD and Rochelle Harper Lentini, MEd

Early educators report that one of their biggest challenges is supporting young children who have problem behavior beyond what might be expected (Buscemi et al. 1995; Hemmeter, Corso, & Cheatham 2005). Some children engage in problem behavior that is typical of a particular stage of development as they build relationships with peers and adults and learn to navigate the classroom environment. For example, a toddler might grab a cracker from another child's plate because she is still learning to use words to ask for what she wants or needs. What troubles teachers is how to meet the needs of children who have persistent problem behavior that does not respond to positive guidance or prevention practices. The extent of this problem is highlighted by recent reports on the rates of expulsion of children from preschool programs (Gilliam 2005).

The Teaching Pyramid

The teaching pyramid model (Fox et al. 2003) describes a primary level of universal practices—classroom preventive practices that promote the social and emotional development of all children—built on a foundation of positive relationships; secondary interventions that address specific social and emotional learning needs of children at risk for challenging behavior; and development of individualized interventions (tertiary level) for children with persistent problem behavior (see the diagram "The Teaching Pyramid"). The model is explained more fully in "The Teaching Pyramid: A Model for Supporting Social Competence and Reinventing Challenging Behavior in Young Children," in the July 2003 issue of *Young Children*.

The foundation for universal practices begins with nurturing and responsive caregiving that supports children in developing a positive sense of self and in engaging in relationships with others. At this level, teachers focus on their relationships with children and families. Universal classroom practices include developmentally appropriate, child-centered classroom environments that promote children's developing independence, successful interactions, and engagement in learning. While universal practices may be enough to promote the development of social competence in the majority of children in the classroom,

teachers may find that there are children whose lack of social and emotional skills or whose challenging behavior requires more focused attention.

In this article we look at the secondary level of the teaching pyramid, which emphasizes planned instruction on specific social and emotional skills for children at risk for developing more challenging behavior, such as severe aggression, property destruction, noncompliance, or withdrawal. Children who may be considered at risk for challenging behavior are persistently noncompliant, have difficulty regulating their emotions, do not easily form relationships with adults and other children, have difficulty engaging in learning activities, and are perceived by teachers as being likely to develop more intractable behavior problems.

> **Teachers may find that there are children whose lack of social and emotional skills or whose challenging behavior requires more focused attention.**

Research shows that when educators teach children the key skills they need to understand their emotions and the emotions of others, handle conflicts, problem solve, and develop relationships with peers, their problem behavior decreases and their social skills improve (Joseph & Strain 2003). Emphasis on teaching social skills is just one component of multiple strategies to support a child at risk for challenging behavior. Additional critical strategies include collaborating with the family; addressing the child's physical and mental health needs; and offering the support of specialists and other resources to address the child or family's individual needs.

Reframing Problem Behavior

The teaching pyramid model guides teachers to view a child's problem behavior as serving a purpose for that child. Some children may use problem behavior instead of socially

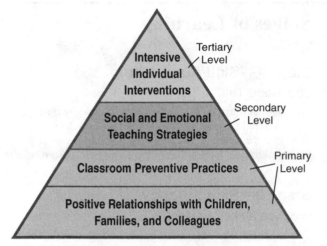

The Teaching Pyramid

Social and Emotional Skills to Teach

- Following rules, routines, and directions
- Identifying feelings in oneself and others
- Controlling anger and impulses
- Problem solving
- Suggesting play themes and activities to peers
- Sharing toys and other materials
- Taking turns
- Helping adults and peers
- Giving compliments
- Understanding how and when to apologize
- Expressing empathy with others' feelings
- Recognizing that anger can interfere with problem solving
- Learning how to recognize anger in oneself and others
- Learning how to calm down
- Understanding appropriate ways to express anger

conventional and appropriate behavior to avoid or join interactions and activities, obtain or avoid attention, and obtain objects. For example, a child who wants another child's toy may hit the other child instead of asking to have a turn with the toy. Other children may use problem behavior to express their disappointment or anger to the teacher, rather than asking for help or sharing their feelings with words. For example, a child may throw toys or destroy materials when frustrated rather than asking a teacher for help.

Reasons for Challenging Behavior

Children may use problem behavior to get their needs met for a variety of reasons. For example, a child may have language development problems, social-emotional delays, difficulties with peer interactions, or developmental disabilities; she may have experienced neglect or trauma; or she may simply have not had opportunities to learn appropriate social or communication skills before entering preschool.

When teachers view challenging behavior as actions children use to get their needs met, they can reframe problem behavior as a skill-learning or skill-fluency issue. *Skill fluency* refers to a child's ability to use a skill consistently and independently. Children with problem behavior may not have appropriate social or communication skills or may not use those skills well in a variety of situations. Reframing problem behavior as a skill-instruction issue opens the door to the development of effective strategies teachers can implement in the classroom: if young children with problem behavior are missing key social and communication skills, then a next step is to teach them those skills!

A Skill-learning Issue

Many skills are important in children's development of relationships with adults and peers. Skills help children learn self-regulation (ability to respond appropriately to anxiety, distress, or uncomfortable sensations) and how to problem solve (see "Social and Emotional Skills to Teach,"). Young children at risk for challenging behavior (children at the secondary interven-

tion level) may not be fluent in or have the ability to use these skills. The teaching pyramid model encourages early educators to teach children these skills systematically, using planned procedures within developmentally appropriate activities and with sufficient intensity to ensure that children learn the skills quickly and can use them when needed (Grisham-Brown, Hemmeter, & Pretti-Frontczak 2005).

Teaching Social Skills

In thinking about how to teach social skills systematically, teachers need to be aware of the three stages of learning (Bailey & Wolery 1992) (see "Stages of Learning"). The first stage is skill acquisition—the skill is introduced to the child; the second stage is fluency—the child has learned the skill and can use it easily; and the final stage of learning is skill maintenance and generalization—the child can use the skill over time and in new situations. In this article, we present strategies for addressing each stage of learning in the instruction of social skills.

It is important to identify the skill, demonstrate or identify when it is used, and link the idea or concept to other skills the child has.

Introducing a New Skill: Show-and-Tell

Explain the new skill. When you first teach a child a social or emotional skill, it is important to ensure that you have explained the skill in concrete terms so the child understands what the skill is and when to use it. Children who have social development challenges may find the nuances of social behavior difficult to interpret. Thus, it is important to identify the skill ("ask to take a turn"), demonstrate or identify when it is used ("Watch Emily ask to play with the water wheel"), and link the idea or concept to other skills the child has ("When you see your friends playing with a toy you want, you can watch them play, you can wait for a turn, or you can ask them for a turn").

Demonstrate it. For many children, it is helpful to provide both a positive example of someone using a skill and an example in which the skill is not used. For example, you may ask children to demonstrate the wrong way to ask for a turn and the correct way to ask for a turn. In this manner, children can practice under a teacher's guidance and receive additional information about how the skill is appropriately used.

Give positive feedback. When children first learn a new skill, they need feedback and specific encouragement on their efforts to use the skill. The importance of feedback cannot be overstated! Think, for example, about a time when you learned something new—such as a language, a sport, or a craft. The instructor most likely gave you feedback: "That's right, you did it" or "That looks good, I think you are getting it." Feedback may provide the support a child needs to persist in practicing a newly learned skill. Have you ever tried to learn a new skill and quit when you were in the early learning stages? Perhaps you did not receive encouragement or maybe those initial attempts were so uncomfortable or awkward that you decided to stop practicing.

Provide opportunities for practice. There are a variety of instructional methods for teaching new social and emotional skills (Webster-Stratton 1999; Hyson 2004; Kaiser & Rasminsky 2007). An important teaching practice at the acquisition stage of learning is providing multiple opportunities for a child to learn a skill in meaningful contexts—that is, in activities that are part of the child's natural play or routines. The more opportunities for practicing, the quicker the child will learn the skill. The box "Classroom Teaching Strategies" lists a variety of ways to teach social and emotional skills within typical classroom activities.

When a child learns a new skill, he needs to practice to build fluency in the skill.

Building Fluency: *Practice Makes Perfect*

When learning to play a new song on the piano, the player must practice before the song becomes easy to play. Similarly, when a child learns a new skill, he needs to practice to build fluency in the skill. When teaching social skills, teachers need to ensure that a skill is not only learned but also practiced often enough

---

Stages of Learning

Stage 1—Skill Acquisition
Show-and-Tell

The teacher introduces a new skill to a child by giving concrete examples of what the skill is and how to use it. For example, the teacher may say, "It's hard to wait until it is your turn to ride a trike. I'm going to help you learn how to wait."

Stage 2—Skill Fluency
Practice Makes Perfect

The teacher provides many opportunities to practice the skill so the child can eventually use it with ease. Practice opportunities may include prompting the child ("How can you ask to play with Brendan?"), helping the child remember to use the skill ("I know you are disappointed and you want a turn right now. What can you do instead?"), and identifying situations that call for the use of the skill ("We have three children who want to sit at the art table and only one chair. What can we do?").

Stage 3—Skill Maintenance and Generalization
"You Got It!"

The teacher continues to promote the child's use of the skill in familiar and new situations. For example, when the child uses his newly learned skill of giving compliments with his mother, the teacher says, "You gave your mom a compliment! Look, she's smiling because you said you like her haircut."

Adapted from D.B. Bailey & M. Wolery, *Teaching Infants and Preschoolers with Disabilities,* 2nd ed. (New York: Macmillan, 1992).

---

that the child becomes fluent in the skill and can easily use it. Consider the following example:

Madison struggles when playing with peers. Recognizing that Madison needs extra help in learning how to ask others to play with toys, her teacher, Mr. Jackson, decides to read the children a story about taking turns and asking to join play during group time. On that same day, several times during center activities and outdoor play, Mr. Jackson reminds Madison to "ask to play." After that day of focused instruction on using the skill, whenever Madison tries to enter a game without asking to play, Mr. Jackson provides corrective feedback or redirection, stating, "Madison, you need to ask to play" or "Madison, you may not grab toys; ask to play." A month later, Madison still has difficulty entering play and asking to play with toys.

Why did Madison have difficulty learning the skill? Perhaps Mr. Jackson did not provide enough opportunities to practice, so

Classroom Teaching Strategies

Instruction is more effective when it is embedded in the meaningful activities and contexts that occur throughout a child's day (Katz & McClellan 1997). Here are suggestions and examples for teaching social skills within classroom activities.

Modeling. Demonstrate the skill while explaining what you are doing. As you pass a block to a child, say, "Look, I am sharing my blocks with my friend."

Modeling with puppets. Use puppets to model the skill while interacting with a child, an adult, or another puppet. A puppet can explain to the teacher and the class how she became angry and hit her brother to get a toy. You can ask the puppet to consider other solutions and then discuss what a child might do when he or she wants a toy that another child is using.

Preparing peer partners. Ask one child to show another child the skill or to help the child use the target skill. You can prompt the peer by saying, "Carmen, Justin is still learning how to wait and take turns. Since you know what to do, can you help him? Show him the line-up picture while you wait for a drink at the water fountain."

Singing. Introduce a new skill through a song. To teach children to trade toys, pass out small toys during a large group activity, then sing the following song to the tune of "Mary Had a Little Lamb" and practice trading:

> I can be a problem solver, problem solver, problem solver, I can be a problem solver, let me show you how. Maybe I can trade with you, trade with you, trade with you, Maybe I can trade with you; let me show you how.

Children then practice trading toys with each other.

Doing fingerplays. Introduce the skill with a fingerplay, then follow up with a discussion or story. While showing fingers, have children recite this rhyme:

> One little friend cried, "Boo-hoo"; a friend gives a hug and then there are two.
> Two little friends share with me; we play together and that makes three.
> Three little friends ask for more; they all say "Please," and then comes four.
> Four little friends take turns down the slide; another comes to play, and that makes five.
> Five little friends have fun at school, because they follow every rule.

Using a flannel board. Introduce a new skill using flannel board activities and stories. For example, to teach turn taking you could have flannel pieces for Humpty Dumpty and change the rhyme so that "All the king's horses and all the king's friends / Work as a team to put Humpty together again." As you say the rhyme, have the children take turns putting the pieces (castle, bricks, Humpty Dumpty pieces, horses, and friends) on the flannel board. When you finish the rhyme, extend the activity by talking about how Humpty felt when he sat on the wall; when he fell; and when his friends helped put him back together.

Using prompts. Give a child verbal, visual, or physical prompts to use a skill during interactions and activities. When a child who has difficulty with initiating play interactions moves toward a group playing together, you might say privately, "Remember to use your words and ask to play."

Giving encouragement. Provide specific feedback when the child uses the skill. For example, describe what the child did: "You asked Joey for a turn. I saw that you two had a good time playing together." Encouragement can be verbal or a signal (a thumbs-up or high five).

Using incidental teaching. Guide the child to use the skill during interactions and activities. Quietly say to the child, "Quan, I see that you are very angry that all the trucks are being used. What can you do when you are angry? Let's go over the steps."

Playing games. Use games to teach problem solving, words that express feelings, identification of others' feelings, friendship skills, and so on. Place photographs of each child in a bag. Have the children take turns pulling a photo out of the bag and offering a compliment to the child in the photo.

Discussing children's literature. Read books to help teach friendship skills, feeling words, problem solving, and so on. While reading a story, pause and ask the children how a character in the story might feel or ask them to suggest ideas for solving the character's problem.

Additional ideas for many of these activities may be found on the Web site of the Center on the Social and Emotional Foundations for Early Learning, at www.csefel.uiuc.edu. Under **Resources,** click on **Practical Strategies.**

Madison quickly forgot to use the new skill. Or possibly Madison had not learned when and how to use the skill: she may not have become fluent in the skill.

Teachers can offer repeated opportunities to practice the skill in familiar and new situations.

To ensure that children learn a skill to the fluency level, teachers can use several strategies. They may offer the child multiple opportunities to practice, help the child link the new concept or skill to other social skills, or remind the child in advance so he or she can use the skill or concept in new situations.

Scaffolding the use of the skill within interactions may be effective. For example, the teacher can monitor child interactions and offer a verbal bridge for problem solving when children have conflicts or face difficulties (Katz & McClellan 1997). The teacher can pose questions like "What else can you do?" to help children problem solve or "How do you think Emily felt when you said that?" to help them take the perspective of the other child. When scaffolding, the teacher need only offer as much support or guidance as the child requires to navigate the situation, and she should be cautious about becoming overly directive or controlling the situation.

Additional teaching techniques to promote fluency include reminding the child, as she goes into a situation, to use the new skill; creating opportunities to practice by staging situations that call for the skill (creating a problem-solving task or planning an activity that requires sharing or taking turns); and providing the child with peer buddies who can remind her to use the new skill.

In the fluency stage of learning, the teacher should continue to offer encouragement when the child is practicing the skill.

Promoting Maintenance and Generalization: "You Got It!"

For a child acquiring a new social skill, the final stage of learning is maintaining and generalizing the skill—learning it to the point that it becomes part of the child's social skill repertoire and he uses it in familiar and in new situations. When teaching children social skills, it is important to ensure that children reach this stage.

For many children, moving from skill acquisition to skill generalization occurs quickly and seamlessly with little teacher effort. However, for children who are at risk for social development delays or challenging behavior, a more systematic approach may be needed.

To ensure maintenance and generalization of a new skill, after introducing the skill and providing practice opportunities, teachers can offer repeated opportunities to practice the skill in familiar and new situations. At this stage of learning, children continue to need occasional encouragement to remember to use the skills, and they need feedback on the successful use of the skill in new situations. The example that follows describes how Ben's teacher supported and encouraged Ben to use his newly learned problem-solving ability in new situations.

Four-year-old Ben tends to get very frustrated when playing with his peers, especially on the playground. He screams, pushes children, and grabs toys. Ms. Mitchell, his teacher, has introduced a four-step problem-solving process to the class, using a puppet (who has a problem to solve) and picture cards depicting the problem-solving process: (1) Ask yourself, What's my problem? (2) Think, think, think of some solutions; (3) What would happen? and (4) Give it a try.

Although Ben uses the process during play times, Ms. Mitchell realizes that he needs additional prompting to problem solve in new situations. Today the class is visiting the children's museum. Before entering, Ms. Mitchell takes Ben aside and reviews the problem-solving steps.

Inside the museum, there are several magnet activity stations, all occupied. Knowing that Ben will want to play with the magnets, Ms. Mitchell moves near him to give him support. She reminds Ben about the problem-solving

steps: "Remember, think, think, think." Ben then says to a child playing with the magnets, "Can I play too?" The child hands him a magnet and they build together. Ms. Mitchell looks at Ben, winks, and smiles.

The goal at this stage of instruction is for children to use the social skills they have learned in a variety of situations, helping them build satisfying relationships with children and adults. They are then motivated by their successes and the joy they experience playing and developing relationships. As children develop new social skills and grow in their social competence, they gain access to a wider variety of play and learning opportunities; increase the duration and complexity of play interactions and engagement in social interactions; build friendships with peers; and feel good about themselves.

Conclusions

It is critically important that early educators identify children who need focused instruction—children who may be considered at risk for challenging behavior. Teachers can guide them to learn new social and emotional skills, teaching them within child-centered, developmentally appropriate activities. It is equally important to design a systematic teaching approach that allows such children to acquire and use their new skills easily, over time, and in a variety of situations.

When young children do not know how to identify emotions, handle disappointment and anger, or develop relationships with peers, a teacher's best response is to teach!

References

Bailey, D.B., & M. Wolery. 1992. *Teaching infants and preschoolers with disabilities.* 2nd ed. New York: Macmillan.

Buscemi, L., T. Bennett, D. Thomas, & D.A. Deluca. 1995. Head Start: Challenges and training needs. *Journal of Early Intervention* 20 (1): 1–13.

Fox, L., G. Dunlap, M.L. Hemmeter, G.E. Joseph, & P.S. Strain. 2003. The teaching pyramid: A model for supporting social competence and preventing challenging behavior in young children. *Young Children* 58 (4): 48–52.

Gilliam, W.S. 2005. *Prekindergarteners left behind: Expulsion rates in state prekindergarten systems.* Online: www.fcdus.org/PDFs/NationalPreKExpulsionPaper03.02_new.pdf.

Grisham-Brown, J., M.L. Hemmeter, & K. Pretti-Frontczak. 2005. *Blended practices for teaching young children in inclusive settings.* Baltimore: Brookes.

Hemmeter, M.L., R. Corso, & G. Cheatham. 2005. Issues in addressing challenging behaviors in young children: A national survey of early childhood educators. Manuscript.

Hyson, M. 2004. *The emotional development of young children: Building an emotion-centered curriculum.* 2nd ed. New York: Teachers College Press.

Joseph, G.E., & P.S. Strain. 2003. Comprehensive evidence-based social-emotional curricula for young children: An analysis of efficacious adoption potential. *Topics in Early Childhood Special Education* 23 (2): 65–76.

Kaiser, B., & J.S. Rasminsky. 2007. *Challenging behavior in young children: Understanding, preventing, and responding effectively.* 2nd ed. Boston, MA: Allyn & Bacon.

Katz, L.G., & D.E. McClellan. 1997. *Fostering children's social competence: The teacher's role.* Washington, DC: NAEYC.

Webster-Stratton, C. 1999. *How to promote children's social and emotional competence.* London: Paul Chapman.

LISE FOX, PhD, is a professor in the Department of Child and Family Studies of the Louis de la Parte Florida Mental Health Institute of the University of South Florida in Tampa. She conducts research and training and develops support programs focused on young children with challenging behavior. **ROCHELLE HARPER LENTINI,** MEd, is a faculty member in the Department of Child and Family Studies of the Louis de la Parte Florida Mental Health Institute. She provides training and technical assistance to early educators and families on supporting young children with challenging behavior and promoting social and emotional competence.

Development of this article was supported by the Center for Evidence-Based Practice: Young Children with Challenging Behavior (Office of Special Education Programs, U.S. Department of Education, Cooperative Agreement #H324Z010001) and the Center on the Social and Emotional Foundations for Early Learning (Administration for Children and Families, U.S. Department of Health and Human Services, Cooperative Agreement #90YD0119/01).

Teaching Pyramid diagram adapted from L. Fox, G. Dunlap, M.L. Hemmeter, G.E. Joseph, & P.S. Strain, "The Teaching Pyramid: A Model for Supporting Social Competence and Preventing Challenging Behavior in Young Children," *Young Children* 58 (July 2003): 49.

Fostering Positive Transitions for School Success

JAYMA FERGUSON MCGANN AND PATRICIA CLARK, PHD

It is the week before school starts, and Ridgeview Elementary is holding a Popsicle Night for children entering kindergarten and their families. As families arrive in the school cafeteria, the principal and a kindergarten teacher welcome each kindergarten child with a T-shirt bearing the school name and logo.

The children excitedly greet their former preschool teachers, who also attend. With their families, the children choose from the variety of activities prepared by the preschool and kindergarten teachers. At an appointed time, the principal gathers the children and reads to them a story about going to kindergarten. Afterward, the families follow the kindergarten teachers to the children's new classrooms for a visit and short talk about kindergarten. The evening ends with Popsicles for everyone.

W hy is it that fewer than 20 percent of U.S. schools have transition practices in place to support children entering kindergarten and welcome their families (Love et al. 1992)? This is an important transition for young children, and its success has a lasting effect on children's school success in later years (Alexander & Entwisle 1988; Ensminer & Slusarcick 1992; Early, Pianta, & Cox 1999; Ramey et al. 2000).

Clearly, educators, schools, and communities must work together to ensure that young children's entry into kindergarten and elementary school is a smooth passage rather than a rocky road. It seems well worth the effort to find ways to support children and families during this crucial transition.

Indiana Steps up to the Challenge

The Indiana Department of Education, through the Ready Schools Initiative, works with 12 communities across the state to help local elementary schools support children's transitions to kindergarten. The communities range from large cities with dozens of elementary schools to small towns and rural areas with one school serving an entire county.

The guiding question has been, "What can we do—in early childhood programs, in elementary schools, with families, and in the community—to facilitate children's successful transition into kindergarten and the elementary grades?" While each community addresses the issue differently based on its resources and needs, in Indiana we have pinpointed some common concerns and found a number of ways to address the transition process.

Encouraging Successful Transitions

Activities for improving children's transitions to school fall into two broad categories: (1) improving connections between early childhood programs and elementary schools, and (2) reaching out to children and families before children enter kindergarten.

Connections between Early Childhood Programs and Schools

Preschool programs and elementary schools need to find ways to communicate. Kindergarten teachers need to know about the early childhood programs their new kindergartners attended, and preschool teachers need to know about kindergarten teachers' expectations for the children. Here are some of the ways the Indiana Ready Schools communities encourage connections:

- Kindergarten teachers visit early childhood programs to get a better idea about the programs, their curricula, and the children.
- Preschool teachers visit kindergarten classrooms, often with the children who will be going to the kindergarten.
- Kindergarten and preschool teachers share dinner and conversation to discuss issues important to both.
- Elementary school districts incorporate procedures for obtaining records from the variety of programs children attend. Schools prepare and distribute to early childhood programs parent permission forms to allow the programs to transfer children's records to the school.
- Communities provide families with a pamphlet that they can read and complete to communicate personal information about their child. These pamphlets are distributed at community fairs, through prekindergarten programs, and

A Read-Aloud for Families

A number of principals read *The Kissing Hand,* by Audrey Penn, at family-welcoming events in Indiana. Parents with tears in their eyes have attested to the power of this story about a young raccoon preparing to go to kindergarten.

Remember, a child going off to kindergarten can be as big a step for the family as it is for the child.

at kindergarten registration, and then are returned to the kindergarten teacher.

- School districts involve early childhood teachers who work in programs outside the schools, as well as those within the schools, and kindergarten teachers in joint professional development experiences.

Connections between Schools and Families

The extent to which families are involved in their children's education is a strong predictor of children's academic success (Henderson & Berla 1994). To facilitate family-school communication and linkages, ready schools reach out to families, establish links *before* the first day of school, and make personal contacts (Pianta & Walsh 1996). However, typical elementary school transition practices often involve experiences taking place *after* the start of school and/or making contact through flyers, brochures, and group open houses.

Here are some of the things that the Indiana Ready Schools communities do to reach out to families before kindergarten:

- Special events held before the school year begins welcome incoming kindergarten children and families. The events often happen in the evening and include a light supper, activities for children and families together, an opportunity to meet the kindergarten teachers and visit the classrooms, and the principal reading a story aloud (see "A Read-Aloud for Families").
- Elementary schools invite preschoolers and their families to Family Night during the school year before the children's kindergarten entry.
- Teachers make home visits before school begins to the families whose children will be starting kindergarten in the fall.
- Communities distribute brochures, videos, and home activity calendars to children and families at community events, through pediatricians and libraries, and with the help of community agencies that work with families (housing authority, social service agencies, etc.). The resources emphasize the importance of the early years and encourage families to contact their local elementary school before their child enters kindergarten.

Conclusion

Nearly half of all kindergarten teachers nationally report that 50 percent of children experience some degree of difficulty in the transition to formal schooling and 16 percent face serious adjustment problems (Rimm-Kaufman, Pianta, & Cox 2000). Strategies to prepare children for change and address the challenges of adjustment can help ensure that children's transitions to school are positive.

The transition to kindergarten is a process among partners rather than an event happening to a child. According to Pianta and Kraft-Sayre, "most important for the transition process are the relationships—those between children and teachers, parents and teachers, children and their peers, and children and their parents" (1999, 52). Effective practices are planned locally, taking into consideration children's cultural backgrounds and the multiple characteristics of the community, including family income levels, cultures, physical location and resources. Using what we know about young children and transitions, teachers, schools, and communities can adapt strategies to local needs and resources to promote children's successful transition to kindergarten and school success in the years after.

References

Alexander, K., & D. Entwisle. 1988. Achievement in the first two years of school: Patterns and processes. *Monographs of the Society for Research in Child Development* 53 (1): 157.

Early, D., R. Pianta, & M. Cox. 1999. Kindergarten teachers and classrooms: A transition context. *Early Education and Development* 10 (1): 25–46.

Ensminer, M., & A. Slusarcick. 1992. Paths to high school graduation or dropout: A longitudinal study of a first-grade cohort. *Sociological Education* 65: 95–113.

Henderson, A., & N. Berla. 1994. *A new generation of evidence: The family is critical to student achievement.* Columbia, MD: National Committee for Citizens in Education.

Love, J., M.E. Logue, J.V. Trudeau, & K. Thayer. 1992. *Transitions to kindergarten in American schools.* U.S. Department of Education report. ED 344693. Hampton, NH: RMC Research Corporation.

Pianta, R., & M. Kraft-Sayre. 1999. Parents' observations about their children's transitions to kindergarten. *Young Children* 54 (3): 47–52.

Pianta, R., & D. Walsh. 1996. *High-risk children in schools: Constructing sustaining relationships.* New York: Routledge.

Ramey, C., S. Ramey, M. Phillips, R. Lanzi, C. Brezausek, C. Katholi, & S. Snyder. 2000. *Head Start children's entry into public school: A report on the National Head Start/Public School Early Childhood Transition Demonstration Study.* Washington, DC: Head Start Bureau.

Rimm-Kaufman, S., R. Pianta, & M. Cox. 2000. Teachers' judgments of problems in the transition to kindergarten. *Early Childhood Research Quarterly* 15 (2): 147–66.

JAYMA FERGUSON MCGANN is director of the Division of Prime Time in the Indiana Department of Education, where she has worked for 10 years. She is responsible for the state's early childhood pre-K to grade 3 initiatives, including Foundations for Young Children and Ready Schools, and issues related to kindergarten and early intervention. E-mail: jferguso@doe.state.in.us. **PATRICIA CLARK**, PhD, is an associate professor in the Department of Elementary Education at Ball State University in Muncie, Indiana. She has worked for the past four years with the Indiana Department of Education on the Ready Schools Initiative and is currently researching its impact. E-mail: pclark@bsu.edu.

A Multinational Study Supports Child-Initiated Learning

Using the Findings in Your Classroom

Jeanne E. Montie, Jill Claxton, and Shannon D. Lockhart

Scenarios like these are found in preschool classrooms all over the world. In a new longitudinal study, researchers observed and followed five thousand four-year-olds and their teachers in preschools and child care centers in 15 countries and diverse cultures. Across all countries, they identified certain classroom practices that related to better language and cognitive skills at age seven, as well as other practices associated later with poorer language and cognitive skills.

Sponsored by the International Association for the Evaluation of Educational Achievement (IEA), the IEA Preprimary Project (Olmsted & Montie 2001; Weikart, Olmsted, & Montie 2003; Montie, Xiang, & Schweinhart 2007) is a multinational study of unprecedented size and scope (see "The IEA Preprimary Project"). At age seven, in primary school, more than eighteen hundred children from 10 of the participating countries had follow-up assessments.

The study affirms that preschool teachers' educational backgrounds and classroom practices matter, that how teachers organize their classrooms and learning activities makes a difference. Four findings, consistent across countries, emerged. At age seven, the children

- whose preprimary teachers or caregivers had had more years of education had higher language scores;
- who had more opportunities in preschool to choose their own activities, rather than spending their time in personal care (such as hand washing, eating, or dressing) and group social activities (like show-and-tell), had higher language scores;
- who spent less time in whole group activities at age four had higher cognitive scores;
- who were in preschool classrooms with a greater number and variety of materials had higher cognitive scores.

The seven-year-olds did better on language assessments if their preschool settings had emphasized free-choice activities and if their teachers had had more years of education.

In other words, the seven-year-olds did better on language assessments if their preschool settings had emphasized free-choice activities and if their teachers had had more years of education. They did better on cognitive assessments if they had spent more preschool time in small group activities, by themselves, or with one or two other children and if they had

The IEA Preprimary Project

The International Association for the Evaluation of Educational Achievement (IEA), a nongovernmental, nonprofit organization of research institutions in more than 50 countries, is well known for its sponsorship of cross-national research in education. The IEA Preprimary Project is its first cross-national study of preschool education. Fifteen countries took part in a preprimary observational study. Ten of those countries (including Finland, Greece, Hong Kong [SAR], Indonesia, Ireland, Italy, Poland, Spain [Catalonia], Thailand, and the United States) participated in the longitudinal study reported here.

The High/Scope Educational Research Foundation served as the international coordinating center for the study. More information about the study is online at www.highscope.org/Content.asp?ContentID=256.

As the teacher, Maria, scans the room during free-choice time, she notes the high level of activity and chatter. Three of the four-year-olds are in the block area, building a garbage truck. Each child offers an idea and all eventually agree to use blocks for the truck body and materials from the art area for "garbage." Now, they hunt for items to serve as the steering wheel and control knobs.

In the house area, a few children pretend to cook dinner using acorns and pinecones, while others make playdough cookies.

A small group gathers to watch the computer screen as two children manipulate the controls. Much discussion ensues as the children consider how to sequence pictures so the volcano will erupt.

The sound of banging diverts Maria's attention to the woodworking table, where a boy and a girl are splitting nuts with hammers and a vise grip. They count the number of nuts they are going to feed the squirrels during outside time.

Maria turns her attention to the art area, where two friends are writing letters to their parents and decorating them with glue, felt, sequins, and foil. They ask Maria how to spell *love, blue,* and *thank you.*

In another preschool, Barbara announces to her class, "Time for show-and-tell!" Seventeen four-year-olds rush to their backpacks to retrieve the items they brought from home and then gather in a circle on the rug.

Barbara asks Paul, "What did you bring today?" Paul stands, holds out a spotted horse, and says that his grandma got it for him. Barbara asks if anyone has a question for Paul. No one responds.

She asks Kim, seated next to Paul, "What did you bring with you today?" Without speaking, Kim holds out her hand, showing a square plastic container. Barbara asks, "What's inside?" Kim doesn't answer. Before Barbara can ask Kim another question, José says, "I didn't see!" and two other children begin talking about why they need a blanket from the house area to cover up the figurines they've brought from home.

For about 30 minutes Barbara continues around the circle, asking each child in turn to present her or his item. Meanwhile, many of the children stare out the window, play with the toys they brought, or talk to a neighbor. Barbara finds herself stopping frequently to ask for their attention.

access to a greater number and variety of materials (Montie, Xiang, & Schweinhart 2006).

It is striking that these relationships between classroom practices and children's skills are found in countries with very different cultures (Ireland and Indonesia, for example). As might be expected, other findings from the study are more complex and vary from one country to another, but the cross-cultural consistency of these four findings is significant. Within the world's diversity, there are common threads that guide development and offer clues as to how to best support children's learning.

Interpreting the Findings for Your Classroom

The fact that teachers' education is positively linked to children's language skills makes intuitive sense and is supported by other research in both home and preschool settings. Children learn language by hearing it and using it. Research (Hart & Risley 1995) shows that parents with higher levels of education use more words and more complex language with their children, and the same is likely to be true for teachers. Teachers with higher levels of education are more likely to introduce rare words—words that children don't encounter every day—and to engage in analytical conversations with children (Dickinson 2001b).

In this study, teachers and care-givers' average years of education ranged from 10 to 16 across the countries. In some countries, there were caregivers who had had as few as three or four years of education.

The informal nature of free play allows teachers to engage children in conversation specific to their play and to introduce new vocabulary relevant to the children's interests.

Concerning the other two findings of this study, what is it about the nature of free-choice and small group and individual activities that leads to better language skills? Children tend to choose activities that are interesting and engaging and of a suitable difficulty level. The first scenario in the article's opening depicts a classroom in which each child can choose from a variety of activities and materials and engage directly in an activity that interests him or her. Free-choice activities provide the opportunity and, often, the necessity for children to talk with other children in one-on-one or small group play—as they assign roles for pretend play, establish rules for games, make plans for block building, and so forth. The informal nature of free play allows teachers to engage children in conversation specific to their play and to introduce new vocabulary relevant to the children's interests.

The authors of a major study exploring the long-term effects of preschool education in England note that "freely chosen play activities often provided the best opportunities for adults to extend children's thinking," and they suggest that child-initiated play is one of the best ways for children to learn (Siraj-Blatchford et al. 2002, 3). Dickinson puts it this way: "Free play is the time when children flex their linguistic and conceptual muscles and contribute to each other's development" (2001a, 253). His research shows positive links between children's performance on literacy measures and child-child interaction and pretend play during free play in preschool.

On the other hand, when teachers like Barbara (in the second scenario) propose a specific activity for the entire class, such as a number lesson or show-and-tell, some children may find the activity too easy or too difficult or simply not interesting. These children may participate, but they are not likely to learn much. As the second scenario illustrates, children who are not directly engaged in showing their treasures tend to get bored and restless if the activity goes on too long. In activities like show-and-tell, preschoolers may learn to express themselves in front of the group, but because they have short attention spans, they soon disengage from the activity. Show-and-tell modifications such as bringing in special items or stories to share are much more engaging.

Learning and creativity grow when situations pique children's interest and stretch their imaginations. By definition, activities for the whole group—with the exception of free play—are not tailored to an individual child's interest or learning ability. To build cognitive skills, young children need to solve problems and explore materials on their own. In settings with an inadequate number or variety of materials, children do not have as many opportunities to experiment and solve problems at their own pace. With enough materials, teachers can promote small group and individual activities that invite all the children to participate (see "Low-Cost Materials for Your Classroom").

Learning and creativity grow when situations pique children's interest and stretch their imaginations.

Making the Most of Whole Group Activities

Whole group activities involve all of the children participating in the same classroom activity at the same time. They occur when the teacher plans and leads a special activity (such as a game, song, or story), or they occur naturally as part of the daily routine (for example, during snack time and cleanup). The challenge for teachers is to plan so that each child is engaged and there is little waiting or down time. The following suggestions may help.

- Have music cued and materials ready for distribution ahead of time.
- Have enough materials for a music and movement activity so that each child has an instrument, ball, scarf, or streamer.

Low-Cost Materials for Your Classroom

A classroom chock-full of varied materials invites children to expand their thinking. Materials need not cost a lot. What we adults might consider junk, young children see as treasures. As they manipulate scraps of wood, plastic bottle caps, or corks, for example, children may sort them by color, stack them on top of each other, or make something by putting the objects together.

Ask families and friends to donate

- fabric, ribbon, leather; and yarn scraps
- bottle caps and small containers
- cardboard boxes of all sizes
- buttons, beads, and costume jewelry
- covers of greeting cards and outdated calendars
- twigs, nuts, pinecones, and shells
- leftover home improvement items, such as plastic plumbing pieces, wood scraps, or nuts and bolts.

For more ideas and sources for reusable resources, visit www.reusableresources.org.

- Act out stories with each child playing a part.
- Ask children to bring in special objects or stories to share on different days, instead of having traditional show-and-tell for all children on the same day.
- Divide the group in half, with one classroom staff member leading the group while the other interacts with the rest of the children.
- Invite children to make up their own variations on familiar songs, games, and stories.
- Find positive ways to use waiting time, such as singing songs or doing finger plays, while most of the class waits for a few children to go to the bathroom or put away their materials.
- Offer self-serve snacks to eliminate waiting during distribution.
- Give several children responsibility for passing out snacks and supplies rather than assigning the task to one child.
- Plan for more than one thing at the same time—for example, some children can wipe off tables and some can put away food as others help set up for the next activity or wash their hands.

Enriching Free-Choice Time

Children need an adequate amount of time for high-level group dramatic play and constructive play to develop during free-choice time. Short periods of time limit the complexity of play and often lead to lower levels of play, such as chase games or children wandering around uninvolved.

Children need an adequate amount of time for high-level group dramatic play and constructive play to develop during free-choice time.

To encourage high-level dramatic play, the classroom schedule should allow for a minimum of 30 minutes of free choice time; however, 45 minutes to an hour is best (Christie & Wardle 1992). This extended period of time allows children to recruit others to join, negotiate roles and rules, agree on a storyline, and so on. In constructive play, children also need time to plan, assemble materials, and build elaborate structures, which over time often become part of dramatic play.

Free-choice time is an opportunity for teachers to talk with individuals or small groups of children about their chosen activities. An engaged adult can help children build on and extend their learning by first observing what the children are doing and saying and then offering specific comments or questions to extend children's thinking and vocabulary.

To make the most of free-choice time in your classroom,

- arrange the schedule so that children have free-choice time both indoors and out;
- avoid scheduling free play solely as a before-school transition; plan another time in the day when children have 45 minutes to an hour of free play;
- provide opportunities for children to explore and use materials at their own developmental level and pace throughout the day;
- make sure there are enough materials for all children to be engaged;
- move around the room and observe each child's choices;
- participate as a play partner, starting by observing and listening to children;
- follow children's leads in play and problem solving;
- give children time to solve problems and offer support if needed;
- get down on children's level and match the complexity of their play;
- offer suggestions for extending play, staying within the play theme;
- ask questions sparingly and make them thought provoking and relevant to what the children are doing;
- allow children time to think and respond;
- introduce new, meaningful vocabulary;
- acknowledge individual work and ideas;
- provide information and examples that help families understand the importance of play and free-play time in supporting children's learning.

Conclusion

The IEA Preprimary Project's findings confirm that, despite the diversity of children's experiences in early childhood settings in different countries, there are common classroom practices that lead to desirable child outcomes. The findings emphasize the importance of child-initiated activities and deemphasize whole group instruction. In addition, they highlight the significance of teacher education. Every country should consider requiring teachers and caregivers to have as much schooling as is feasible.

Although a limited number of countries participated in the longitudinal study and many cultures and regions were not represented, the IEA Preprimary Project is the largest study of its kind ever conducted. Its findings are consistent with the developmentally appropriate practices and active learning long advocated by NAEYC and others (Head Start Bureau 1984; Bredekamp 1987; Isenberg & Quisenberry 1988; European Commission 1995; Bredekamp & Copple 1997). We hope that teachers and caregivers can use the practical information in this article to enhance the time they spend with young children and enrich learning.

References

Bredekamp, S. 1987. *Developmentally appropriate practice in early childhood programs serving children from birth through age 8.* Washington, DC: NAEYC.

Bredekamp, S., & C. Copple, eds. 1997. *Developmentally appropriate practice in early childhood programs.* Rev. ed. Washington, DC: NAEYC.

Christie, J.F., & F. Wardle. 1992. How much time is needed for play? *Young Children* 47 (3): 28–32.

Dickinson, D.K. 2001a. Large-group and free-play times. In *Beginning literacy with language,* eds. D.K. Dickinson & P.O. Tabors, 223–55. Baltimore: Brookes.

Dickinson, D.K. 2001b. Putting the pieces together. In *Beginning literacy with language,* eds. D.K. Dickinson & P.O. Tabors, 257–87. Baltimore: Brookes.

European Commission. 1995. *Pre-school education in the European Union—Current thinking and provision.* Luxembourg: Office for Official Publication of the European Communities. ERIC document ED 439975.

Hart, B., & T.R. Risley. 1995. *Meaningful differences in the everyday experience of young American children.* Baltimore: Brookes.

Head Start Bureau. 1984. *Head Start Performance Standards.* DHHS Publication No. ACF 92-31131. Washington, DC: Department of Health and Human Services.

Isenberg, J., & N. Quisenberry. 1988. Play: A necessity for all children. A position paper of the Association for Childhood Education International. Olney, MD: ACEI. Online: http:www.acei.org/playpaper.htm.

Montie, J.E., Z. Xiang, & L.J. Schweinhart. 2006. Preschool experience in 10 countries: Cognitive and language performance at age 7. *Early Childhood Research Quarterly* 21: 313–31.

Montie, J.E., Z. Xiang, & L.J. Schweinhart. 2007. *The role of preschool experience in children's development: Longitudinal findings from 10 countries.* Ypsilanti, MI: High/Scope Press.

Olmsted, P.P., & J. Montie. 2001. *Early childhood settings in 15 countries: What are their structural characteristics?* Ypsilanti, MI: High/Scope Press.

Siraj-Blatchford, I., K. Sylva, S. Muttock, R., Gilden, & D. Bell. 2002. *Researching effective pedagogy in the early years.* Research Brief No. 356. London: Department for Educational Studies, Oxford University. Online: www.dfes.gov.uk/research/data/uploadfiles/RB356.pdf.

Weikart, D.P., P.P. Olmsted, & J. Montie. 2003. *A world of preschool experience: Observations in 15 countries.* Ypsilanti, MI: High/Scope Press.

JEANNE E. MONTIE, PhD, is a senior research associate at the High/Scope Educational Research Foundation in Ypsilanti, Michigan. For more than a decade she has served as part of the team coordinating the IEA Preprimary Project. E-mail: jmontie@highscope.org. **JILL CLAXTON,** MA, is a senior research assistant at High/Scope. She has served as a classroom teacher, project trainer, data collection coordinator, instrument developer, and data manager. E-mail: jclaxton@highscope.org. **SHANNON D. LOCKHART,** MA, is a senior early childhood specialist with High/Scope. She has served as a national and international researcher, curriculum developer and trainer, teacher, and educational consultant in the United States and abroad. E-mail: slockhart@highscope.org.

From *Young Children*, November 2007, pp. 22–26. Copyright © 2007 by National Association for the Education of Young Children. Reprinted by permission.

The Power of Documentation in the Early Childhood Classroom

A parent eyes something on the wall in the hallway near her child's classroom. She stops and looks across the entire wall, as if trying to determine where to start. She moves to the left a bit and scans the bulletin board posted farther down. At one point she nods as if in agreement and mouths a yes. Another parent approaches and turns to see what is on the wall. He too is mesmerized by the documentation of what one child discovered about pussy willows by using an I-scope lens.

HILARY SEITZ

Early childhood educators might ask, "What is documentation?" or "Is this documentation?" They sometimes wonder, "Can my bulletin board be documentation?"

What Is Documentation?

Knowing what is documentation is the first stage of understanding the process. Katz and Chard offer this explanation: "Documentation typically includes samples of a child's work at several different stages of completion: photographs showing work in progress; comments written by the teacher or other adults working with the children; transcriptions of children's discussions, comments, and explanations of intentions about the activity; and comments made by parents" (1996, 2).

Effective Communication

An effective piece of documentation tells the story and the purpose of an event, experience, or development. It is a product that draws others into the experience—evidence or artifacts that describe a situation, tell a story, and help the viewer to understand the purpose of the action.

When used effectively, consistently, and thoughtfully, documentation can also drive curriculum and collaboration in the early childhood classroom setting.

Formats That Work

A bulletin board can be a form of documentation, but there are any number of other possible formats, including a presentation board containing documentation artifacts and/ or evidence (documentation panels), class books, portfolios, slide shows, movies, and other creative products.

The format that documentation takes can be as varied as the creator's mind permits. Because documentation should provide evidence of a process with a purpose, whatever the format, it should fully explain the process, highlighting various aspects of the experience or event.

Audience and Purposes

Successful documentation formats reflect the intended audience and purposes. In addition, the format selected will depend on the individual preparing the documentation and how the children are involved in the experience.

For example, if one teacher wants to highlight for families and administrators how the class is meeting a particular math or science standard, she would use examples of children participating in experiences that align with the standard. As evidence, she might include photographs of children measuring plant stems with a ruler, children's comments about measuring the stems, background information about how the children learned about measurement (or plants), and the specific learning standard the children are meeting by participating in this experience. To best combine all of these elements, the teacher may choose a documentation panel as the format to help the audience understand how children are learning.

If children in the class are the intended audience, however, and the purpose of the documentation is to help children reflect on their math and science learning and connect them to future lessons, then the teacher would select different artifacts and evidence. A documentation panel could again be appropriate, but different artifacts and evidence might include a web of children's ideas: for instance, why an elephant should not live at the Alaska Zoo, children's comments about the elephant, and questions for further exploration, such as, "Where should an elephant live?" Add related photographs and work samples.

Again, an explanation about where the learning began and where it is intended to go will help any audience better

Documentation Artifacts and Evidence

- Teacher's description and overview of an event/experience/skill development, such as photographs and descriptions of a field trip
- Photographs of children at work—for example, conducting a science experiment
- Samples of children's work, like a writing sample from the beginning of the year
- Children's comments, such as "All the rocks have sparkles in them," in writing or as recorded by the teacher
- Teacher or parent comments about a classroom event—for instance, "It was really fun helping the children measure the ingredients for playdough"
- Teacher transcriptions of conversations during small group time when children are exploring a new topic, such as why snow melts indoors
- Important items or observations relating to an event/experience/development, such as "Johnny can now write his own name on his work"

Possible Topics to Document

- Individual child growth and development, such as language development progression
- Expected behaviors (at group time, in using a certain toy, while eating together)
- Curriculum ideas or events (field trips, presentations, special activities, celebrations)
- Curriculum projects, such as learning about plant life cycles
- Families and relationships (different types of family structures and characteristics of the families in the classroom community)
- Evidence of meeting learning standards (by posting work samples)
- Questions and answers of the children, teachers, and families about such topics as classroom routines (like how to wash your hands)

understand the documentation. In both cases, the quality of the end product will depend on the teacher's understanding of children, the curriculum, and the standards, along with his or her effective use of technology and observation.

What Should We Document?

A variety of experiences and topics are appropriate to document, but documentation should always tell a complete story. To stay on track, carefully select one topic and explore it to the fullest rather than trying to do a little of everything. For example, if the class is learning about plants (and studying plant parts, how to grow particular plants, types of plants, and so on), it would be best to document fully just one aspect of children's learning.

To stay on track, carefully select one topic and explore it to the fullest rather than trying to do a little of everything.

Choosing a Focus

The teacher might choose to document only the children's study of plant parts, for example, and could start by providing a learning spark, such as a new plant in the classroom (Seitz 2006). As children comment on the plant parts, the teacher can create a web to record what they know and to help them formulate questions. The children might also draw and label the various plant parts.

Presenting the Topic and Learning

The teacher can combine all of these pieces to make a documentation panel. This panel would illustrate the children's knowledge and understanding more thoroughly than a panel displaying every child's worksheet on plant parts, all of their water-color paintings of a plant, and every brainstormed list of vegetable plants. Offering specific examples of how children came to their understandings about just one aspect of a lesson—in this case, plant parts—achieves more than offering an overview of several experiences.

Showing Developmental Progress

One important and common topic for documentation is individual child growth and development. As previous examples have shown, the documenter is a researcher first, collecting as much information as possible to paint a picture of progress and outcomes. Documenting individual growth requires a great deal of research, as the teacher must observe each child in a variety of areas of development (such as social-emotional, cognitive, language, and motor) over a substantial length of time. Only then can the teacher create a documentation piece that tells an accurate story about each child.

The documenter is a researcher first, collecting as much information as possible to paint a picture of progress and outcomes.

A teacher should be careful to avoid displaying private or confidential information in public forums. There are times when documentation may be more appropriately shared in other, more private venues, such as a portfolio.

Portfolios used for individual assessment of children make a particularly good format for documenting developmental progress. Teachers select several domains to research. They then collect evidence of a child's interaction with other children (photographs and written observations), record the child's reflections about their friendships and cognitive abilities in interviews or group discussions, collect work samples, and tie the documentation together by writing a narrative describing the child's abilities (not deficits) in the selected domains. Even though the portfolio focuses on a child's abilities, teachers may want to consider sharing the documentation/portfolio in a private setting, such as a parent/child/teacher conference, so that parents do not feel compelled to compare their child to others in the class.

Why Should We Document?

There are several important reasons for using documentation in early childhood classrooms.

Showing Accountability

Accountability is one reason for documentation. Teachers are accountable to administrators, families, community members, and others, and documentation helps to provide evidence of children's learning. In addition, documentation can improve relationships, teaching, and learning. Use of this tool helps educators get to know and understand children, and it allows them to reflect on the effectiveness of their teaching practices (Kroeger & Cardy 2006).

Extending the Learning

Consider the following example of how one thoughtful teacher could use documentation to prolong and extend an unexpected learning opportunity. A group of children finds some miscellaneous nuts and bolts on a playground, and their teacher, noting their curiosity, carefully observes their responses and listens to and documents their conversations (by using written notes, photographs, and video). She listens to learn what the children know about the items and what they wonder, such as "Where do these come from?" Then she facilitates a conversation with the children to learn more about their ideas and theories behind the purpose of the nuts and bolts and how they came to be on the playground.

Later the teacher incorporates the initial comments, the photographs, and the conversations in a documentation source (panel, notebook, PowerPoint, or other creative product). The children and teacher revisit the encounter through the documentation and reflect on the experience, which helps the children continue their conversation and drives forward their interest. This back-and-forth examination of the documentation helps the teacher and children negotiate a curriculum that is based on the children's interests (Seitz 2006).

Making Learning Visible

When expected to provide evidence that children are meeting learning standards, documentation is a natural way to make learning visible. Helm, Beneke, and Steinheimer (1998) call this idea "windows on learning," meaning that documenting offers an insight into children's development and learning. Moreover, they observe, "When teachers document children's learning in a variety of ways, they can be more confident about the value of their teaching" (1998, 24).

How Should We Document?

The documentation process is best done in collaboration with other teachers, parents, and, in some cases, children soon after the experience. The information and product become richer when two or more teachers, children, and parents work together to understand an event. Collaboration also helps build a classroom community, which is important because it engages teachers, parents, and children in thinking about the process of learning.

The documentation process is best done in collaboration with other teachers, parents, and, in some cases, children soon after the experience.

When two or more people discuss an event, each brings a different perspective and a new level of depth. The photo below shows two teachers discussing a possible change to the classroom environment. They have discussed aspects that are necessary and that work and things they would like to change based on the children's needs, such as repositioning the furniture. Together they share how they have observed young children using the space. This environment plan would look very different if just one individual had created it. Carlina Rinaldi discusses this notion of working together and building community: "To feel a sense of belonging, to be part of a larger endeavor, to share meanings—these are rights of everyone involved in the educational process, whether teachers, children, or parents . . . working in groups is essential" (1998, 114).

Stages of the Documenter

First and foremost, documentation is a process that is learned, facilitated, and created in stages. I would even go so far as to say that documenters go through their own stages as they learn more about documenting and using documentation to support their ideas. Many early childhood educators already document children's development and learning in many ways, and most communicate a variety of messages in diverse formats to families (Brown-DuPaul, Keyes, & Segatti 2001).

There are six stages that most early childhood educators, including college students and practicing teachers, move through both individually and collaboratively (see "Stages of Documenter Experience"). Educators who collaborate to learn more about documentation tend to have more positive experiences than those who work on their own.

Stages of Documenter Experience

Stage	Experience	Value
1. Deciding to document	Documenters ask, "What should I document?" They collect artwork from every child but at first tend to create busy bulletin boards with too much information. Concerned with equity, many include every item rather than being selective.	Documenters show pride in the children's work.
2. Exploring technology use	Documenters explore how to use equipment and photographs from various events and experiences. Most of the photos are displayed on bulletin boards or inserted in photo albums. The video clips are placed in slideshows or movies and shown to children and parents.	Documenters work hard to learn more about technology. They show pride in the children's actions by displaying photos and video clips.
3. Focusing on children's engagement	Documenters learn to photograph specific things and events with the intent of capturing a piece of the story of children engaged in learning.	Documenters become technologically competent and able to focus on important learning events and experiences.
4. Gathering information	Documenters title the photographs, events, and experiences and begin to write descriptions that tell the story of children's learning.	Documenters begin to connect children's actions and experiences.
5. Connecting and telling stories	Documenters combine work samples, photographs, descriptions, and miscellaneous information in support of the entire learning event. They tell the whole story with a beginning, middle, and an end, using supporting artifacts.	Documenters continue to use documentation artifacts to connect children's actions and experiences to curriculum and learning standards.
6. Documenting decision making	Documenters frame questions, reflect, assess, build theories, and meet learning standards, all with the support of documentation.	Documenters become reflective practitioners who document meaningful actions/events, explain why they are important, and push themselves and others to continue thinking about these experiences.

Conclusion

Documentation can be a rewarding process when educators understand the value associated with collecting evidence and producing a summary presentation, whether in a bulletin board, panel, video, or other format. To become a documenter, one must first understand what to observe and what to do with the information collected. It takes time and practice to learn which experiences support effective documentation and how to collect artifacts and evidence.

Next, as documenters learn why the information is important, they begin to understand the value of documentation for different audiences and come to recognize why certain aspects of child development are important to assess. In addition, documenters learn that administrators and parents value this information, yet it also has value to the children and the teacher in planning authentic curriculum that meets children's needs.

Often the documentation provides insights into children's thinking and helps drive the future curriculum.

Finally, the documenter learns how best to interpret and display the information gathered. Often the documentation provides insights into children's thinking and helps drive the future curriculum. Deepening children's learning is the ultimate reward of documentation.

References

Brown-DuPaul, J., T. Keyes, & L. Segatti. 2001. Using documentation panels to communicate with families. *Childhood Education* 77 (4): 209–13.

Helm, J.H., S. Beneke, & K. Steinheimer. 1998. *Windows on learning: Documenting young children's work.* New York: Teachers College Press.

Katz, L.G., & S.C. Chard. 1996. The contribution of documentation to the quality of early childhood education. ED 393608. www.eric-digests.org/1996-4/quality.htm

Kroeger, J., & T. Cardy. 2006. Documentation: A hard-to-reach place. *Early Childhood Education Journal* 33 (6): 389–98.

Rinaldi, C. 1998. Projected curriculum construction through documentation—*Progettazione*. In *The hundred languages of children: The Reggio Emilia approach—Advanced reflections,* 2nd ed., eds. C. Edwards, L. Gandini, & G. Forman, 114. Greenwich, CT: Ablex.

Seitz, H. 2006. The plan: Building on children's interests. *Young Children* 61 (2): 36–41.

Further Resources

Chard, S.C. 1998. *The Project Approach: Making curriculum come alive.* New York: Scholastic.

Curtis, D., & M. Carter. 2000. *The art of awareness: How observation can transform your teaching.* St. Paul, MN: Redleaf.

Edwards, C., L. Gandini, & G. Forman, eds. 1998. *The hundred languages of children: The Reggio Emilia approach—Advanced reflections.* 2nd ed. Greenwich, CT: Ablex.

Fraser, S., & C. Gestwicki. 2002. *Authentic childhood: Exploring Reggio Emilia in the classroom.* Albany, NY: Delmar/Thomson Learning.

Fu, V.R., A.J. Stremmel, & L.T. Hill. 2002. *Teaching and learning: Collaborative exploration of the Reggio Emilia approach.* Upper Saddle River, NJ: Merrill.

Gandini, L., & C.P. Edwards, eds. 2001. *Bambini: The Italian approach to infant/toddler care.* New York: Teachers College Press.

Hill, L.T., A.J. Stremmel, & V.R. Fu. 2005. *Teaching as inquiry: Rethinking curriculum in early childhood education.* Boston: Pearson/Allyn & Bacon.

Jones, E., & J. Nimmo. 1994. *Emergent curriculum.* Washington, DC: NAEYC.

Katz, L.G., & S.C. Chard. 2000. *Engaging children's minds: The project approach,* 2nd ed. Greenwich, CT: Ablex.

Oken-Wright, P. 2001. Documentation: Both mirror and light. *Innovations in Early Education: The International Reggio Exchange* 8 (4): 5–15.

Reed, A.J., & V.E. Bergemann. 2005. *A guide to observation, participation, and reflection in the classroom.* 5th ed. Boston: McGraw-Hill.

Shores, E.F., & C. Grace. 2005. *The portfolio book: A step-by-step guide for teachers.* Upper Saddle River, NJ: Pearson.

Wurm, J. 2005. *Working the Reggio way: A beginner's guide for American teachers.* St. Paul, MN: Redleaf.

HILARY SEITZ, PhD, is the early childhood coordinator in the Department of Teaching and Learning at the University of Alaska in Anchorage. Her wide range of early childhood experiences includes teaching in child care centers, a public preschool, and elementary schools. hilary@uaa.alaska.edu

UNIT 7

Curricular Issues

Unit Selections

35. **Got Standards?: Don't Give up on Engaged Learning!,** Judy Harris Helm
36. **The Plan: Building on Children's Interests,** Hilary Jo Seitz
37. **One Teacher, 20 Preschoolers, and a Goldfish: Environmental Awareness, Emergent Curriculum, and Documentation,** Ann Lewin-Benham
38. **Fostering Prosocial Behavior in Young Children,** Kathy Preusse
39. **Constructive Play: A Value-Added Strategy for Meeting Early Learning Standards,** Walter F. Drew et al.
40. **Early Literacy and Very Young Children,** Rebecca Parlakian
41. **Using Picture Books to Support Young Children's Literacy,** Janis Strasser and Holly Seplocha
42. **Calendar Time for Young Children: Good Intentions Gone Awry,** Sallee J. Beneke, Michaelene M. Ostrosky, and Lilian G. Katz

Key Points to Consider

- How can teachers use an emergent curriculum planning approach to plan their work?

- Can teachers support prosocial development, and if so, how?

- What information should teachers send parents about their children's early literacy experiences?

- Give some reasons for why picture books should be a big part of children's learning?

Student Web Site

www.mhcls.com

Internet References

Action for Healthy Kids
www.actionforhealthykids.org

Awesome Library for Teachers
http://www.neat-schoolhouse.org/teacher.html

The Educators' Network
http://www.theeducatorsnetwork.com

The Family Involvement Storybook Corner
http://www.gse.harvard.edu/hfrp/projects/fine.html

Grade Level Reading Lists
http://www.gradelevelreadinglists.org

Idea Box
http://theideabox.com

International Reading Association
http://www.reading.org

PE Central
http://www.pecentral.org

The Perpetual Preschool
http://www.ecewebguide.com

Phi Delta Kappa
http://www.pdkintl.org

Teacher Quick Source
http://www.teacherquicksource.com

Teachers Helping Teachers
http://www.pacificnet.net/~mandel/

Tech Learning
http://www.techlearning.com

Technology Help
http://www.apples4theteacher.com

Increasingly, preschool teachers are becoming aware of the tremendous responsibility to plan learning experiences which are aligned with state and national standards to allow children to develop a lifelong love of learning along with the necessary skills they will need to be successful. "Got Standards?: Don't Give up on Engaged Learning!" addresses early learning standards. Standards help guide teachers as they plan appropriate activities that will allow their students to gain the necessary skills to continue to learn as they move through school. It is the responsibility of any teacher of young children to be very familiar with standards. If you are unaware of where to start, try your state Department of Education, many of which have standards for programs serving preschool children. Become familiar with the standards and incorporate them into your planning.

There is a major difference between eating frozen dinners every night vs. meals that have been prepared using the freshest local ingredients. The same holds true for planning curriculum. The "generic one-curriculum-package for all classrooms" approach allows for little, if any, local flavor. Curriculum that is jointly developed by the teachers and students brings the best of the children's interest coupled with what is happening in their world for meaningful, authentic learning. "One Teacher, 20 Preschoolers, and a Goldfish: Environmental Awareness, Emergent Curriculum, and Documentation," provides an excellent overview on the use of an emergent curriculum for young children. Teachers who carefully observe and listen to their children and know the events of their local community will find plenty of possibilities for topics of investigation. Young children are most interested in authentic curriculum that is meaningful to their lives. We wouldn't want to eat frozen dinners every night for the rest of our lives; neither would we want to teach from a pre-packaged curriculum. Get out there and choose some local flavor and spice up the teaching and learning experience in your classroom.

"Using Picture Books to Support Young Children's Literacy" by Janis Strasser and Holly Seplocha provides the reader with additional information on this most important of early childhood skills. The article includes suggestions for shared book experiences, emergent writing, and conversations with children in a variety of settings.

There are two articles, each addressing an important curricular content issue for teachers of young children. Healthy discussion can take place about the role of math and science, and physical fitness. Beginning and veteran teachers alike need to be well versed in a variety of topics affecting young children. The unit ends with "Calendar Time for Young Children: Good Intentions Gone Awry." The traditional calendar time, where children sit for long periods of time as phrases, dates, or songs that are often meaningless to young children are repeated, is in desperate need of updating. Learning experiences should be meaningful and applicable to the lives of children. Children

© Photodisc/PunchStock

simply parroting back to the teacher the full date including day of the week, month, date, and year has little application to young children. They instead could benefit from tracing the weather, counting the number of days until important events, or using vocabulary that will be relevant to their daily lives.

A number of the articles in unit 7 provide opportunities for the reader to reflect on the authentic learning experiences available for children. How can they investigate, explore, and create while studying a particular area of interest? Make children work for their learning or as noted early childhood author Lilian Katz says, "Engage their minds." As a teacher of young children, acquaint yourself with the importance of firsthand experiences. Teachers often confuse firsthand and hands-on experiences but they are very different. Firsthand experiences are those where the children have a personal encounter with an event, place, or activity. Firsthand experiences include a visit to a firehouse, looking for life at the end of a small pond, and touring a local art gallery. After children have these firsthand experiences they are then able to incorporate them into their play, investigating and exploring in the classroom. Hand-on experiences allow the children to actually use their hands and manipulate materials as they learn about the activity such as making a batch of play-dough, building a garage with the blocks, or investigating bubbles in the water table.

This unit is full of articles addressing different curriculum areas. Active child involvement leads to enhanced learning. Suggestions for project-based activities in literacy, movement, and technology are also included. Again, the theme runs deep. Hands on = Minds on!

Professional organizations, researchers, and educators are reaching out to teachers of young children with a clear message that what they do in classrooms with young children is extremely important for children's future development and learning capabilities. Of course, the early childhood community will continue to support a hands-on experiential learning environment, but teachers must be clear in their objectives and have standards that will lead to future school success firmly in mind. Only when we are able to effectively communicate to others the importance of what we do and receive proper recognition and support for our work, will the education of young children be held in high regard. We are working toward that goal, but need adults who care for and educate young children to view their job as building a strong foundation for children's future learning. Think of early childhood education as the extremely strong and stable foundation for a building that is expected to provide many decades of active service to thousands of people. If we view our profession in that light, we can see the importance of our jobs. Bring passion and energy to what you do with young children and their families and you will be rewarded ten times over. Enjoy your work, for it is so important.

Got Standards?

Don't Give up on Engaged Learning!

JUDY HARRIS HELM

As the children enter the kindergarten classroom, they gleefully pull pairs of shoes from their backpacks for a project on shoes. There are big shoes and small ones, sneakers and ballet slippers, galoshes and flip-flops. There are new shoes and old shoes, shiny shoes and dull shoes. One child has even brought in dog shoes! The children become more excited with each pair that is added to the class collection. When the teacher gathers the group for morning meeting, the children cry out: "Our shoes are all different sizes!" "Jason brought Nikes!" "We've got boys' shoes and girls' shoes!" "When can we play with our shoes?" The teacher explains that they have to do their math lesson and reading work first, and then they can decide what to do with the shoes. The children look longingly at the shelf of shoes.

The teacher sighs inwardly. She loves the interest and curiosity generated by projects and rich thematic units, but she feels the pressure of covering curriculum and meeting kindergarten standards. "If only I could be sure they would learn what they need to know, I could harness this enthusiasm."

Like many early childhood teachers today, this kindergarten teacher is overwhelmed by early learning standards and the required curriculum experiences and commercial programs that have accompanied the standards movement into early childhood education. Faced with a literacy program and a math program with prescribed time allocations, she feels challenged to "get it all in the day." She is hesitant to engage children in integrated learning experiences because she wants to be sure they are acquiring the knowledge and skills she is responsible for teaching.

The Importance of Integrated Learning

Even in classrooms in which standards and required curriculum are prominent, there is still a place for rich, integrated learning experiences that truly engage children, such as projects. When children are engaged they are excited, curious, and intensely involved in learning experiences that are meaningful to them (Jones et al. 1994); they take responsibility for their own learning and feel energized. They develop and practice strategies for learning and become collaborative. Engagement increases the ability of the brain to remember; adrenaline created through emotional involvement activates the amygdala, a part of the brain that decides which information is important enough to retain. Over time, a stronger and more lasting memory is created when the brain is emotionally involved (McGaugh 2003). Engagement is a valid criterion for selecting learning experiences to include in the young child's day.

Learning is easier for children when new information is connected to what they already know, not taught in isolation.

Learning is easier for children when new information is connected to what they already know, not taught in isolation. Research in early cognition indicates that by the time children are 4 years old, they have developed a complex, interconnected knowledge base about the world and how it works. Catherwood (1999), in a review of early cognition research, concludes that the task of early educators supporting cognitive development may be to help children articulate their knowledge and link that knowledge to verbal expression. For example, before reading a book about puppies, a teacher might ask the children if they have a puppy or know someone who does. If a child doesn't know about puppies but does know something about dogs, this could be the focus. A discussion about puppies and dogs will activate those parts of the brain where the children have stored knowledge and vocabulary from previous experiences. This discussion will help children connect what they already know with the new information they will gain. Experiences that support a child in making connections, according to Catherwood, "enhance the richness of neural networks in the child's brain" (1999, p.33).

For children in the early years of schooling, teachers can provide engaged and integrated learning experiences through the *project approach,* a three-phase structure for in-depth investigation of a topic that interests children (Katz & Chard 2000; Helm & Katz 2001). Integrated learning experiences, such as projects, enable children to connect the knowledge and skills specified in standards (such as counting or reading and writing) to their world. Through project work children see the value of new skills and have opportunities to practice them as they investigate topics of interest to them. Learning experiences in project work are authentic (real world) and integrative, both characteristics of engaged learning (Jones et al. 1994). Engagement and integration increase when children have an opportunity to investigate something of great interest to them and have a say in what they want to learn about the topic.

The Role of Child Initiative and Decision Making

Effective early childhood teachers use many different approaches to teaching knowledge and skills. One way to think about these approaches is to place them on a continuum of how child initiated they are, meaning how much of a role children have in determining the direction of study.

All approaches on the continuum are valuable and valid ways to teach young children. The approach used may be determined by the content to be taught. For example, when teaching children how to cross the street (to meet a standard on "knowing and using safety rules"), it is best if the teacher determines the content and the most efficient way for children to learn this valuable information. Children can easily learn knowledge about and skills for "collecting and using data to answer questions" during project work, when they will find these skills useful in completing their work. Sometimes the choice of approach is based on how much time is available to teach the concept or skill.

Teachers most often combine approaches to curriculum as they plan their week. For example, a teacher may plan for a unit on magnets in the science area; a lesson on learning how to stop, drop, and roll during large group time; and independent child choice time during which children may choose to continue their work on a project on turtles. These events may occur in the classroom during the same week, the same day, or even the same hour. By using multiple approaches, teachers introduce children to much knowledge and many skills and offer children opportunities to practice and extend their learning.

Even though all approaches are valuable, teaching approaches on the left side of the continuum (teacher-determined content, narrow units and instruction in single skills and concepts) should not be the only ones used in prekindergarten and primary classrooms. Spending too little time on the child-initiated side of the continuum may actually be harmful. When learning experiences never venture into directed inquiry or project work, children are less likely to develop the higher-level thinking skills of analyzing, hypothesizing, predicting, and problem solving (Katz & Chard 2000). Teacher-centered approaches can limit children's vocabulary development. These approaches can also be less motivating for children learning and practicing academic skills. For example, a child who wants to know how many children have shoes with Veicro fasteners versus shoes with laces is motivated to count and write numerals. A child who is making a model of a drink machine is motivated to identify words that indicate the kinds or brands of drinks and to copy and practice reading those words. These experiences not only motivate but provide an opportunity and an authentic reason to practice counting, reading, and writing. Unfortunately, teaching on the single-concept, teacher-centric side of the continuum is often recommended, and in some cases mandated, by school district administrators or directors of early childhood programs.

Even for learning to read, which requires mastering many specific skills, research supports the importance of a balanced approach that emphasizes children's engagement.

Exclusive use of teacher-directed teaching approaches is especially problematic for children at risk. Martin Haberman (2004) labels these teacher-controlled approaches *directive pedagogy,* part of an ineffective *pedagogy of poverty* that focuses teachers on compliance and low-level thinking skills, which limit children's achievement and thirst to learn. Research also suggests that formal, didactic instruction in basic skills may produce more positive results on standardized measures in the short term compared to approaches that give children more initiative and choice, but will not produce higher school achievement in the long term (Marcon 1995, 2000; Golbeck 2001). Even for learning to read, which requires mastering many specific skills, research supports the importance of a balanced approach that emphasizes children's engagement (Cummins 2007).

Most teachers understand that children need learning experiences all along the continuum. Unfortunately today's emphasis on standards and required curriculum is resulting in squeezing most of the children's day into the left side of the continuum.

Integrating Standards into Engaged Learning

It is possible to teach required content and skills through project work and other child-initiated learning experiences such as a shoe project. For example, the shoes need to be sorted so they can be placed on the shelves of a pretend shoe store created by the class. As the children discuss and decide how to label the shelves, how to arrange shoes on the shelves, and where to place each pair of shoes, they learn and practice the math skills of sorting, classifying, and reading numerals. If the teacher has anticipated and prepared for the experience by providing photos of the aisles of a shoe store and shoe catalogs and flyers for children to use as resources, they will also be engaged in literacy. The teacher can take the first step to rich integration of standards and required curriculum into engaging learning experiences by making sure he has a clear understanding of *what* children need to learn and then anticipating *how* they might learn these in the learning experience.

Anticipating the opportunities for integration enables teachers to be prepared with introductory lessons, materials, and supplies and also to interact supportively with children as they do their project work. For example, while children are looking at and talking about the shoes in their shoe collection, the teacher can extend vocabulary by introducing names for the parts of shoes, encouraging children to compare parts of shoes, encouraging children to compare parts of shoes on different models, or even spontaneously showing children how they could create a chart comparing shoe parts. These supportive interactions are more likely to occur if the teacher has anticipated vocabulary and skills possible in the project.

There are specific strategies that teachers who do project work have found helpful in doing this anticipatory planning. The strategies described below can be helpful for rich thematic units or teacher-directed inquiry also.

Know the Content, Skills, and Dispositions You Are Supposed to Teach—Make a List

A first step in anticipating opportunities for integration is to analyze curriculum goals and standards and make a comprehensive list of the knowledge, skills, and dispositions children need to develop. Often teachers do not have a clear understanding of exactly what children need to learn and what they are to teach. There may be learning standards (from the state), a teacher's manual for a math or literacy program, and sometimes another list from the report card.

Often standards are global but children's progress is assessed using a checklist that is more specific. For example, there may be a global standard ("Use concepts that include number recognition, counting, and one-to-one correspondence," from the Illinois Early Learning Standards—Kindergarten), but children will be evaluated on a report card including items to be checked, such as "Recognizes and writes numerals 1–30" and "Can make sets." Sometimes a content program (such as a math book or reading book) may contain additional knowledge and skills that are not required to be taught in every local program. Textbook publishers include everything they feel that any school might want so that their books are applicable to a large number of schools. Sometimes topics in a required curriculum program are introduced to build awareness; mastery is not expected. Just because there is a page on reading pie charts in the manual, this doesn't mean that a teacher is responsible for teaching it or that all children must master that concept at this time.

A teacher who finds herself in a program that has manuals for required curriculum materials, a separate list of standards, and an assessment system with another list of goals (which may or may not be coordinated) will find it less frustrating and more effective to work with a consolidated comprehensive list. For example, a teacher might find that a state standard indicates that children "Count with understanding and recognize 'how many' in sets of objects." However, a curriculum guide may indicate that 4-year-olds should be able to count 10 items before entering kindergarten. A list distributed to families of incoming kindergartners may indicate that children should be able to count to 10. The teacher can make one consolidated list of all math requirements and their sources and then seek assistance from supervisors to clarify discrepancies. This list will be very helpful as the teacher integrates standards and required curriculum goals into engaged learning. A clear understanding of what is to be taught is essential. Training on integration of standards may be available for teachers, or they may find published tables that correlate required curriculum programs with local or state standards. Such resources will help with this consolidation task.

Align the Introduction of Skills and Concepts with Children's Engagement

Once teachers know what children need to learn and do, they can look at their curriculum guides and see if there is a particular sequence for the introduction of concepts. In multiage early childhood classrooms, this is not usually an issue. Kindergarten and primary curriculum guides, however, are usually arranged chronologically. Look to see if the knowledge or skill has to be introduced in a particular sequence. Often the order is flexible so teachers may introduce skills when they are most meaningful to children instead of following the order in the manual.

Often the order is flexible so teachers may introduce skills when they are most meaningful to children instead of following the order in the manual.

For example, in the shoe project, measuring feet to determine the correct shoe size is relevant to the children. If learning how to use standard units of measurement (such as inches) or even nonstandard units (such as Unifix cubes or straws) is a curriculum goal, then this is a perfect opportunity to teach the skill. Anticipating what skill might be needed, then teaching it at the time children must use it maximizes the children's engagement. Even when the skill requires explicit teaching, you can teach it during more formal times of your day, then use the project work as the "practice time" for integration and application of the newly developed or previously taught skill. As teachers create the comprehensive list of what they are supposed to teach, they can note what knowledge and skills will require explicit teaching or must be introduced in sequence and those that can be moved to take advantage of children's engagement.

Create an Anticipatory Planning Web That Includes Knowledge and Skills from Your List of Standards and Required Curriculum Goals

Creating anticipatory planning webs when preparing for project work makes it easier to integrate required curriculum in response to children's interests and lessens the chance that teachers will miss opportunities for skill building and practice. Teachers or teaching teams create planning webs in anticipation of all the possible opportunities for curriculum integration.

To Make an Anticipatory Planning Web

Write the main study topic in the center of a blank page using a marker. In the same color add *concepts about the topic* in a web format. For example, for the topic *shoes,* concepts might include "Shoes have parts," "Shoes come in different sizes," "Shoes are bought" (see "Step 1: Concepts about Shoes"). Keep your focus on concepts about shoes; do not list activities for children to do with the shoes. If this is difficult, imagine a book titled *All about Shoes* for elementary-age children, and think of the concepts you might find in that book. The book would not include activities to do with shoes, only content about the world of shoes.

Review your comprehensive list of knowledge and skills related to the standards and required curriculum goals; compare with your concept web. Determine which concepts would *naturally* and *authentically* provide opportunities for children to learn specific knowledge or skills. For example, the world of shoes is a natural topic in which children would use numeral recognition ("Use concepts that include number recognition," from Illinois Early Learning Standards—Prekindergarten). Learning opportunities could include reading the shoe sizes printed in the shoes and on the boxes or the prices of shoes shown in store ads or signs in shoe stores.

It is important to use this stage of the webbing to discover the most authentic and meaningful opportunities for children to

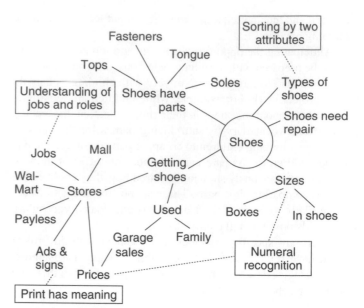

Step 2: Opportunities to Learn Required Knowledge and Skills.

learn; do not start thinking of teacher-directed activities. Write an abbreviated version of the appropriate standard (skill or knowledge) next to the concepts for which a learning opportunity is likely to occur. For example, next to "Prices" you would write "Numeral recognition" (see "Step 2: Opportunities to Learn Required Knowledge and Skills").

Keep your focus on situations in which children might see the value of relevant knowledge and skills or times when they might naturally practice their application. Do not write possible lessons or learning experiences. The goal of this step is to find authentic intersections between the topic concepts and the knowledge and skills you are to teach. In the next step you will begin to think of possible learning experiences.

Look at the web, which now has *concepts* in one color and *knowledge* and *skills* in *another*. Select an area where a concept and a standard or goal come together, such as "Sizes" and "Numeral recognition." Think of a possible authentic learning experience for children that combines these two. For example, you could show children where sizes are located on shoes, and they could then sort the shoes by sizes as they would be in a store. This is an authentic, or real, task performed in shoe stores. This activity shows children the usefulness of numerals and motivates them to learn. They are likely to repeat the activity at home, gaining additional practice with numerals. The task is highly engaging for children.

Contrast this with a shoe theme activity that is not authentic. A teacher prepares construction paper cutouts of pairs of shoes. On one shoe in each pair she places dots. On the other shoe in the pair she writes a numeral. She asks the children to make pairs of shoes by matching numerals and dots. This activity fails to engage the children in the same way, does not demonstrate the value of learning numerals or using them in the real world, and requires teacher monitoring for children to complete the task.

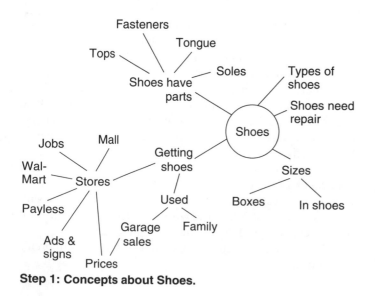

Step 1: Concepts about Shoes.

Look at each place on your web where concepts and knowledge and skills come together. Make a list of possible engaging learning experiences.

Choose one or two possible learning experiences from the list you have generated. The children may create a shoe store in the classroom, visit a shoe store, collect shoes, or even dissect shoes. As children become more involved with the experiences, you can easily integrate the appropriate knowledge and skills because you have anticipated the opportunities to do so. You will be prepared to "teach on the fly," incorporating content or extending learning as children become more involved with the topic. For example, you might teach children how they can use a graph to record data in response to a child's observation that there are almost as many slip-on shoes as shoes with Velcro fasteners.

Identify which concepts are of the most interest to the most children by observing children's involvement in the initial learning experiences. If children appear to be more interested in *shoe repair* than *shoe stores* or *where shoes come from,* then shoe repair can become the topic of the project, maximizing the children's initiation, engagement, and decision making. You can cut out that section of the planning web that addresses shoe repair and move it to the center of the web to remind everyone of the new topic. Instead of the *shoe* project, the children are participating in the *shoe repair* project (see "Step 5: Maximizing Engagement by Adjusting Topic Focus," p. 20).

When you cut out and move the repair section to the center of the knowledge and skills web, many of the concepts and useful and meaningful applications of the knowledge and skills will remain applicable to this new, more narrow topic. Other concepts or applications will be replaced, dropped, or moved to another, newly added concept. Selecting the topic to match the children's engagement and then encouraging children to develop questions and find answers to their questions increases

child decision making and engagement and moves the learning experience to the right on the continuum to teacher-guided inquiry or project work.

As the learning experience progresses, you can determine whether to introduce knowledge and skills before children need them or during an experience, or whether the learning experience itself will provide mainly practice. For some children each of these methods must be used; you must introduce the knowledge or skill before the child will use it, demonstrate and provide coaching at the time it will be used, and then allow the child plenty of time for practice.

Plan for Documentation

It is important for teachers to keep track of which ideas they have introduced to children and what children are and are not learning. Just because a learning experience occurs does not mean that a particular child will be engaged in it or learn the knowledge and skills you have planned to teach. As in all learning experiences, both teacher-directed and child-directed, the teacher must observe to see if each child is meeting the standards. The use of observation notes and photographs, plus the collection of children's work, enables the teacher to be sure that anticipated learning becomes actual learning, that children master knowledge and skills, and that each individual child is participating in some way and moving toward the required curriculum goals or standards (Helm & Beneke 2003; Helm, Beneke, & Steinheimer 2006). Anticipatory planning should also include preparing materials for documentation.

Making Time for Engagement

As the kindergarten teacher at the beginning expressed, time is an important issue when deciding to include engaging learning experiences like the shoe project. However, if a teacher plans what children should know and should be taught, anticipates opportunities to integrate and organize explicit teaching, and documents each child's achievement, then she can be confident that children are achieving standards and learning required knowledge and skills. Teaching time previously reserved for directly teaching these skills becomes free for more active learning experiences. Children can once again be excited about what they are learning in school.

References

Catherwood, D. 1999. New views on the young brain: Offerings from developmental psychology to early childhood education. *Contemporary Issues in Early Childhood Education* 1 (1). www.wwwords.co.uk/rss/abstract.asp?j=ciec&aid=1501

Cummins, J. 2007. Pedagogies for the poor? Realigning reading instruction for low-income students with scientifically based reading research. *Educational Researcher* 36 (9): 564–72.

Golbeck, S. L. 2001. Instructional models for early childhood: In search of a child-regulated/teacher-guided pedagogy. In *Psychological perspectives on early childhood education: Reframing dilemmas in research and practice,* ed. S.L. Golbeck, 153–80. Mahwah, NJ: Erlbaum.

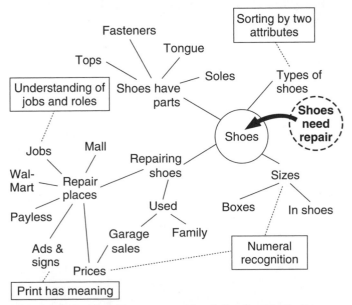

Step 5: Maximizing Engagement by Adjusting Topic Focus.

Haberman, M. 2004. *Star teachers: The ideology and best practice of effective teachers of diverse children and youth in poverty.* Houston, TX: Haberman Educational Foundation.

Helm, J.H., & S. Beneke, eds. 2003. *The power of projects: Meeting contemporary challenges in early childhood classrooms—Strategies and solutions.* New York: Teachers College Press.

Helm, J.H., S. Beneke, & K. Steinheimer. 2006. *Windows on learning: Documenting young children's work.* New York: Teachers College Press.

Helm, J.H., & L.G. Katz. 2001. *Young investigators: The project approach in the early years.* New York: Teachers College Press.

Jones, B., G. Valdez, J. Nowakowski, & C. Rasmussen. 1994. *Designing learning and technology for educational reform.* Oak Brook, IL: North Central Regional Educational Laboratory.

Katz, L.G., & S.C. Chard. 2000. *Engaging children's minds: The project approach.* 2nd ed. Stamford, CT: Ablex.

Marcon, R. 1995. Fourth-grade slump: The cause and cure. *Principal* 74 (5): 17–20.

Marcon, R. 2000. Impact of preschool models on educational transitions from early childhood to middle-childhood and into early adolescence. Poster session at the Conference on Human Development, Memphis, TN, April 16.

McGaugh, J. L. 2003. *Memory and emotion: The making of lasting memories.* New York: Columbia University Press.

JUDY HARRIS HELM, EdD, provides consultation and professional development to school districts and early childhood centers. She is the author of seven books on the project approach and documentation and provides training on integrating standards and engaged learning. judyhelm@bestpracticesinc.net. This article is available online in **Beyond the Journal,** July 2008, at www.journal.naeyc.org/btj/200807.

The Plan

Building on Children's Interests

HILARY JO SEITZ, PhD

During outdoor playtime four-year-old Angela discovers a loose metal nut about half an inch in diameter. She shows the nut to her teacher.

Angela: Look what I found. It looks just like the big one on our workbench.

Teacher: Yes, it sure does, Angela. It's called a nut.

Angela: I wonder where it came from.

Teacher: Where do you think it may have come from?

Angela: Well, actually it is the same as the ones in the workbench inside.

Teacher: This nut looks very similar to the nuts and bolts inside. I think this nut might be bigger than the nuts and bolts we have inside.

Angela: Maybe it came off of something out here.

Teacher: What do you think it is from?

Angela: Umm, I don't know—something out here.

Teacher: Maybe you should check.

Angela: Okay.

Holding the nut tight in her fist, Angela walks around, stopping to examine the play equipment, the tables, the parked trikes, and anything else she thinks might have a missing nut. She can find only bolts with nuts on the trikes. She spies a large Stop sign, puts her special treasure in her pocket so other children cannot see it, and sets up a roadblock for the busy trike riders so she can check the nuts and bolts on their trikes.

Edmund stops and asks her what she is doing, and she explains. Edmund says he needs to see the nut. When Angela shows it to him, he gets off his trike and starts helping her inspect the other trikes. They eventually find the one that is missing the nut. Other children, curious, crowd around.

While incidents such as this are common in early childhood settings, teachers may not listen for them, seize upon them, and build on them. When teachers do pay attention, these authentic events can spark emergent curriculum that builds on children's interests. This kind of curriculum is different from a preplanned, "canned" thematic curriculum model. In emergent, or negotiated, curriculum, the child's interest becomes the key focus and the child has various motivations for learning (Jones & Nimmo 1994). The motivations are intrinsic, from deep within, meaningful and compelling to the child. As such, the experience is authentic and ultimately very powerful.

This article outlines a plan that teachers, children, and families can easily initiate and follow to build on children's interests. It is a process of learning about what a child or a class is interested in and then planning a positive authentic learning experience around and beyond that interest. Teachers, children, and parents alike are the researchers in this process. All continuously observe and document the process and review the documentation to construct meaning (Edwards, Gandini, & Forman 1998). Documentation is the product that is collected by the researchers. It may include work samples, children's photos, children's dialogues, and the teacher's written interpretations.

The Plan

"The Plan," as it became known in my classroom, is a simple four-step process of investigation, circular in nature and often evolving or spinning off into new investigations. (See diagram) The Plan consists of

1. **Sparks** (provocations)—Identify emerging ideas, look at children's interests, hold conversations, and provide experiences. Document the possibilities.
2. **Conversations**—Have conversations with interested participants (teachers, children, and parents), ask questions, document conversations through video recordings, tape recordings, teacher/parent dictation, or other ways. Ask "What do we already know? What do we wonder about? How can we learn more? What is the plan?"
3. **Opportunities and experiences**—Provide opportunities and experiences in both the classroom and the community for further investigation. Document those experiences.
4. **More questions and more theories**—Think further about the process. Document questions and theories.

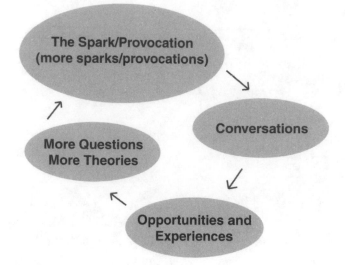

Figure 1

In other words, teachers, children, and parents identify something of interest; we discuss what we know about it or what we want to know about it; we experience it or have opportunities to learn about the idea; and then we discuss what we did and either ask more questions or make new theories. We document our understandings throughout the whole process.

The initial spark can come from anywhere or anything. For example, we might overhear children talking about the lawnmower at the park. The class, or sometimes a smaller group of children, then sits down and devises a plan with the help of interested adults.

Step 1: Sparks

Sparks can be things, phenomena, conversations—anything that provokes deeper thought. The sparks are what trigger a child (and adult) to want to know more, to investigate further. These sparks can occur at any time. They can be as simple as finding a pebble in one's shoe, grabbing an idea or story line from a book, or finding a nut on the playground. Young children have these sparks of interest all day long.

Sparks can be things, phenomena, conversations—anything that provokes deeper thought.

How Do Teachers See/Catch These Sparks?

I often hear teachers say, "How can I learn what the children are interested in?" or "How do we find out what the children want to know?" My response is always, Talk with the children, listen to them, and observe. For some teachers, it can be difficult to sit back and trust that ideas will naturally emerge. But once teachers become familiar with the process, they begin noticing how easily sparks appear.

Teachers in preschools, Head Start programs, and public school classrooms are expected to meet state standards or curriculum content goals. It is possible (although sometimes challenging) to integrate these standards and goals into emergent themes. Teachers who know and understand the "big picture" of standards and goals are more likely to *fit* a topic or emerging idea/plan into the curriculum. They document the process of The Plan (through photographs as well as descriptive narrative) to provide evidence of meeting standards and content goals.

Can We Provoke the Sparks?

Triggering sparks is sometimes helpful and can have exciting implications. Teachers can provoke children's thinking by suggesting ideas through stories, specific items, or experiences. Again, when a teacher is knowledgeable about standards and content goals, she knows when to provide appropriate sparks. For example, reading a book such as *If You Give a Moose a Muffin*, by Laura Numeroff, may trigger thinking and conversations about several different ideas (moose and what they eat and where they live, baking, puppet shows, painting, and others) as well as support literacy development. Owocki, in discussing teachable moments in literacy development, says, "Teachable moment strategies involve knowledgeably observing children and seeking out relevant opportunities to help them extend their understandings" (1999, 28).

Introducing an item into the classroom is another way of triggering sparks of thought. Watch children's eyes light up when you place a large beetle on a table or pluck an unfamiliar stringed instrument.

Finally, we can trigger sparks by offering experiences such as a neighborhood walk or a visit to the grocery store. Authentic experiences with meaningful things interest children (Fraser & Gestwicki 2001). The following is an excerpt of an observation from an early childhood classroom.

Teachers can provoke children's thinking by suggesting ideas through stories, specific items, or experiences.

A small group of four-year-olds and their teacher prepare to visit the park across the street. The teacher locks the gate and turns toward the children. She leans down and says, "Please stay on the sidewalk." Pointing to the nearby intersection, she adds, "We are going to walk over there to the crosswalk." The teacher holds hands with one child while the others pair off and walk behind her.

> Kayla: What's a crosswalk?
>
> José: It's over there.
>
> Teacher: At the corner, we are going to walk inside the lines of the crosswalk. The lines show people where to walk. That way, cars know to stop. It is safer for us to cross in the crosswalk than in the middle of the street.
>
> Tiana: My mom and me always cross over there by our car.
>
> José: That's the middle of the street.
>
> Michael (*motioning*): See that red sign? It says STOP, so you gotta stop at it.

As the small group negotiates the crosswalk and heads down the sidewalk on the other side of the street, José points out three more signs (a No Parking sign, a street name sign, and a Caution sign). The children are puzzled by the Caution sign and stop to try to figure it out.

The teacher documents this interest in street signs and crosswalks in writing and by drawing a sketch of the situation. Later, back in the classroom with the whole class, she brings up the subject of signs. The topic stirs interest and lots of conversation—triggering a new classroom investigation and the beginning of a new plan.

Step 2: Conversations and Writing a Plan

Formal meetings, built into the daily classroom routine, are ideal times for children, teachers, and family volunteers to have large group conversations about forming and writing a plan. In these routine meetings, children already know what to expect; they understand the process as well as the expectations. Our class meetings generally include a variety of fairly predictable experiences (reading stories, singing songs, conversations). Depending on the time of the meeting, we always discuss what has happened earlier or what is about to happen. While one teacher facilitates this meeting, another adult (teaching assistant or parent) writes down ideas, questions, and thoughts about the conversations. The adults later review this documentation to help plan and provide appropriate experiences.

Conversations also take place in settings such as activities or mealtimes. Small group conversations can be very meaningful to children and adults alike. Here is one snack time conversation:

Five girls, ages three and four, are seated at a small table, eating crackers. One child mentions going to the state fair the night before with her family. Two of the other children had been to the fair the previous week, so the teacher considers where to go with this spark of interest.

Kamie: It was cold at the fair, but the animals weren't cold 'cause they got fur on them.

Stacy: I touched the goats and the baby pig!

Kamie: Me too!

Karla: I went on a ride, but next time I'm gonna see the animals.

Teacher: Where are the animals?

Stacy: They are in this big tent, and you gotta wait real long to go inside. But you can put a penny or a dollar in the machine to get food, then you can feed the goats and pigs.

Teacher: What do they eat?

Kamie: They eats lots of stuff.

Karla: Yeah, like rice and leaves.

Stacy: The pony has big teeth and a tongue. It gets your hand sticky.

Teacher: Do all the animals eat the same food? (Kamie nods yes.) Maybe we could go to the petting zoo and feed the goats and sheep.

All the girls: Yes!

Teacher: Let's make a plan.

Karla and Stacy jump out of their seats to get a big sheet of paper and markers. Kamie reminds them to bring a clipboard too.

The teacher writes THE PLAN at the top of the paper. She prints the five girls' names under it. Then she begins writing a list, speaking the words at the same time she writes them.

1. Goats and pigs and ponies eat food.
2. What do they eat?

Karla: Where do they sleep? (The teacher makes this No. 3.)

4. Go to library to get books.
5. Go to petting zoo and talk to zoo keeper.

The Plan is set and displayed on the wall. As a form of documentation, it is revisited frequently and adjusted to meet the needs of the children (Project Zero & Reggio Children 2001). Children, teachers, and families continuously reassess The Plan to guide inquiries. Often children and teachers add revisions to the plan.

Formal Planning

Teachers should also prepare a more formal lesson plan. This planning process works best when teachers, teaching assistants, and parents have opportunities to discuss ideas together. The teacher, who usually assumes the role of facilitator, needs to be prepared. She should know and understand standards and content goals; gather documentation, including photographs, observational records, and work samples; and guide the process of creating the formal plan.

The group discusses why the emerging ideas are important and how to further the investigations. Lesson plans should include the children's questions or inquiries as well as the teacher's; both are integrated into a formal plan.

Step 3: Opportunities and Experiences

Essential in a good plan is providing, facilitating, and initiating *meaningful* and *authentic* opportunities and experiences to help children further understand ideas. The word *meaningful* is the critical element here. Significant experiences create a sense of purpose for the child. John Dewey cautioned, "Attentive care must be devoted to the conditions which give each present experience a worthwhile meaning" (1938, 49).

One way to promote meaningful experiences is to find opportunities for authentic experiences that allow young children to see, negotiate, and participate in the real world. The experiences should be based on ideas that emerge from conversations or the written plan. For example, when the children initiated the conversation about street signs, their authentic experience of seeing and learning about street signs prompted a written plan for deeper understanding. The class began to take walks to explore different signs. Several children created a map showing where the street signs were located. Another group drew all the street signs they saw. Back in the classroom, everyone shared their information. Two children created signs and posted them in the classroom. There was a Stop sign and one that looked like a stop sign but read Quiet in the Library. At the sink, a yellow sign said Wash Hands.

One way to promote meaningful experiences is to find opportunities for authentic experiences that allow young children to see, negotiate, and participate in the real world.

The children also decided they needed road signs on the trike paths in the outdoor play area. Some confusion arose during this phase of the experience. Children began arguing about where signs should be placed and if they had to follow the direction on the signs. This discomfort led to the next phase of the plan (see Step 4).

Several content goals were acknowledged in the above experience. Children drew and created maps of a familiar setting; they practiced writing letters and putting together sounds; they used their knowledge of street signs to create classroom rules. In all, the children experienced authentic, meaningful learning.

Step 4: More Questions, More Theories

During this phase, the teacher carefully outlines the theories and documents new questions. As children raise new questions, they are forced to deepen their thinking about the situation. These thoughts become new sparks or provocations for future plans.

In the continuing sign investigation, the teacher called a large group meeting when the arguing about the trike signs and rules persisted. She posted a large piece of paper on the wall and said, "I noticed some confusion on the trike roads today. Jacob, tell me your plan with the signs." She was careful to focus the conversation on the plan rather than encouraging a blame game ("So-and-so went the wrong way"). Jacob expressed his concern of following the sign rules for safety. The teacher wrote on the paper, "If we follow the street signs, we will stay safe." Kayla added another theory: "People who make the signs get to

make the rules, but they have to write them out." Another child brought up additional safety issues, such as wearing helmets and keeping the trikes on the path. The children and teacher decided to post several signs on the roadway to direct traffic in a clockwise pattern.

Summary

Young children learn best through active participation and experience. When helped, allowed, and encouraged to follow an interest and construct a plan to learn more, children are empowered and become intrinsically motivated. They fully engage in the experience when it is their own (Jones & Nimmo 1994). Meaningful ideas are intrinsically motivating.

A caring, observant teacher can easily promote motivation by facilitating the planning process. As the four-step process described here becomes more familiar to children, teachers, and families, The Plan gets easier. Through collaboration, they document, reflect, and interpret ideas to form deeper meanings and foster lifelong learning.

References

Dewey, J. 1938. *Experience and education*. New York: Collier.

Edwards, C., L. Gandini, & G. Forman. 1998. *The hundred languages of children: The Reggio Emilia approach—Advanced reflections*. 2nd ed. Westport, CT: Ablex.

Fraser, S., & C. Gestwicki. 2001. *Authentic childhood: Experiencing Reggio Emilia in the classroom*. Albany, NY: Delmar.

Jones, E., & J. Nimmo. 1994. *Emergent curriculum*. Washington, DC: NAEYC.

Owocki, G. 1999. *Literacy through play*. Portsmouth, NH: Heinemann.

Project Zero & Reggio Children. 2001. *Making learning visible: Children as individual and group learners*. Reggio Emilia, Italy: Project Zero.

HILARY JO SEITZ, PhD, is an assistant professor at University of Alaska, Anchorage. She has worked in early childhood settings for the past 18 years as a teacher, administrator, and instructor.

One Teacher, 20 Preschoolers, and a Goldfish

Environmental Awareness, Emergent Curriculum, and Documentation

ANN LEWIN-BENHAM

Teaching preschoolers about the environment is hard. Many complex concepts are involved: the interactions among everything on the planet—air, land, water, and all living things; the systems that determine weather and climate, food supply, energy resources, and the quality of life for every plant and animal; systems operating on a planetary scale or in geologic time; the organisms living in a single water drop. Chemistry, geology, physics, and biology all intersect in discussions on the environment.

This article shares the experiences of one teacher in helping preschoolers learn about the environment. The article is based on my lifelong concerns for the environment, on my own experience helping children learn to take care of a goldfish in a preschool classroom, and on a composite of many different efforts—my own and other teachers'—helping children learn about the environment. It is also based on three of my own beliefs:

1. Most young children are eager to learn about the environment.
2. A teacher who lives an environmentally friendly life can be effective in teaching young children about the environment.
3. The emergent curriculum approach (Rinaldi 1992; Jones & Nimmo 1994), including documentation, is well suited for encouraging children to develop environmentally aware behavior.

These beliefs are reflected in this article through enthusiastic children, a teacher respectful of environmental concerns, and the success of the emergent curriculum in arousing and building on children's interests.

Social Constructivist Theory

The theoretical base for the use of an emergent curriculum is social constructivist theory. Briefly, we can infer from the theory that learning occurs when children are engaged in collaborative activity about something that deeply interests them and that the teacher's role is to collaborate with the children in their exploration so her knowledge can scaffold their understanding.

"Learning and development emerge from the dynamic interaction of social and individual factors" (John-Steiner, Panofsky, & Smith 1994, 6). Today numerous psychologists and social theorists have confirmed the idea, first proposed by Lev Vygotsky, that learning is a social process (Feuerstein, Klein, & Tannenbaum 1991; John-Steiner, Panofsky, & Smith 1994; Resnick & Hall 1998; Bronfenbrenner 2004).

Social constructivist theory is robustly practiced in the schools of Reggio Emilia, Italy. In these schools projects emerge through teacher collaboration with small groups of children. The projects are based on teachers' thoughtful listening to children's conversations to determine their deep interests and on subsequent focused talk with the children about these interests. The Reggio structure also involves a carefully designed classroom that functions as a "third teacher," and as such frees the teacher to engage in projects. Literature describing these schools and certain Web sites will acquaint those unfamiliar with the Reggio Emilia approach (see Jones & Nimmo 1994; Edwards, Gandini, & Forman 1998; Lewin-Benham 2006; visit the Web sites of NAREA and Reggio Children).

Ms. Putnam, 20 Children, and a Goldfish

Ms. Putnam, a preschool teacher, wanted to arouse children's concern for the environment and to inspire them to think and act in ecologically sound ways. An evolving chain of experiences about the environment emerged from the introduction of a goldfish to her class.

Projects are based on teachers' thoughtful listening to children's conversations to determine their deep interests and on subsequent focused talk with the children about these interests.

Emergent Curriculum

Rather than sets of lesson plans and objectives, emergent curriculum is a *process* that roughly follows these steps:

1. Select a topic that reflects interests expressed by children in their conversations or that you as their teacher suspect may be of high interest. Ms. Putnam brought a goldfish to school with the idea that the children's care of the fish might interest them in exploring environment-related subjects.
2. Brainstorm, alone or with colleagues, the many ways the experience could develop to ensure that the topic has rich "generative" (Perkins 1992, 92–95) potential. As it evolves, the project may or may not follow what you brainstormed.
3. Use something concrete—from the children, their families, or the teacher—to pique initial interest and to maintain it. The concrete "thing" may be children's own words as recorded by the teacher. Ms. Putnam used children's questions about the goldfish as the starter for many pursuits. Throughout the year she recorded, saved, and studied the children's conversations and kept using their words to arouse further interest.
4. Tape or take notes of the children's words as they react. Study their words to determine what *really* grabs their attention. You may let a day or more pass to heighten the children's anticipation and to allow yourself time to study their words.
5. Continue to bring the children's own words back to them: "On Monday you said the fish's water was really dirty. Joey said, 'It's full of poop.' Would you like to help me clean the fishbowl?"
6. Brainstorm what might happen before any new activity. Knowing she wanted to build environmental awareness, Ms. Putnam had a container available to save the dirty water. When the children asked why she was saving it, she asked, "What do you think we could do with this water?" Again she recorded and studied the children's answers, and brought back those that she had selected for their potential to spark environmental awareness.
7. Use children's words, some particular things they have made, or photo(s) taken during the process as the stimulus for the next steps.
8. Document the experience as each step happens. Record the story of the emerging project as *it emerges,* using children's words, photos of them, their drawings or other work, and a photojournalistic-type retelling. (See "Documentation.").

Documentation

Documentation is the process of recording children's thoughts and actions on a topic to maintain their focus and expand their interest. It works like this:

1. As an experience begins, create a large panel out of sturdy cardstock or illustration board. Write a question, repeat a child's comment, or make up a title as a headline for the panel. Include a photo, a drawing, or an object to show what sparked the project.
2. Continue to add information to the panel as the experience continues. Information can be key words from the teacher or children, a child's drawing, or a photo or series of photos of the children, even an object. The information should reflect a pivotal moment which led to next steps. Ms. Putnam added a photo of the full class at the first group meeting with the fishbowl in the center, one child's comment, and one question each from two other children. As the project continued, she added drawings of children's ideas for how to clean the fish bowl—one a theory, the other the process the class eventually adopted.
3. Whenever a panel is hung or words or photos are added, and before continuing the experience, gather the children who were involved, and read the panel to them (or have them "read"—retell—to you) what has happened thus far. This is called *revisiting.* Ms. Putnam and the small group revisited the panel at least once a day.
4. Add whatever photos and comments or questions bring the experience to a conclusion. In this case, Ms. Putnam added a series of photos—cleaning the fishbowl, discovering Big Eyes dead, everyone crying, and the fish's grave. At the end she added two children's questions which stimulated new projects: "What are we going to do with the dirty water?" and "What will happen to the dead fish?"

A finished documentation panel should convey what started the experience, how it developed and why, and its outcome or the open-ended questions it sparked. As children revisit panels, they begin to retell the experience to themselves, to one another, and to their parents or classroom visitors. Revisiting helps the experience move forward, keeps the children focused, and deepens their understanding of their experiences. Documentation gives parents and visitors a window into life in the classroom and builds both appreciation for and trust in the school.

In September Ms. Putnam made five commitments. During the coming year she would:

- bring into the classroom things related to the environment.
- listen closely to children's conversations and observe their activities and explorations around the items, then use the children's interests as the basis for projects.
- use related vocabulary often and read aloud books on the environment twice weekly.
- keep parents informed so they could reinforce the topic at home.
- follow an emergent curriculum approach—teaching through small group projects, documenting the projects, and revisiting the documentation.

Where do subjects for in-depth projects come from? Ms. Putnam knew that the information she needed for projects to emerge would come from a variety of sources: actively conversing with the children, listening to their conversations with each other to determine what they already knew and what else they wanted to know, and studying her notes on these conversations. Having decided to bring a goldfish to the classroom—because she believed it would be of great interest to the children—she brainstormed concepts that might emerge over time. Her list included the following areas:

- the ecosystem a goldfish requires
- energy sources for living things
- clean and unclean water
- waste disposal
- relationships between living things and the environment

The Goldfish Arrives

On the day Ms. Putnam brought the goldfish to school, Joey, the most active four-year-old in the class, spotted it immediately: "Ms. Putnam, what have we got?" She knew his enthusiasm would spread. During group time she asked Joey to describe what he had seen: "It's orange, and it's swimming, and . . ." jumping up and pointing, "it's THERE!"

Carefully, Ms. Putnam carried the bowl to the full class meeting. Immediately, an animated conversation ensued. Ms. Putnam made notes on the children's comments and, over the next few days, took photos of them observing the fish. After analyzing this information she determined which children were most interested in the goldfish. She created a documentation panel with the heading "Joey Discovered a New Fish" and two photos of children observing the fish, and she hung the panel in the classroom. Later she discussed the panel with the small group of children whom she had observed were most interested. Revisiting the panel with the children revealed more of their ideas because it sparked another conversation.

As the children and teacher discussed the panel, questions tumbled out:

- Where did the goldfish come from? The stream near the school?
- Where did you get the bowl?
- Can we feed the fish from our lunchboxes?
- How does it poop?
- Can I hold it?
- Will it have babies?
- Can I take it home?
- Will it get old and die?
- What do you do with a dead fish?

Like most children, the four-year-olds in Ms. Putnam's class are interested in everything around them. Even by age 4 they have had many experiences, and know more than adults may realize. They are naturally empathetic, know instinctively if living things feel sad or are hurt, and express their concern with words and hugs. Ms. Putnam felt certain she could focus their empathy on the environment, helping them to acquire a sense of what the environment is, an awareness of all living things'

needs, and some knowledge of how those needs relate to the environment (Gardner 1991). From the children's comments, she added this one to the documentation panel: "How can we get this poop out of the water?" She also added a photo of the fishbowl with its dirty water.

That evening Ms. Putnam matched the concepts she had originally brainstormed with the children's questions. The comparison convinced her to use the children's own questions to begin exploring environmental issues with them. She added two of their most fertile questions to the panel: "How can we clean the water?" and "What will we do with the dirty water?"

Planning for Learning

In educating children about anything, a teacher needs to determine what they already know and find the intersections between her perceptions and their interests. Teachers use this information to decide what to do next (Vecchi 1994). Through analyzing her own brainstorming list and comparing it to the interests children expressed, Ms. Putnam hypothesized that an environmental curriculum in her classroom, sparked by the children's interest in the goldfish, could cover these topics: ecosystem; land, water, and air; food and energy; pollution. The curriculum would emerge as children's investigations and activities led to the evolution of old interests and the development of new ideas. How she prepared the classroom environment and documented the children's experiences would be critical. Ms. Putnam asked herself if she could also:

- Care for an animal in addition to the plants already maintained in the classroom?
- Model environmentally conscious behaviors for the children consistently? For example, could she
  — make sure to turn out lights *whenever* the class left the classroom or sunshine provided adequate light and each time tell the children her actions were taken to save energy?
  — teach the children to conserve by running only a trickle of water then turning it off while soaping hands or brushing teeth?
  — set up a system to segregate leftover food, paper, glass, and plastic, and with the children analyze which leftovers could be reused and how? During meals, Ms. Putnam began to play a game with the children, Compost Collection, in which they discussed what leftovers would make good compost. This sparked the children's curiosity about what to do when the compost container was full, and led to a project to develop a compost pile in a remote corner of the play yard.
- Reach beyond the classroom to engage in environmentally friendly efforts? For example, she
  — toured the school with the children to detect how to save resources.
  — asked parents to send to school examples of community environmental activities. One family sent an article about the installation of energy-saving light bulbs in the local public libraries. Ms. Putnam read every item to the whole class, and discussed it in depth with those children

who were most interested. Often the children had their own theories, which Ms. Putnam recorded, studied, and later discussed with them. On subsequent days she had them draw pictures or represent their ideas in other materials, like paper, cardboard, clay, wire, or blocks.

— invited parents to help on field trips. One involved a visit to the city's waste recycling plant, another to a nearby stream to look for effects of pollution.

Using Observations and Conversations to Facilitate Learning

For several days after introducing the goldfish, Ms. Putnam left a tape recorder next to the fishbowl to capture the children's comments. As the children observed the fish, she took photos and added two to the panel. All the children visited the fishbowl at least once a day, most two or three times; five children were regulars, sometimes checking on the fish several times a day and naming it Big Eyes. Children's comments on tape ranged from how fish are born to fish weddings, death, play, and fighting. Most often the children wondered how fish get food, what happens when they poop in the water, and how to clean the water.

After observing and revisiting the panel with the children and while excitement was still high, Ms. Putnam revisited the panel again with the five most interested children and asked, "What else would you like to know about the fish?" Questions poured out. Ms. Putnam then asked another question: "How can we find out?" "These two questions are powerful and universally applicable. The first taps the wealth of experiences even very young children have already accumulated. The second stretches them to make connections from one particular bit of information to their other ideas, which adults cannot intuit" (Lewin-Benham 2006, p. 51).

From this discussion Ms. Putnam realized the children knew these things: the fish should be fed just once daily, it pooped a lot, and its water was already dirty. This bothered them, and they wanted to do something about it.

Ms. Putnam asked the five children, "Can you draw pictures showing how we could clean the bowl?" She added two of the children's drawings to the panel. Two days later, she gathered the five children again, revisited the panel, and asked them to use their drawings to describe to one another how to clean the bowl. Their ideas ranged from fantasy—using a magic vacuum that unrolled from a long tube—to reality—finding ways to clean the bowl without hurting Big Eyes, since cleaning utensils might be rough and cleansers could poison him. Danielle, one of the children, had been to a pet store where she gleaned this information, which she then shared with the others during one of their many small group discussions.

Ms. Putnam suggested that the group discuss which method would be best and then make one drawing to represent it. Several more days passed as the children debated among themselves, sometimes arguing fiercely, often joined by Ms. Putnam. They finally agreed on how to clean the bowl: Catch Big Eyes in a fish net (Danielle had seen this in the pet store also), put him quickly into a pitcher of clean water, empty the old water, carefully scour the bowl, then pour in Big Eyes,

clean water and all. The group collaborated on making one drawing of this process, which Ms. Putnam added to the panel.

Big Eyes Dies!

Because the class had not allowed the changing water to stand overnight so the chlorine could evaporate, Big Eyes did not survive the change. Ms. Putnam had not told the children this vital knowledge, something she knew but, in the excitement, had forgotten to share with them. The children were distraught. Ms. Putnam blamed herself. The children saw how sad she was.

"Hey! I know," Joey exclaimed. "Let's go to the pet store and buy a new fish!"

Teacher and children cried—all still sad about Big Eyes, Donnie and Charles in distress at Ms. Putnam's sadness, Danielle and Darrell not to be left out, Ms. Putnam upset at her omission and deeply moved by the children's compassion.

"What are we gonna do with Big Eyes?" asked Joey. Crying ceased as the children began a conversation that became animated. Many ideas later, they toured the yard and found an ideal spot to bury Big Eyes—under the pussy willow, their favorite with its soft, silky-haired blooms. Ms. Putnam added a photo of Big Eyes's grave to the documentation panel. She saw the echoes of this powerful experience in many of the projects that emerged later that year.

Emerging Projects

The experience with Big Eyes sparked a new project on the environment with these themes: What happens when dirty water is poured on the earth? What is earth? What would happen to Big Eyes in the earth? Ms. Putnam documented the earth project on a second panel. A small group went with her to the pet store to buy a new fish in response to Joey's suggestion (the subject of a third panel). The children were full of questions about how stores find fish. This led to a project on ecosystems that support different fish. By year's end the children's evolving interests led to:

- Questioning what's in water and how evaporation works.
- Reading the fish food label, which prompted a big project on food sources.
- Carefully watching the ceaseless swimming of the new fish, which led to a project on energy.
- Discussing how pollutants get into air and water.
- Studying the labels on cleansers, which resulted in a search for environmentally friendly cleaning products and replacing commercial cleansers with homemade solutions of baking soda, vinegar, and water, natural products that the children learned would not pollute.

When the children learned how dangerous plastic can be to wild animals, they organized a Plastic Patrol and involved their families in a clean-up day.

When the children learned how dangerous plastic can be to wild animals, they organized a Plastic Patrol and involved their families in a clean-up day. When they learned that fish poop makes good fertilizer, they went on a hunt for other waste to recycle, and visited their town's recycling center.

Each project involved only a small group, generally different for each project. Ms. Putnam documented every project on its own panel. Usually the entire class toured each panel, led in small groups by the children involved. With one group, Ms. Putnam wrote to parents discussing how to use the classroom's environmentally friendly practices at home. The whole class read the letter; several children added words and drawings, and everyone carried a copy home.

It was possible for Ms. Putnam to teach to a small group for two reasons. First, there were two adults in the classroom. Second, the classroom environment was richly prepared. "In practice this means . . . [the teachers] trust the environment as much as they trust one another, and create a three-member team from two teachers and an environment. Their painstaking organization results in environment-guided activity that is as valuable as teacher-guided activity" (Lewin-Benham 2006, 14–15).

A Year in Review

At the end of the year Ms. Putnam reviewed her teaching and the children's learning. Projects on a wide range of areas covered 10 different panels. She had learned to be more thoughtful about when to add her own knowledge to the children's explorations. This is the essence of emergent curriculum: the learning that results for children and teacher from the teacher's knowledge and skills through collaboration with the children. Because the teacher scaffolds the children's ability, it makes it possible for her knowledge to merge with, expand, or alter their knowledge. What the children learned was evident in their

- favorite books, like *Cactus Hotel,* about a saguaro's life cycle and relationship to other desert plants and animals;
- daily vocabulary, which now included words like *environment, relationship, impact, pollutant, and earth-friendly;*
- drawings, which showed increasingly thoughtful ideas about the environment;
- interest in food content, concern about clean air and water, and knowledge of the plants and animals that lived near the school;
- comments, like Joey's after burying Big Eyes: "You see, we're all connected to everything, fish to insects, insects to earth, earth to goldfish, what we eat to earth. It's all connected."

Conclusion

Ms. Putnam's experience illustrates how to raise preschool children's environmental awareness. Her approach was grounded in the social constructivist theory that we learn through relationships with others who mediate our interactions with things around us. Her approach was influenced by Reggio Emilia

school practices, especially belief in children's ability; attentive listening to children's ideas; collaborative small-group projects including the teacher; the use of a well-designed environment as a third teacher; extensive use of various materials as vehicles for children to express and reformulate ideas; and documentation.

Teachers wanting to raise children's environmental awareness can use a fish, a plant, an insect, a book, an environmentally focused local event, or many other things. Wherever they start, teachers should allow plenty of time for conversation and should use the children's own reactions, comments, and questions as the basis for what they do next.

The interconnectedness of everything on our planet dovetails with a teaching approach based on collaboration and a theory of learning based on relationships. In this case the children's interest in the life and death of a goldfish enabled the teacher to arouse their concern for the well-being of the environment and to help the children think and act in ecologically sound ways.

References

Bronfenbrenner, U. 2004. *Making human beings human.* London: Sage.

Edwards, C., L. Gandini, G. Forman, eds. 1998. *The hundred languages of children: The Reggio Emilia approach—Advanced reflections.* 2nd ed. Greenwich, CT: Ablex.

Feuerstein, R., P. Klein, A. Tannenbaum. 1991. *Mediated learning experience (MLE): Theoretical, psychosocial and learning implications.* London: Freund.

Gardner, H. 1991. *The uschooled mind.* New York: Basic Books.

John-Steiner, V., C.P. Panofsky, & L.W. Smith. 1994. *Sociocultural approaches to language and literacy.* New York: Cambridge University Press.

Jones, E., & J. Nimmo. 1994. *Emergent curriculum.* Washington, DC: NAEYC.

Lewin-Benham, A. 2006. *Possible schools: The Reggio approach to urban education.* New York: Teachers College Press.

NAREA (North American Reggio Emilia Alliance). Online: www.reggioalliance.org.

Perkins, D. 1992. *Smart schools.* New York: Free Press.

Reggio Children. Online: http://zerosei.comune.re.it/inter/reggiochildren.htm.

Resnick, L.B., & M.W. Hall. 1998. Learning organizations for sustainable education reform. *Daedalus* 127 (4): 89–118. Online: www.instituteforlearning.org/media/docs/learningorgforsustain.pdf.

Rinaldi, C. 1992. Lecture. Ida College, Newton Centre, Massachusetts, June.

Vecchi, V. 1994. Lecture/Study Seminar. "Experience of the Municipal Infant-Toddler Centers and Preprimary Schools." June. Reggio Emilia, Italy.

ANN LEWIN-BENHAM, AB, was founder/director of the Model Early Learning Center (MELC) and Capital Children's Museum in Washington, D.C. Her recent book, Possible Schools: The Reggio Approach to Urban Education, tells MELC's story. Ann writes and lectures on early education.

Further resources on environmental education—a bibliography and a listing of curriculum activities—are available through *Beyond the Journal* at www.journal.naeyc.org/btj.

From *Young Children*, March 2006, pp. 28–34. Copyright © 2006 by National Association for the Education of Young Children. Reprinted by permission.

Fostering Prosocial Behavior in Young Children

KATHY PREUSSE

According to the National Center for Education Statistics (2001), there are over 21 million children under the age of six in center-based child care programs in the United States. Programs vary in their content, but one of the aspects common to all is the social context in which learning and care occurs. All early childhood teachers have a tremendous responsibility to meet the developmental needs of the whole child, and more than that, to help children develop the prosocial skills necessary to succeed in a group setting, as well as in society.

Social Development in Young Children

From infancy, children are active participates in a complex world. Interactions with parents are the first type of social exchange infants experience. Healthy exchanges create a bond or attachment. Attachment is a sense of connection between two people that forms the foundation for a relationship (Pruitt, 1998). Exchanges such as facial expressions, movements, and verbal interactions help create an attachment or bond. Experts feel that the first year of life is a critical period for bonding. Bonds create a sense of trust that supports an infant's exploration of the world and serves as a base for future development (Raikes, 1996). "Numerous studies have shown that infants with secure attachments to their mothers and fathers are at an advantage for acquiring competencies in language and in cognitive, social, and emotional development" (Raikes, 1996, p. 59). If attachment does not occur, children may have problems later in life and may display asocial behaviors (Wardle, 2003).

Today, with an increasing number of children enrolled in center-based programs, educators and caregivers play an important role in promoting the development of prosocial skills. "The teacher-child relationship is an extension of the primary parent-child relationship, and teachers invest in building supportive relationships with families around their common interest, the child" (Edwards & Raikes, 2002, p. 12). Many programs have been designed based on the principle that attachment is vital to the social development of young children. Some centers have focused on the importance of attachment and relationships by

creating small groups or 'families.' In these programs, an early childhood teacher is assigned to a group of children over an extended period of time, sometimes several years, which is called looping. Primary caregivers provide children predictability, consistency and a secure base, which helps promote the development of trust. It is from this base the child can explore his physical and social environment. According to Howes and others (cited in Raikes, 1996, p. 61) "There are multiple advantages of secure-based behavior for infants: infants explore more, have more productive play, and interact more and more resourcefully with adults in group settings when their attachments to teachers are secure." Furthermore, children with a secure teacher-child relationship tended to have more positive peer relationships (Raikes, 1996).

During the preschool years, children are developing a sense of independence and capacity for cooperation. As they become more verbal, self-aware, and able to think about another person's point of view, they become more able to interact with peers (Berk, 2002). Furthermore, children at this age move from parallel play to more advanced levels such as associative and cooperative play. It is through cooperative play that children experience play in groups in which they must set aside their needs for the good of the group (Wardle, 2003). Thus, they are developing positive social skills.

Early social development is complex and closely intertwined with other areas of development: cognitive, physical, emotional, linguistic, and aesthetic. The National Association for the Education of Young Children (NAEYC; Bredekamp & Copple, 1997) emphasizes the need for socialization and the development of social skills as a vital part of early childhood education. They advocate principles that educators should use as a guide to developmentally appropriate practices. Listed below are five of these principles. As you can see socialization is intertwined and important to each of these principles (as well as the remaining ones not listed).

- Development and learning occur in and are influenced by multiple social and cultural contexts.
- Children are active learners, drawing on direct physical and social experiences as well as culturally transmitted

knowledge to construct their own understandings of the world around them.

- Development and learning result from interaction of biological maturation and the environment, which includes both the physical and social worlds that children live in.
- Play is an important vehicle for children's social, emotional, and cognitive development as well as a reflection of their development.
- Children develop and learn best in the context of a community where they are safe and valued, their physical needs are met, and they feel psychologically secure (cited in Bredekamp & Copple, 1997, p. 10).

Prosocial behaviors are crucial to children's well being. Thus, it is our responsibility as early childhood educators to provide opportunities for the development of necessary social skills.

Play

Play is a common form of interaction between and among children. "Children do not construct their own understanding of a concept in isolation but in the course of interaction with others" (Bredekamp and Copple 1997, p. 114). Some of the social skills fostered through play are the ability to work towards a common goal, initiating and/or keeping a conversation going, and cooperating with peers. Attachments are formed with other children of similar interests and can lead to friendships. Friendship can be defined as "a mutual relationship involving companionship, sharing, understanding of thoughts and feelings, and caring for and comforting one another in times of need" (Berk, 2002, p. 377). Many of the social skills children develop at this time are listed in this definition. As social skills become more developed, friendships and interactions can become more complex.

Prosocial Skills

Prosocial behaviors allow a child to interact with adults and children in a successful and appropriate manner (Wardle, 2003). The interaction should be beneficial to one, the other, or both parties involved. An added component is the "individual's ability to perceive the situation and be aware when a particular set of behaviors will result in positive outcomes" (cited in Cartledge & Milburn, 1986, p. 7). According to this, a child needs more than specific skills. A child also needs the ability to navigate specific situations.

Prosocial behaviors can be grouped into three distinct categories: sharing (dividing up or bestowing), helping (acts of kindness, rescuing, removing distress), and cooperation (working together to reach a goal) (Marion, 2003). Other experts include showing sympathy and kindness, helping, giving, sharing, showing positive verbal and physical contact, showing concern, taking the perspective of another person, and cooperating. Kostelnik et al. (1988) placed prosocial behavior in two categories: cooperation and helpfulness. The authors defined cooperation as the act of working together for a common goal. Helpfulness was defined as the act of removing distress from another person.

Developing Prosocial Skills

Many experts have looked at the process of developing prosocial skills. A child must develop cognitive competencies, emotional competencies, and specific skills in order to develop prosocial behavior (Marion, 2003). For example, in order to share a child must have: 1) The cognitive ability to recognize him/herself as able to make things happen; 2) The emotional capacity to empathize with the other person; and 3) The ability to perform a specific skill.

It is the combination of these three elements that result in the formation of a social skill such as sharing.

Another expert, Vygotsky, viewed socialization as two fold. First, cognition is related to social engagement, and secondly, language is a critical tool for communication within a social context (cited in Berk & Winsler, 1995). Vygotsky emphasized the importance of sociodramatic play. Play is a means by which children interact, but it is also through this social interaction that cognitive development occurs. Researchers have found that preschoolers who spend more time at pretend play are more advanced in intellectual development, have a higher capacity for empathy, and are seen by teachers as more socially competent (Berk & Winsler, 1995).

The development of prosocial skills can be viewed as a three-part process. In the *recognition* step, a child must be able to determine if someone needs help. Secondly, the child must *decide* whether to help or not to act. Thirdly, a child must *act* by selecting and performing an appropriate behavior for that situation (Kostelnik et al., 1988).

Click and Dodge looked at the social problem solving aspect of social development (cited in Berk, 2002). They developed an information-processing model that looked at 1) a child's ability to engage in several information-processing activities at a time, 2) a child's mental state, and 3) peer evaluation and response. They listed the activities a child must do in order to deal with the problem and come up with a solution. They are: "Notice social cues; Interpret social cues; Formulate social goals; Generate possible problem solving strategies; Evaluate probable effectiveness of strategies; Enact response" (cited in Berk, 2002, p. 378).

In addition, the child must have knowledge of social rules, memory of past experiences, and expectations for future experiences. Lastly, peer perspectives and responses to a child's problem solving techniques greatly impact future interactions between the children involved (Berk, 2002).

The Teacher's Role

It is the teacher's role to facilitate and encourage prosocial behaviors, provide activities that foster appropriate skills, provide necessary assistance, and develop a social network that supports children in their efforts. Teachers must provide activities that help children identify various social skills and help them understand why the skill is needed (Johnson et al., 2000).

The National Association for the Education of Young Children (NAEYC) pointed out that "preschoolers are capable of engaging in truly cooperative play with their peers and forming real friendships. However, development of these important social skills is not automatic for children. They need coaching and supervision to learn and maintain appropriate behaviors with others" (cited in Bredekamp & Copple, 1997, p. 116).

How can teachers help children develop the skills and behaviors needed to act in a prosocial manner? According to NAEYC the classroom is a place to learn about human relationships. Children should have the opportunity to:

- Play and work with others
- Make choices and encounter the consequences of those choices
- Figure out how to enter play situations with others
- Negotiate social conflicts with language
- Develop other skills that characterize socially competent human beings (cited in Bredekamp & Copple, 1997, p. 118).

Facilitating Positive Interactions

Teachers can facilitate positive play interactions for children through the use of a variety of strategies. These strategies include: 1) emphasizing cooperation rather than competition, 2) teaching games that emphasize cooperation and conflict resolution, 3) setting up classroom spaces and materials to facilitate cooperative play, 4) using literature to enhance empathy and caring, and 5) encouraging social interactions between children of different abilities whether it is social, emotional, or physical (Honig & Wittmer, 1996). Research has shown children benefit greatly from effective, positive play situations. Klein, Wirth, and Linas (2003) listed several approaches for facilitating quality play situations. These approaches include: 1) Focusing on the process by asking exploratory questions; 2) Building on children's interests and elaborate on their play; 3) Labeling emotions and feelings that children are expressing through their play; 4) Providing materials that encourage and extend exploration and 5) Providing open-ended materials such as blocks or pretend props.

Howes and Stewart (cited in Honig & Wittmer, 1996) found that children who are involved in high-quality care and have supportive parents learn how to recognize and regulate emotional signals when playing with peers.

Helping Children Make Choices

Teachers should help children make choices and deal with the consequences of their decisions. The teacher's role is to plan activities that help children think through a problem. It is also necessary to repeat the learning activity or similar activity several times (Kostelnik et al. 1988). Through this repeated step-by-step process children can learn how to identify the different path choices, apply reasoning to the process, and formulate a decision.

Promoting Entry into Play Groups

Young children frequently need encouragement to enter playgroups, whether it is to enter an ongoing group, initiate a contact with a friend or being approached by others. Children enter playgroups in a variety of ways, some more successfully than others. Preschoolers tend to enter groups in one or a combination of ways: 1) approaching and watching with no verbal or nonverbal attempt to participate, 2) starting the same activity as another child and blending into the ongoing activity, 3) making social greetings or invitations, 4) offering informational statements or questions, 5) making overt requests to join, or 6) approaching and trying to control group or get attention (Ramsey, 1991).

Preschool playgroups can be fluid, with children entering and leaving quite frequently. Teachers can respond to these already formed groups to "insure the equal participation of all children, help the group work towards a desired goal, and enrich the activity so that all the children can have a meaningful role" (Ramsey, 1991, p. 120). In some instances teachers may prefer arranging playgroups. This helps reduce children's anxiety and widens their range of contacts. Again, equal and active participation by all members and a common goal are important (Ramsey, 1991).

Helping Negotiate Conflict

Teachers need to help children develop negotiating skills to handle conflict situations. Children must use social problem solving skills to resolve issues in a matter that benefits them and is acceptable to others (Berk, 2002). Marion (2003, p. 56) suggested six steps for teaching conflict resolution:

- Identify and define the conflict.
- Invite children to participate in solving the problem.
- Work together to generate possible solutions.
- Examine each idea for how well it might work.
- Help children with plans to implement the solution.
- Follow up to evaluate how well the solution worked.

Peer mediation is another strategy used by teachers to negotiate conflicts. Peer leaders are seen by other children as being credible and serve as role models (Wardle, 2003). This method is used most effectively in elementary schools because of the skills required to implement the process. The "friendship table, or talk-it-over table," is suggested for preschoolers. The teacher's role is to remove the children to a neutral site, and facilitate the conflict resolution process (Wardle, 2003, p. 393).

Promoting Self-Control

Teachers should provide as many opportunities for young children to develop other necessary skills needed to achieve social competency. Self-control is one of the skills. Harter and Shaffer (cited in Marion, 2003, p. 56) said, "Self-control is an essential part of how children learn, is important in a child's growth and development, and is fundamental in preserving social and moral order." Self-control or self-discipline refers to the ability to internally regulate one's own behavior rather than depending on others to enforce it (Kostelnik et al., 1988). Children demonstrate self-control when they 1) control their impulses, wait, and suspend action, 2) tolerate frustration, 3) postpone immediate gratification, and 4) initiate a plan and carry it out over time (Marion, 2003).

If it is an internal process, how can teachers foster the development of self-control? Kostelnik et al. (1988) suggested four strategies:

- Use direct instruction to let children know what are appropriate behaviors, inappropriate behaviors, and alternative behaviors. For example, restricting certain behaviors ("Five more minutes on the swing.") or redirecting children's behaviors ("Don't bounce that ball inside. Go outdoors instead.").
- Model right from wrong so children can learn by example. Modeling can be nonverbal (returning library books on time) or verbal ("I'm petting the kitten very gently.").
- Introduce logical consequences to influence future behavior ("Wear an apron so paint doesn't get on your shirt.").
- Integrate emotions, development, and experience to help children make an internal map. A child can use this chart to categorize past events, interpret cues, envision various responses, and then respond appropriately ("When you share the chalk with Tommy it makes him happy.").

Self-control evolves over time. Teachers should provide repeated experiences for children to practice self-control and refine their behavior.

Environment and Curriculum

The teacher's role should include preparing the classroom environment for optimal prosocial learning opportunities and providing a comprehensive curriculum that enhances the development of prosocial skills. Opportunities for prosocial skill development should be evident in all classroom areas. To illustrate, here are some examples:

- Placing marble mazes (or other exploratory activities) in the science area that can be played by two or more children. Encourage verbal discussion as well as problem solving.
- Introducing a variety of books that deal with perspective taking, feelings and emotions in the literacy corner.
- Arranging the housekeeping area to include a dollhouse with people of many cultures represented.
- Providing rainbow ribbons in the music area so children can come together in dance to express themselves.
- Placing giant floor puzzles in the manipulative area so that children can work together toward a common goal.
- Playing a parachute game where cooperation is necessary during large motor times.
- Promoting helping skills and acts of kindness by setting up opportunities in the dramatic play area such as a pet hospital.

- Preparing muffins and sharing them as a cooking experience.
- Including open-ended materials in the block area.
- Facilitating play groups for those reluctant to join in.
- Setting up bath time for baby dolls in the sensory table. Model caring and helping behaviors.
- Supplying paint, brushes and a very large piece of paper for the whole class to make a mural in the art area.
- Displaying children's work in the classroom at their level.

Teachers must also implement curriculum that emphasizes prosocial themes and concepts. Activities and experiences should focus on the development of self-worth as well as respecting others. One such curriculum is Moozie's Kindness Curriculum which is distributed by Children's Kindness Network (moozie@childrenskindnessnetworkorg). The curriculum emphasizes respect for self, family, friend, community, animals, and the environment. Activities included promote kindness, caring and sharing (Herr et al., 2004).

Conclusion

Prosocial behavior is essential to the well being of children. Children must learn to act in an appropriate manner, one that is both beneficial to them and to others. With so many children participating in group settings, positive interactions are a necessity. The development of these skills allows children to interact with others in a socially accepted manner.

The development of prosocial skills begins in infancy with the development of healthy attachments to parents and caregiver(s). The early years are the time for children to develop prosocial skills by interacting with other children. Moreover, it is the role of early childhood teachers to facilitate the development of these behaviors in young children. Positive play opportunities, modeling, coaching, optimal room environments, and carefully designed curriculums lay the foundation.

References

Berk, L. (2002). *Infants, children, and adolescents.* Boston, MA: Allyn & Bacon.

Berk, L., & Winsler, A. (1995). *Scaffolding children's learning: Vygotsky and early childhood education.* Washington, DC: NAEYC.

Bredekamp, S., & Copple, C. (Eds.; 1997). *Developmentally appropriate practice in early childhood programs.* Washington, DC: NAEYC.

Cartledge, G., & Milburn, J. (Eds.; 1986). *Teaching social skills to children.* New York, NY: Pergamon Books, Inc.

Edwards, C., & Raikes, H. (2002). Extending the dance: Relationship-based approaches to infant/toddler care and education. *Young Children, 57* (4), 10–17.

Herr, J., Lynch, J., Merritt, K., Preusse, K, Wurzer, R. (2004). *Moozie s Kindness Curriculum: Preschool.* Breckenridge, CO: Children's Kindness Network.

Honig, A., & Wittmer, D. (1996). Helping children become more prosocial: Ideas for classrooms, families, and communities. *Young Children*, 51 (2), 62–70.

Johnson, C., Ironsmith, M., Snow, C., & Poteat, G. (2000). Peer acceptance and social adjustment in preschool and kindergarten. *Early Childhood Education Journal*, 27 (4), 207–212.

Klein, T., Wirth, D., & Linas, K. (2003). Play: Children's context for development. *Young Children*, 58 (3), 38–45.

Kostelnik, M., Stein, L., Whiren, A., & Soderman, A. (1988). *Guiding children of social development*. Cincinnati, OH: South-Western Publishing Co.

Marion, M. (2003). *Guidance of young children*. Columbus, OH: Merrill Prentice Hall.

National Center for Education Statistics. (2001). *Table 44. Percentage distribution of preschool children under 6 years old*. Retrieved June 24, 2004, from: www.nces.ed.gov/programs/digest/d01/dt044.asp

Pruitt, D. (Ed.; 1998). *Your child: Emotional, behavioral, and cognitive development from birth through preadolescence.* New York, NY: HarperCollins.

Raikes, H. (1996). A secure base for babies: Applying attachment concepts to the infant care setting. *Young Children*, 51 (5), 59–67.

Ramsey, P. (1991). *Making friends in school: Promoting peer relationships in early childhood*. New York, NY: Teachers College Press.

Wardle, F. (2003). *Introduction to early childhood education: A multidimension al approach to child-centered care and learning.* Boston, MA: Pearson Education, Inc.

KATHY PREUSSE is the Senior Instructional Specialist and the Head Teacher for the Child and Family Study Center at the University of Wisconsin–Stout in Menomonie, WI.

Constructive Play

A Value-Added Strategy for Meeting Early Learning Standards

WALTER F. DREW ET AL.

This was one of the children's first days using turkey basters in water play. We try to add only one new thing at a time. The children started hooking the funnel to the turkey baster and found ways to fill the baster and squirt out water. They were so excited to discover they had made a fountain. They named it Water Spout. We had read the book *I Wish that I Had Duck Feet,* and the children remembered the water spout in the story.

—Trisha McCunn, Preschool Teacher

Constructive play involves building and making things no one has ever seen before. As young children fiddle with, sort, and arrange materials, ideas and imagination begin to flow. Questions arise naturally. They wonder: What will happen if I put this here? How tall will it go? Where did the bubble come from? In this way, constructive play serves to focus the minds of children through their fingertips and leads them to invent and discover new possibilities, to fulfill their sense of purpose.

Play in a Standards-oriented World

In many early childhood programs across the country, time for play is dwindling away. The field of early childhood education is in the midst of a major shift in orientation toward a standards base. Early learning standards specify what young children should know and be able to do in academic areas such as science, literacy, and mathematics. These standards have rapidly become an integral part of state systems of early childhood education. All the states plus the District of Columbia have approved early learning standards for preschoolers. As a structural element of education reform, early learning standards shape the content of instructional curriculum, set the goals of professional development, and establish the focus of outcomes assessment. Standards are increasingly seen as a powerful lever for improving preschool instruction and children's school readiness.

This rise of state early learning standards has alarmed many early childhood educators, especially advocates of play-based approaches to teaching and learning. Play has long had a central role in early childhood education, where it has been viewed as an effective means for promoting all aspects of child development. Many early childhood teachers are concerned that the standards movement and its narrowing of educational goals are pushing aside classroom learning through play in favor of more didactic forms of instruction.

Reconciling Play and Standards

In this article, we take a more positive, pragmatic approach and propose to reconcile constructive play with the standards movement. Recognizing that standards have become an integral part of early education, we believe that mature forms of play, such as the examples presented in which children are focused and intentional, can be effective strategies for helping children learn academic skills stressed in state standards (Kagan & Lowenstein 2004; Van Thiel & Putnam-Franklin 2004; Christie & Roskos 2006). Mature play is mindful make-believe and reasonably self-regulated.

Our proposals are based on field research, observations, interviews, and vignettes focused on constructive play that uses a variety of open-ended materials to promote learning and development. We share educators' stories, experiences, and ideas around principles of constructive play and include specific suggestions for practice.

Three Principles for Using Constructive Play to Meet Early Learning Standards

We identify three key principles that explain why developmentally appropriate constructive play is an ideal instructional strategy for meeting early learning standards. These principles are derived from our own experiences as play researchers and teacher educators.

1. During the preschool years, constructive play merges with exploration and make-believe play and becomes a mature form of play that allows children to strengthen inquiry skills and build conceptual understanding.

Constructive play is organized, goal-oriented play in which children use play materials to create or build something (Johnson, Christie, & Wardle 2005). It often begins during the toddler years and becomes increasingly complex with age. Constructive play involves open-ended exploration, gradually becoming more functional in nature, then evolving to make-believe transformations. Four- and 5-year-olds often switch back and forth between constructive and dramatic play, and it can be difficult to distinguish between the two forms of play. According to Bodrova and Leong (2004), the type of mature play that promotes learning and development has three critical components: imaginary situations, explicit roles, and implicit rules.

Mature play has three critical components: imaginary situations, explicit roles, and implicit rules.

We typically think of constructive play as building with blocks and other three-dimensional materials. Building a road or castle with wooden blocks, shaping a ball out of clay, constructing a spaceship with recycled materials, and putting a puzzle together are all examples of constructive play. But how is the water play, described at the beginning of this article, constructive play (see "Water Play" below)?

Trisha McCunn, a teacher of 3- to 5-year-olds at Lollipop Pre-School in rural Iowa, uses *Exploring Water with Young Children,* the Young Scientist series, and records observations of the children:

> The children discovered that a little squeeze of a water-filled baster made the water bubble, but with a big squeeze the water shot up with great force. They had made water play rules, and one was that the water had to stay in the water table. For today, we decided to set aside the rule because the water could be wiped up. Everyone wiped up water most of the afternoon, but how exciting it was to make a fountain in preschool.

> When I added clear plastic hoses, the children discovered that if they pushed the hose into the water and stuck their thumbs or fingers on the top end, they could make a bubble go up and down inside by moving the hose up or down like a steering wheel. One boy exclaimed, "Look, I'm driving a car!" He drove the car for 20 minutes, pretending the moving air bubble was the road and imagining he was following it.

For Ms. McCunn and the children in her class, constructive play is a form of hands-on inquiry, a way of meeting early learning standards. She knows the children have an innate need to understand their worlds, physically explore, and manipulate materials, and she values the exploring, inventing, and discovering they do together.

Inquiry is a way of looking at the world, according to Parker (2007), a questioning stance we take when we seek to learn something we don't yet know. And when we are truly into inquiring about something, whatever it may be, we drive ourselves to learn more and more because we seek answers to our own questions. This definition captures the very heart of inquiry-based learning and aptly relates what the children in Trish's class are doing.

Water Play

. . . is about physical science, the study of fluid dynamics. Understanding how the water spout works involves design technology, which is part of the construction of simple systems. It requires a different kind of knowledge than constructing with blocks.

If children have a goal in mind in relation to water flow, they are motivated to learn about forces of gravity, water pressure, and fluids in motion to be successful at what they are doing.

When teachers encourage children to explore and think about what they are doing and talk and plan together, there is potential for skill development in a lot of areas . . . language, science, social competence, as well as positive dispositions toward learning and learning how to learn.

—Ingrid Chalufour, Young Scientist Series Author

Believing that all children have the desire and capacity to explore and better understand their worlds is the foundation of constructive play and inquiry-based teaching in early childhood.

Trisha McCunn provided the kinds of simple constructive play materials that appeal to the children's natural desire to question and find out things for themselves. She set the stage in a way that encouraged children to construct new knowledge and thus initiated the learning process.

According to Chouinard (2007), humans' ability to seek out information from one another seems to give us a particular evolutionary advantage and allows us to learn efficiently. Chouinard's research also substantiates the belief that children need to take an active role in the questioning and information-gathering process. When children are actively involved, they remember the information they gather better than information simply given to them. Children build knowledge through active questioning and information gathering combined with hands-on experiences and direct personal-social interactions. This process of active learning and acquisition of knowledge occurs during play with materials, play with ideas, and play with others.

Vygotsky and other well-known theorists have stressed the importance of play in the learning process of young children (Bodrova & Leong 2004). Play provides an intrinsically motivating context in which children come together to understand their world. Constructive play, with its emphasis on hands-on inquiry, is ideally suited for helping children learn the academic skills and concepts found in states' early learning standards (see "Connections between Arizona Early Learning Standards and Constructive Play").

2. Teachers who are knowledgeable about the purposeful use of materials, the process of constructive play, and intentional strategies for interacting with children succeed in helping children develop essential concepts and skills in all content areas.

Making things is an activity that is key to successful learning for young children. They combine the dexterity of their little fingers with the power of their brains to develop a knack for

Connections between Arizona Early Learning Standards and Constructive Play

Early Learning Standards (Arizona)	Constructive Play, Research Supported
Language and Literacy	
Strand 2: Pre-Reading Processes, **Concept 5:** Vocabulary Development—The child understands and uses increasingly complex vocabulary.	Research by Cohen (2006) shows that children learn new vocabulary words as they socially interact with partners and in groups during constructive play.
Strand 2: Pre-Reading Processes, **Concept 1:** Print Awareness—The child knows that print carries meaning.	Literacy-enriched play centers contain theme-related reading and writing materials. For example, a block center might contain pencils, pens, materials for making signs, storage labels (for large blocks, Legos), and so on. Research indicates that when children play in print-enriched settings, they often learn to read play-related print (Neuman & Roskos 1993; Vukelich 1994).
Strand 3: Pre-Writing Processes, **Concept 1:** Written Expression—The child uses writing materials to communicate ideas.	Research by Pickett (1998) shows that adding writing materials to block centers results in a large increase in emergent writing, including making signs to identify function and ownership, regulate behavior, and communicate messages.
Mathematics	
Strand 4: Geometry and Measurement, **Concept 1:** Spatial Relationships and Geometry—The child demonstrates an understanding of spatial relationships and recognizes attributes of common shapes.	Recent research by Miyakawa, Kamii, and Nagahiro (2005) confirms that block building can help children learn important spatial relationships.
Social-Emotional	
Strand 2: Social Interactions with Others, **Concept 2:** Cooperation—The child demonstrates the ability to give and take during social interactions.	Creasey, Jarvis, and Berk (1998) contend that a two-way relationship exists between group play and social development: the social environment influences children's play, and play acts as an important context in which children acquire social skills and social knowledge needed to engage in group play. Children learn attitudes and skills needed for this play from their parents, teachers, and other children. At the same time, play with others has a key role in social development by providing a context in which children can acquire many important social skills, such as turn taking, sharing, and cooperation, as well as the ability to understand other people's thoughts, perceptions, and emotions.
Strand 4: Approaches to Learning, **Concept 5:** Problem-solving—The child demonstrates the ability to seek solutions to problems.	Bruner (1972) proposes that play contributes to children's ability to solve problems by increasing their behavioral options and suggests that block play encourages inventive thinking and logical reasoning while constructing three-dimensional patterns. Copely and Oto (2006) find that young children demonstrate considerable problem-solving knowledge during block play.

Source: Arizona Early Learning Standards, www.azed.gov/earlychildhood/downloads/EarlyLearningStandards.pdf.

representation and the capacity for creative visual symbolizing. It is interesting to consider this as the ability to imagine the future. The ability to physically construct new connections between thoughts and objects is the act of innovation and change. Teachers who understand and encourage this process of learning help children develop a very important talent.

By taking known elements and creating new connections, children demonstrate the lifelong process of accommodation and improvisation. In this regard, current research emphasizes the importance of school readiness factors covering all developmental domains and including active approaches to learning (Bowman & Moore 2006). Child-focused inquiry learning that involves constructive play with an array of three-dimensional materials, fosters positive learning, such as enthusiasm, resilience, creativity, decision making, and persistence in completing tasks (Day 2006).

For optimal learning to occur through play, children need support, time, and open-ended materials that stimulate the brain to think imaginatively. The materials teachers choose to bring into the classroom reveal the choices they have made about knowledge and what they think is important for children to learn, including the content of applicable learning standards.

Pauline Baker, a cooperating early childhood resource teacher in the Tucson Unified School District, supports the constructive play of 4-, 5-, and 6-year-olds who come to her studio.

I pick up interesting materials all the time . . . sticks, stones, wire, wood, and use them all with the children.

I organize materials by color and keep them in baskets, bins, boxes, and lettuce trays. Some materials are organized by "circleness," both man-made and nature-made.

Quality early childhood programs reflect the knowledge of teachers, like Ms. Baker, who understand their roles during children's constructive play and learning and routinely allocate ample time for children to choose and engage in a wide variety of play-related activities, including constructive play with different types of blocks and other open-ended materials (Drew & Rankin 2004).

By age 4, children begin to move from sorting, lining up, stacking, and pushing blocks to constructing and symbolically representing a tree house, for instance, as in the classroom description. As children practice building, their constructions become more detailed, more complex, more coordinated, and balanced.

In addition, constructions are more likely to be used in dramatic pretense. Children may use foam blocks to make a forest of trees, while using other materials to represent people and animals that have adventures in the forest. Constructive play becomes more popular with age, accounting for more than 50 percent of play activity in pre-school settings (Rubin, Fein, & Vandenberg 1983).

Linda Vinson, a pre-K teacher of children with disabilities in Brevard County, Florida, offers a variety of materials to the children in her class.

The eight 2- to 4½-year-olds in my class are socially and emotionally developmentally delayed. At the beginning of the year they did not know how to play. I put something in their hands to get them started.

Gradually, I've offered more open-ended and natural materials to help the children express their thinking through words and actions and gain a sense of competence. Now the children have wooden blocks, foam rectangles, purple cylinders, stretchy fabric scraps, soft wire, cardboard tubes, colorful plastic caps, and mat board, all collected from our local reusable resource center. The materials are arranged in straw baskets that add a homelike atmosphere to my classroom.

Yesterday, after reading the Three Little Pigs, we talked about the wolf and the forest and the different houses the pigs built. The children retold the story, using stuffed animals and puppets. Afterwards, they went to the shelves of materials and began building. Kevin made a tree house of foam rectangles. He built it up and knocked it down 15 or 20 times—each time confidently building it a little higher, laughing as it toppled, and exclaiming, "I can build anything all the way to the sky!"

In construction play activities, children do both science and mathematics.

Linda Vinson's account of the children's play shows the opportunity for conceptual understanding in the area of structural engineering as Kevin makes his tree house. He explores the forces of gravity, compression, tension, and the relationship between the characteristics of materials and successful design to achieve balance, stability, and even aesthetic sensibility. During construction play, Kevin discovers the science of quantity (arithmetic) and shape (geometry) in the making and testing of different design patterns. In short, in construction play activities, children do both science and mathematics. Ms. Vinson is aware of the value-added benefits that come from joyful play—like Kevin's feeling a sense of personal power, competence, and a positive disposition about himself and learning.

3. Professional development experiences that feature hands-on constructive play with open-ended materials help early childhood educators extend and deepen their understanding of constructive play as a developmentally appropriate practice for meeting early learning standards.

Providing professional development opportunities that supply rich, hands-on play experiences using a variety and abundance of open-ended materials, time for reflection on those experiences, and guidance in applying new insights to teaching practice is a powerful strategy for helping teachers develop deeper understandings of developmentally appropriate practice and the essential role of constructive play in quality early childhood programs. Adults who engage in active inquiry and construct knowledge through creative exploration with materials are more positively disposed to encouraging children to do the same. In this way teachers come to understand and appreciate how play helps children develop character virtues, such as tenacity, flexibility, creativity, courage, and resilience—all are characteristics practiced in constructive play, by child and adult.

The adults' hands-on experience is consistent with recommended developmentally appropriate practices for young children. Just as with children, constructive play stimulates an inner dialogue between the teacher and the materials. Ideas, feelings, questions, and relationships begin to take form. The teacher becomes the protagonist—exploring, assuming control through objects, creatively inventing, and becoming the empowered initiator of inquiry and self-discovery.

In *The Ambiguity of Play,* play scholar Brian Sutton Smith describes play not only as about learning important concepts and skills but also as about playing with interpreting one's own feelings and thoughts instead of primarily representing the external world. He says, "What is adaptive about play, therefore, may be not only the skills that are a part of it but also the willful belief in acting out one's own capacity for the future" (2001, 198). Teachers and children who are most likely to succeed are the ones who believe in possibilities—optimists, creative thinkers, people who have flexibility along with a sense of power and control. Adult constructive play helps to inform teachers of the kinds of insights, issues, and feelings children experience during their play. Teachers discover new ways of thinking about play and compelling new insight into children's learning. Constructive play becomes an effective self-reflective professional practice that stimulates the creativity of teachers to construct new play strategies to meet early learning standards.

In *Teaching Adults Revisited: Active Learning for Early Childhood Educators,* Betty Jones reminds us that, "Wherever they are in their educational journey, teachers of young children need to tell their stories, hear other stories, and practice reflective thinking about children's development—over and over again" (2007, ix).

Conclusion

Professional development activities in which teachers play together using construction materials can foster a deeper understanding of how to employ materials and engage young children in positive constructive play. Play can be a bridge to school readiness and academic success for all children. Three key principles in using constructive play to meet early learning standards are interrelated in this way.

Players are active agents in learning, imagining, and creating together. This kind of mature or quality play involves imaginary situations, explicit roles, and implicit rules and is recognizable by its persistence and tendency to become more elaborate over time.

Social interaction and shared imaginings often emerge in the context of constructive play, adding values over and above the benefits of reaching academic standards. These extra benefits include creativity, imagination, problem solving, eagerness to learn, ability to cooperate and stay on task, and learning how to self-regulate and be more responsible overall for one's own learning and development in general.

Finally, setting up and supporting positive constructive play in the early educational setting rests on teachers' creativity, sound judgments, and wise decisions. Although constructive play involves objects, good teachers do not focus on these per se but instead on the actions that take place and especially on the children playing. Learningful play, or "play learning" as it is called by some (PramlingSamuelsson 2007), occurs when children have teachers who are empathic, playful, and intentional. Open-ended, fluid, and natural materials for creative constructive play are important. In addition, teachers must guide exploration and play, helping children as needed, stepping in and out at the right times, and scaffolding in appropriate ways during constructive play episodes.

Constructive play must connect to other kinds of play and activities and be networked with different aspects of the curriculum to maximize its value. To be sure, for the benefit of young children, we must see clearly the value-added connection between constructive play and meeting early learning standards. The challenges are great, as is the reward. Teachers will be helping to restore play to its proper place in early education.

References

Bodrova, E., & D. Leong. 2004. Observing play: What we see when we look at it through "Vygotsky's eyes"? *Play, Policy and Practice Connections* 8 (1–2).

Bowman, D., & E.K. Moore, eds. 2006. *School readiness and social-emotional development: Perspectives on cultural diversity.* Washington, DC: National Black Child Development Institute.

Bruner, J. 1972. The nature and uses of immaturity. *American Psychologist* 27: 687–708.

Cohen, L. 2006. Young children's discourse strategies during pretend block play: A sociocultural approach. PhD diss., Fordham University, New York.

Copely, J., & M. Oto. 2006. An investigation of the problem-solving knowledge of a young child during block construction. www.west.asu. edu/cmw/pme/resrepweb/PME-rr-copley.htm

Chouinard, M.N. 2007. Children's questions: A mechanism for cognitive development. Serial no. 286. *Monographs of the Society for Research in Child Development* 73 (1).

Christie, J., & K. Roskos. 2006. Standards, science, and the role of play in early literacy education. In *Play = learning: How play motivates and enhances children's cognitive and social-emotional growth,* eds. D. Singer, R. Golinkoff, & K. Hirsh-Pasek, 57–73. Oxford, UK: Oxford University Press.

Creasey, G., P. Jarvis, & L. Berk. 1998. Play and social competence. In *Multiple perspectives on play in early childhood education,* eds. O. Sara-cho & B. Spodek, 116–43. Albany: State University of New York Press.

Day, C.B. 2006. Leveraging diversity to benefit children's social-emotional development and school readiness. In *School readiness and social-emotional development: Perspectives on cultural diversity,* eds. D. Bowman & E.K. Moore, 23–32. Washington, DC: National Black Child Development Institute.

Drew, W., & B. Rankin. 2004. Promoting creativity for life using open-ended materials. *Young Children* 59 (4): 38–45.

Johnson, J., J. Christie, & F. Wardle. 2005. *Play, development, and early education.* New York: Allyn & Bacon.

Jones, E. 2007 *Teaching adults revisited: Active learning for early childhood educators.* Washington DC: NAEYC.

Kagan, S.L., & A.E. Lowenstein. 2004. School readiness and children's play: Contemporary oxymoron or compatible option? In *Children's play: The roots of reading,* eds. E. Zigler, D. Singer, & S. Bishop-Josef, 59–76. Washington, DC: Zero to Three Press.

Miyakawa, Y., C. Kamii, & M. Nagahiro. 2005. The development of logico-mathematical thinking at ages 1–3 in play with blocks and an incline. *Journal of Research in Child Development* 19: 292–301.

Neuman, S., & K. Roskos. 1993. Access to print for children of poverty: Differential effects of adult mediation and literacy-enriched play settings on environmental and functional print tasks. *American Educational Research Journal* 30: 95–122.

Parker, D. 2007. *Planning for inquiry: It's not an oxymoron!* Urbana, IL: National Council of Teachers of English.

Pickett, L. 1998. Literacy learning during block play. *Journal of Research in Childhood Education* 12: 225–30.

Pramling-Samuelsson, I. 2007. A research-based approach to preschool pedagogy: Play and learning integrated. *Play, Policy, and Practice Connections (*Newsletter of the Play, Policy, & Practice Interest Forum of NAEYC) 10 (2): 7–9.

Rubin, K., G. Fein, & B. Vandenberg. 1983. Play. In *Socialization, personality, and social development,* vol. 4, *Handbook of child psychology,* ed. E. Hetherington, series ed. P. Mussen, 693–774. New York: Wiley.

Sutton-Smith, B. 2001. *The ambiguity of play*. Cambridge, MA: Harvard University Press.

Van Thiel, L., & S. Putnam-Franklin. 2004. Standards and guidelines: Keeping play in professional practice and planning. *Play, Policy, and Practice Connections* 8 (2): 16–19.

Vukelich, C. 1994. Effects of play interventions on young children's reading of environmental print. *Early Childhood Research Quarterly* 9 (2): 153–70.

Walter F. Drew, EdD, is executive director of the Institute for Self-Active Education and cofounder of the Reusable Resources Association. He chairs the Play Committee for the Early Childhood Association of Florida and is creator of Dr. Drew's Discovery Blocks. drdrew@cfl.rr.com. **James Christie,** PhD, is a professor of curriculum and instruction at Arizona State University in Phoenix. He is past president of the Association for the Study of Play and a member of the board of directors of Playing for Keeps. jchristie@asu.edu. **James E. Johnson,** PhD, is professor-in-charge of early childhood education at Penn State University in University Park. He is the current series editor of *Play and Cultural Studies* and the former president of the Association for the Study of Play. **Alice M. Meckley,** PhD, professor in early childhood education at Millersville University, Pennsylvania, researches the social play of young children. She is a member of the NAEYC Play, Policy, and Practice Interest Forum's Research Group and TASP (The Association for the Study of Play). Alice.Meckley@millersville.edu. **Marcia L. Nell,** PhD, is assistant professor in the Elementary and Early Childhood Department at Millersville University. Marcia has been a public school teacher for 25 years in kindergarten through second grade classrooms.

Early Literacy and Very Young Children

REBECCA PARLAKIAN

Early (or emergent) literacy is what children know about reading and writing before they can actually read and write. It encompasses all the experiences—good and bad—that children have had with books, language, and print from birth onward. Because these experiences unfold in the context of relationships, they are linked to and dependent on social–emotional development.

When one imagines an infant or toddler, it is often difficult to conceptualize what early literacy "looks like" for such young children. Schickedanz (1999) has identified several commonly observed early literacy behaviors for infants and toddlers that providers may use to recognize the emergence and progression of very young children's early literacy skill development. These behaviors include:

1. *Handling books:* Physically manipulating books (e.g., page turning and chewing).
2. *Looking and recognizing:* Paying attention to and interacting with pictures in books (e.g., laughing at a picture); recognizing and beginning to understand pictures in books (e.g., pointing to pictures of familiar objects).
3. *Comprehending pictures and stories:* Understanding pictures and events in a book (e.g., imitating an action seen in a picture or talking about the events told in a story.
4. *Reading stories:* Verbally interacting with books and demonstrating an increased understanding of print in books (e.g., babbling in imitation of reading or running fingers along printed words).

What does research tell us about early literacy development in the first 3 years of life? The short answer is, not enough. There are several significant gaps in our understanding of the antecedents of early literacy skills, one being the period from birth to 3. Few longitudinal studies follow children into kindergarten or elementary school to confirm the ways and extent to which early interventions, either in the home or caregiving setting, shape later competencies in reading and writing.

The National Early Literacy Panel (NELP), funded by the National Institute for Learning and administered by the National Center for Family Literacy, has been charged with synthesizing the existing research regarding the development of early literacy in children ages birth to 5. The NELP does plan to analyze preschool children separately from kindergarten children. Although the NELP's report is not yet released, researchers Strickland

At a Glance

- [F]or infants and toddlers, education and care are "two sides of the same coin."
- Instructional strategies that are most appropriate to the early years include *intentionality* and *scaffolding*.
- Intentionality means thoughtfully providing children with the experiences they need to achieve developmentally appropriate skills in early literacy.
- Scaffolding is the continuum of supportive learning experiences that more competent others (adults or peers) offer to children as they master a new strategy or skill.

and Shanahan recently shared preliminary findings highlighting the skills and abilities that "have direct links to children's eventual success in early literacy development" (2004). These skills included oral language ability, alphabetic knowledge, and print knowledge.

Oral Language Development and Literacy

Language development provides the foundation for the development of literacy skills. Speaking, reading aloud, and singing all stimulate a child's understanding and use of language. Studies linking oral language to literacy address vocabulary growth and listening comprehension. Oral language development is facilitated (a) when children have many opportunities to use language in interactions with adults, and (b) when they listen and respond to stories that are read and told to them (Strickland & Shanahan, 2004). A growing body of research affirms this link between children's early language skills and later reading abilities (Strickland & Shanahan, 2004).

Parents are essential supports of their children's language development. The more time that parents spend talking with their children, the more rapidly their children's vocabulary will grow (Hart & Risley, 1999). Listening to books being read—and having the opportunity to discuss illustrations, characters, and storylines—is also important. The experience of shared reading, whether with parents or other caring partners, is integral to language development. Research in this area finds that the repeated reading and discussion of a story enhances a child's receptive and expressive vocabulary (Senechal, 1997).

Being able to communicate and being understood by those around them is a powerful achievement for very young children.

Language development occurs gradually across the first 3 years of life, and indeed, throughout childhood. Speaking, reading, and writing are reciprocal, interactive skills, each supporting the other's development. For example, toddlers engaged in a pretend-play dramatic scenario (e.g., talking into a plastic banana "phone") possess not only the oral language skills required for this "conversation" but also the ability for symbolic thought, which is integral to understanding that letter symbols can represent sounds and vice versa.

Being able to communicate and being understood by those around them is a powerful achievement for very young children. It is also a critical social–emotional skill originating in the reflexive communication (such as crying, cooing, body and facial movements) that is apparent from birth. Intentional communication emerges as very young children are increasingly able to use gestures and words to convey needs, desires, and ideas. Most important expressive language (such as spoken speech) helps children communicate, to connect with another: to request, protest, greet or take leave of someone, respond to a comment, ask a question, solve a problem, and share their feelings and ideas (Weitzman & Greenberg, 2002). These interactions form the basis of the child's relationships with family members and the outside world.

Alphabetic Knowledge and Literacy

By listening to others and speaking themselves, children develop phonemic awareness—the insight that every spoken word can be conceived as a sequence of phonemes (Snow, Burns, & Griffin, 1998). An example of phonemic awareness is recognizing that *bug, bear*, and *button* all start with "b." Because phonemes are the units of sound that are represented by the letters of an alphabet, an awareness of phonemes is key to understanding the logic of the alphabetic principle. Learning the letters of the alphabet and recognizing the sounds within words are two skills that form the foundation for later decoding and spelling—which is linked to learning to read. Research has shown that phonemic awareness and alphabetic knowledge (an understanding of the names and shapes of the alphabet) predict whether a child will learn to read during his first 2 years of school (National Reading Panel, 2000).

Print Knowledge and Literacy

Print knowledge is a recognition of the many uses of the printed word and an understanding of how printed language works. The research base here emphasizes the importance of infusing the caregiving environment with print. For example, when children are provided literacy "props" (menus, newspapers, magazines, tablets, writing utensils, etc.), they will incorporate these items into their play (e.g., "reading" a menu and playing restaurant; Neuman & Roskos, 1992). This play offers repeated opportunities for children to practice and expand early literacy skills.

Exposure to environmental print—the print that appears on signs, labels, and products in our everyday environment—also contributes to a child's early literacy skills (Kuby, Goodstadt-Killoran, Aldridge, & Kirkland, 1999). Often, awareness of environmental print emerges organically in a child's life—for example, when a toddler learns to "read" a fast-food sign or recognizes the meaning behind a stop sign. Infant–family professionals can promote children's awareness of and facility with recognizing environmental print by pointing it out, discussing it with children, or integrating it into play activities (e.g., pointing out street signs on walks or noting labeled play spaces).

Social–Emotional Development and Literacy

For babies and toddlers, all learning happens within a relationship. The social–emotional context of a child's most important relationships—parents, family members, and infant–family professionals—directly affects young children's motivation to learn to read and write. In short, for infants and toddlers, the learning of a new skill and the emotional context in which the learning takes place are equally important (National Research Council, 2001).

Social–emotional skills are an integral part of school readiness because they give very young children the skills they need to communicate, cooperate, and cope in new environments. Over the long term, social–emotional skills contribute to a successful first year of school. For example, research has shown that the quality of children's relationships with their kindergarten teachers predicts how well those children adapt and learn, that year *and* the next (Bowman, 2001). In addition, at the end of the kindergarten year, the children who were considered to have made a positive adjustment to school also had the most friends, were able to maintain those friendships over time, and established new friendships across that first year (National Education Goals Panel, 1997). A positive adjustment to kindergarten is an important achievement: Children who are not successful in the early years of school often fall behind from the start (Peth-Pierce, 2000).

Children who are not successful in the early years of school often fall behind from the start.

School readiness means that children enter the classroom able to form relationships with teachers and peers, listen and communicate, cooperate with others, cope with challenges, persist when faced with difficult tasks, and believe in their own competence. The relationship between school readiness and social–emotional development can be summarized in five key points (adapted from Bowman, 2001):

1. Responsive, supportive relationships with parents, caregivers, and other significant adults nurture a child's desire to learn.
2. Learning requires a solid foundation of social–emotional skills.
3. The development of social–emotional skills depends on, and is responsive to, experience.
4. Children acquire new experiences within the context of relationships with the significant adults in their lives; this is why, for infants and toddlers, education and care are "two sides of the same coin."
5. Social–emotional development and academic achievement *are united priorities*. They represent a developmental continuum, a gathering-up of all the skills, abilities, and attributes that children need to succeed in school and, later, in life.

Social–emotional skills help children to adapt and be resilient, to resolve conflict, to make sense of their feelings, and to establish a new network of supportive satisfying relationships to depend on and grow within. Social–emotional skills enable children to concentrate on learning.

Cognitive Development and Literacy

Cognitive development—a crucial part of school readiness—is the natural product of warm and loving families, experienced and well-trained caregivers and enriching environments. Infants and toddlers do not need organized instruction to develop their cognitive skills. Young children's everyday activities and experiences provide ample opportunity for infusing learning into play.

It is possible to introduce cognitive skills such as literacy during the infant and toddler years. Rote learning, flash cards, and one-size-fits-all approaches, however, are developmentally inappropriate for very young children. Drill and practice may reduce children's natural curiosity and enthusiasm for the learning process and so undermine their interest in learning. Toddlers who feel pushed to read, for example, may become frustrated and fearful, and they may begin to associate those negative feelings with books. Although introducing emergent literacy skills is important, these abilities are unlikely to flourish in very young children when presented out of context as isolated skills (National Association for the Education of Young Children, 1995).

Until the body of research on the early learning skills of the birth-to-3 population becomes more robust, infant–family professionals are challenged to "translate" successful, research-based instructional strategies for older children to meet the needs of infants and toddlers. Instructional strategies that are most appropriate to the early years include *intentionality* and *scaffolding* (Collins, 2004). Rather than use a didactic approach, adults who work with infants and toddlers can creatively integrate these strategies into the day-to-day "teachable moments" that unfold during their natural interactions with very young children.

Intentionality, in this context, means thoughtfully providing children with the support and experiences they need to achieve developmentally appropriate skills in early literacy (and other domains). For example, an intentional provider may offer 14-month-olds the opportunity to pick up raisins and cereal by themselves (which builds fine motor skills critical to writing) and then later offer children crayons to experiment with (which gives them direct experience with writing and drawing). Intentionality is at play here when the provider recognizes the relationship between these experiences, offers these experiences purposefully, and understands the shared developmental goal they both support.

Infants and toddlers learn best when the adults in their lives provide opportunities for exploration and learning in their everyday routines and interactions. The concept of intentionality underscores the role that planning, knowledge, and expertise play in devising and introducing these opportunities. It is the cumulative effect of intentional teaching—the thoughtful repetition of early literacy experiences, the introduction of literacy props into play, modified teacher behavior (e.g., pointing to words on the page), and the creation of language-rich, stimulating environments—that yields the early and important learning that takes place in very young children ages birth to 3.

Scaffolding, a concept introduced by Vygotsky (1962), refers to the continuum of supportive learning experiences that more competent others (adults or other children) offer to children as they master a new strategy or skill (Kemple, Batey, & Hartie, 2004). Children need engaged, responsive adults in their lives who offer them appropriate opportunities to question and problem solve, to hypothesize and take action, to (safely) fail and try again. The richest opportunity for learning—in which children experience a challenge as they pursue a task but do not struggle so intensely as to become frustrated—is called the one of proximal development (Vygotsky, 1962). To help children perform in this zone, teachers must provide scaffolding that incorporates the development of new skills and concepts on the foundation of established ones. This scaffolding requires that teachers know each child in their care—their skills, achievements, and needs—and offer a careful balance of planned, teacher-initiated activities and child-initiated ones, as well. In working with infants and toddlers, a teacher could initiate the practice of reading to children one-on-one each day while placing books at the child's level to enable child-initiated, spontaneous exploration, as well.

The more time that parents spend talking with their children, the more rapidly their children's vocabulary will grow.

Introducing Literacy Concepts to Young Children

Teachers can introduce early literacy concepts to infants and toddlers in a variety of fun, meaningful, and developmentally appropriate ways.

Oral Language

Read to very young children: The most important thing that providers can do to support children's emerging literacy skills is read to them and discuss the stories, at the children's pace and based on their cues.

Talk to children: Children learn language when adults talk to them and with them.

Rhyme and sing: Rhyming activities such as songs and poems promote very young children's knowledge of sounds of speech.

"Narrate" the child's day: Providers can describe what happened that day, which creates opportunities to expand children's vocabulary.

Alphabetic Knowledge

Repeat letter sounds: Providers can point out and say the letters they see in signs or books.

Make a game of repetition: Children love knowing what comes next in a story and anticipating a picture or phrase.

Sing the ABC song and read alphabet books: Both verbal and visual experience with letters help children learn the alphabet.

Play with letters: Arranging and rearranging magnetic letters, alphabet blocks, and puzzles help children with letter recognition and letter sounds.

Use the child's name: Providers can teach children their own names and the sounds that make up their names.

Print Awareness

Make literacy part of playtime: Providers can stock children's play spaces with literacy "props."

Encourage children's own writing: Make paper and writing utensils (markers, crayons, fingerpaint, chalk) available to children. Let infants "write" in applesauce or yogurt.

Point out signs in your neighborhood: When taking walks, providers can look for opportunities to point out stop signs, street signs, and school crossing signs.

Show how adults use writing: Providers can encourage children to watch as they write notes to themselves or colleagues, make a shopping list, or compose the class's weekly update for parents. Providers can also give older toddlers the opportunity to "write" (dictate) notes to one another and family members.

Help children "read" their food: When preparing meals and snacks, providers should read children the words on the food labels, or ask them to "read" the labels to themselves.

Read while you're out and about: Pointing out and reading the signs that say "women" and "men," "exit" and "entrance," and "open" and "closed" are easy ways of sensitizing children to environmental print. Point to the words while reading them aloud to children.

In working with older toddlers, skilled teachers can combine a child-initiated interest that arises in the classroom—for example, a passion for castles—and create a series of teacher-initiated early literacy activities that are responsive and flexible. Using the castle example, such activities might include:

- drawing pictures of castles (which helps build fine motor skills for writing);
- reading books about castles; asking older toddlers to dictate stories to the teacher about castles; and
- making a cardboard box castle for the classroom and encouraging children to "act out" storylines using the castle prop (which creates opportunities to expand vocabulary—*moat, knight, king, queen, drawbridge*, etc.).

This "castle" project may last for several days (or weeks), depending on the children's intensity of interest. By remaining observant and responsive to the children's engagement with the topic and activities, teachers can gauge when the children's interest has shifted and when it might be time to introduce a set of early literacy-based activities around a new theme.

Supporting and nurturing early literacy and language skills in infants and toddlers is complex. These skills cannot be developed in isolation but, rather, emerge together with a child's growing competency in all domains—including the social–emotional, motor, and cognitive domains. When providers can recognize and observe each child's current stage of development, they are better positioned to use the strategies above to appropriately extend and build upon a child's existing skills and abilities.

Parents, School Readiness, and Early Literacy

Relationships—especially those between parent and child—play a critical role in ensuring that infants and toddlers are adequately prepared for school. Parents' beliefs about the appropriate ways to express emotion, resolve conflict, persuade, and cooperate with others have a profound influence on toddlers' abilities to get along with peers, follow rules, and cooperate with adults—and ultimately, to be ready for school (Morisset, 1994). In addition, children's positive, satisfying relationships with parents set the tone for equally positive, secure relationships with preschool teachers (DeMulder, Denham, Schmidt, & Mitchell, 2000). This crucial achievement is an important predictor of a successful transition to early education environments (Bowman, 2001).

Parents are the most important people in a child's life. Parents' attitudes toward education, their aspirations for children, the language models and literacy materials they provide, and the activities they encourage all contribute to children's language development. Parental behaviors also influence children's early learning. For example, research shows that the type of at-home language environment is the most powerful influence on children's language growth (Educational Research Service, 1998). Preschool children who live in homes where literacy is supported amass 1,000 to 1,700 hours of informal reading and writing encounters before entering school, whereas children without similar family support may enter school with only about 25 hours of literacy experiences (Adams,1990). Not surprisingly, most children who have difficulties learning to read have been read to one tenth as much as those who are the most successful with acquiring this skill (Adams, 1990).

When infants and very young children receive what they need from their parents, they learn to believe that the world is a good place, that it is safe to explore, and that loving adults will provide comfort, affection, and security. Children who do not receive this loving care expend a great deal of energy trying to ensure that these needs are fulfilled by someone, sometime. How much energy do these children have left for learning and exploration—and, later, for the new concepts and challenges that are a part of going to school?

The Role of Infant–Family Professionals in Supporting Early Literacy

The adults who populate the lives of very young children (including family members and the professionals who support them) make important contributions to children's school readiness. In working with infants and toddlers, teachers and child-care providers are reminded that care and education are not separate activities. They unfold together—one leading to the other, one supporting the other.

Children begin kindergarten with 5 years of accumulated life experiences. Because each set of experiences is unique, children have different perspectives on education, different approaches to relationships with adults and peers, and different levels of competency with social–emotional and academic skills. The ability of direct-service professionals to individualize their approaches to specific children and families is crucial to ensuring that services are meaningful and effective.

Infant–family professionals can support the development of very young children's school readiness skills in several ways.

Responding to children's individual needs and temperaments. Staff members in all infant–family fields can respond to children as individuals, build on their strengths, and support their development. Staff members in infant–family programs must be excellent observers of children. Responsive staff members search for the meaning behind infants' and toddlers' gestures, gurgles, cries, and glances. They wonder why particular behaviors occur, come up with educated guesses to explain why, and interact with children to determine whether their guesses are correct.

Encouraging children's curiosity and exploration. If caregivers select all the "lessons" that are to be learned or provide an environment that is not stimulating, children will push to do activities that interest them or to create their own stimulation.

Often children are told "No," "Stop," or "Bad"—not because these children are not learning, but because they are following their own learning agenda or searching for experiences that interest them. Although setting some limits is important and helps keep children safe, it is equally important to allow children to engage in self-directed learning—that is, to follow their interests and allow them to become immersed in new ideas. This approach supports their development of persistence, motivation, critical thinking, and logical thinking skills.

Introducing early literacy and numeracy concepts in developmentally appropriate ways. A program that serves infants and toddlers can introduce literacy concepts in ways that are fun, meaningful, and developmentally appropriate for very young children (Collins, 2004).

Appreciating the magic of everyday moments. Children often develop social–emotional skills not in specially planned lessons but in the context of their daily interactions and experiences— such as napping, eating, playing, and diapering (Lerner, Dambra, & Levine, 2000). When staff members use these everyday moments to support and expand children's current repertoire of social–emotional skills, they help prepare young ones to enter the larger world with all of its demands.

To help parents do the same, staff members should emphasize the important learning that takes place in everyday interactions. For example, the give-and-take of parents imitating their babies' babbling teaches children about turn-taking and communication and, from a social–emotional perspective, that they are important, loved, and listened to. Observing this ongoing, daily learning also encourages parents' pride in and enjoyment of their children.

Establishing strong working relationships with families. When interactions between parents and staff members are open and collaborative, parents receive the support they need to learn and grow in their new roles as mothers and fathers. Parents are then better able to support their children's development with affection, responsiveness, and sensitivity. Staff members can provide parents with an outlet in which to explore the questions and challenges associated with child rearing; wonder about their children's behavior, needs, and motivations; and brainstorm about how best to respond.

Recognizing and respecting family culture. By entering a dialogue with parents about how they want their child raised and what family or cultural practices they value, staff members let families know that they are respected partners in the program. If it is difficult to incorporate families' wishes into program practices, a solid foundation of respect and openness makes negotiating these differences easier and more helpful for everyone.

Reducing parents' anxiety about school success. A newborn does not need expensive "developmental" toys or flash cards to become intellectually curious and academically successful. Staff members can help parents understand that the foundation of school readiness is in supportive, nurturing relationships that provide children with a safe "home base" from which they can explore, learn, and grow. This close parent–child bond also helps children develop the key social–emotional competencies that are necessary for a successful transition to school.

Providing anticipatory guidance. When staff members help parents anticipate their children's developmental changes, parents are better prepared to support their children's learning. Armed with accurate information, parents can respond to their children's changing developmental needs in appropriate ways. Parents' ability to meet their children's needs contributes to a greater sense of competency and confidence, which in turn strengthens the family as a whole.

Speaking, reading, and writing are reciprocal, interactive skills, each supporting the other's development.

Supporting inclusive environments. Very young children with special needs may face unique challenges in achieving the skills (social–emotional or otherwise) necessary to enter school. Inclusion is an important intervention because it draws children with disabilities into the mainstream. Ongoing interactions with typically developing children may help support the development of children with disabilities. Inclusion is also important for children whose development is more typical, because diversity helps them to broaden their experiences and learning and to develop empathy.

Conclusion

Developing early literacy skills across the first 3 years of life is a critical ingredient in ensuring that children are school-ready at age 5. By using all domains of development as well as all their senses, children develop the foundational skills necessary for cultivating a lifelong love of literacy. Supported by healthy relationships formed early in life with parents and caregivers, children experience the world as both safe and exhilarating, they view new challenges as exciting, and they believe themselves to be competent learners. In short, infants and toddlers have a lust for life and learning. When we reject the notion of children as passive "sponges," we are able to truly follow in "the wake of a curious, motivated, social child who is dying to learn" (Lally, 2001).

References

Adams, M. J. (1990). *Beginning to read: Thinking and learning about print.* Cambridge, MA: MIT Press.

Bowman, B. (2001, December). *Eager to learn.* Plenary presentation at the 16th Annual National Training Institute of ZERO TO THREE, San Diego, CA.

Collins, R. (2004, April). *Early steps to language and literacy.* Workshop presented at the meeting of the National Head Start Association, Anaheim, CA.

DeMulder, E. K., Denham, S., Schmidt, M., & Mitchell, J. (2000). Q-Sort assessment of attachment security during the preschool years: Links from home to school *Developmental Psychology, 36*(2), 274–282.

Educational Research Service. (1998). *Reading aloud to children.* ERS Info-File #F1-342. Arlington, VA: Author.

Hart, B., & Risley, T. R. (1999). *The social world of children learning to talk.* Baltimore: Paul H. Brookes.

Kemple, K. M., Batey, J. J., & Hartie, L. C. (2004). Music play: Creating centers for musical play and exploration. *Young Children, 59*(4), 30–37.

Kuby, P., Goodstadt-Killoran, I., Aldridge, J., & Kirkland, L. (1999). A review of the research on environmental print. *Journal of Instructional Psychology, 26*(3), 173–183.

Lally, R. (2001, December). *School readiness.* Plenary presentation at the 6th Annual National Training Institute of ZERO TO THREE, San Diego, CA.

Lerner, C., Dombro, L., & Levine, K. (2000). *The magic of everyday moments'* [series]. Washington, DC: ZERO TO THREE.

Morisset, C. E. (1994, October). *School readiness: Parents and professionals speak on social and emotional needs of young children* [Report No. 26]. Center on Families, Communities, Schools, and Children's Learning. Retrieved January 25, 2002, from http://readyweb.crc.uiuc.edu/library/1994/cfam-sr/cfam-sr.html

National Association for the Education of Young Children. (1995). *NAEYC position statement on school readiness.* Revived January 24, 2002, from www.naeyc.org/resources/position_statements/psredy98.htm

National Education Goals Panel. (1997). *Getting a good start in school.* Retrieved January 23, 2002, from http://www.negp.gov/Reports/good-sta.htm

National Reading Panel. (2000). *Report of the National Reading Panel. Teaching children to read: An evidence-based assessment of the scientific research literature on reading and its implications for reading instruction.*

This article was adapted from *Before the ABCs: Promoting School Readiness in Infants and Toddlers,* a publication written by Rebecca Parlakian for Zero to Three's Center for Program Excellence.

Using Picture Books to Support Young Children's Literacy

JANIS STRASSER AND HOLLY SEPLOCHA

Five-year-old Levi is listening to his teacher read *Why Epossumondas Has No Hair on His Tail* (Salley, 2004). This richly woven and engaging tale includes several unfamiliar words, like "lollygagging," "skedaddle," and "persimmon." It also contains phrases that Levi has never heard before, including "my sweet little pattootie" and "no sirree." Because the art and text so beautifully express the joy of eating a persimmon, Levi asks questions about the fruit once the teacher has finished the story. The next day, the teacher brings several persimmons to class. As the children examine them, cut them, and taste them, they recall the events in the story, sing the song that is part of the story, and remember such rich descriptive terms as "powder-puff tails." Later, in the art area, Levi draws a sketch of a persimmon and tries to write the word, coming up with "PRSMN." The children ask to sing the song about persimmons for the next several days. The teacher suggests that they change the words to create their own version. She writes their version on large chart paper. In the library area, two weeks after the initial whole-group story reading, three children are making the "RRRRRR" sound of Papapossum's stomach as they point to the text in the book that matches the sound. Two of them decide to go into the art area and make puppets to act out the story. As the teacher watches them glue wiggly eyes and a tail made out of yarn onto a large oval shape they have cut out from cardboard, she asks, "What do you think are some good things about not having hair on your tail?"

This example shows the multiple ways in which a picture book can support literacy in the classroom. Literacy skills can be embedded when using an engaging children's picture book, as in the example above, instead of focusing on skills in isolation (as in "letter of the week" types of activities).

Literacy skills can be embedded when using an engaging children's picture book instead of focusing on skills in isolation.

How Do Picture Books Support Literacy?

The benefits of storybook reading are well documented (Aram & Biron, 2004; Neuman, 1999; Neuman, Copple, & Bredekamp, 2000; Strickland & Morrow, 1989). As preschoolers, children should be active participants in picture book reading—chiming in on the refrain of predictable books, dramatizing stories they love, and reciting the text of books "so familiar that they have been committed to memory" (Jalongo, 2004, p. 91).

A joint position paper issued by the National Association for the Education of Young Children and the International Reading Association (cited in Neuman, Copple, & Bredekamp, 2000) states, "The single most important activity for building . . . understandings and skills essential for reading success appears to be reading aloud to children" (p. 8). Neuman (1999) explains how storybook reading helps children gain general knowledge, practice cognitive thinking, and learn about the rhythms and conventions of written language.

Vygotskian theory supports the notion that through interaction with text (written by other authors or themselves), "children transfer the understandings and skills they have gleaned from dialogues with others to their own literacy-related discourse . . . they converse not just with themselves but also with the text narrative" (Berk & Winsler, 1995, p. 115). Creating opportunities for young children to explore literature, individually and in small groups, helps this discourse to flourish. Through such activities as looking through new books, rereading (or "pretend reading") stories that the teacher has read, imagining new endings for popular stories, or creating artistic renderings of favorite stories, young children can interact with text in meaningful ways. In considering extension activities for literature, teachers should consider whether the activity grows naturally out of the literature, encourages students to thoughtfully reexamine the book, and/or demonstrates something the reader has gained from the book (Routman, 1991, p. 87).

Definition of a Picture Book

A picture book is different from a children's book that contains illustrations. In a picture book, both the picture and text are equally important. There exists "a balance between the pictures and text . . . neither of them is completely effective without the other" (Norton, 1999, p. 214). They contain at least three elements: what is told with words, what is told through the pictures, and what is conveyed from the combination of the two (Jalongo, 2004). A fourth element is the child's personal association with the book. Anyone who has read a good picture book has experienced the unique magic and beauty of this relationship. The story line is brief (about 200 words) and straightforward, with a limited number of concepts; the text is written in a direct, simple style; illustrations complement the text; and the book is usually 32 pages long (Jalongo, 2004). Classic picture books that fit these criteria include Keats' *The Snowy Day* (1962), Numeroff's *If You Give a Mouse a Cookie* (1985), and Ringgold's *Tar Beach* (1996). They are more than "cute little books" or useful teaching tools, however; they "also exist as an art form that transcends the functions of informing, entertaining and providing emotional release" (Jalongo, 2004, p. 13). They can be fiction or nonfiction and the illustrations can be photographs as well as drawings, paintings, or collage.

Language Learning with Picture Books

Picture books not only expose young children to words and pictures, they also provide the following experiences that support the dispositions and feelings in learning how to read (Jalongo, 2004):

- Holding Attention: with powerful, vivid illustrations
- Accommodating Difference: within the developmental differences of individual children
- Giving Pleasure: within an intellectually stimulating context
- Challenging the Brain: as the brain seeks patterns out of the complexity of stimulation from text and illustrations at the same time
- Provoking Conversation: hearing stories increases children's vocabulary
- Connecting Experiences: from home and family to stories

Oral language is a key area of literacy development in early childhood. The components of language skills include: Communication, Forms and Functions, Purposeful Verbal Interactions, and Play With Language (Isenberg & Jalongo, 2001). In one classroom of 3-year-olds, the teacher has read Vera B. Williams' *"More More More" Said the Baby* (1997) to individual children and small groups many times, at their request, over a two-week period. She has documented the ways in which the children have practiced the four components of language skills as they connect with elements of the picture book (about the ways that three families show their love for the children in their family):

- Communication: The children pretend to be mommies, grandmothers, and uncles putting their babies to bed, singing to them and kissing them goodnight.

- Forms and Functions: Some children scold the "babies" when they don't go right to sleep, others sing in a gentle voice, and some pretend to laugh as they tickle the "babies."
- Purposeful Verbal Interaction: In their play, the children problem solve how to undress the "baby" and put her in the cradle quietly, as she has fallen asleep while the "grandma" sang to her. Two other children figure out what materials to use to make a blanket when they can't find the blanket that used to be in the dramatic play area.
- Play With Language. The children make up funny names for the babies (with reference in their play to one of the babies in the book who was called "Little Bird"). They call the babies "Little Quacky Duck" and "Puppy Poo Poo."

Picture books should be a part of every day in the early childhood years. Reading to children and engaging them in activities that encourage the use of expressive language, phonological awareness, and high-level thinking is critical for the development of the skills and dispositions that are necessary for reading and writing.

In another classroom, the teacher supported one child's language and cognitive development after reading Ehlert's *Eating the Alphabet* (1993). She watched the child begin to create "vegetables" by cutting orange, brown, and green pieces of foam and gluing them onto her paper. The child then said to the teacher, "When you do this, you have to use your imagination." The teacher responded, "That's very true when creating art. I like how you used the word 'imagination.'" The child then went over and brought back Sendak's *Where the Wild Things Are* (1998) and said, "This is an imagination book, because you can see in the pictures that his room changes. It's pretend." The child was clearly responding to the illustrations and text of the two books, and synthesizing the information in her conversation. The classroom environment had supported this learning through its accessible art area, rich selection of books, flexibility allowing children to bring books into the art area, and the scaffolding conversation between the child and the adult.

Rich Vocabulary

A preschool teacher is reading *Giraffes Can't Dance* (Andreae, 1999) to her class of 4-year-olds. The lavish, colorful illustrations help to illuminate the rich text describing animals dancing in a contest. Verbs like "prance" and "sway" and phrases like "buckled at the knees" and "swishing round" are new for the children. Rhyme and alliteration appear throughout the book; for example:

The warthogs started waltzing and the rhinos rock'n'rolled.

The lions danced a tango

That was elegant and bold.

When the children ask about the waltz and tango, the teacher downloads these two types of music from the computer for the children to listen to during center time. She puts the book into the music center so that the children can look at the illustrations of the warthogs, rhinos, and lions dancing as they listen to different types of music. She stays in the music center for a while so that she can explain which type of music is played for each type of dance. Her questions invite the children to compare and contrast the two different styles. They don't have to ask about "buckled at the knees." The illustration clearly shows what this means.

The fact that reading to young children supports language development is clearly evidenced in the literature (Aram & Biron, 2004; Bus, van IJzendoorn, & Pelligrini, 1995; Hargrave & Senechal, 2000; Koralek, 2003; Schickedanz, 1999). When the story reading includes explanations of particular words, dialogue about new vocabulary, high-level questions, and other active participation by children, that language development is further enhanced (Hargrave & Senechal, 2000).

Although such wordless picture books as *Good Dog, Carl* (Day, 1989) do not fit the traditional definition of a picture book, they are a wonderful way to encourage children to use expressive language, as they use visual literacy and knowledge of story sequence to become the author of the story (Owocki, 2001). Teachers can audiotape children's voices as they "read" the story to their friends and keep the tape in the listening area with the book.

Phonological and Phonemic Awareness

Phonological awareness is "the ability to hear, identify and manipulate the sounds of spoken language (hearing and repeating sounds, separating and blending sounds, identifying similar sounds in different words, hearing parts of syllables in words)" (Seplocha & Jablon, 2004, p. 2). It includes "the whole spectrum[,] from primitive awareness of speech sounds and rhythms to rhyme awareness and sound similarities and, at the highest level, awareness of syllables or phonemes" (Neuman, Copple, & Bredekamp, 2000, p. 124).

As children listen to songs, nursery rhymes, poems, and books with repetitive words and phrases, they begin to play with language. For example, when chanting alliterative phrases, such as, "Splash, splosh, splash, splosh, splash, splosh" to describe the river and "Squelch, squerch, squelch, squerch, squelch, squerch" to describe the "thick, oozy mud" in Rosen's *We're Going on a Bear Hunt* (1997), children revel in the sounds and begin to want to create their own descriptive, playful phrases. Teachers can begin by reading the book, inviting children to join in the repetitive parts with their voices while slapping their knees to the rhythm, and helping them to create their own versions of the story (hunting other animals in other environments). A perfect companion to this book is Axtell's *We're Going on a Lion Hunt* (1999). This version, situated in the jungle, also contains lots of alliteration and rhythm as the suspense builds to a crescendo. Using both books, followed by a compare and contrast discussion, encourages higher order thinking and promotes ample use of rich descriptive language, as well as analysis and attention to phonological awareness.

Children learn to pay attention to the sounds in spoken language through rhymes, chants, nonsense words, and poetry. Many picture books, such as the Dr. Seuss books, contain predictable rhymes, rhythms, alliteration, and a great deal of word play that invite children to complete lines, make up nonsense words, and engage in other types of phonological-based activities, when these types of activities are promoted by the teacher.

Phonemes are the building blocks of words. They are "perceivable, manipulable units of sound; they can be combined and contrasted with one another in ways that matter to language users, that is, in ways that make possible the production and perception of words" (McGee & Richgels, 2004, p. 20). The ability to hear phonemes (i.e., words that begin or end with the same sounds) is called phonemic awareness. It is more finite, more related to specific letters and sounds, and usually develops later than phonological awareness. It is a critical skill for reading and writing. It usually does not develop spontaneously, but is supported as teachers plan activities and interactions that draw attention to the phonemes in spoken words (Neuman, Copple, & Bredekamp, 2000).

As mentioned above, phonological and phonemic awareness can be supported when teachers choose books to read aloud that focus on sounds. Many picture books are based on songs that children love to sing. Among them are *Miss Polly Has a Dolly* (Edwards, 2003), *The Itsy Bitsy Spider* (Trapani, 1997), and *Miss Mary Mack* (Hoberman, 1998). Reading/singing these books, and making up new words to the familiar tunes, promote the development of phonological and phonemic awareness.

In a mixed-age class (3- to 5-year-olds), 3-year-old Jacob runs over to his teacher, bringing a piece of paper that is colored with red marks and taped to two Popsicle sticks. He says, "Look, I made a stop sign for our bus." His older friend Deshawn says, "No. You have to put S on the sign and some other letters if you want it to be a real stop sign." Deshawn shows him where and how to add the letters SDP. The teacher had read *Don't Let the Pigeon Drive the Bus* (Willems, 2003) several days earlier, and some of the children were making "things that go" in various areas of the classroom. The main character of the story, the pigeon, is just like a 3-year-old: impulsive, easily frustrated, and seeing the world only from his own perspective. The children, like the pigeon, wish they could really drive. So, they make a three-dimensional bus from a dishwasher crate that the teacher placed in the art area (after moving around some furniture), an airplane from some chairs in the dramatic play area, and a train in the block area. The teacher had suggested that 5-year-olds Rebecca and Devone write instructions for how to drive their train. They are writing on large chart paper taped to the wall in the block area. They are figuring out how to write "Don't Go Too Fast." Devone says, "Don't starts like Devone, with D." They make some other marks on the paper, followed by FS and an exclamation mark. Their teacher had pointed out the many exclamation marks contained in the book. She draws their attention to the page on which the pigeon describes the sound of the bus as "Vroom-vroom, vroomy-vroom!," and suggests they try to figure out how to write some noises that their train makes. Five-year-old Aisha decides to write "CHKU CHKU CHU! CHU!" on a separate piece of paper. The exclamation mark was used in this picture as well as on the large chart made by the children. This example shows how easily the children transfer the phonemic and phonological awareness skills linked to prior knowledge, engaging picture books, and play.

Teachers can support language development and cognitive thinking through such activities as reading multiple versions of the same folktale (e.g., a traditional version of "The Three Little Pigs," Lowell's *The Three Little Javelinas* (1992), and Scieszka's *The True Story of the Three Little Pigs!* (1989)) and asking children to compare and contrast the versions. Creating new endings to favorite stories and/or planning open-ended art projects that synthesize knowledge (e.g., a mural depicting metamorphosis, as explained in Eric Carle's *The Very Hungry Caterpillar* (1981), helps children learn to synthesize information. Assembling diverse collections of subjects of interest from particular books, such as *Bread, Bread, Bread* (1993) or *Hats, Hats, Hats* (1993), both by Ann Morris, and charting which are the favorites, help children learn to evaluate and discuss others' opinions.

Print-Rich Environments

Research has shown that when additional literacy props and tools are added to various centers in preschool classrooms, children's conversations and understanding of written language are enhanced (Neuman & Roskos, 1991; Schickedanz, 1999). Literacy props include the types of things that would naturally occur in each of the centers, such as recipe cards, coupons, cookbooks, pencils, and notepads in the kitchen area. Using picture books to support these literacy tools makes play scenarios even richer. For example, one teacher read *The Little Red Hen Makes a Pizza* (Sturges, 2002). The book contains funny and interesting ingredients from the hen's kitchen, such as pickled eggplant, anchovies, and blue cheese. The teacher saw how eager the children were to make their own shopping lists, copying words from the labels of the variety of strange and interesting items that the teacher brought into the kitchen area (marinated artichokes, hearts of palm, Kalamata olives, etc). The children and teacher ultimately made real individual pizzas, choosing their own toppings.

In order for children to extend the experiences they read about in books, they must have many other literacy tools to do so. Art areas with open-ended materials from which children can choose, writing/drawing tools and other implements, a variety of types of paper, paint, three-dimensional materials, and long periods of time to work on independent or collaborative projects are important. For example, one kindergarten teacher always finds several of her children engaged in book-making activities after she reads high-quality picture books. After reading *The Napping House* (Wood, 1994), some of the children made felt figures of the characters in the book in order to reenact the story with their flannel board. Additionally, the children made their own version of the book, called "The Kindergarten Napping House," in which each child contributed a page with various texts, according to their writing abilities and interests.

Picture books focused on writing, such as *Click, Clack, Moo: Cows That Type* (Cronin, 2000), offer a perfect vehicle through which teachers can introduce writing for a purpose. Just as the cows type their complaints to the farmer, children can voice their opinions in print on issues related to classroom problems or concerns.

Exploring picture books and creating lists of the types of literacy tools (or making prop boxes) that would support the content of specific books is a valuable exercise. Additionally, thinking about which books should be included in *each* of the early childhood interest areas (changed regularly, to allow for changes in children's interests, themes, etc.) is important.

Teachers also should consider the needs and interests of specific children when considering which books to read to individuals. One teacher noted that Quincy was having difficulty creating rhymes. So, she read Trapani's (1998) *The Itsy Bitsy Spider* to him. Then, using a flannel board, Quincy acted out the song with a flannel spider and other props. The next day, the teacher extended this activity even further. She put other felt animals next to the flannel board and invited Quincy and Fatima to change the animals and make up a new song. Together, the two children giggled as they sang, *"The itsy bitsy kitty went up the water spout. Down came the water and cried the kitty out. Out came the sun and the kitty cried away and the itsy bitsy spider went out the day-de-day."*

Conclusions

The text and illustrations of high-quality picture books weave rich stories that can excite and surprise children, make them laugh, make them wonder, and make them think. Turning each page brings another element to the magic. Whether the pictures are photographs, black-and-white line drawings, unusual designs, paintings, woodcuts, or collage, the visual art form excites the young audience. Whether the text is factual, fictional, historical, readily identifiable to the listener, or something from another culture, the stories fill young children with a multitude of ideas, words, and questions.

Using the wealth of classic and new picture books available, adults can support literacy in ways that are engaging to children. Picture books should be a part of every day in the early childhood years. Reading to children and engaging them in activities that encourage the use of expressive language, phonological awareness, and high-level thinking is critical for the development of the skills and dispositions that are necessary for reading and writing.

In the picture book *Book!* (George, 2001), a preschool child opens a present and falls in love with his new picture book. He typifies the relationship young children can have with books when he says:

I'll take you on a wagon ride to my secret place, Where both of us can hide.
After that, we'll find an empty lap before I take my nap.
We'll read you warm and snug, Book!
I'll give you a hug, Book!
Open wide.
Look inside.
Book!

References

Andreae, G. (1999). *Giraffes can't dance*. New York: Orchard Books.

Aram, D., & Biron, S. (2004). Joint storybook reading and joint writing interventions among low SES preschoolers: Differential contributions to early literacy. *Early Childhood Research Quarterly, 19*, 588–610.

Axtell, D. (1999). *We're going on a lion hunt*. New York: Henry Holt and Company.

Berk, L. E., & Winsler, A. (1995). Scaffolding children's learning: *Vygotsky and early childhood education*. Washington, DC: National Association for the Education of Young Children.

Bosschaert, G. (2000). *Teenie bird and how she learned to fly*. New York: Harry N. Abrams, Inc.

Bus, A. G., van IJzendoorn, M. H., & Pelligrini, A. D. (1995). Joint book reading makes for success in learning to read: A meta-analysis on intergenerational transmission of literacy. *Review of Educational Research, 65*, 1–21.

Carle, E. (1981). *The very hungry caterpillar*. New York: Philomel Books.

Cronin, D. (2000). *Click, clack, moo: Cows that type:* New York: Simon & Schuster.

Day, A. (1989). *Good dog, Carl*. New York: Simon & Schuster.

Edwards, P. D. (2003). *Miss Polly has a dolly*. New York: Penguin Young Readers Group.

Ehlert, L. (1993). *Eating the alphabet*. New York: Harcourt Brace Company.

George, K. O. (2001). *Book!* New York: Clarion Books/Houghton Mifflin.

Hargrave, A. C., & Senechal, M. (2000). A book reading intervention with preschool children who have limited vocabularies: The benefits of regular reading and dialogic reading. *Early Childhood Research Quarterly, 15*, 75–90.

Hoberman, M. A. (1998). *Miss Mary Mack*. Hong Kong: Little Brown.

Isenberg, J. P., & Jalongo, M. R. (2001). *Creative expression and play in early childhood*. Upper Saddle River, NJ: Merrill.

Jalongo, M. R. (2004). *Young children and picture books* (2nd ed.). Washington, DC: National Association for the Education of Young Children.

Keats, E. J. (1962). *The snowy day*. New York: Viking Juvenile.

Koralek, D. (Ed.). (2003). *Spotlight on young children and language*. Washington, DC: National Association for the Education of Young Children.

Lowell, S. (1992). *The three little javelinas*. Flagstaff, AZ: Rising Moon.

McGee, L. M., & Richgels, D. J. (2004). *Literacy's beginnings: Supporting young readers and writers*. New York: Pearson, Allyn and Bacon.

Morris, A. (1993). *Bread, bread, bread*. New York: HarperCollins.

Morris, A. (1993). *Hats, hats, hats*. New York: William Morrow & Company.

Neuman, S. B. (1999). Books make a difference: A study of access to literacy. *Reading Research Quarterly, 34*, 286–311.

Neuman, S. B., Copple, C., & Bredekamp, S. (2000). *Learning to read and write: Developmentally appropriate practices for young children*. Washington, DC: National Association for the Education of Young Children.

Neuman, S. B., & Roskos, K. (1991). Peers as literacy informants: A description of young children's literacy conversations in play. *Early Childhood Research Quarterly, 6*, 23–248.

Norton, D. E. (1999). *Through the eyes of a child: An introduction to children's literature* (5th ed.). Columbus, OH: Merrill.

Numeroff, L. J. (1985). *If you give a mouse a cookie*. New York: HarperCollins.

Owocki, G. (2001). *Make way for literacy: Teaching the way young children learn*. Portsmouth, NH: Heinemann & Washington, DC: National Association for the Education of Young Children.

Ringgold, F. (1996). *Tar beach*. New York: Dragonfly.

Rosen, M. (1997). *We're going on a bear hunt*. New York: Simon and Schuster Children's Publishing Division.

Routman, R. (1991). *Invitations: Changing as teachers and learners K-12*. Portsmouth, NH: Heinemann.

Salley, C. (2004). *Why Epossumondas has no hair on his tail*. New York: Harcourt.

Schickedanz, J. A. (1999). *Much more than the ABC's: The early stages of reading and writing*. Washington, DC: National Association for the Education of Young Children.

Scieszka, J. (1989). *The true story of the three little pigs*. New York: Penguin Group.

Sendak, M. (1998). *Where the wild things are*. San Diego: HarperCollins.

Seplocha, H., & Jablon, J. (2004). *New Jersey early learning assessment system: Trainer's box*. Trenton, NJ: New Jersey Department of Education.

Strickland, D.S., & Morrow, L. M. (1989). *Emerging literacy: Young children learn to read and write*. Newark, DE: International Reading Association.

Sturges, P. (2002). *The little red hen makes a pizza*. New York: Puffin.

Trapani, I. (1997). *The itsy bitsy spider*. New York: Charlesbridge.

Williams, V. B. (1997). *"More more more," said the baby*. New York: HarperCollins.

Willems, M. (2003). *Don't let the pigeon drive the bus!* New York: Scholastic.

Wood, A. (1994). *The napping house*. New York: Harcourt.

JANIS STRASSER is Associate Professor of Early Childhood Education and **HOLLY SEPLOCHA** is Associate Professor of Early Childhood Education, Willam Paterson University, Wayne, New Jersey.

Thank you to Darcee Chaplick, Christina Komsa, Lisa Mufson, Joe Murray, and Sage Seaton for sharing their experiences with children.

Calendar Time for Young Children
Good Intentions Gone Awry

SALLEE J. BENEKE, MICHAELENE M. OSTROSKY, AND LILIAN G. KATZ

Why do the children struggle to answer Ms. Kelsey correctly, when they have participated in this routine for months? What is the long-term impact on children when they engage regularly in an activity they do not fully understand? Here is a fresh look at calendar time in light of what we know about child development and best practices.

Young Children's Development of a Sense of Time

Adults use calendars to mark and measure time, such as scheduling appointments, remembering birthdays, and anticipating upcoming special events (spring break, a basketball tournament). However, if we look at the development of children's understanding of time (sometimes referred to as *temporal understanding*), there is little evidence that calendar activities that mark extended periods of time (a month, a week) are meaningful for children below first grade (Friedman 2000). However, there *are* some temporal concepts that preschoolers can grasp in the context of their daily activities—concepts such as *later, before,* and *after.*

Barriers to Meaningful Participation

To participate meaningfully in calendar activities, young children must understand that time is sequential. The sequences include yesterday, today, and tomorrow; morning, afternoon, and evening; Sunday, Monday, Tuesday, and so on. Children also must be able to conceptualize *before* and *after* and think about future and past events. Three-year-olds typically "have established object permanence and can recall past events, even though they do not understand the meaning of the words 'yesterday,' 'today,' or 'tomorrow'" (CTB/McGraw-Hill 2002, 9). Thus, young children can talk about things that have happened or will happen, but they cannot yet understand or talk about these events in terms of units of time (days, weeks) or sequence. This child development knowledge draws into question the usefulness of calendar activities for children under age 6.

Heather, a student teacher, watches as Ms. Kelsey begins calendar time with the 4-year-olds seated in a semicircle on the rug. "What day is it today?" Ms. Kelsey asks, gesturing toward the large calendar on an easel next to her. When no one responds, she asks, "Well, what day was it yesterday?" The children show little enthusiasm for the exercise, but finally Mindy offers, "Yesterday was Friday!" Ms. Kelsey says, "No, it wasn't Friday, Mindy. Does someone else know what day it was yesterday?" Terrance suggests, "Wednesday?" to which Ms. Kelsey responds, "Right! And if it was Wednesday yesterday, then what day is it today?" Several wrong guesses later, the correct answer emerges.

Ms. Kelsey then asks Terrance to cross out the corresponding date on the calendar. When he hesitates, she prompts, "Just look at the date we crossed out yesterday." Terrance still seems confused, so Ms. Kelsey points to a box and says, "That's the one for today." Although the children are quite restless and appear indifferent to the solution to the date problem, Ms. Kelsey succeeds in getting them to say in unison, "Today is Thursday, February 15th."

Shortly after large group time, Heather meets with her faculty supervisor, who suggests that when helping the children get ready to go home, Heather might casually ask them what day it will be when they get home. She also suggests that when a child gives the correct answer, Heather should ask, "Are you sure?"

Later, following this advice, Heather finds that about a third of the children do not know what day it will be when they get home. Among those who get the day right, about half are unsure of their answer. Heather wonders about the calendar activity. After all, it is February, and calendar time has been part of the children's daily routine since September.

Young children can talk about things that have happened or will happen, but they cannot yet understand or talk about these events in terms of units of time or sequence.

Distance in Time

Calendar use requires children to understand not only concepts such as *before* and *after* but also the relative lengths of time or distance of past or future events from the present (Friedman 2000). For example, how far away is October 30 when today is October 5? How long is the weekend? Preschoolers cannot usually judge such distances or lengths of time. A 4-year-old who learns that there will be a field trip in five days will not judge the temporal distance of this event any differently than if he were told it is in eight days. In fact, it is difficult for preschoolers to judge length of time within a given day (with hours as the unit of time), such as "in two hours" versus "in four hours." Perhaps this is the reason children on a car trip repeatedly ask, "How long until we get there?"

According to Friedman (2000), the ability to judge the relative time from a past event or until a future event in terms of the calendar year is not in place until sometime between 7 and 10 years of age. The following anecdote about 6-year-olds' attempts to understand time concepts associated with birthdays and age illustrate Friedman's point.

As Joey's grandparents arrive for his birthday, Joey runs to greet them, saying, "I can't believe I'm gonna be 6." "So, you're going to be 6. Six what?" his grandmother asks. Joey responds, "It's my birthday. I'm gonna be 6." "Yes, I know," she replies, "but six what? You're not six books." At that point Joey's 9-year-old brother whispers in his ear, "You're gonna be 6 years old, dummy!" and Joey says, "I'm gonna be 6 years old."

Three days later, as Joey's friends assemble for the traditional noisy birthday party, a discussion begins about who is already 6 and who is not. Marta states, "Well, I'm 6½." Joey asks her, "Six-and-a-half what?" Marta responds, "I don't know." Another child says to 6½-year-old Marta, "Wait a minute. When were you a baby?" She hesitates and then answers, "I don't know, maybe 10 years ago."

True understanding of dates and the calendar comes with maturity. Given the above information on the level of thinking required to grasp the time concepts of the calendar and the developmental abilities of young children, teachers may want to reconsider the calendar routine and their expectations for young children's comprehension.

Teaching Using the Calendar—or Not?

Early childhood educators may use the calendar to teach concepts other than time, including numeracy, vocabulary (*month, year, weekend*), sequencing (yesterday, today, tomorrow), and patterning (Monday, Tuesday, Wednesday). Additionally, as children attend to the visual calendar, teachers may hope they will learn numeral recognition and one-to-one correspondence. Early childhood specialists have cited numbers, spatial reasoning, patterning, logical relations, measurement, and early algebra as key components of young children's mathematical

growth (for example, Greenes 1999; NCTM 2000). However, most 4-year-olds are not ready to grasp the complex concepts involved in dates (Etheridge & King 2005).

Math Concepts

Learning experiences that center on mathematical concepts should not only be enjoyable and meaningful but also direct children's thinking toward, and focus it on, important mathematical ideas (Trafton, Reys, & Wasman 2001). Giving preschool children opportunities to explore and experiment individually with math concepts, using concrete materials with a responsive adult to question and guide learning, is likely to be more meaningful and beneficial than having young children participate in a whole group discussion of such concepts centered on the calendar.

For example, a teacher can help children notice patterns in the environment and in their work and explain the process of patterning both at circle time and individually. A teacher might join a child who is stringing beads and say, "I think I will make a pattern with my beads. My pattern is blue, yellow, red; blue, yellow, red. What kind of pattern can you make with your beads?" These approaches can help children build their own patterning abilities.

Other Knowledge and Skills

Many teachers use calendar time to teach skills unrelated to math, such as colors, letters, emergent writing, and social skills. While each of these concepts and skills is important for young children to learn, the calendar routine is not the most useful format for teaching them. For example, it is difficult for teachers to individualize instruction to meet the diverse needs of young learners during a large group activity such as calendar time.

Better Alternatives at Group Time

If focusing on the calendar is not an appropriate way to introduce young children to time concepts, numeracy, and the other concepts mentioned above, then what are some better ways?

The following evidence-based practices are likely to be more effective than calendar activities in presenting time concepts to young children.

Picture Schedules

Although young children have difficulty judging the length of time between events (for example, how long the time between snack and outside play will be), they can understand a sequence of events (for example, snack comes after circle time). Young children generally have a strong sense of narrative and the way a story progresses. Pictures illustrating the schedule of class activities are often recommended for children with particular disabilities. Similarly, a poster with illustrations or photos of the day's activities in sequence can be helpful for all young children.

A poster with illustrations or photos of the day's activities in sequence can be helpful for all young children.

Classroom Journal

Using a digital camera, the teacher can take frequent photographs of classroom events, projects, or field trips, then invite the children to help select photos for a classroom journal. Attach the photos to a dated page (one photo per page or multiple photos on a page) or tuck them into a plastic sleeve. Post or display them in a designated place—on a wall or bulletin board or in a binder—to clearly reflect the sequence of activities: "On Tuesday, we went to the park, we made pancakes, and we read *Pancakes, Pancakes!* by Eric Carle." As the children add new pictures chronicling recent events, they can revisit and discuss past shared events.

Along these same lines, the teacher can collect samples of children's work in a notebook as a visual record of shared events. Children can take turns contributing work to this community notebook. When teachers encourage children to tell peers or their families the story of their project, the children strengthen their understanding of the way an event unfolds, with the various activities taking place in a time sequence.

Documentation Displays

Displaying documentation of shared class events can lead to meaningful discussions that involve time-linked vocabulary. For example, when looking at a documentation display about the class construction of a giant papiermâché butterfly, one child said, "See, there's the butterfly we made that other time." Her teacher responded, "Yes, we made the giant butterfly two weeks ago. Here [pointing to a photograph on the display] is a picture of the frame we built the first day, and the picture next to it shows you adding the papiermâché on the second day."

Linear Representations

Linear representations also can help children begin to understand and conceptualize that a day is a unit of time and talk about it with increasing clarity. For example, to count the number of days they have been in kindergarten, children can add a link to a paper chain each day, or number a pattern of colored Post-it notes and place them on the classroom wall, or add a Unifix cube to a stack of cubes. The teacher can emphasize time-linked vocabulary, such as *before, after, later, earlier,* as the children add the new link. Unlike calendars, linear representations do not require the left-to-right orientation.

Games

Games are another way for children to begin to get a feel for the length of various units of time and the vocabulary associated with them. For example, children might guess how many seconds it takes to walk from one side of the playground to the other, and the teacher or another child can time it with a watch. Or a teacher might ask the children to guess how many minutes it will take for a snowball to melt indoors and then time it with a clock. They might guess how many hours it will be until story time, tally the hours as they pass, and then compare the result with their estimate. These experiences with units of time (seconds, minutes, hours) can lead to discussions about points in time during the school day and the relative distance in the future of these points in time. For example, the teacher might say, "We are going to the library at nine o'clock, and we will go outside at ten o'clock. Where are we going first?"

Project Work

Project work, in which children actively engage in ongoing investigations of events and phenomena around them, is another way to give children opportunities to acquire many concepts and skills related to time (Helm & Beneke, 2003). In project work, calendar concepts are useful rather than ritualistic in nature. Project work lends itself to planning future events and keeping a record of events that happen over time. For example, in a mixed-age preschool, the children investigated eggs. They incubated mallard duck eggs, and each day they added to a tally of days until the ducklings would hatch. As children plan for investigation and reflect on what they have learned and when they learned it in the meaningful context of a project, they naturally begin to develop a sense of the relative lengths of time in the past and future.

Project work lends itself to planning future events and keeping a record of events that happen over time.

Intellectual Development and Calendar Time

A teacher's actions can enhance or inhibit young children's learning. Communication, classroom support, activities, and interactions all play a part. If young children participate frequently in activities they do not really understand, they may lose confidence in their intellectual powers. In this case, some children may eventually give up hope of understanding many of the ideas teachers present to them. Certainly all children will experience some degree of not fully understanding activities at some point. However, in such cases it is helpful for the teacher to reassure learners that fuller understanding will come and that it often takes practice to master a concept, and to indicate in other ways that feeling "out of it" happens to us all sometimes and will be overcome. "Curriculum goals must be both challenging and achievable for all children . . . one size does not fit all. Children will learn best if curriculum content connects with what they already know and have experienced, while introducing them to important new ideas and skills" (Hyson 2000, 61).

In a joint position statement on best practices in early childhood mathematics learning, NAEYC and the National Council of Teachers of Mathematics (NCTM) (2002) stated,

It is vital for young children to develop confidence in their ability to understand and use mathematics—in other words, to see mathematics as within their reach. In addition, positive experiences with using mathematics to solve problems help children to develop dispositions such as curiosity, imagination, flexibility, inventiveness, and persistence that contribute to their future success in and out of school. (p. 5)

Lengthy daily calendar sessions in which a teacher expresses the expectation that young children will understand the workings of a calendar run counter to this position. Teachers who intend to keep calendar a part of their daily classroom routine will be more effective if they develop ways to incorporate the calendar that require little time and reflect young children's limited development of time concepts.

Conclusion

As teachers reflect on their practice, they may experience an inner conflict in terms of what they believe about children's development and how and what they teach. Understanding how children learn should enable teachers to focus on calendar-related constructs such as patterning, sorting, and seriating during more natural and appropriate routines. In fact, many teachers will likely realize they already address these fundamental concepts during other parts of the classroom day.

As we return to the opening vignette, considering the information in this article, the discussion Ms. Kelsey has with her class might look something like this:

As Heather watches, Ms. Kelsey addresses the 4-year-olds seated on the rug in front of her: "It's time for us to add another link to our chain. Who would like to attach the link that stands for today?" Mindy volunteers, and Ms. Kelsey says, "Wonderful! Pick someone for your partner, and you two can take care of that." Mindy holds out her hand to Ginelle, and Ginelle joins her in attaching the latest link.

"Now, let's look at our picture chart. Who can tell me what we are going to do after circle time?" Terrance offers, "We're going to the library." Ms. Kelsey responds, "Right! Does anyone remember what are we going to do after that?" Althea enthusiastically states, "We're going out for recess!" Ms. Kelsey cheerfully responds, "Yes, that's right, Althea."

Ms. Kelsey then says, "Mindy and Ginelle have added a link for today to the paper chain. How far does the chain reach, now?" Ginelle responds, "It's almost to the window. It's really getting long." Many of the children voice their agreement.

Not long after circle time, Heather's faculty supervisor suggests that when she helps the children get ready to go home, she might ask them what they are going to

tell their parents they did that day at school. Most of the children plan to tell their parents about the day's sequence of activities, and when Heather prompts them with, "Are you sure?" several children refer to the picture chart to verify their statements.

References

CTB/McGraw-Hill. 2002. *Pre-kindergarten standards: Guidelines for teaching and learning.* Executive summary. www.ctb.com/media/articles/pdfs/resources/PreKstandards_summary.pdf

Etheridge, E.A., & J.R. King. 2005. Calendar math in preschool and primary classrooms: Questioning the curriculum. *Early Childhood Education Journal* 32 (5): 291–96.

Freidman, W.J. 2000. The development of children's knowledge of the times of future events. *Child Development* 71 (4): 913–32.

Greenes, C. 1999. The Boston University-Chelsea project. In *Mathematics in the early years,* ed. J.V. Copley, 151–55. Washington, DC: NAEYC.

Helm, J.H., & S. Beneke. 2003. *The power of projects.* New York: Teachers College Press.

Hyson, M. 2000. "Is it okay to have calendar time?" Look up to the star—Look within yourself. *Young Children* 55 (6): 34–36.

NAEYC & NCTM (National Council of Teachers of Mathematics). 2002. Early childhood mathematics: Promoting good beginnings. A joint position statement of NAEYC and NCTM.www.naeyc.org/about/positions/mathematics.asp

NCTM (National Council of Teachers of Mathematics). 2000. *Principles and standards for school mathematics.* Reston, VA: Author.

Trafton, P., B.J. Reys, & D.G. Wasman. 2001. Standards-based mathematics curriculum materials: A phrase in search of a definition. *Phi Delta Kappan* 8 (3): 259–64.

SALLEE J. BENEKE is the author and coauthor of several books on the project approach. She is a doctoral student in the Department of Special Education at the University of Illinois and provides professional development for school districts and child care centers. **MICHAELENE M. OSTROSKY**, PhD, is on faculty in the Department of Special Education at the University of Illinois at Urbana-Champaign. She collaborates with other faculty in the Center on Social and Emotional Foundations for Early Learning and is involved with The Autism Program in Illinois. Micki is involved in research on social interaction interventions, naturalistic language interventions, social-emotional competence, challenging behavior, and transitions. ostrosky@uiuc.edu. **LILIAN G. KATZ**, PhD, is codirector of the Clearinghouse on Early Childhood and Parenting and professor emerita at the University of Illinois, Urbana-Champaign. Lilian served as vice president and president of NAEYC in the 1990s. She has lectured in more than 60 countries and served as visiting professor in a half dozen countries.

Test-Your-Knowledge Form

We encourage you to photocopy and use this page as a tool to assess how the articles in *Annual Editions* expand on the information in your textbook. By reflecting on the articles you will gain enhanced text information. You can also access this useful form on a product's book support Web site at *http://www.mhcls.com*.

NAME: _____   DATE: _____

TITLE AND NUMBER OF ARTICLE:
_____

BRIEFLY STATE THE MAIN IDEA OF THIS ARTICLE:
_____
_____

LIST THREE IMPORTANT FACTS THAT THE AUTHOR USES TO SUPPORT THE MAIN IDEA:
_____
_____
_____
_____

WHAT INFORMATION OR IDEAS DISCUSSED IN THIS ARTICLE ARE ALSO DISCUSSED IN YOUR TEXTBOOK OR OTHER READINGS THAT YOU HAVE DONE? LIST THE TEXTBOOK CHAPTERS AND PAGE NUMBERS:
_____
_____
_____
_____

LIST ANY EXAMPLES OF BIAS OR FAULTY REASONING THAT YOU FOUND IN THE ARTICLE:
_____
_____
_____
_____

LIST ANY NEW TERMS/CONCEPTS THAT WERE DISCUSSED IN THE ARTICLE, AND WRITE A SHORT DEFINITION:

We Want Your Advice

ANNUAL EDITIONS revisions depend on two major opinion sources: one is our Advisory Board, listed in the front of this volume, which works with us in scanning the thousands of articles published in the public press each year; the other is you—the person actually using the book. Please help us and the users of the next edition by completing the prepaid article rating form on this page and returning it to us. Thank you for your help!

ANNUAL EDITIONS: Early Childhood Education 09/10

ARTICLE RATING FORM

Here is an opportunity for you to have direct input into the next revision of this volume.
We would like you to rate each of the articles listed below, using the following scale:

1. **Excellent: should definitely be retained**
2. **Above average: should probably be retained**
3. **Below average: should probably be deleted**
4. **Poor: should definitely be deleted**

Your ratings will play a vital part in the next revision.
Please mail this prepaid form to us as soon as possible.
Thanks for your help!

RATING	ARTICLE
	1. Early Education, Later Success
	2. The Changing Culture of Childhood: A Perfect Storm
	3. Joy in School
	4. Accountability Comes to Preschool: Can We Make It Work for Young Children?
	5. No Child Left Behind: Who's Accountable?
	6. Preschool Comes of Age: The National Debate on Education for Young Children Intensifies
	7. Class Matters—In and Out of School
	8. Meeting of the Minds
	9. Making Long-Term Separations Easier for Children and Families
	10. Supporting Grandparents Who Raise Grandchildren
	11. Children of Teen Parents: Challenges and Hope
	12. Whose Problem Is Poverty?
	13. Learning in an Inclusive Community
	14. Including Children with Disabilities in Early Childhood Education Programs: Individualizing Developmentally Appropriate Practices
	15. Creative Play: Building Connections with Children Who Are Learning English
	16. Twelve Characteristics of Effective Early Childhood Teachers
	17. Health = Performance
	18. Which Hand?: Brains, Fine Motor Skills, and Holding a Pencil
	19. What Can We Do to Prevent Childhood Obesity?
	20. When Girls and Boys Play: What Research Tells Us
	21. What Research Says about . . . Grade Retention
	22. Back to Basics: Play in Early Childhood
	23. Scripted Curriculum: Is It a Prescription for Success?
	24. Using Brain-Based Teaching Strategies to Create Supportive Early Childhood Environments That Address Learning Standards

RATING	ARTICLE
	25. Successful Transition to Kindergarten: The Role of Teachers and Parents
	26. *Rethinking* Early Childhood Practices
	27. The Looping Classroom: Benefits for Children, Families, and Teachers
	28. Play: Ten Power Boosts for Children's Early Learning
	29. Ready or Not, Here We Come: What It Means to Be a Ready School
	30. "Stop Picking On Me!": What You Need to Know about Bullying
	31. "You Got It!": Teaching Social and Emotional Skills
	32. Fostering Positive Transitions for School Success
	33. A Multinational Study Supports Child-Initiated Learning: Using the Findings in Your Classroom
	34. The Power of Documentation in the Early Childhood Classroom
	35. Got Standards?: Don't Give up on Engaged Learning!
	36. The Plan: Building on Children's Interests
	37. One Teacher, 20 Preschoolers, and a Goldfish: Environmental Awareness, Emergent Curriculum, and Documentation
	38. Fostering Prosocial Behavior in Young Children
	39. Constructive Play: A Value-Added Strategy for Meeting Early Learning Standards
	40. Early Literacy and Very Young Children
	41. Using Picture Books to Support Young Children's Literacy
	42. Calendar Time for Young Children: Good Intentions Gone Awry

NO POSTAGE
NECESSARY
IF MAILED
IN THE
UNITED STATES

BUSINESS REPLY MAIL
FIRST CLASS MAIL PERMIT NO. 551 DUBUQUE IA

POSTAGE WILL BE PAID BY ADDRESSEE

McGraw-Hill Contemporary Learning Series
501 BELL STREET
DUBUQUE, IA 52001

ABOUT YOU

Name

Date

Are you a teacher? ❑ A student? ❑
Your school's name

Department

Address

City

State

Zip

School telephone #

YOUR COMMENTS ARE IMPORTANT TO US!

Please fill in the following information:
For which course did you use this book?

Did you use a text with this ANNUAL EDITION? ❑ yes ❑ no
What was the title of the text?

What are your general reactions to the Annual Editions concept?

Have you read any pertinent articles recently that you think should be included in the next edition? Explain.

Are there any articles that you feel should be replaced in the next edition? Why?

Are there any World Wide Web sites that you feel should be included in the next edition? Please annotate.

May we contact you for editorial input? ❑ yes ❑ no
May we quote your comments? ❑ yes ❑ no